THE ASSOCIATION FOR OFFICE PROFESSIONALS™

# THE
# PROFESSIONAL SECRETARY'S

## Book of
## LISTS
## & TIPS

### MARY A. DE VRIES

**PRENTICE HALL**

**Library of Congress Cataloging-in-Publication Data**

De Vries, Mary A.
    Professional secretary's book of lists and tips / Mary A. De Vries.
       p.   cm.
    Includes bibliographical references.
    ISBN 0-13-149345-0
    1. Office practice—Handbooks, manuals, etc.   2. Secretaries—Handbooks,
manuals, etc.   I. Title.
    HF5547.5.D393   1996                          95-24338
    651.3'741—dc20                                   CIP

*Printed in the United States of America*

*10  9  8  7  6  5  4*

Jacqueline Roulette, Production Editor
Interior Design by William Ruoto

ISBN 0-13-149345-0

---

---

**PRENTICE HALL**
**Paramus, NJ 07652**

On the World Wide Web at http://www.phdirect.com

## ALSO BY THE AUTHOR

*The Complete Office Handbook*

*Complete Secretary's Handbook*

*The Complete Word Book*

*Elements of Correspondence*

*Guide to Better Business Writing*

*How to Run a Meeting*

*Internationally Yours: Writing and Communicating Successfully in Today's Global Marketplace*

*Legal Secretary's Complete Handbook*

*The New American Dictionary of Abbreviations*

*The New American Handbook of Letter Writing*

*New Century Vest-Pocket Secretary's Handbook*

*The New Robert's Rules of Order*

*The Office Sourcebook*

*The Practical Writer's Guide*

*The Prentice Hall Complete Book of Model Letters, Memos, and Forms for Secretaries*

*The Prentice Hall Style Manual*

*Professional Secretary's Encyclopedic Dictionary*

# ACKNOWLEDGMENTS

In preparing this book, I talked to many secretaries and other office professionals who helped me decide what to include. I also consulted with Professional Secretaries International (PSI®).

I especially want to acknowledge the contributions of three people who worked on the book from beginning to end: Judith Grisham, laboratory administrator at Harvard University, who reviewed the chapters and offered detailed suggestions and corrections; Carmen Riepe, former member of the Foreign Service and now a communications consultant, who assisted with the research and proofreading of many chapters; and Alice Hubbard, former teacher and now manager of her own word processing service, who prepared the manuscript on disk and provided research for several chapters.

In addition, I want to thank Susan Fenner, Ph.D., manager of Education and Professional Development at PSI®, who reviewed the manuscript, made numerous valuable suggestions, and supplied important survey material and other useful information.

# A WORD ABOUT PSI®

Since 1942, PSI® has set the standard for secretarial professionals throughout the world. The organization, headquartered in Kansas City, Missouri, provides ongoing education and training, offering an entry-level certification through the Office Proficiency Assessment and Certification® (OPAC) program and the coveted Certified Professional Secretary® (CPS®) rating. The efforts of students in business education are supported with PSI® membership and through high school and college organizations under the guidance of the PSI® Institute for Education. In addition to offering newsletters, research findings, and other essential material, PSI® publishes *The Secretary* magazine, one of many PSI® sources consulted in preparing this book.

# PREFACE

*The Professional Secretary's Book of Lists and Tips* is an invaluable desk reference for busy office professionals. It is a storehouse of information that you will use daily to settle virtually any on-the-job question or problem.

This easy-to-use list format helps you find the answers you need quickly and easily. You will also find useful illustrations and actual samples you can use like letter formats and time charts.

The book is divided into three parts. The first part deals with a wide range of secretarial and office skills. It has nine chapters that cover secretarial careers, personal interaction at work, telecommunication practices, correspondence, mail processing, word processing, accounting, meetings, and travel. Here you'll find practical, interesting, and enlightening topics such as the following:

- Crucial Strategies for Success in Office Careers (Chapter 1)
- Simple Listening Strategies That Will Pay Big Dividends (Chapter 2)
- Eighteen Ways to Cope with Telemarketing Fraud (Chapter 3)
- General Rules for Using Forms of Address Correctly (Chapter 4)
- Common Mailing Abbreviations for Proper Addressing (Chapter 5)
- How to Use Ergonomics to Prevent Injuries in the Office (Chapter 6)
- Seven Commands You Can Use to Manipulate Data with Spreadsheet Software (Chapter 7)
- A Meeting-Preparation Checklist to Make Your Job Easier (Chapter 8)
- Two Dozen Domestic Trip-Preparation Guidelines (Chapter 9)

The second part of the book deals with language skills. It has seven chapters that cover grammar, spelling, punctuation, proofreading, word usage, and foreign language. Here you'll find essential language and communications guidelines such as the following:

- The Six Verb Tenses That Denote Time (Chapter 10)
- How to Use Familiar Prefixes in Business Writing (Chapter 11)
- General Rules to Help You Use the Principal Marks of Punctuation Correctly (Chapter 12)
- Two Dozen Common Errors That Expert Proofreaders Find (Chapter 13)
- Three Hundred Positive Words That Will Help You Influence People (Chapter 14)
- Discriminatory Language That Could Get You in Trouble (Chapter 15)
- Anglicized Foreign Words That Need No Accents (Chapter 16)

The third part of the book is the reference section. Its two chapters include the metric system and an office recycling guide. Here you'll find a variety of facts and figures such as the following:

- Metric Measurement Conversions (Chapter 17)
- Hints for Establishing a Recycling Program (Chapter 18)

As more and more businesses are involved in international trade, secretaries are being asked to handle international communications and to research various matters involving other countries. *The Professional Secretary's Book of Lists and Tips* has a wealth of international subject matter that will save you many hours in the library paging through directories, travel guides, and other books. For example,

- Chapter 2: The Essential Do's and Don'ts of International Business Etiquette; Valuable Suggestions for Proper International Gift Giving
- Chapter 3: Telephone Codes You Will Need to Make Domestic and International Calls
- Chapter 9: Important International Trip-Preparation Guidelines; A Simple Guide to Calculating Time Around the World; Currencies Used in the Major Countries of the World; U.S. Embassies in Other Countries; Foreign Embassies in the United States

- Chapter 16: Two Hundred Foreign Words and Phrases That You Should Know

Check the Table of Contents for a complete listing of the 128 section topics, and consult the index for specific information.

I hope you will enjoy using *The Professional Secretary's Book of Lists and Tips* as much as I enjoyed working on it. It's packed cover to cover with a wide range of topics and ideas, both traditional and new, practical and innovative.

# CONTENTS

Preface v

## PART ONE: OFFICE SKILLS 1

## 1. Career Enhancement and Personal Development 3

The Ten Most Common Secretarial Titles • Common Job Tasks Performed by Office Professionals • Positive Steps That Will Make You a More Productive Employee • Crucial Strategies for Success in Office Careers • Tested Goal-Setting Guidelines That Will Enhance Your Career • A Dozen Practical Steps to Improve Your Organizational Abilities • Two Dozen Proven Ways to Manage Your Time Better at Work • Fourteen Helpful Tips for Overcoming Procrastination • The Five Commandments of Successful Body Language • Effective Networking Ideas for Exchanging Useful Information • Easy-to-Learn Speed-Reading Techniques • Fourteen Useful Tips for Reducing Stress at Work • Putting It All Together: Office Skills Testing and Certification

## 2. Interpersonal Relations 22

Simple Listening Strategies That Will Pay Big Dividends • Basic Guidelines to Ensure Success in Training Others • A Dozen Practical Hints for Criticizing Others Constructively • The Eight Most Important Delegating Guidelines • Sensible Strategies for Controlling Office Politics • Fourteen Key Pointers for Dealing with Sexual Harassment at Work • The Essential Do's and Don'ts of International Business Etiquette • Valuable Suggestions for Proper International Gift Giving

## 3. Telecommunications 34

The Ten Telephone Company Services You Will Most Often Use • Six Advanced Telecommunications Services That Save Time • Efficient and Effective Practices in Handling Incoming Calls • Valuable Tips for Handling Voice-Mail Messages • Practical Measures for Better Telecommunications Time Management • Eighteen Ways to Cope with Telemarketing Fraud • The Most Often Used Telephone and Fax Numbers at Work • Telephone Codes You Will Need to Make Domestic and International Calls

## 4. Correspondence 72

Three Common Ways to Format a Business Letter • Two Common Ways to Format a Memo • Two Common Ways to Format an Envelope • How to Write the Fifteen Principal Parts of a Business Letter • How to Write the Eight Principal Parts of a Standard Memo • Four Common Sizes of Letter and Memo Stationery • General Rules for Using Forms of Address Correctly

## 5. Electronic and Conventional Mail 130

Effective Procedures for Processing Incoming Mail • Effective Procedures for Processing Outgoing Mail • Ten Steps to Ensure That Mail Is Addressed Properly • The Chief Do's and Don'ts of E-Mail Etiquette • Sixteen Ways to Save Money in the Mail Room • A Checklist of Ways to Improve Mail Room Security • Frequently Used Classes of Private-Courier and Postal Mail • Common Mailing Abbreviations for Proper Addressing

## 6. Word Processing 152

The Eight Basic Steps in Creating Documents Electronically • Important Guidelines for Drafting Manuscripts to Be Typeset • How to Organize the Sixteen Principal Parts of a Business Report • How to Organize the Eight Principal Parts of a Business Proposal • Where to Place the Seven Principal Parts of a Table • Common Styles for Basic Reference Forms • An Easy Way to Review Your Work Using an Editing Checklist • Common Business Applications for Desktop Publishing (DTP) • Thirteen Ways to Improve Your DTP Documents • Simple Procedures That Will Promote Better Scanning Results • Effective Methods for Handling Transcription Duties More Efficiently • Useful Hints for Selecting the Right Paper for Business Documents • Nine Things You Can Do to Protect Diskettes • Crucial Computer-Security Guidelines for the Office • How to Use Ergonomics to Prevent Injuries in the Office

## 7. Information Processing and Accounting 178

The Three Crucial Components of the Accounting Process • Basic Rules for Using Debit and Credit Entries in Bookkeeping • Three Essential

Financial Statements That You May Need to Prepare • The Five Major
Components of a Spreadsheet • Seven Commands You Can Use to
Manipulate Data with Spreadsheet Software • The Four Major
Components of a Database • Five Ways You Can Process Information
with Database Software • The Four Principal Types of Storage Media
Used in an Office • Useful Tips for Filing Information Electronically •
Useful Tips for Filing Information Manually

## 8. Meetings 192

A Meeting-Preparation Checklist to Make Your Job Easier • A Dozen
Useful Tips for Preparing Effective Presentations • Meeting-
Attendance Strategies That Will Boost Your Benefits • Four Principal
Teleconferencing Methods • A Dozen Essential Steps in Arranging a
Teleconference • Key Agenda Topics and How to Organize Them •
Timesaving Suggestions for Taking the Meeting Minutes • Important
Guidelines for Preparing the Minutes Properly • Twenty-eight Basic
Parliamentary Motions and What They Mean

## 9. Travel 209

A Useful Checklist to Help You Select the Best Possible Travel Agent • Two
Dozen Domestic Trip-Preparation Guidelines • A Valuable Collection of
Travel-Safety Tips • Important International Trip-Preparation Guidelines •
A Simple Guide to Calculating Time Around the World • Currencies Used
in the Major Countries of the World • U.S. Embassies in Other Countries •
Foreign Embassies in the United States

## PART TWO: LANGUAGE SKILLS 243

## 10. Grammar 245

The Eight Parts of Speech That You Use Every Day • The Most
Important Grammatical Terms • The Most Familiar Prepositions in the
English Language • A Sampler of Common Coordinate, Subordinate, and
Correlative Conjunctions • The Present, Past, and Past Participle of More
than One Hundred Common Irregular Verbs • The Six Verb Tenses That
Denote Time • A Guide to the Nouns and Adjectives That Denote
Nationality Around the World

## 11. Spelling 268

One Thousand Most Often Misspelled Words • How to Use Familiar Prefixes in Business Writing • One Hundred Common Prefixes • How to Use Familiar Suffixes in Business Writing • One Hundred Common Suffixes • The Preferred Spelling of Common Compound Terms • Three Hundred Common Compound Terms


## 12. Punctuation 296

General Rules to Help You Use the Principal Marks of Punctuation Correctly • The Nine Basic Diacritical Marks


## 13. Proofreading 307

Standard Proofreader Marks to Use in Correcting and Editing Documents • Two Dozen Common Errors That Expert Proofreaders Find


## 14. Useful Language 312

Three Hundred Positive Words That Will Help You Influence People • Two Hundred Fifty Action Words That Will Make Your Messages More Forceful • Examples of Transition Words and Phrases to Help Your Writing Flow Smoothly


## 15. Troublesome Language 321

Stilted Expressions That Should Never Be Used in Your Messages • Examples of Redundant Expressions and the Preferred Shortened Forms • Negative Words That May Make You Sound Pessimistic or Rude • A Guide to Homophones That Often Cause Problems • Discriminatory Language That Could Get You in Trouble • A Collection of Cliches That Will Make You Sound Out of Date • Examples of Jargon That Should Not Be Used Outside the Workplace • Three Hundred Commonly Misused Words

16. Foreign Language 391

Two Hundred Foreign Words and Phrases That You Should Know • Two Dozen Overused Foreign Terms • Anglicized Foreign Words That Need No Accents

PART THREE: REFERENCE SECTION 401

17. Weights, Measures, and Values 403

Units in the Metric System • Spelling and Symbols for Units • Prefixes of Metric Units • Metric Prefixes and Multiplication Factors • Traditional Weights, Measures, and Values and the Metric Equivalents • Metric Measurement Conversions

18. Office Recycling Guide 418

Hints for Establishing a Recycling Program • Recycling Product List • What You Can Do

# — PART ONE —

# OFFICE SKILLS

# —1—
# CAREER ENHANCEMENT
# AND PERSONAL DEVELOPMENT

## THE TEN MOST COMMON SECRETARIAL TITLES

Professional secretaries hold a wide variety of position titles, usually selected by employers without regard to any universal set of standards. A *general secretary* in one firm, for example, may have the same duties and responsibilities as an *administrative secretary* in another organization. Numerous other titles, many of which no longer use the word *secretary* in the title, also indicate secretarial work, such as *office administrator* and *professional assistant*. Specialized secretarial titles are commonly used to designate a particular profession *(medical secretary)* or industry *(construction secretary)*, as well as a specific area of secretarial activity *(correspondence secretary)*. The following positions indicate ten of the most commonly advertised titles pertaining to secretarial work.

*1.* Secretary (general)
*2.* Secretary (specialized)
*3.* Executive secretary
*4.* Executive assistant
*5.* Administrative assistant
*6.* Administrative secretary

7. Office manager                    9. Educator/instructor

8. Senior secretary                  10. Coordinator

## Common Job Tasks Performed by Office Professionals

A total of seventy-four office tasks were identified in a study conducted by Professional Secretaries International® with the Department of Business Education and the University of Georgia Survey Research Center. The study was titled the *PSI Career Path for Office Professionals*. Of the seventy-four job tasks, sorted into twenty-one categories, it was found that there were more tasks performed by *all* office workers than tasks performed by specific groups. For more information about career opportunities and job requirements pertinent to the following outline, contact PSI®.

*Scheduling Tasks*

- Schedule appointments
- Maintain calendar
- Organize schedule
- Schedule meetings/conferences
- Make travel arrangements via agents
- Prepare meeting materials
- Maintain expense reports

*Supervisory Tasks*

- Supervise staff
- Train others
- Prioritize/assign work
- Interview personnel
- Input on physical layout of office

*Equipment-Purchasing/Maintenance Tasks*

- Recommend office equipment
- Recommend office furniture
- Coordinate maintenance
- Recommend computers

*Data-Collection/Analysis Tasks*

- Analyze spreadsheets
- Research and summarize data
- Collect budget data
- Format statistical reports/tables
- Compile annual report data

*Participation and Communication Activities*

- Participate in task forces
- Make oral presentations
- Participate in staff meetings
- Represent supervisor
- Compose articles

*Financial-Management Tasks*

- Process payroll
- Process accounts
- Maintain petty cash
- Compile time sheets
- Collect overdue bills

*Routine Office Tasks*

- Receive visitors

- Answer/screen calls
- Sort/distribute mail
- Provide information
- Maintain manual files

*Network Tasks*

- Transfer/receive files
- Maintain server
- Send/receive E-mail
- Maintain electronic files

*Mass-Mailing Tasks*

- Prepare mass mailings
- Coordinate mass mailings

*Information-Distribution Tasks*

- Send/receive voice mail
- Send facsimiles

*Document Preparation*

- Proofread documents
- Edit documents
- Key correspondence/reports

*Decisional Tasks*

- Compose correspondence
- Serve as liaison
- Make decisions during absences
- Handle confidential material
- Use symbol shorthand

- Abstract documents

*Document Design*

- Design office forms
- Design tables/graphs
- Use desktop publishing

*Manual Documentation*

- Maintain procedures manuals
- Create procedures manuals

*Database Maintenance*

- Search databases
- Create databases

*Conference Scheduling*

- Arrange videoconferences
- Arrange audioconferences

*Programming Tasks*

- Design Gant/PERT charts
- Write/modify software

*Transcription Tasks*

- Transcribe from dictaphone
- Transcribe from notes
- Maintain library

*Dictating to Word Processing Center*

- Dictate to word processing center

*Information Gathering*
- Rapid note taking
- Optically scan documents

*Photocopying*
- Photocopy documents

## POSITIVE STEPS THAT WILL MAKE YOU A MORE PRODUCTIVE EMPLOYEE

Employers use productivity as a measure of employee worth. The more efficiently and effectively you perform your duties, the more valuable you are to your employer. Although secretaries have a right to know what is or is not expected of them, those who want to enhance their worth will do what is required and more. This list contains positive steps you can take to increase your productivity at work.

- Arrive at work on time or early and be willing to stay late or cut short your breaks and lunches.
- Practice strict time management, and let coworkers know your schedule and needs.
- Pace yourself with heavy work loads to avoid time-wasting fatigue and errors.
- Use criticism and mistakes as a guide to more effective and more accurate performance in the future.
- Apply creativity and ingenuity to each task.
- Actively investigate ways to perform each task better.
- Block out distractions and personal worries so that you can focus fully on the task at hand.
- Pay close attention even to small details to avoid costly mistakes.
- Don't be afraid to ask questions when something isn't clear.

- Communicate your expectations clearly to temps, assistants, and other coworkers.
- Keep your emotions in check at all times so that you will respond to situations maturely and sensibly.
- Remain flexible in your work so that you can adjust to change at a moment's notice.
- Be self-motivated, working carefully and accurately without supervision.
- Improve your job skills through practice, self-study, education and training, networking, and other means.

## CRUCIAL STRATEGIES FOR SUCCESS IN OFFICE CAREERS

Secretaries who are concerned with career enhancement and personal development need to devise effective strategies to ensure success. All too often, useful steps are overlooked, sometimes because they are too obvious or too simple to attract attention. To avoid missing an important opportunity, imagine that you must activate each of the following strategies to open the door to success.

- Identify your strengths and weaknesses, listing ways to increase the former and compensate for the latter.
- Set standards of excellence that you want to achieve, such as earning the CPS® rating.
- Show pride in your accomplishments without appearing conceited.
- Define your career goals and the specific steps (e.g., education, training) required to reach them.
- Volunteer for new responsibilities.
- Be a willing and enthusiastic team player.
- Be firm but fair with temps, assistants, and other coworkers.
- Attend to personal needs and involvements after work or outside the office.

- Offer to help coworkers in need, such as finding transportation or day care for someone.

- Express your appreciation when others help you.

- Be willing to meet pressing deadlines, but speak up when expectations are unrealistic.

- Don't be afraid to try something new (when company policies permit) and to fail.

- Develop and improve computer skills needed to manage new technologies.

- Adopt a positive attitude toward your work, using positive words to discuss it with others.

- Polish your speech (e.g., tone, enunciation) to improve your professional image.

- Learn to speak "with a smile."

- Be a good listener, letting others finish their thoughts and express views that may be contrary to yours. (See Chapter 2.)

- Maintain a cheerful, optimistic outlook under stressful, demanding conditions.

- Be imaginative and resourceful in problem solving.

- Maintain the highest possible ethical standards regardless of pressure or temptation from coworkers and outsiders.

- Follow through when you have a good idea (before someone else does) if company policy allows.

- Dress for success with a professional, businesslike appearance appropriate for your office.

## TESTED GOAL-SETTING GUIDELINES THAT WILL ENHANCE YOUR CAREER

Most people who want to achieve something must take deliberate steps to make it happen. The number of steps that may be needed depends on the objective, but the more clearly you define your goals and follow a concrete plan to reach them, the more likely it is that you will achieve the desired results. Whether your goal is as large as being promoted or as small as finishing a letter, some or all of the following guidelines will help you set and achieve professional and personal goals.

- State *in writing* clearly and precisely what you want to accomplish, including specific details.

- *Visualize* what you want to do or achieve (picture yourself actually doing or achieving it).

- Accept personal responsibility for each goal or act, without blaming others or circumstances for any failures.

- Decide who should or should not know about your goals (who might help you or be an obstacle).

- Set goals in harmony and consistent with the goals of your employer and coworkers (professional goals) or with those of family and friends (personal goals).

- Distinguish between short-term and long-term personal and professional goals, listing them by priority and rank.

- Set a *realistic* deadline for achieving each goal, not so short that you might fail and not so long that you might lose interest.

- Create a practical step-by-step plan to achieve each goal, listing *in writing* the steps you must take.

- Review your written lists of goals frequently, making adjustments as needed.

- Keep a *written* record of the accomplishments that bring you closer to a desired goal.


## A DOZEN PRACTICAL STEPS TO IMPROVE YOUR ORGANIZATIONAL ABILITIES

Common sense tells us that the better organized we are, the more efficiently and effectively we can perform our duties. Unnecessary interruptions and searches are time wasters. Although, presumably, everyone knows that better organization is directly linked to better performance, not everyone knows how to become better organized.

Following these twelve steps has helped many secretaries improve the organization of both their work and their workstations.

1. Take a periodic inventory of files, instruction manuals, supplies, and other materials, reorganizing, replacing, or disposing (when authorized) of items as appropriate.

2. Use daily to-do lists, scheduling tasks by priority.

3. Use baskets, color-coded folders, or other means to segregate work in progress or pending.

4. Color-code paper files for quick identification and retrieval and easy discovery of misfiles.

5. Use your computer and appropriate software to organize and manage filing, scheduling, and other daily activities.

6. Maintain an up-to-the-minute paper or electronic calendar, recording even tentative matters as they arise.

7. Keep an up-to-date printed index of computer disks so that you do not have to scan the directories of numerous disks to locate a particular file.

8. Try to file daily or semiweekly, but at least sort material by general category, indicating the file name on each document.

9. Organize all supplies you use regularly in nearby desk drawers and cabinets rather than in a more remote storage area.

10. Use bulletin boards or wall space to post large project charts for organizing and tracking tasks and deadlines.

11. Write down ideas, messages, and so on immediately on proper message sheets rather than assume you will recall something later.

12. Organize supplies, documents, messages, and other material in your workstation at the end of each day so that everything will be set up for use the next morning.

## TWO DOZEN PROVEN WAYS TO MANAGE YOUR TIME BETTER AT WORK

Time is a precious and limited resource in a busy office. Lack of time, or poor time management, has caused many secretaries to be controlled by problems and activities. This type of situation leads to ineffective performance and a failure to focus on results. Time-management experts recommend, first, that you be highly critical about *which* activities you spend your time on (priority) and, second, that you be concerned with how to perform the high-priority tasks better to achieve the desired results. To take this approach, here are two dozen proven ways to manage your time better.

1. Set specific, realistic objectives (in writing), listed according to priority.

2. Put a per-hour price on your time to calculate whether each task is worth the cost (cost per hour times the number of hours it takes).

3. Schedule work appropriately according to low- or high-energy periods whenever company policy and deadlines will allow this flexibility.

4. Take time to organize work, equipment, and supplies at the beginning of a task to ensure minimum timewasting interruptions later.

5. Do a detailed time analysis (recording for two or three weeks every task you do, when you do it, and how much time it takes) to search for more efficient scheduling practices.

6. Use readily available resources, such as on-line databases, coworker expertise, and secretarial networks.

7. Use computers, dictation equipment, and other timesaving equipment as much as possible.

8. Use communication tools, such as voice mail and fax messages, to reduce the number of mail-processing steps.

9. Group and handle similar activities in time blocks whenever possible so that you do not have to repeat setup procedures unnecessarily.

10. Use priority-ranked to-do lists, activity schedules, daily planners, and other paper or electronic organizers that encourage orderly, efficient, timesaving procedures.

11. Break large projects into smaller, manageable tasks.

12. Use holding periods, when you are waiting for someone or something, to work on to-do lists, schedules, and other useful organizational aids.

13. Don't procrastinate (see the next list) and allow difficult or unpleasant tasks to pile up.

14. Inquire regularly about new techniques, systems, and procedures that save time and increase productivity.

15. Develop good communications, including listening carefully to others and making your own comments clear, to avoid time-wasting misunderstandings.

16. Delegate routine work to assistants, temps, or others whenever you can.

17. Cope with occasional work overloads by delegating to others or asking for temporary help.

18. Say no to requests you cannot reasonably handle yourself or delegate.

19. Set deadlines whenever possible that allow you to work steadily at a comfortable pace in which errors are less likely to occur.

20. Benefit from criticism and previous mistakes by taking steps to avoid similar problems in the future.

21. Process papers faster by grouping similar tasks and by reducing the number of times you handle each one.

22. Discourage unnecessary interruptions or personal visits by friends and coworkers (say that you are running late or have a deadline to meet).

23. Treat meetings and conferences as business discussions that must follow an agenda without social visiting or unplanned digressions.

24. Reward yourself periodically for successful time management with something meaningful or enjoyable, such as a movie, to encourage further efforts.

## FOURTEEN HELPFUL TIPS FOR OVERCOMING PROCRASTINATION

Procrastination is a serious threat to productivity. Contrary to popular opinion, few people procrastinate because they are lazy and unconcerned. Most people delay necessary tasks for other reasons, such as fear of failure or a sense of being overwhelmed by the complexity or difficulty in handling a task. Whatever the reason, the result is the same: lost time and disruption of work schedules that together create inefficiency and lowered productivity. The following fourteen tips will help you gain extra hours that previously were lost to the very serious problem of procrastination.

1. Analyze your feelings to determine what frightens you about a project and what is the worst that could happen (write it down).

2. Create a two-column reality-check list, writing each excuse for procrastination in one column and a rational rebuttal in the second column.

3. Develop realistic schedules and deadlines so that you don't begin a task with the feeling that completion on schedule is impossible.

4. Develop a routine in handling tasks so that completing all of your work, including unappealing tasks, will become a habit.

5. Take whatever steps are necessary to calm yourself as a deadline approaches so that your fear does not become debilitating.

6. Think of large or complex tasks as challenging rather than difficult or frightening.

7. Divide a large or difficult project that tends to overwhelm you into a group of smaller, less intimidating individual tasks.

8. Start with a very short, easy task; build on your sense of confidence after handling it, by taking another, slightly larger step. (*Note:* Some people prefer to do the most difficult task first.)

9. Record the time each component in a large project takes as a reminder the next time that individual steps are limited and manageable.

10. Schedule difficult or unpleasant tasks during high-energy, high-confidence times if possible so that you are less likely to quit or delay work.

11. Promise yourself that whenever you start to procrastinate, you will immediately work five or ten minutes on the project before putting it aside.

12. Be strict concerning diversions, refusing to allow yourself to handle low-priority work until you have eliminated the high-priority tasks.

13. Praise or reward yourself upon completing each step, task, or project, no matter how small.

14. Recognize the difference between irrational procrastination and intelligent rescheduling of difficult tasks to a more appropriate time.

## THE FIVE COMMANDMENTS OF SUCCESSFUL BODY LANGUAGE

Before you open your mouth, others notice the way you look—how you sit or stand, the way you dress, the expression on your face, and other visual qualities. Body language can suggest that you are confident or unsure, friendly or unfriendly, happy or sad, and many other things. To project a favorable image, follow the five commandments of successful body language.

1. Sit, stand, and walk straight, without fidgeting or making nervous gestures, to project a sense of confidence, poise, and capability.

2. Learn to smile not only with your mouth but also with your eyes to avoid any suggestion of insincerity or deceptiveness.

3. Make eye contact with each person you meet to indicate genuine interest in and concern for the other person as well as to avoid projecting a sense of timidity and lack of confidence.

4. Maintain a pleasant expression on your face that masks any anxiety, impatience, irritation, or other unappealing emotion you may be experiencing.

5. Maintain a clean, neat, well-groomed, professional appearance in hairstyle, clothing, and nail care, observing any other requirements in your office.

## EFFECTIVE NETWORKING IDEAS FOR EXCHANGING USEFUL INFORMATION

Networks connect people with similar interests. They provide an excellent avenue for the exchange of ideas, factual information, and other useful material. Informal networks, such as daily or weekly lunches with coworkers, are sometimes as helpful as formal, structured networks. When a more formal connection is desired, the type of network you join or start will depend on your needs and interests, as well as available connections. You may, for example, make contact by postal mail, E-mail, telephone, local area network, or on-line subscriber service. In all cases, it is important to take advantage of these strategies and opportunities to make networking a valuable learning tool.

- Participate in outside networks as well as in-house networks.

- Expand the number of contacts you make by letting each new contact lead you to another contact.

- Encourage communication by asking other network participants what type of information they can and want to exchange.

- Offer to provide information whether or not you will receive something in return.

- Seek diversity among your contacts to ensure the receipt of new ideas and other information that will broaden your knowledge base.

- Earn the trust of other network participants by keeping confidences and respecting the privacy of others.

- Keep records (computer, Rolodex, and so on) of networking activities to identify contacts, sources of information, and other useful material.

- Consider using a sorting program if you want to maintain extensive contact lists by computer.

- Use your off-network time to expand your knowledge through reading, study, and other means.

- Join a professional association like PSI®, or network via Professional Secretaries On-Line on the Internet, to increase your knowledge and also provide an opportunity for further information exchange.

- Send E-mail communications to contacts to reduce the amount of paperwork to be processed and the time required to process it.

- Work on computer documents simultaneously with other network participants through document conferencing without physically circulating disks or printouts.

## EASY-TO-LEARN SPEED-READING TECHNIQUES

Almost every aspect of secretarial work involves reading—reading the incoming mail, proofreading printouts for errors, reading file material to determine file location, reading handwritten material before typing it, and reading newspapers, magazines, and other material for information. Therefore, the faster you can read, the more work you can do in a short time, increasing your productivity. Here are some suggestions for increasing your reading speed.

- Read for *both* speed and comprehension, not speed alone.
- Adjust your lighting and seating arrangements for maximum comfort and benefit.
- Preview the material quickly before reading, to note who wrote it, how it is written and formatted, and so on.
- Scan the material quickly to get a general idea of the content, glancing at the table of contents, headings, illustrations, and other items.
- Force your eyes to move ahead from one line to another without pausing and without moving back to reread an earlier line.
- Focus on key words or ideas, and group associated words into single thought units rather than read and focus on each word, one at a time.
- Mark unfamiliar words and abbreviations, waiting until you are finished reading to look them up.
- Annotate, underline, or highlight key points mentally or with a pen as you read.
- Rescan material after reading it to be certain you have gleaned everything you want or need to know.

- Try reading faster with each new session, without sacrificing comprehension.

## FOURTEEN USEFUL TIPS FOR REDUCING STRESS AT WORK

Tension, anxiety, stress—very few secretaries escape the pressures of the workplace and the adverse way that they affect performance. Errors in work, irritability, frustration, and even physical ailments result when stress gains the upper hand. Rather than wait for quieter days that never come, you may want to try the following tips for reducing stress at work.

1. List stressful tasks, projects, and other problems along with possible solutions that would alleviate the pressure (e.g., revising schedules and deadlines).

2. Ask coworkers or your employer for suggestions on how to cope with stressful problems such as an unmanageable work load or simultaneous deadlines.

3. Ask friends or coworkers for help (and offer to reciprocate) with nuisance matters such as finding transportation to work.

4. Remind yourself continually that you are not required to be superwoman or superman, only a competent, professional secretary.

5. Don't feel guilty if you must say no to a personal or professional request that you cannot handle or delegate.

6. Pick something to work on that will enable you to become wholly absorbed in the task to the point that you temporarily forget about everything else.

7. Take a refreshment break, go for a walk, or go to the company exercise room (if any) when the stress becomes too severe for you to work.

8. Start work early or stay late to handle occasional overloads or to compensate for unexpected interruptions that ruin your schedule.

9. Transfer pertinent items (e.g., a dental appointment) from your home calendar to your work calendar so that you won't forget when you plan your daily work schedule.

10. Consider a long commute to and from work as free time that you can use—without feeling guilty—to relax and unwind.

11. Focus regularly on the positive aspects of your personal and professional life, such as your achievements (small ones included) or the challenge of a new project.

12. Make it a habit *each* day to do at least one thing that you enjoy, such as reading a chapter in a new book or listening to a favorite tape.

13. Look for humor in demanding, difficult situations, using megadoses of laughter as a tonic.

14. Keep up your health and physical stamina by exercising several times a week and eating sensibly each day.

## PUTTING IT ALL TOGETHER: OFFICE SKILLS TESTING AND CERTIFICATION

Employers frequently assess the competencies of entry-level workers to screen job applicants and test new employees. A key objective is to identify areas where training will strengthen them as office workers. One notable program is the Office Proficiency Assessment and Certification® (OPAC®) program, originally developed by PSI® and now distributed through Biddle & Associates, Inc., in Sacramento, California. OPAC measures keyboarding and word processing, language arts, records management, financial record keeping, spreadsheets, and database skills.

PSI® also created, and continues to offer, the Certified Professional Secretary® (CPS®) rating. Secretaries who have earned this rating have reported pride in accomplishment, increased self-esteem, greater respect from employers and peers, increased confidence, pay increases and bonuses, and more opportunities for advancement. Those who would like to qualify for the CPS® rating must complete and verify educational and secretarial employment experience requirements and pass a three-part, one-day exam. Candidates may request an application form, review materials for taking the exam, a list of testing centers throughout the world, and colleges and universities giving academic credit for having passed the exam. For full details on exam dates (May and November), expenses (expenses are covered by some companies), review materials and other matters, write to the Institute for Certification, CPS Department, 10502 N.W. Ambassador Drive, P.O. Box 20404, Kansas City, MO 64195-0404, telephone 816-891-6600, fax 816-891-9118 or E-mail-Internet cps@psi.org. The following subjects are covered in the CPS® Examination.

*Part I. Finance and Business Law*

30 percent economics

35 percent accounting

35 percent business law

120 items, 2 hours 30 minutes

*Part II. Office Systems and Administration*

50 percent office technology

25 percent office administration

25 percent business communications

150 items, 2 hours

*Part III. Management*

36 percent behavioral science in business

19 percent human resources management

45 percent organizations and management

150 items, 2 hours

# — 2 —
# INTERPERSONAL
# RELATIONS

## SIMPLE LISTENING STRATEGIES THAT WILL PAY BIG DIVIDENDS

Although one-half of the communications equation involves listening, most people focus on the other half—talking and writing. Yet secretaries and other office professionals spend a substantial amount of time listening to clients and customers, other callers and visitors, coworkers, executives, and various other contacts, such as service repairpeople and sales representatives. How well you listen will significantly affect your ability to assimilate and convey information, make decisions, and carry out instructions. This list, therefore, outlines important strategies that will make you a better listener.

- Think of listening as an active process rather than a passive activity.

- Look for expressions, body-language signs, and other indicators of what someone means rather than concentrating solely on the person's words.

- Listen seriously and fully to other people's ideas without prejudging the importance of a concept or proposal.

- Demonstrate interest in what someone is saying through eye contact and other receptive body language, such as leaning forward toward the person.

- Give your undivided attention to the other person when he or she is speaking without interrupting or letting your thoughts wander.

- Focus on the complete message rather than on isolated fragments that may be misleading or appear unimportant when taken out of context.

- Don't tune out information you hear just because it conflicts with your own views or appears to duplicate something you already know.

- Don't mentally alter other people's messages to fit your own needs, prejudices, or perceptions.

- Watch for facial clues (e.g., wandering eyes) and other signs (e.g., attempts to interrupt) that it is time for you to stop talking and start listening.

- Don't distract the speaker's communication with arguments, criticisms, or other comments and facial expressions.

- Encourage the flow of information by using pauses to ask questions and clarify points the speaker has made.

## BASIC GUIDELINES TO ENSURE SUCCESS IN TRAINING OTHERS

Training others is a regular activity for many secretaries who must train their own assistants or temps as well as help other coworkers learn various techniques and procedures. Since a well-trained employee will save time for you in the future and will help to prevent, not create, problems, it is worth the time and energy initially required to provide useful, effective instruction. Here are some guidelines that will help you to become a more successful trainer.

- Prepare written lists of steps for handling a technique or procedure, going through the list one step at a time.

- Demonstrate the technique or procedure you are explaining.

- Find out what the person already knows before you begin.

- Develop a routine with clear limitations and expectations so that the person will know how much time and what type of instruction and assistance you will provide.

- Be patient when you provide instruction so that you won't have to keep repeating your explanations.

- Resist the temptation to do the work yourself rather than take time to train someone else.

- Use humor to defuse the nervous tension that people often feel when learning something new.

- Ask the person to restate your instructions from time to time and to demonstrate a technique or procedure so that you can check his or her comprehension and progress.

- Pause frequently to ask if the person understands or has any questions.

- Be prepared to try more than one method of instruction until you find the one that best fits the individual.

- Find out why your previous instruction failed each time it is necessary to repeat an explanation or demonstration.

- Provide adequate reference material for equipment, software, and other aspects of the training, including additional sources for independent study.

- Motivate the individual by emphasizing the interesting, challenging, and rewarding features of the work.

- Compliment the person frequently on work well done, encouraging him or her to keep up the good work.

- Phrase criticisms carefully to avoid discouraging the individual and weakening his or her confidence and enthusiasm.

- Don't make judgmental, critical comments about others in the company that might prejudice the individual and create troublesome working barriers.

- Realize that it may take a while for the person to become proficient and work at a faster pace.

## A Dozen Practical Hints for Criticizing Others Constructively

One of the most difficult things a secretary occasionally has to do is criticize others. Unless an error is so minor that it is not worth mentioning, it is usually helpful and necessary to point out mistakes so that they won't cause problems for the company or embarrassment for the person making them. Most people would rather know about an error they have made so that they can correct it before it becomes public knowledge. But they don't want to be humiliated or scolded like a child. The utmost care is needed in criticizing someone to avoid hurt feelings and counterproductive results. Here are a dozen practical hints for criticizing others constructively.

1. Take steps immediately, while facts and events are still clear in everyone's mind, when it is necessary to point out a mistake or unacceptable practices.

2. Be very clear and specific in explaining precisely what is wrong and why the mistake must be corrected or the unacceptable practice discontinued.

3. Use positive words such as "a good approach would be" instead of negative words such as "that was a bad approach."

4. Criticize only one problem at a time to avoid confusing or overwhelming the person.

5. Analyze problems before discussing them so that you are better prepared to discuss why the situation developed and how it can be corrected.

6. Word your criticism carefully to attack the problem instead of the person.

7. Find something to commend to take the sting out of the criticism.

8. Include suggestions and resolutions with your criticism to emphasize a positive outcome.

9. Don't overstate or exaggerate a situation by belaboring a point or by treating one instance of a mistake or problem as a trend or regular occurrence.

10. Never humiliate someone by criticizing the person in front of others.

11. Try to find out if someone making a mistake or causing a problem has been temporarily affected by an outside problem, such as a family illness.

12. Don't let someone's mistake or unacceptable practice cloud your objectivity about the rest of the person's work.

## THE EIGHT MOST IMPORTANT DELEGATING GUIDELINES

Secretaries who have assistants or who supervise temporary help during periods of a heavy work load need to master the art of delegating effectively. Delegating work to others—particularly when you are responsible for what they do—isn't so easy as it might at first seem. Also, many secretaries feel more confident doing everything themselves and resent the need to let certain tasks go to others. But sometimes there is no choice; some of the work must be given to others to cope with a hectic schedule. Learning how to delegate effectively to others, even to your supervisor, is essential in a busy office, and every secretary should know these eight guidelines.

1. Evaluate both the work and the person to whom you delegate, to be certain that you have the best possible match of duties and capabilities.

2. Distribute the work load fairly among all employees and according to skills, to be certain that no one feels overworked or mistreated.

3. Let the individuals know exactly what the task is and what is expected, including quality as well as quantity of work.

4. Set realistic deadlines for each task.

5. Encourage each person to ask questions, to make suggestions, and to keep you informed of progress and problems.

6. Demonstrate your interest and support by regularly monitoring the progress of each person.

7. Schedule regular meetings to review the work, answer questions, and solve problems.

8. Adopt a tactful tone of requesting help rather than issuing orders or instructions when you are delegating work to peers or upward to a supervisor.

## SENSIBLE STRATEGIES FOR CONTROLLING OFFICE POLITICS

Although office politics can be used unfairly to gain an advantage at work, the implication that all activities designed to help you advance are negative is misleading. Honest, ethical steps to enhance your career not only are legitimate but also are necessary. There is no need to shy away from competition or to avoid opportunities simply because others are also maneuvering to gain an advantage and advance in their careers. It is virtually impossible for a secretary to avoid office relationships, and often it is impossible to succeed without taking deliberate steps to influence others in your favor. The following strategies may help you control office politics and use opportunities wisely.

- Recognize other people's cultural, social, and economic backgrounds and the values they have developed.
- Develop your skills in handling interpersonal relationships while avoiding overdependence on others.
- Remain alert to signs of selfish, adversarial behavior in office relationships.
- Cultivate a friendly, cooperative, professional relationship with key players at all levels in your company who can help you.

- Use networking and other forms of collaboration to increase your knowledge and encourage constructive assistance in reaching your goals.

- Find a mentor, someone in an influential position who will help and support you in your efforts to create and make good use of opportunities.

- Demonstrate a strong loyalty and commitment to your company in your attitude, conversations, and responses to others.

- Reveal your performance to your employer and other key people by, for example, making useful suggestions and writing brief status reports about your projects.

- Offer to expand your regular duties and responsibilities.

- Look for opportunities to help coworkers, new employees, and others.

- Gain visibility by volunteering for committee assignments, special-project work, and high-profile public duties.

- Develop your leadership skills, including decision making and conflict resolution.

- Seek support for new ideas before you distribute them widely so that they will have a better chance of acceptance.

- Learn how to offer genuine praise without overdoing it.

- Learn how to criticize constructively and tactfully.

- Treat rumors as gossip or unsubstantiated information (sometimes warranting further investigation) rather than fact.

- Decide how much you are willing to risk (lose) when an uncertain situation exists.

- Be willing to risk failure within the limits you establish.

- Keep private documentation of problems so that you can support any analysis or recommendation you might make if a conflict escalates.

# Fourteen Key Pointers for Dealing with Sexual Harassment at Work

Sexual harassment includes any unwelcome attention or behavior that focuses on a worker's sex rather than his or her status as an employee. This includes essentially any language, expression, gesture, or physical contact that in any way has to do with sex. The guidelines of the Equal Opportunity Employment Commission consider sexual harassment a form of sexual discrimination, which is prohibited by Title VII of the 1964 Civil Rights Act. According to the guidelines, the unwelcome attention or behavior constitutes sexual harassment (1) when submission to the conduct is explicitly or implicitly made a term or condition of the person's employment, (2) when submission or rejection of the conduct is used as the basis for making decisions that affect the person's employment, and (3) when the conduct unreasonably interferes with the person's performance or creates an intimidating, hostile, or offensive working environment. Here are fourteen key pointers for dealing with sexual harassment at work.

1. Assert yourself immediately when offensive behavior occurs.

2. Clearly and firmly state that you strongly object to the behavior and do not wish to participate.

3. Write a letter to the harasser if your verbal rejection is ignored.

4. Deliver the letter in person, if possible, accompanied by a supportive friend or coworker.

5. Document each incident in detail, including copies of offensive literature as well as the date, time, location, and a clear description of what was said and done.

6. Keep copies of your documentation in secure places.

7. Document your job performance, including written descriptions of your responsibilities and accomplishments and copies of correspondence that reveal your efforts and commendations you received.

8. Seek the support and help of both male and female coworkers, some of whom may also be victims and will join you in a collective complaint.

9. Discuss the problem with the designated official, a manager, or other influential person in the company.

10. Acknowledge in writing any promises of action on your behalf by these people.

11. Consider seeking additional help from the outside, such as from a minister or from the media.

12. Consider discussing the matter with an attorney if the harassment does not stop.

13. File a complaint (with or without legal representation) with a nearby office of the Equal Employment Opportunity Commission within 180 days (300 in some states) of the first incident.

14. Look for another job if you cannot find resolution or protection within the company, but ask for letters of reference before you submit your resignation.

## THE ESSENTIAL DO'S AND DON'TS OF INTERNATIONAL BUSINESS ETIQUETTE

As international business contacts increase, the need for greater cultural awareness and sensitivity also increases. Secretaries who work for organizations that do business with firms in other countries need to expand their knowledge of business and social customs around the world. Differences abound, and it is necessary to adapt to the requirements of each situation with the realization that what is preferred in one country may be taboo in another. Local libraries and bookstores may have books and tapes on the various countries, and schools and government departments and agencies may also be helpful. Most major countries also maintain embassies or consulates in the United States where you can seek additional information, or you may contact a U.S. embassy office or consulate in a particular country (see the address list in Chapter 9). In spite of the vast differences from country to country, the following general guidelines apply.

- Respect the religious, social, and business customs of each country.

- Never make critical observations of or jokes about the people and their practices, even if you are not serious (people may not appreciate your sense of humor).

- Use the preferred form of address for a man or woman in another country, including the correct personal or professional title.

- Use the correct order in stating first, middle, and last names.

- Keep language that would be unfamiliar to someone in another country, such as idioms, clichés, and jargon, out of your conversations and letters.

- Use appropriate formality in conversations and letters unless you know that a foreign contact desires less formality.

- Follow the practices of the country in regard to appointments, punctuality, business hours, and holidays.

- Have the reverse side of business cards printed in the language of the other country, without abbreviations or other information that might be unclear.

- Determine whether physical contact with someone in another country, such as shaking hands, is a sign of respect or disrespect.

- Keep in mind that eye contact or the lack of it means different things, such as aggression or respect, in different countries.

- Learn how much physical distance you should maintain between you and the other person, being careful not to move farther away or closer while talking.

- Watch your American gestures, some of which in certain countries might have entirely different, even obscene, meanings.

- Study the practices pertaining to handling food and utensils and to eating meals in both restaurants and homes.

- Observe a country's prohibitions on or your contact's beliefs concerning dress style, alcohol, cigarettes, and certain foods, such as meat.

- Avoid topics of conversation, such as sex, religion, and politics, that might disturb or offend someone in another country.

- Find out what are considered proper and improper gifts for social and business occasions (see the next section).

- Observe a country's practices concerning the role occupied by women in social and business settings.

- Be aware of the different attitudes toward money, including the proper amount for gifts and gratuities and the handling of financial matters in business negotiations.

- Use the universal signals that are viewed favorably by almost everyone in any country—a smile, a compliment, and an expression of appreciation.

## VALUABLE SUGGESTIONS FOR PROPER INTERNATIONAL GIFT GIVING

Selecting the right gift for someone in another country requires a thorough knowledge of gift-giving practices in that country. In many cultures, gift giving is an essential act that must be carried out at the right time and in the right way. Although American companies often have policies that affect the acceptance and disposition of valuable gifts and may have certain standard gifts that are always given, it is important to review the practices in the other country to be certain that the American gift-giving ideas don't conflict with those of someone in another country. Etiquette books and books on international communication often deal with this subject, and some travel guides provide tips for individual countries. The following general guidelines should also be considered in all cases of international gift giving.

- Giving the wrong gift may be worse than giving none (e.g., liquor is forbidden in the Islamic religion).

- Giving a gift that is too expensive will usually cause more embarrassment than giving one that is too modest.

- Although most flowers are a welcome gift in the United States, certain ones may be a poor choice in some countries (e.g., chrysanthemums are associated with death in France).

- In most countries, you should enclose a blank card with your gift, rather than a business card, containing a hand-written note.

- Generally, avoid very personal gifts, such as perfume and cologne.

- In some countries, such as in Japan, business gifts are exchanged at the first meeting, whereas in other areas, such as in western Europe, that would be considered too forward.

- One should always take a gift to a person's home on the first or any other visit.

- When in doubt, let your contact make the first gesture or initiate the gift giving.

- In the Arab world and in other countries where women occupy a traditional, subservient role, it is inappropriate to give a gift to a wife or wives.

- Use simple wrapping for a gift going through Customs since it may be unwrapped there for inspection.

- Gifts that are made in the United States are especially appreciated by people in other countries.

- In certain places, such as in the Middle East, if you admire someone's possessions too much, he or she may feel obliged to give them to you.

- If you give a visitor a large gift, offer to ship it to the person's home or office.

- If guide books do not offer enough suggestions, telephone or write the cultural attaché in the embassy of the particular country (see Chapter 9 for addresses).

# — 3 —

# TELECOMMUNICATIONS

## THE TEN TELEPHONE COMPANY SERVICES YOU WILL MOST OFTEN USE

Telecommunications, which include voice, data, and image transmission, form the basis of most business communication, especially long-distance communication. Although telephone company services may vary from one company to another, all of them provide the basic requirements for local, national, and international communication. Secretaries and other office professionals, who spend a substantial portion of each day with telephone-related activities, make heavy use of the services provided by telephone companies, including these ten common business services.

1. *Direct-distance dialing.* Using this least expensive form of service, you dial a number directly, without operator assistance, and speak with anyone who answers.

2. *Person-to-person calls.* This type of call, placed with operator assistance and thus more expensive, is used when you want to speak only with a particular person.

3. *International calls.* Direct-dialed calls may be placed to any participating country by dialing the international access code, country code, city code, and local telephone number (see the list of codes in this chapter).

4. *Conference calls.* To talk with several people in different locations simultaneously, dial the local operator and ask for the conference-call operator, give the date and time desired, and state the names and telephone numbers of the participants.

5. *Credit-card calls.* Using a telephone-company calling card or an approved credit card, you can charge calls by dialing the operator, by dialing direct and entering the card number, or by inserting the card in a card-reader telephone.

6. *Marine radiotelephone.* (1) To use operator assistance to talk with someone on a ship, dial the local operator; ask for the marine operator; and give the name of the ship, the ocean, and the ship's telephone number. (2) To use a satellite connection for international calls, dial the international access code, ocean code, and ship's telephone number, and press the # key.

7. *Airfone and railfone service.* When airplanes and trains have special equipment, you can place card-reader calls, with the connection made by an operator who takes the number and places the call from a telephone company ground station.

8. *Outbound WATS.* Companies that frequently make calls to a particular area may request an outbound line, with the calls often made by first dialing a standard code followed by the telephone number.

9. *Inward WATS.* Companies that receive or want to encourage a lot of incoming calls may have an inbound line with an 800 number that callers may use to place calls without charge to them.

10. *Leased lines.* Companies that have heavy traffic between two points may lease a private line, such as a foreign-exchange line to a another city or a tie line connecting two private branch exchanges in distant cities.

# Six Advanced Telecommunications Services That Save Time

Telephones and computers are used together to create advanced technologies that make it possible for organizations to conduct business faster and, often, at lower costs. Secretaries use these technologies every day either directly or indirectly by making arrangements for their employers to use them. These six advanced telecommunications services are especially noteworthy for the time they save and the greater speed they provide compared with older forms of communication and transmission.

1. *Voice mail.* A voice-mail system provides for the automated storage and delivery of voice messages through the computerized processing of the speaker's voice.

2. *E-mail.* Using a computer, a modem, and the telephone lines, electronic messages can be sent to a receiving computer, where the received message may be stored in an electronic mailbox, read on screen, or printed out.

3. *Fax mail.* A paper document, both text and graphics, can be sent over the telephone lines from one fax machine to another, or an electronic version can be sent by a properly equipped computer.

4. *Cellular telephone service.* Cellular technology, which divides a city into cells containing transmitting and receiving equipment, enables callers to place and receive calls from a moving vehicle.

5. *Telecomputing.* By using the telephone lines to connect remote computers or fax machines to those in a main office, one can perform computerized tasks from the remote location and interact with other computer users.

6. *Teleconferencing.* Through connections of people and equipment made over the telephone lines or by satellite, the three common options are (1) *audioconferencing* (voice exchange only), (2) *videoconferencing* (audio and visual exchange), and (3) *document conferencing* (on-screen processing and document exchange).

## EFFICIENT AND EFFECTIVE PRACTICES IN HANDLING INCOMING CALLS

The way you handle telephone calls will reveal a great deal about you, your boss, and your company. Even if your organization provides the best product or service in the city, some customers or clients will form a negative impression if you sound impatient, disinterested, irritable, uninformed, defensive, or argumentive. Someone who has never seen you and doesn't know you at all may make sweeping—perhaps incorrect—judgments about you and the people and organization you represent solely on the basis of how you act and sound on the telephone. It is, therefore, essential to project the best possible image, which the following practices should help you to do.

- Answer the telephone promptly, by the second or third ring.

- Answer calls with the mouthpiece rather than a speaker, which unfairly compromises a caller's need for privacy and may additionally create a poor connection.

- When you answer someone else's telephone, identify yourself and the absent person, take a message (write legibly), and later ask the absent person if he or she found the message.

- When someone is absent and a caller does not want you to take a written message, give the absent person's voice-mail number (if any), offering to transfer the call when possible.

- When you don't have time to handle a call, tactfully explain that you aren't free now but can transfer the call to someone else who might be (give an approximate time).

- When you will be absent, leave a personalized voice-mail message if possible.

- When you must ask someone to answer your telephone, provide clear instructions about what to say, leaving a pen or pencil and a message pad.

- Identify yourself when you answer: "Good morning, Shipping Department. This is Carol. May I help you?"

- Ask your employer if you should screen calls, following instructions as diplomatically as possible: "May I ask who is calling?" "May I tell Mr. Bentley what this is in reference to?"

- Write down a caller's name (ask how to spell it if necessary) immediately, recording the date, time, and message as soon as possible.

- Keep an adequate supply of pens, pencils, and message forms by your telephone.

- Devote all your attention to a caller, postponing other, even simple, tasks until you are finished with the call.

- Use a caller's name during the call both to make the caller feel good and to help you remember it: "Do you happen to know your customer number, Ms. Nelson?"

- Respond to a caller's message rather than his or her emotional state.

- Listen patiently, without interrupting, without clipping off the ends of or finishing a caller's sentences, and without asking for clarification before the caller has had a chance to finish.

- When a caller speaks too rapidly or doesn't enunciate clearly, ask for clarification or spelling of names if necessary, after he or she has finished talking.

- Learn to smile as you speak, since a pleasant facial expression often creates a similarly pleasant tonal quality that callers detect.

- Avoid embarrassing a caller ("You're *really* out of touch") even when he or she is incorrect; rather, respond by saying, for example, "You're right; there used to be an office in Dayton, but it's no longer open."

- Take a positive, concerned, helpful approach to problems, so that you will project an image of a company that cares: "I certainly understand your concern, Mr. Porter."

- Phrase all your remarks in a positive manner: "We expect to finish on October 30" rather than "We won't be able to finish until October 30."

- Provide essential information: "Ms. Anderson is away from her desk at the moment, but is expected back at 2 o'clock."

- Do not reveal confidential or nonessential facts: "Ms. Anderson is having a tooth capped between now and 2 o'clock."

- Speak slowly and enunciate clearly, without eating, drinking, chewing gum, humming, playing the radio, or doing anything else that is annoying and distracting to callers.

- When you must speak to someone by your desk while you are on the telephone, ask the telephone caller to excuse you for a moment.

- If you are talking to someone in the office when the telephone rings, excuse yourself to the visitor so that you can promptly answer the call.

- When you must end a rambling conversation or a personal call, wait for a pause and quickly, but politely, give an excuse for ending the call, such as an incoming call on another line.

- When persistent callers that your employer refuses to talk to become annoying, ask them to put their messages in writing, and offer to deliver their letters promptly to the appropriate person.

- If you often provide information to callers, learn in advance about the business you discuss (keep notes handy), answering as many questions as possible before referring a caller to someone else.

- Ask for permission to put someone on hold before doing so, giving the caller a chance to leave a message instead.

- When you have a caller temporarily on hold, check in about every 30 seconds to ask if he or she wants to continue holding, leave a message, or have you return the call.

- If a caller will have to be on hold a long time, ask for a message, offer to transfer the call to someone else who can help more quickly, or offer to call back as soon as possible (give an approximate time).

- When you must transfer a call, give the caller the extension in case the call is cut off.

- When practical, let a person to whom a call is transferred know the background so that the caller won't have to repeat everything.

- When a conversation is ended, let the caller hang up first, if possible.

- Listen to yourself on tape to determine how you sound to others.

- Call in to your company from the outside to determine how calls are handled.

## VALUABLE TIPS FOR HANDLING VOICE-MAIL MESSAGES

*Voice mail*, or *voice messaging*, is a means of storing and distributing telephone messages electronically. In a typical system, a user has a private voice file or mailbox, and only the user can retrieve his or her messages. Although some people object to hearing an automated operator take a call and recite a list of options and the correct button to push for each, other people enjoy the benefits of freeing workers for other tasks. However, since voice mail is not the same as direct human interaction, special requirements apply to this type of communication. The following tips will help users overcome some of the fear and frustration of using voice messaging.

*Your Recorded Message to Callers*

- When possible, record messages in your own voice, including your name, office or department, company name, and any other essential information.

- Make your recorded messages as personal as possible: "I'll be in a meeting from 1 to 3 o'clock today, Wednesday, July 1."

- Change your recorded message daily or throughout the day when practical: "It's January 6, and I'll be in the office from 9 A.M. to 1 P.M. and from 3 to 4:30 P.M."

- State that you regularly check your mailbox for incoming calls if you are able to do that: "I'll be traveling today but will check my mailbox several times throughout the day."

- Indicate how soon you'll be able to respond to an incoming call: "I'll be hosting an out-of-town delegation until 2 P.M. and will return calls after that. Let me know the best time to call you back."

- Let callers know when you won't be able to respond the same day.

- If you will be away for the day, offer to return calls the following day; if you will be away for three to five days, offer to respond within a week or suggest another person and number to the caller.

- If you can most easily be reached at certain times, let callers know: "The best time to reach me is between 7:30 and 9:00 in the morning."

- State any important requests or requirements, such as when a caller may begin a fax transmission.

- When you are absent, refer callers to another number in case of emergency.

- Notice the good and bad points of other people's recordings, and try to use the good features while avoiding the bad.

*Leaving a Message When You Are the Caller*

- Speak clearly and slowly, spelling out difficult names.

- Leave enough basic facts, including your name, telephone number, and company, as well as specific details of your request or comment.

- When you're responding to someone's earlier call to you, refresh the person's memory: "This is Marlene Douglas in Mr. Eddings' office. You called this morning to ask when Mr. Eddings would be returning from his field trip. . . ."

- When you're calling to report bad news, don't reveal the details in your voice message: "Jane, I noticed something in the new software program that I'd like to discuss with you. Could you please call me this afternoon? Thanks much."

- If you have a long, detailed message, send the main message by fax or E-mail, and use your voice message simply to announce it: "This is Tim. I'll be faxing you the X100 specifications by 4 o'clock today. Call me at 555-3366 if you have any questions. Thanks."

- If you previously left a message asking for something but no longer need it, notify the person immediately: "This is Beverly Leoni at ABC Consultants. I called at 9 this morning to ask for a price list. Since then, someone found a copy for me, so I won't need you to send it. Thanks anyway."

## PRACTICAL MEASURES FOR BETTER TELECOMMUNICATIONS TIME MANAGEMENT

When telephone usage is handled properly, the telephone can be a significant time and money saver in a busy office. But when it is handled improperly, it can be an expensive time waster. Just as secretaries need to apply effective time-management principles to general office work (see Chapter 1), they also need to improve their telecommunications time management. Many managers believe that the telephone is the most abused piece of equipment in the office and that strict cost-control and time-management practices are essential. Here are some practical measures for better telecommunications time management.

- Use the telephone as a quick substitute for more time-consuming tasks such as preparing a letter.

- Jot down the time or use a clock with a second hand or quiet timer to remind you to halt (tactfully) certain conversations, such as excessive small talk and rambling.

- Place calls during slow periods, if possible, when you won't be interrupted and have to repeat the call later.

- Return all calls in the same time block when possible.

- Be aware of different time zones to avoid wasting time placing calls when someone is not likely to be available (see the map in this chapter).

- Program fax machines for lower-cost after-hours transmission when possible.

- Don't call people during lunch periods or other times when they are not likely to be available.

- Have detailed written notes in front of you when placing a call to avoid wasting time back-tracking or pausing repeatedly to think of the next point.

- Listen carefully so that you will not have to waste time repeating information.

- Speak clearly so that the other party will not have to ask you to take time to repeat something.

- Evaluate your telephone usage by studying bills or by recording your incoming and outgoing calls for a week or more: date, start and finish times, total time spent, person called or calling, and personal or business purpose.

- Establish time-management guidelines for assistants, temps, and others, letting coworkers and your employer know what you are trying to accomplish.

## EIGHTEEN WAYS TO COPE WITH TELEMARKETING FRAUD

Both homes and businesses are targets of telemarketing fraud, and the secretary is often the first person to talk to a swindler. The Federal Trade Commission in Washington, D.C., estimates that fraudulent telemarketers swindle consumers out of more than a billion dollars each year. It publishes a variety of free "Facts for Consumers" publications explaining fraudulent sales practices and what precautions you can take. Here are some of the ways you can cope with telemarketing fraud.

1. Remember the old adage that if an offer sounds too good to be true, it probably is.

2. Avoid making any purchase if you don't understand something.

3. Remember that swindlers are persuasive and deceptive.

4. Beware of high-pressure sales tactics and a salesperson's refusal to accept no for an answer.

5. Be skeptical when someone insists that you make an immediate decision.

6. Beware of statements offering something free followed by a requirement that you also pay for something.

7. Reject any claim of a proposed investment without risk.

8. Reject any request to make a purchase on trust.

9. Refuse to give your credit-card number unless you initiated a call to a reputable firm from which you are authorized to make purchases by telephone.

10. Refuse to allow a caller to send someone to your office or home to pick up your money.

11. Request written information by mail about an unknown organization and its product or service before you consider making a purchase.

12. Ask for written details about guarantees and refund policies before you buy.

13. Insist on knowing what state or federal agencies regulate the organization.

14. Insist that duplicate material be sent to your accountant or attorney if you are considering a large purchase.

15. Beware of sellers who have excuses why they cannot provide *written* references and other material that you can investigate.

16. Ignore testimonials that you cannot verify.

17. Investigate the references and other material if you actually receive them.

18. Fill out an order form even when you order by telephone, keeping a dated copy available for later reference.

# THE MOST OFTEN USED TELEPHONE AND FAX NUMBERS AT WORK

Secretaries usually have an electronic or paper address list containing the names and numbers of their employer's associates, clients and customers, and other contacts. In addition to these numbers, the numbers of various business services should be on file, including the following frequently called places.

- Airlines and air shuttles
- Amtrak
- Associations
- Banks (business)
- Brokers
- Building manager/supervisor
- Buses and airport shuttle buses
- Business organizations and clubs
- Car-rental agencies
- Catering services
- Credit-card companies
- Emergency calls (fire, police, ambulance, and so on)
- Equipment dealers and service departments
- Express-mail offices
- Garages and service stations
- Highway Patrol or State Police (road conditions and so on)
- Hotels and motels
- Hot lines
- Libraries
- Maintenance service
- Messenger/courier services

- Office-personnel residences
- Office-supply stores
- On-line services
- Other common carriers
- Post offices
- Regional telephone company
- Security-alarm service
- Subcontract services (e.g., printers)
- Taxis
- Temporary help agencies
- Theater ticket agencies
- Travel agent
- Weather
- Western Union

## TELEPHONE CODES YOU WILL NEED TO MAKE DOMESTIC AND INTERNATIONAL CALLS

Secretaries need to know domestic area codes and international country and city codes for two reasons: (1) to be able to dial direct and (2) to be able to identify the location of incoming calls and other communications. The lists in this chapter can be used for quick reference when you don't have time to consult various telephone books and other directories and don't want to take time to call Directory Assistance (Information). The first listing consists of a map of domestic area codes and time zones for the United States and Canada, as well as a numerical cross-index to the area codes given on the map. The second listing consists of international access codes and the country and city codes for all major countries of the world and their principal cities, as well as a chart showing time differences for different parts of the world. Since both domestic and international codes change from time to time, update the following lists as you learn about such changes.

# AREA CODES AND TIME ZONES

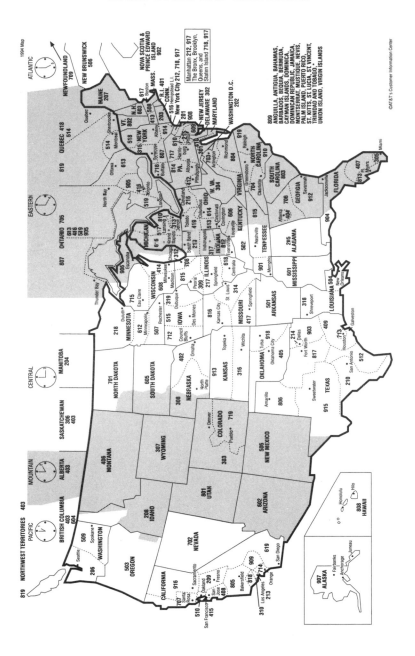

Courtesy of Payne Publishers, Manassas, Virginia

## AREA CODES FOR THE UNITED STATES, CANADA, AND OTHER LOCATIONS

| Area Code | Location | Area Code | Location |
|---|---|---|---|
| 201 | New Jersey | 313 | Michigan |
| 202 | District of Columbia | 314 | Missouri |
|  |  | 315 | New York |
| 203 | Connecticut | 316 | Kansas |
| 204 | Manitoba | 317 | Indiana |
| 205 | Alabama | 318 | Louisiana |
| 206 | Washington | 319 | Iowa |
| 207 | Maine | 401 | Rhode Island |
| 208 | Idaho | 402 | Nebraska |
| 209 | California | 403 | Alberta, British Columbia, Northwest Territories, Saskatchewan, and Yukon |
| 210 | Texas |  |  |
| 212 | New York |  |  |
| 213 | California |  |  |
| 214 | Texas | 404 | Georgia |
| 215 | Pennsylvania | 405 | Oklahoma |
| 216 | Ohio | 406 | Montana |
| 217 | Illinois | 407 | Florida |
| 218 | Minnesota | 408 | California |
| 219 | Indiana | 409 | Texas |
| 301 | Maryland | 410 | Maryland |
| 302 | Delaware | 412 | Pennsylvania |
| 303 | Colorado | 413 | Massachusetts |
| 304 | West Virginia | 414 | Wisconsin |
| 305 | Florida | 415 | California |
| 306 | Saskatchewan | 416 | Ontario |
| 307 | Wyoming | 417 | Missouri |
| 308 | Nebraska | 418 | Quebec |
| 309 | Illinois | 419 | Ohio |
| 310 | California | 501 | Arkansas |
| 312 | Illinois | 502 | Kentucky |

| Area Code | Location | Area Code | Location |
|-----------|----------|-----------|----------|
| 503 | Oregon | 618 | Illinois |
| 504 | Louisiana | 619 | California |
| 505 | New Mexico | 701 | North Dakota |
| 506 | New Brunswick | 702 | Nevada |
| 507 | Minnesota | 703 | Virginia |
| 508 | Massachusetts | 704 | North Carolina |
| 509 | Washington | 705 | Ontario |
| 510 | California | 706 | Georgia |
| 512 | Texas | 707 | California |
| 513 | Ohio | 708 | Illinois |
| 514 | Quebec | 709 | Newfoundland |
| 515 | Iowa | 712 | Iowa |
| 516 | New York | 713 | Texas |
| 517 | Michigan | 714 | California |
| 518 | New York | 715 | Wisconsin |
| 519 | Ontario | 716 | New York |
| 520 | Arizona | 717 | Pennsylvania |
| 601 | Mississippi | 718 | New York |
| 602 | Arizona | 719 | Colorado |
| 603 | New Hampshire | 801 | Utah |
| 604 | British Columbia | 802 | Vermont |
| 605 | South Dakota | 803 | South Carolina |
| 606 | Kentucky | 804 | Virginia |
| 607 | New York | 805 | California |
| 608 | Wisconsin | 806 | Texas |
| 609 | New Jersey | 807 | Ontario |
| 610 | Pennsylvania | 808 | Hawaii |
| 612 | Minnesota | 809 | Caribbean Islands |
| 613 | Ontario | 810 | Michigan |
| 614 | Ohio | 812 | Indiana |
| 615 | Tennessee | 813 | Florida |
| 616 | Michigan | 814 | Pennsylvania |
| 617 | Massachusetts | 815 | Illinois |

| Area Code | Location | Area Code | Location |
|---|---|---|---|
| 816 | Missouri | 907 | Alaska |
| 817 | Texas | 908 | New Jersey |
| 818 | California | 909 | California |
| 819 | Quebec and North-west Territories | 910 | North Carolina |
|  |  | 912 | Georgia |
| 901 | Tennessee | 913 | Kansas |
| 902 | Nova Scotia and Prince Edward Island | 914 | New York |
|  |  | 915 | Texas |
|  |  | 916 | California |
| 903 | Texas | 917 | New York |
| 904 | Florida | 918 | Oklahoma |
| 905 | Ontario | 919 | North Carolina |
| 906 | Michigan | 941 | Florida |

### International Dialing Codes

To dial direct to another country, dial "011" (international access code), the country code, the city code, and the local number. To dial direct to the United States *from* another country, dial the local international access code listed below, the U.S. country code "1," the area code, and the local number. For countries that do not have international direct dialing, dial the operator and give the country code, city code, and local number.

### INTERNATIONAL ACCESS CODES

*Note:* Place calls through the operator for countries that have no access code.

| Country | Access Code | Country | Access Code |
|---|---|---|---|
| Australia | 0011 | Bahrain | 0 |
| Austria-Linz | 00 | Belgium | 00 |
| Austria-Vienna | 900 | Brazil | 00 |

| Country | Access Code | Country | Access Code |
|---|---|---|---|
| Colombia | 90 | Monaco | 19 |
| Costa Rica | 00 | Morocco | 00 |
| Cyprus | 00 | The Netherlands | 09 |
| Czech Republic | 00 | Netherlands Antilles | 00 |
| Denmark | 009 | | |
| El Salvador | 0 | New Zealand | 00 |
| Finland | 990 | Nicaragua | 00 |
| France | 19 | Norway | 095 |
| French Antilles | 19 | Panama | 00 |
| Germany | 00 | Philippines | 00 |
| Greece | 00 | Portugal (Lisbon) | 097 |
| Guam | 001 | | |
| Guatemala | 00 | Qatar | 0 |
| Honduras | 00 | Saudi Arabia | 00 |
| Hong Kong | 001 | Senegal | 12 |
| Hungary | 00 | Singapore | 005 |
| Iran | 00 | Slovakia | 00 |
| Iraq | 00 | South Africa/ Namibia | 09 |
| Ireland | 16 | | |
| Israel | 00 | Spain | 07 |
| Italy | 00 | Sweden | 009 |
| Ivory Coast | 00 | Switzerland | 00 |
| Japan | 001 | Taiwan | 002 |
| Korea, South | 001 | Thailand | 001 |
| Kuwait | 00 | Tunisia | 00 |
| Lebanon | 00 | Turkey | 99 |
| Libya | 00 | United Arab Emirates | 00 |
| Liechtenstein | 00 | | |
| Luxembourg | 00 | United Kingdom | 010 |
| Malaysia (Kuala Lumpur and Penang) | 00 | Vatican City | 00 |
| | | Venezuela | 00 |

# Time Differences Around the World

| Location | | | | | | | | | | | | | | | | | | | | | | | | | |
|---|---|---|---|---|---|---|---|---|---|---|---|---|---|---|---|---|---|---|---|---|---|---|---|---|---|
| Aleutian Islands, Tutuila, Samoa | 1:00pm | 2:00pm | 3:00pm | 4:00pm | 5:00pm | 6:00pm | 7:00pm | 8:00pm | 9:00pm | 10:00pm | 11:00pm | MIDNIGHT | 1:00am | 2:00am | 3:00am | 4:00am | 5:00am | 6:00am | 7:00am | 8:00am | 9:00am | 10:00am | 11:00am | NOON | 1:00pm |
| Hawaiian Islands, Alaska | 2:00pm | 3:00pm | 4:00pm | 5:00pm | 6:00pm | 7:00pm | 8:00pm | 9:00pm | 10:00pm | 11:00pm | Medianoche | 1:00am | 2:00am | 3:00am | 4:00am | 5:00am | 6:00am | 7:00am | 8:00am | 9:00am | 10:00am | 11:00am | Mediodia | 1:00pm | 2:00pm |
| Tahiti | 2:00pm | 3:00pm | 4:00pm | 5:00pm | 6:00pm | 7:00pm | 8:00pm | 9:00pm | 10:00pm | 11:00pm | MINUIT | 1:00am | 2:00am | 3:00am | 4:00am | 5:00am | 6:00am | 7:00am | 8:00am | 9:00am | 10:00am | 11:00am | MIDI | 1:00pm | 2:00pm |
| San Francisco & Pacific Coast | 4:00pm | 5:00pm | 6:00pm | 7:00pm | 8:00pm | 9:00pm | 10:00pm | 11:00pm | MIDNIGHT | 1:00am | 2:00am | 3:00am | 4:00am | 5:00am | 6:00am | 7:00am | 8:00am | 9:00am | 10:00am | 11:00am | NOON | 1:00pm | 2:00pm | 3:00pm | 4:00pm |
| Chicago, Central America (except Panama), Mexico, Winnipeg | 6:00pm | 7:00pm | 8:00pm | 9:00pm | 10:00pm | 11:00pm | Medianoche | 1:00am | 2:00am | 3:00am | 4:00am | 5:00am | 6:00am | 7:00am | 8:00am | 9:00am | 10:00am | 11:00am | Mediodia | 1:00pm | 2:00pm | 3:00pm | 4:00pm | 5:00pm | 6:00pm |
| Bogota, Havana, Lima, Montreal, Bermuda, New York, Panama | 7:00pm | 8:00pm | 9:00pm | 10:00pm | 11:00pm | MINUIT | 1:00am | 2:00am | 3:00am | 4:00am | 5:00am | 6:00am | 7:00am | 8:00am | 9:00am | 10:00am | 11:00am | MIDI | 1:00pm | 2:00pm | 3:00pm | 4:00pm | 5:00pm | 6:00pm | 7:00pm |
| Buenos Aires, Santiago, Puerto Rico, Lapaz, Asuncion | 8:00pm | 9:00pm | 10:00pm | 11:00pm | Medianoche | 1:00am | 2:00am | 3:00am | 4:00am | 5:00am | 6:00am | 7:00am | 8:00am | 9:00am | 10:00am | 11:00am | NOON | 1:00pm | 2:00pm | 3:00pm | 4:00pm | 5:00pm | 6:00pm | 7:00pm | 8:00pm |
| Rio, Santos, Sao Paulo | 9:00pm | 10:00pm | 11:00pm | MIDNIGHT | 1:00am | 2:00am | 3:00am | 4:00am | 5:00am | 6:00am | 7:00am | 8:00am | 9:00am | 10:00am | 11:00am | Mediodia | 1:00pm | 2:00pm | 3:00pm | 4:00pm | 5:00pm | 6:00pm | 7:00pm | 8:00pm | 9:00pm |
| Iceland | 11:00pm | MINUIT | 1:00am | 2:00am | 3:00am | 4:00am | 5:00am | 6:00am | 7:00am | 8:00am | 9:00am | 10:00am | 11:00am | MIDI | 1:00pm | 2:00pm | 3:00pm | 4:00pm | 5:00pm | 6:00pm | 7:00pm | 8:00pm | 9:00pm | 10:00pm | 11:00pm |
| Algiers, Lisbon, London, Paris, Madrid | MIDNIGHT | 1:00am | 2:00am | 3:00am | 4:00am | 5:00am | 6:00am | 7:00am | 8:00am | 9:00am | 10:00am | 11:00am | NOON | 1:00pm | 2:00pm | 3:00pm | 4:00pm | 5:00pm | 6:00pm | 7:00pm | 8:00pm | 9:00pm | 10:00pm | 11:00pm | MIDNIGHT |
| G.M.T. | 0000 | 0100 | 0200 | 0300 | 0400 | 0500 | 0600 | 0700 | 0800 | 0900 | 1000 | 1100 | 1200 | 1300 | 1400 | 1500 | 1600 | 1700 | 1800 | 1900 | 2000 | 2100 | 2200 | 2300 | 2400 |
| Bengasi, Berlin, Oslo, Rome, Tunis, Tripoli, Warsaw, Stockholm | 1:00am | 2:00am | 3:00am | 4:00am | 5:00am | 6:00am | 7:00am | 8:00am | 9:00am | 10:00am | 11:00am | Mediodia | 1:00pm | 2:00pm | 3:00pm | 4:00pm | 5:00pm | 6:00pm | 7:00pm | 8:00pm | 9:00pm | 10:00pm | 11:00pm | Medianoche | 1:00am |
| Cairo, Capetown, Istanbul, Moscow | 2:00am | 3:00am | 4:00am | 5:00am | 6:00am | 7:00am | 8:00am | 9:00am | 10:00am | 11:00am | MIDI | 1:00pm | 2:00pm | 3:00pm | 4:00pm | 5:00pm | 6:00pm | 7:00pm | 8:00pm | 9:00pm | 10:00pm | 11:00pm | MINUIT | 1:00am | 2:00am |
| Ethiopia, Iraq, Madagascar | 3:00am | 4:00am | 5:00am | 6:00am | 7:00am | 8:00am | 9:00am | 10:00am | 11:00am | NOON | 1:00pm | 2:00pm | 3:00pm | 4:00pm | 5:00pm | 6:00pm | 7:00pm | 8:00pm | 9:00pm | 10:00pm | 11:00pm | MIDNIGHT | 1:00am | 2:00am | 3:00am |
| Bombay, Ceylon, New Delhi | 5:30am | 6:30am | 7:30am | 8:30am | 9:30am | 10:30am | 11:30am | 12:30pm | 1:30pm | 2:30pm | 3:30pm | 4:30pm | 5:30pm | 6:30pm | 7:30pm | 8:30pm | 9:30pm | 10:30pm | 11:30pm | 12:30am | 1:30am | 2:30am | 3:30am | 4:30am | 5:30am |
| Chungking, Changtu, Kunming | 7:00am | 8:00am | 9:00am | 10:00am | 11:00am | Mediodia | 1:00pm | 2:00pm | 3:00pm | 4:00pm | 5:00pm | 6:00pm | 7:00pm | 8:00pm | 9:00pm | 10:00pm | 11:00pm | Medianoche | 1:00am | 2:00am | 3:00am | 4:00am | 5:00am | 6:00am | 7:00am |
| Celebes, Hong Kong, Manila, Shanghai | 8:00am | 9:00am | 10:00am | 11:00am | NOON | 1:00pm | 2:00pm | 3:00pm | 4:00pm | 5:00pm | 6:00pm | 7:00pm | 8:00pm | 9:00pm | 10:00pm | 11:00pm | MIDNIGHT | 1:00am | 2:00am | 3:00am | 4:00am | 5:00am | 6:00am | 7:00am | 8:00am |
| Korea, Japan, Adelaide | 9:00am | 10:00am | 11:00am | MIDI | 1:00pm | 2:00pm | 3:00pm | 4:00pm | 5:00pm | 6:00pm | 7:00pm | 8:00pm | 9:00pm | 10:00pm | 11:00pm | MINUIT | 1:00am | 2:00am | 3:00am | 4:00am | 5:00am | 6:00am | 7:00am | 8:00am | 9:00am |
| Brisbane, Guam, Melbourne, New Guinea, Sydney | 10:00am | 11:00am | Mediodia | 1:00pm | 2:00pm | 3:00pm | 4:00pm | 5:00pm | 6:00pm | 7:00pm | 8:00pm | 9:00pm | 10:00pm | 11:00pm | Medianoche | 1:00am | 2:00am | 3:00am | 4:00am | 5:00am | 6:00am | 7:00am | 8:00am | 9:00am | 10:00am |
| Solomon Islands, New Caledonia | 11:00am | MIDI | 1:00pm | 2:00pm | 3:00pm | 4:00pm | 5:00pm | 6:00pm | 7:00pm | 8:00pm | 9:00pm | 10:00pm | 11:00pm | MINUIT | 1:00am | 2:00am | 3:00am | 4:00am | 5:00am | 6:00am | 7:00am | 8:00am | 9:00am | 10:00am | 11:00am |
| Wellington, Auckland | 12:30pm | 1:30pm | 2:30pm | 3:30pm | 4:30pm | 5:30pm | 6:30pm | 7:30pm | 8:30pm | 9:30pm | 10:30pm | 11:30pm | 12:30am | 1:30am | 2:30am | 3:30am | 4:30am | 5:30am | 6:30am | 7:30am | 8:30am | 9:30am | 10:30am | 11:30am | 12:30pm |

Source: Mary A. De Vries, Professional Secretary's Encyclopedic Dictionary, 5th ed. (Englewood Cliffs, NJ: Prentice Hall, 1994), p. 57. Reprinted by permission of the publisher, Prentice Hall/A Division of Simon & Schuster.

## Country and City Codes

*Note:* An asterisk by the country name and in the city column means that no city code is needed. Dial 1 + 809 + local number for Anguilla, Antigua and Barbuda, Bahamas, Barbados, Bermuda, British Virgin Islands, Cayman Islands, Dominica, Dominican Republic, Grenada and Carriacou, Jamaica, Montserrat, Nevis, St. Kitts, St. Lucia, St. Vincent and the Grenadines, Trinidad and Tobago, Turks and Caicos Island. (Refer to the international time chart for a guide to determining time differences in selected locations around the world.)

| Country | Country Code | City Code |
|---|---|---|
| **Albania** | 355 | |
| Durres | | 52 |
| Tirana | | 42 |
| **Algeria*** | 213 | * |
| **American Samoa*** | 684 | * |
| **Andorra** | 33 | 628 |
| **Angola** | 244 | |
| Luanda | | 2 |
| **Anguilla** | 809 | |
| **Antigua and Barbuda** | 809 | |
| **Argentina** | 54 | |
| Buenos Aires | | 1 |
| Cordoba | | 51 |
| Mendoza | | 61 |
| San Juan | | 64 |
| Santa Fe | | 627 |
| **Armenia** | 7 | |
| Yerevan | | 8852 |
| **Aruba** | 297 | 8 |
| **Ascension Island*** | 247 | * |
| **Australia** | 61 | |
| Adelaide | | 8 |
| Brisbane | | 7 |

| Country | Country Code | City Code |
|---|---|---|
| Canberra | | 6 |
| Gold Coast | | 75 |
| Melbourne | | 3 |
| Perth | | 9 |
| Sydney | | 2 |
| **Austria** | 43 | |
| Graz | | 316 |
| Innsbruck | | 512 |
| Salzburg | | 662 |
| Vienna | | 1 |
| **Azerbaijan** | 7 | |
| Baku | | 8922 |
| **Bahamas** | 809 | |
| **Bahrain\*** | 973 | \* |
| **Bangladesh** | 880 | |
| Dhaka | | 2 |
| Rajshaki | | 721 |
| **Barbados** | 809 | |
| **Belarus** | 7 | |
| Minsk | | 391 |
| **Belgium** | 32 | |
| Antwerp | | 3 |
| Brussels | | 2 |
| Ghent | | 91 |
| Mons | | 65 |
| **Belize** | 501 | |
| Belize City | | 2 |
| Belmopan | | 8 |
| Punta Gorda | | 7 |
| San Ignacio | | 92 |
| **Benin\*** | 229 | \* |
| **Bermuda** | 809 | |
| **Bhutan\*** | 975 | \* |
| **Bolivia** | 591 | |

| Country | Country Code | City Code |
|---|---|---|
| Cotoga | | 388 |
| La Paz | | 2 |
| Santa Cruz | | 33 |
| Sucre | | 64 |
| Trinidad | | 46 |
| **Bosnia and Herzegovina** | 387 | |
| Sarajevo | | 71 |
| **Botswana** | 267 | |
| Francistown | | 21 |
| Gaborone | | 31 |
| Orapa | | 27 |
| **Brazil** | 55 | |
| Brasília | | 61 |
| Port Alegre | | 512 |
| Rio De Janeiro | | 21 |
| São Paulo | | 11 |
| Vitoria | | 27 |
| **British Virgin Islands** | 809 | |
| **Brunei** | 673 | |
| Bandar Seri Begawan | | 2 |
| Kuala Belait | | 3 |
| **Bulgaria** | 359 | |
| Plovdiv | | 32 |
| Sofia | | 2 |
| Varna | | 52 |
| **Burkina Faso*** | 226 | * |
| **Burundi** | 256 | |
| Bujumbura | | 2 |
| **Cambodia** | 855 | |
| Phnom Penh | | 23 |
| **Cameroon*** | 237 | * |
| **Cape Verde Islands*** | 238 | * |
| **Cayman Islands** | 809 | |
| **Central African Republic*** | 236 | * |

| Country | Country Code | City Code |
|---|---|---|
| **Chad*** | 235 | * |
| **Chile** | 56 | |
| Concepcion | | 41 |
| Santiago | | 2 |
| Valparaiso | | 32 |
| Vina del Mar | | 32 |
| **China** | 86 | |
| Beijing | | 1 |
| Peking | | 1 |
| Shanghai | | 21 |
| **Colombia** | 57 | |
| Bogotá | | 1 |
| Cali | | 23 |
| Cartegena | | 59 |
| Medellin | | 4 |
| Palmira | | 31 |
| **Comoros*** | 269 | * |
| **Congo*** | 242 | * |
| **Cook Islands*** | 682 | * |
| **Costa Rica*** | 506 | * |
| **Croatia** | 385 | |
| Zagreb | | 41 |
| **Cyprus** | 357 | |
| Morphou | | 71 |
| Nicosia | | 2 |
| Platres | | 54 |
| **Czech Republic** | 42 | |
| Brno | | 5 |
| Kosice | | 95 |
| Pizen | | 19 |
| Prague | | 2 |
| **Denmark** | 45 | |
| Aalborg | | 8 |
| Copenhagen | | 3 |

| Country | Country Code | City Code |
|---|---|---|
| Haderslav | | 4 |
| Oddense | | 7 |
| Vorgod | | 7 |
| **Djibouti*** | 253 | * |
| **Dominican Republic** | 809 | |
| **Ecuador** | 593 | |
| Cuenca | | 7 |
| Esmeraldas | | 2 |
| Manta | | 4 |
| Quito | | 2 |
| Santo Domingo | | 2 |
| **Egypt** | 20 | |
| Alexandria | | 3 |
| Aswan | | 97 |
| Cairo | | 2 |
| Port Said | | 66 |
| **El Salvador*** | 503 | * |
| **Equatorial Guinea** | 240 | |
| Malabo | | 9 |
| **Eritrea** | 291 | |
| Asmara | | 1 |
| **Ethiopia** | 251 | |
| Addis Ababa | | 1 |
| Dire Dawa | | 5 |
| Jimma | | 7 |
| Nazareth | | 2 |
| **Falkland Islands*** | 500 | * |
| **Fiji Islands*** | 679 | * |
| **Finland** | 358 | |
| Helsinki | | 0 |
| Lappeenranta | | 53 |
| Pori | | 39 |
| Vaasa | | 61 |
| **France** | 33 | |

| Country | Country Code | City Code |
|---|---|---|
| Bordeaux | | 56 |
| Cannes | | 93 |
| Grenoble | | 76 |
| Marseille | | 91 |
| Nancy | | 8 |
| Nice | | 93 |
| Paris | | 1 |
| Tours | | 47 |
| **French Antilles*** | 596 | * |
| **French Guiana*** | 594 | * |
| **French Polynesia (incl. Tahiti and Moorea)*** | 689 | * |
| **Gabon Republic*** | 241 | * |
| **Gambia*** | 220 | * |
| **Georgia** | 7 | |
| Tbilisi | | 8832 |
| **Germany** | 49 | |
| Berlin | | 30 |
| Bonn₁ | | 228 |
| Cologne | | 221 |
| Dresden | | 51 |
| Dusseldorf | | 211 |
| Frankfurt | | 69 |
| Hamburg | | 40 |
| Heidelberg | | 6221 |
| Munich | | 89 |
| Neubrandenburg | | 90 |
| Potsdam | | 33 |
| Schwerin | | 84 |
| Stuttgart | | 711 |
| Weisbaden | | 6121 |
| **Ghana** | 233 | |
| Accra | | 21 |
| Kumasi | | 51 |

| Country | Country Code | City Code |
|---|---|---|
| **Gibraltar*** | 350 | * |
| **Greece** | 30 | |
| Athens | | 1 |
| Corinth | | 741 |
| Rodos | | 241 |
| Sparti | | 731 |
| Tripolis | | 71 |
| **Greenland*** | 299 | |
| Godthaab | | 2 |
| Nuuk | | * |
| **Grenada (incl. Carriacou)** | 809 | |
| **Guadeloupe*** | 590 | * |
| **Guam*** | 671 | * |
| **Guantanamo Bay (U.S. Naval Base)*** | 53 | * |
| **Guatemala** | 502 | |
| Guatemala City | | 2 |
| All other locations | | 9 |
| **Guinea** | 224 | |
| Conakry | | 4 |
| Labe | | 51 |
| **Guinea-Bissau*** | 245 | * |
| **Guyana** | 592 | |
| Bartica | | 5 |
| Georgetown | | 2 |
| Linden | | 4 |
| New Hope | | 3 |
| **Haiti*** | 509 | |
| Cap-Haitien | | 3 |
| Cayes | | 5 |
| Gonaive | | 2 |
| Port Au Prince | | * |
| **Honduras*** | 504 | * |
| **Hong Kong*** | 852 | * |

| Country | Country Code | City Code |
|---|---|---|
| **Hungary** | 36 | |
| Budapest | | 1 |
| Derbrecen | | 52 |
| Kaposvar | | 82 |
| Szolnok | | 56 |
| **Iceland** | 354 | |
| Akureyri | | 6 |
| Hafnarfjorour | | 1 |
| Keflavik N. B. | | 2 |
| Reykjavik | | 1 |
| Varma | | 1 |
| **India** | 91 | |
| Bangalore | | 812 |
| Bhopal | | 755 |
| Bombay | | 22 |
| Calcutta | | 33 |
| Madras | | 44 |
| New Delhi | | 11 |
| **Indonesia** | 62 | |
| Cirebon | | 231 |
| Denpasar (Bali) | | 361 |
| Jakarta | | 21 |
| Malang | | 341 |
| Semarang | | 24 |
| **Iran** | 98 | |
| Ahwaz | | 61 |
| Ghome | | 251 |
| Mashad | | 51 |
| Tehran | | 21 |
| **Iraq** | 964 | |
| Baghdad | | 1 |
| Basra | | 40 |
| Kerbela | | 32 |
| Najaf | | 33 |

| Country | Country Code | City Code |
|---|---|---|
| **Ireland** | 353 | |
| Cork | | 21 |
| Dublin | | 1 |
| Galway | | 91 |
| Kildare | | 45 |
| Killarney | | 64 |
| Tipperary | | 62 |
| Waterford | | 51 |
| **Israel** | 972 | |
| Haifa | | 4 |
| Jerusalem | | 2 |
| Nazareth | | 65 |
| Tel Aviv | | 3 |
| **Italy** | 39 | |
| Capri | | 81 |
| Florence | | 55 |
| Genoa | | 10 |
| Milan | | 2 |
| Naples | | 81 |
| Palermo | | 91 |
| Pisa | | 50 |
| Rome | | 6 |
| Trieste | | 40 |
| Venice | | 41 |
| Verona | | 45 |
| **Ivory Coast*** | 225 | * |
| **Jamaica** | 809 | |
| **Japan (includes Okinawa)** | 81 | |
| Hiroshima | | 82 |
| Kyoto | | 75 |
| Nagasaki | | 958 |
| Naha (Okinawa) | | 988 |
| Osaka | | 6 |
| Tachikawa (Tokyo) | | 425 |

| Country | Country Code | City Code |
|---|---|---|
| Tokyo | | 33 |
| Yokohama | | 45 |
| **Jordan** | 962 | |
| Amman | | 6 |
| Jerash | | 4 |
| Sult | | 5 |
| **Kazakhstan** | 7 | |
| Alma-Ata | | 3272 |
| **Kenya** | 254 | |
| Anmer | | 153 |
| Kiambu | | 154 |
| Mombasa | | 11 |
| Nairobi | | 2 |
| **Kiribati*** | 686 | * |
| **Korea (South)** | 82 | |
| Icheon | | 361 |
| Osan | | 339 |
| Osan (Military) | | 333 |
| Pusan | | 51 |
| Seoul | | 2 |
| **Kuwait*** | 965 | * |
| **Kyrgyzstan** | 7 | |
| Frunze | | 3312 |
| **Lesotho*** | 266 | * |
| **Liberia*** | 231 | * |
| **Libya** | 218 | |
| Derna | | 81 |
| Jamahiriya | | 218 |
| Tripoli | | 21 |
| Tripoli Int'l Airport | | 22 |
| **Liechtenstein** | 41 | 75 |
| **Luxembourg*** | 352 | * |
| **Macau*** | 853 | * |
| **Macedonia** | 389 | |

| Country | Country Code | City Code |
|---|---|---|
| Skopje | | 91 |
| **Madagascar** | 261 | |
| Antananarivo | | 2 |
| **Malawi*** | 265 | |
| Domasi | | 531 |
| Lilongwe | | * |
| Luchenza | | 477 |
| Thornwood | | 486 |
| **Malaysia** | 60 | |
| Alor Star | | 4 |
| Broga | | 3 |
| Kuala Lumpur | | 3 |
| Port Dickson | | 6 |
| **Maldives*** | 960 | * |
| **Mali*** | 223 | * |
| **Malta*** | 356 | * |
| **Marshall Islands** | 692 | |
| Majuro | | 625 |
| **Mauritania*** | 222 | * |
| **Mauritius*** | 230 | * |
| **Maristat (Atlantic East)** | 871 | |
| **Maristat (Atlantic West)** | 874 | |
| **Maristat (Indian)** | 873 | |
| **Maristat (Pacific)** | 872 | |
| **Mexico** | 52 | |
| Acapulco | | 74 |
| Cancun | | 988 |
| Chihuahua | | 14 |
| Guadalajara | | 36 |
| Mexico City | | 5 |
| Monterrey | | 83 |
| Puerto Vallarta | | 322 |
| Veracruz | | 29 |
| **Micronesia** | 691 | |

| Country | Country Code | City Code |
|---|---|---|
| **Moldova** | 373 | |
| Kishinev | | 2 |
| **Monaco** | 33 | 93 |
| **Montserrat** | 809 | |
| **Morocco** | 212 | |
| Agadir | | 8 |
| Casablanca | | 2 |
| Marrakech | | 4 |
| Rabat | | 7 |
| Tangiers | | 99 |
| **Mozambique** | 258 | |
| Maputo | | 1 |
| Tete | | 52 |
| Xai-Xai | | 22 |
| **Namibia** | 264 | |
| Gobabis | | 681 |
| Mariental | | 661 |
| Windhoek | | 61 |
| Windhoek Airport | | 626 |
| **Nauru*** | 674 | * |
| **Nepal*** | 977 | * |
| **The Netherlands** | 31 | |
| Amsterdam | | 20 |
| Haarlem | | 23 |
| Hoensbroek | | 50 |
| Rotterdam | | 10 |
| The Hague | | 70 |
| **Netherlands Antilles** | 599 | |
| Curacao | | 9 |
| St. Maarten | | 5 |
| Willemstad | | 9 |
| **New Caledonia*** | 687 | * |
| **New Zealand** | 64 | |
| Auckland | | 9 |

| Country | Country Code | City Code |
|---|---|---|
| Christchurch | | 3 |
| Invercargill | | 21 |
| Palmerston North | | 63 |
| Tauranga | | 75 |
| Wellington | | 4 |
| **Nicaragua** | 505 | |
| Leone | | 311 |
| Managua | | 2 |
| San Juan Del Sur | | 466 |
| San Marcos | | 43 |
| **Niger*** | 227 | * |
| **Nigeria** | 234 | |
| Abuja | | 9 |
| Lagos | | 1 |
| **Norway** | 47 | |
| Arendal | | 41 |
| Bergen | | 5 |
| Larvik | | 34 |
| Oslo | | 2 |
| Tonsberg | | 33 |
| **Oman*** | 968 | * |
| **Pakistan** | 92 | |
| Bahawalpur | | 621 |
| Islamabad | | 51 |
| Okara | | 442 |
| Quetta | | 81 |
| Sukkur | | 71 |
| **Panama*** | 507 | * |
| **Papua New Guinea*** | 675 | * |
| **Paraguay** | 595 | |
| Asunción | | 21 |
| Encarnacion | | 71 |
| Ita | | 24 |
| Pilar | | 63 |

| Country | Country Code | City Code |
|---|---|---|
| Villeta | | 25 |
| **Peru** | 51 | |
| Arequipa | | 54 |
| Cuzco | | 84 |
| Iquitos | | 94 |
| Lima | | 14 |
| Trujillo | | 44 |
| **Philippines** | 63 | |
| Angeles | | 455 |
| Clark Field (Military) | | 4535 |
| Manila | | 2 |
| Pampanga | | 45 |
| Tarlac City | | 452 |
| **Poland** | 48 | |
| Crakow | | 12 |
| Gdansk | | 58 |
| Lublin | | 81 |
| Poznan | | 61 |
| Warsaw | | 22 |
| **Portugal** | 351 | |
| Lajes AFB | | 95 |
| Lisbon | | 1 |
| Madeira Islands | | 91 |
| Santa Cruz | | 92 |
| **Qatar*** | 974 | * |
| **Reunion Island*** | 262 | * |
| **Romania** | 40 | |
| Bacau | | 31 |
| Bucharest | | 0 |
| Craiova | | 41 |
| Pitesti | | 76 |
| **Russia** | 7 | |
| Moscow | | 095 |
| **Rwanda*** | 250 | * |

| Country | Country Code | City Code |
|---|---|---|
| **St. Kitts and Nevis** | 809 | |
| **St. Lucia** | 809 | |
| **St. Vincent and the Grenadines** | 809 | |
| **San Marino** | 39 | 549 |
| **São Tomé and Príncipe*** | 239 | * |
| **Saudi Arabia** | 966 | |
| Dhahran | | 3 |
| Jeddah | | 2 |
| Riyadh | | 1 |
| Yenbu | | 4 |
| **Senegal*** | 221 | * |
| **Seychelles*** | 248 | * |
| **Sierra Leone** | 232 | |
| Freetown | | 22 |
| All other points | | 232 |
| **Singapore*** | 65 | * |
| **Slovakia** | 42 | |
| Bratislava | | 427 |
| **Slovenia** | 386 | |
| Ljubljana | | 61 |
| **Solomon Islands*** | 677 | * |
| **South Africa** | 27 | |
| Cape Town | | 21 |
| East London | | 431 |
| Gordons Bay | | 24 |
| Johannesburg | | 11 |
| Port Elizabeth | | 41 |
| Pretoria | | 12 |
| Welkom | | 171 |
| **Spain** | 34 | |
| Barcelona | | 3 |
| Cadiz | | 56 |
| Las Palmas (Canary Islands) | | 28 |

| Country | Country Code | City Code |
|---|---|---|
| Madrid | | 1 |
| Pamplona | | 48 |
| Seville | | 5 |
| Valencia | | 6 |
| **Sri Lanka** | 94 | |
| Colombo Central | | 1 |
| Kandy | | 8 |
| Matara | | 41 |
| **Suriname*** | 597 | * |
| **Swaziland*** | 268 | * |
| **Sweden** | 46 | |
| Goteborg | | 31 |
| Helsingborg | | 42 |
| Karlstad | | 54 |
| Stockholm | | 8 |
| Uppsala | | 18 |
| **Switzerland** | 41 | |
| Baden | | 56 |
| Bern | | 31 |
| Geneva | | 22 |
| Interlaken | | 36 |
| Lucerne | | 41 |
| Lugano | | 91 |
| St. Moritz | | 82 |
| Zurich | | 1 |
| **Syria** | 963 | |
| Damascus | | 11 |
| Hasake | | 521 |
| Kerdaha | | 492 |
| Tarous | | 431 |
| **Taiwan** | 886 | |
| Chunan | | 36 |
| Fengyuan | | 45 |
| Lotung | | 39 |

| Country | Country Code | City Code |
|---|---|---|
| Taipei | | 2 |
| **Tajikistan** | 7 | |
| Dushanbe | | 3772 |
| **Tanzania** | 255 | |
| Dodoma | | 61 |
| **Thailand** | 66 | |
| Bangkok | | 2 |
| Cheingrai | | 54 |
| Lampang | | 54 |
| Tak | | 55 |
| **Togo*** | 228 | * |
| **Tonga*** | 676 | * |
| **Trinidad and Tobago** | 809 | |
| **Tunisia** | 216 | |
| Beja | | 8 |
| Gafsa | | 6 |
| Medenine | | 5 |
| Tunis | | 1 |
| **Turkey** | 90 | |
| Ankara | | 4 |
| Istanbul | | 1 |
| Izmir | | 51 |
| Konya | | 331 |
| Samsun | | 361 |
| **Turkmenistan** | 7 | |
| Ashkhabad | | 3632 |
| **Uganda** | 256 | |
| Entebbe | | 42 |
| Kampala | | 41 |
| **Ukraine** | 7 | |
| Kiev | | 044 |
| **United Arab Emirates** | 971 | |
| Abu Dhabi | | 2 |
| Ajman | | 6 |

| Country | Country<br>Code | City<br>Code |
|---|---|---|
| Al Ain | | 3 |
| Aweer | | 58 |
| Dubai | | 4 |
| Fujairah | | 70 |
| Ras-al-Khaimah | | 77 |
| Sharjah | | 6 |
| Umm-al-Quwain | | 6 |
| **United Kingdom** | 44 | |
| **(Channel Islands, England,** | | |
| **Isle of Man, Northern Ireland,** | | |
| **Scotland, and Wales)** | | |
| Belfast | | 232 |
| Cardiff | | 222 |
| Durham | | 385 |
| Edinburgh | | 31 |
| Glasgow | | 41 |
| Gloucester | | 452 |
| Liverpool | | 51 |
| London (Inner) | | 171 |
| London (Outer) | | 181 |
| Manchester | | 61 |
| Nottingham | | 115 |
| Southampton | | 703 |
| **Uruguay** | 598 | |
| Caneleones | | 332 |
| Maldonado | | 42 |
| Mercedes | | 532 |
| Montevideo | | 2 |
| Paysandu | | 722 |
| **Uzbekistan** | 7 | |
| Tashkent | | 3712 |
| **Vatican City** | 39 | 6 |
| **Venezuela** | 58 | |
| Barcelona | | 81 |
| Caracas | | 2 |

| Country | Country Code | City Code |
|---|---|---|
| Ciudad Bolivar | | 85 |
| Maracaibo | | 61 |
| Puerto Cabello | | 42 |
| San Cristobal | | 76 |
| **Vietnam** | 84 | |
| Hanoi | | 4 |
| **Western Samoa*** | 685 | * |
| **Yugoslavia** | 38 | |
| Belgrade | | 11 |
| Dubrovnik | | 50 |
| Maribor | | 62 |
| **Zaïre** | 243 | |
| Kinshasa | | 12 |
| Lubumbashi | | 2 |
| **Zambia** | 260 | |
| Chingola | | 2 |
| Kitwe | | 2 |
| Luanshya | | 2 |
| Lusaka | | 1 |
| Ndola | | 2 |
| **Zimbabwe** | 263 | |
| Bulawayo | | 9 |
| Harare | | 4 |
| Mutare | | 20 |

# — 4 —
# CORRESPONDENCE

## THREE COMMON WAYS TO FORMAT A BUSINESS LETTER

The three most common business-letter formats are the simplified, full-block, and modified-block setups, although they may be known by other names. The modified-block layout, for example, is sometimes called a semiblock format. Businesses often require employees to use one of the formats consistently. Professional Secretaries International®, for example, has adopted the simplified format and recommends it for its ease of setup, requiring fewer keystrokes. To see how each element described in the following sections would appear on a page (line spacing, margins, and so on), refer to the appropriate model. When a particular element is not illustrated in one of the models, an example is provided within the list description. The appropriate writing style (spelling, punctuation, and capitalization) for each element is described later in this chapter.

## SIMPLIFIED FORMAT

[LETTERHEAD]

January 2, 1995

Your reference:   12345
Our reference:   54321

Confidential


Mr. Bryant R. Hamrick
Manager, Accounting and Finance
Friendly Businesses, Inc.
300 Marsh Street
New York, NY 10017

Attention Edith Jarand


SALARY SCHEDULES


Thanks, Bryant, for your detailed proposal to revise
the salary schedules in four of our departments.

I agree that we need to be competitive and would like
to discuss this with you and the other department heads
later this month.  I'll ask my secretary to contact
everyone this week to arrange a convenient time.

Sincere thanks for your keen observations and useful
suggestions, Bryant.



MARTHA K. BENTLEY--General Manager

MKB:cj
Enc.:  Brochure
By messenger
Copy:  Harold Ginsburg

P.S.  Are you planning to attend the wholesalers'
exhibition next month?  See enclosed brochure.  MKB

## FULL-BLOCK FORMAT

**[LETTERHEAD]**

January 2, 1995

Your reference:   12345
Our reference:   54321

Confidential


Mr. Bryant R. Hamrick
Manager, Accounting and Finance
Friendly Businesses, Inc.
300 Marsh Street
New York, NY 10017

Attention Edith Jarand

Dear Bryant:

SALARY SCHEDULES

Thanks for your detailed proposal to revise the salary
schedules in four of our departments.

I agree that we need to be competitive and would like
to discuss this with you and the other department heads
later this month.  I'll ask my secretary to contact
everyone this week to arrange a convenient time.

Sincere thanks for your keen observations and useful
suggestions, Bryant.

Best regards,


Martha K. Bentley
General Manager

MKB:cj
Enc.:  Brochure
By messenger
Copy:  Harold Ginsburg

P.S.  Are you planning to attend the wholesalers'
exhibition next month?  See enclosed brochure.  MKB

## MODIFIED-BLOCK FORMAT

[LETTERHEAD]

January 2, 1995

Your reference: 12345
Our reference: 54321

Confidential


Mr. Bryant R. Hamrick
Manager, Accounting and Finance
Friendly Businesses, Inc.
*300 Marsh Street*
New York, NY 10017

Attention Edith Jarand

Dear Bryant:

SALARY SCHEDULES

Thanks for your detailed proposal to revise the salary schedules in four of our departments.

I agree that we need to be competitive and would like to discuss this with you and the other department heads later this month. I'll ask my secretary to contact everyone this week to arrange a convenient time.

Sincere thanks for your keen observations and useful suggestions, Bryant.

Best regards,


Martha K. Bentley
General Manager

MKB:cj
Enc.: Brochure
By messenger
Copy: Harold Ginsburg

P.S. Are you planning to attend the wholesalers' exhibition next month? See enclosed brochure. MKB

*Simplified Format (see model)*

<u>DATE</u>

- Place the date flush left, two to four line spaces below the letterhead (more if the letter is very short).

<u>REFERENCE</u>

- Place the addressee's reference (if any) flush left, two line spaces below the date.
- Place your reference (if any) immediately beneath the addressee's reference.
- If the stationery has a printed line (e.g., "In reply please refer to"), fill in your reference after it, and put the addressee's reference immediately beneath it.

<u>PERSONAL OR CONFIDENTIAL NOTATION</u>

- Place the word *Personal* or *Confidential* (if used) flush left about four line spaces above the inside address or about two line spaces below the reference (if any).

<u>INSIDE ADDRESS</u>

- Place the addressee's name and complete address flush left, two to twelve line spaces beneath the date or reference line (if any).

<u>ATTENTION LINE</u>

- Place the attention line (if any) flush left, two line spaces below the inside address.

<u>SALUTATION</u>

- Omit the salutation.
- Instead of a salutation, mention the addressee's name in the first paragraph.

## SUBJECT

- Place the subject flush left, three line spaces below the inside address or attention line (if any).

## BODY

- Begin the body three line spaces below the subject.
- Place all paragraphs flush left and single-spaced.
- Leave one blank line space between paragraphs.
- Space before and after an extract and each item in a list, both of which may be flush left or indented 1/2 to 1 inch from both margins or the left only.

## COMPLIMENTARY CLOSE

- Omit the complimentary close.
- Instead of a close, mention the addressee's name in the last paragraph.

## SIGNATURE

- Place a person's typed signature flush left, about five line spaces after the body.
- If a firm name is included, place it three line spaces after the body and the person's name about four line spaces below the firm name. Follow the example provided for a company signature in the full-block format (but without the line for the close).

## IDENTIFICATION

- Place the identification initials (if any) flush left, two line spaces below the last line of the signature.

## ENCLOSURE NOTATION

- Place the enclosure notation (if any) flush left, one or two line spaces below the signature or identification initials (if any), depending on available space.

- Either single-space or double-space *all* notations that appear after the body.

### MAILING NOTATION

- Place the mailing notation (if any) flush left one or two line spaces below the previous notation.

### COPY-DISTRIBUTION NOTATION

- Place the copy-distribution notation flush left one or two line spaces below the previous notation.

### POSTSCRIPT (P.S.)

- Place the postscript flush left two line spaces below the last line or notation of the letter.

*Full-Block Format (see model)*

### DATE

- Same as in the simplified format.

### REFERENCE

- Same as in the simplified format.

### PERSONAL OR CONFIDENTIAL NOTATION

- Same as in the simplified format.

### INSIDE ADDRESS

- Same as in the simplified format.

### ATTENTION LINE

- Same as in the simplified format.

## SALUTATION

- Place the salutation (greeting) flush left two line spaces below the inside address or attention line (if any).

## SUBJECT

- Place the subject (if any) flush left two line spaces below the salutation.

- In professional practices where the words *In re* are used, place the subject flush left two line spaces *above* the salutation.

## BODY

- Begin the body two line spaces below the salutation or subject (if any).

- Place all paragraphs flush left and single-spaced.

- Leave one blank line space between paragraphs.

- Space before and after an extract and each item in a list, both of which may be flush left or indented 1/2 to 1 inch from both margins or the left only.

## COMPLIMENTARY CLOSE

- Place the complimentary close flush left two line spaces after the body.

## SIGNATURE

- Place a person's typed signature flush left about four line spaces after the complimentary close.

- When a firm name is used, as illustrated here, place it two line spaces after the close and place the person's name about four line spaces below the firm name.

```
Sincerely,

MAGIC ACCOUNTING, INC.


John Marler, CPA
```

### IDENTIFICATION

- Same as in the simplified format.

### ENCLOSURE NOTATION

- Same as in the simplified format.

### MAILING NOTATION

- Same as in the simplified format.

### COPY-DISTRIBUTION NOTATION

- Same as in the simplified format.

### POSTSCRIPT (P.S.)

- Same as in the simplified format.

*Modified-Block Format (see model)*

### DATE

- Place the date slightly right of the page center two to four line spaces below the letterhead (more if the letter is very short).

### REFERENCE

- Place the addressee's reference (if any) slightly right of the page center two line spaces below the date.
- Place your reference (if any) immediately beneath it.

- If the stationery has a printed line (e.g., "In reply please refer to"), fill in your reference after it, and put the addressee's reference immediately beneath it.

### PERSONAL OR CONFIDENTIAL NOTATION

- Same as in the full-block format.

### INSIDE ADDRESS

- Same as in the full-block format.

### ATTENTION LINE

- Same as in the full-block format.

### SALUTATION

- Same as in the full-block format.

### SUBJECT

- Place the subject (if any) two line spaces below the salutation.

- Indent the subject line the same amount of indention used for the body's paragraphs.

- In professional practices where the words *In re* are used, also indent the subject line the same amount of indention used for the body's paragraphs, but place it two line spaces *above* the salutation.

### BODY

- Begin the body two line spaces below the salutation or subject (if any).

- Indent each paragraph 1/2 to 1 inch.

- Single-space the paragraphs, with one blank line space between them.

- Space before and after an extract and each item in a list, both of which should be indented the same as each paragraph (or more) from both margins or the left only.

## COMPLIMENTARY CLOSE

- Place the complimentary close slightly right of the page center, aligned with the date, two line spaces after the body.

## SIGNATURE

- Place a person's typed signature slightly right of the page center, aligned with the complimentary close, about four line spaces after the close.

- When a firm name is used, follow the line spacing described for a firm in the full-block letter, except for positioning the entire signature block slightly right of the page center in the modified-block setup.

## IDENTIFICATION

- Same as in the full-block format.

## ENCLOSURE NOTATION

- Same as in the full-block format.

## MAILING NOTATION

- Same as in the full-block format.

## COPY-DISTRIBUTION NOTATION

- Same as in the full-block format.

## POSTSCRIPT

- Place the postscript two line spaces below the last line or notation of the letter.

- Indent the postscript the same as the body's paragraphs.

## TWO COMMON WAYS TO FORMAT A MEMO

Memo formats vary widely in business. Some organizations use standard commercial forms available in office-supply stores. Others design their own specially printed memo letterheads. Still others use regular business letterhead and type in the necessary guide-words, such as *To, From,* and *Subject.* Since memos are used for interoffice communication or informal messages to outside associates, customers, or clients, ease of setup is a principal consideration in selecting a practical format. One of the two formats described and illustrated here may be adapted to most situations.

*Interoffice Memo Stationery Format (see model)*

### GUIDE WORDS

- Have as many or as few guide words as you need printed on interoffice memo stationery (e.g., *Date, To, From, Subject, Attention,* and *Reference*).
- Begin guide words flush left two to four line spaces below the letterhead data.
- Depending on the number of guide words used, arrange them in a single column or side by side in two columns.
- Leave at least one blank line space between entries.
- Begin the fill-in information one or two character spaces or one tab space after the colon following each guide word.

### BODY

- Begin the memo body three to five line spaces below the last line of the guide words.
- Follow the requirements for a letter regarding the arrangement of paragraphs within the body.

### SIGNATURE

- Use any ruled line that is printed on the page. (*Note*: Commercial styles sometimes have one or more lines at the bottom of the sheet for signatures.)

## INTEROFFICE MEMO STATIONERY FORMAT

[INTEROFFICE MEMO LETTERHEAD]


**TO:**        Distribution   **FROM:**    Martha K. Bentley

**DEPT:**         --          **DEPT:**    General Mgr. Office

**FLOOR:**        --          **FLOOR:**   9th

**SUBJECT:** Salary Sched.    **DATE:**    January 2, 1995


Thanks for your detailed proposal to revise the salary
schedules in four of our departments.

I agree that we need to be competitive and would like
to discuss this with each of you later this month.
I'll ask my secretary to contact everyone this week to
arrange a convenient time.

Sincere thanks for your keen observations and useful
suggestions.

                                          MKB

MKB:cj

Enc.: Brochure

Distribution
Bryant Hamrick
Harold Ginsburg
Danielle Yaeger
John Wondolski

P.S. Are you planning to attend the wholesalers'
exhibition next month?  See enclosed brochure.  MKB

## STANDARD BUSINESS STATIONERY MEMO FORMAT

**[STANDARD BUSINESS LETTERHEAD]**

DATE:     January 2, 1995

TO:       Bryant Hamrick

FROM:     Martha K. Bentley

SUBJECT:  Salary Schedules


Thanks for your detailed proposal to revise the salary schedules in four of our departments.

I agree that we need to be competitive and would like to discuss this with you and the other department heads later this month.  I'll ask my secretary to contact everyone this week to arrange a convenient time.

Sincere thanks for your keen observations and useful suggestions, Bryant.

                                    MKB

MKB:cj

Enc.:  Brochure

Copies:   Harold Ginsburg
          Danielle Yaeger
          John Wondolski

P.S.  Are you planning to attend the wholesalers' exhibition next month?  See enclosed brochure.  MKB

- When there is no ruled line, type the sender's initials (or have the sender handwrite them) about two line spaces below the body, positioned slightly right of the page center.

- As an older-style alternative, have the sender handwrite the initials after his or her name in the guideword section.

### IDENTIFICATION

- Same as in a letter format.

### ENCLOSURE NOTATION

- Same as in a letter format.

### MAILING NOTATION

- Same as in a letter format when used. (*Note*: Memos that are hand-delivered by mail room messengers do not need this notation.)

### COPY-DISTRIBUTION NOTATION

- Same as in a letter format or handled as a distribution list. See the next point.

- To use a distribution list, type the word *Distribution* after the guideword *To* and list the names flush left at the end of the memo after the word *Distribution*.

### POSTSCRIPT

- Place the postscript two line spaces below the last line or notation of the memo.

- Start flush left or indent the postscript according to the paragraphing style of the body.

*Standard Business Stationery Memo Format (see model)*

### GUIDE WORDS

- If desired, type the same guide words that are printed on interoffice memo stationery on standard business letterhead stationery. (*Note:* Often fewer guide words are used on regular letter stationery.)

- Follow the instructions for printed guide words in the previous section.

### BODY

- Same as in the interoffice memo stationery format.

### SIGNATURE

- Same as in the interoffice memo stationery format.

### IDENTIFICATION

- Same as in a letter format.

### ENCLOSURE NOTATION

- Same as in a letter format.

### MAILING NOTATION

- Same as in a letter format when used. (*Note:* Memos that are hand-delivered by mail room messengers do not need this notation.)

### COPY-DISTRIBUTION NOTATION

- Same as in a letter format or, if a distribution list is used, the same as in the interoffice memo stationery format.

### POSTSCRIPT

- Same as in the interoffice memo stationery format.

## TWO COMMON WAYS TO FORMAT AN ENVELOPE

Two types of envelope addressing are common: (1) the traditional format, often used with social-business correspondence; and (2) the optical character reader (OCR) format, used for most general business messages and required by the U.S. Postal Service for OCR processing. Both types of formatting are illustrated here.

## TRADITIONAL ENVELOPE FORMAT

---

**[Return Address]**                              **[Postage]**

   Personal                                    SPECIAL DELIVERY


         Mr. J. T. Hollingsworth
         Western Manufacturing Co.
         14 East 63 Street, Room 2001
         Melrose Park, IL 60160

---


## OCR ENVELOPE FORMAT

---

**[Return Address]**                              **[Postage]**

**ADDRESS CORRECTION REQUESTED**

                 SPECIAL DELIVERY


         JTV:6077-9-44
         WESTERN MANUFACTURING CO
         ATTN MR JT HOLLINGSWORTH
         14 EAST 63 ST RM 2001
         MELROSE PARK IL 60160

---

## Traditional Envelope Format *(see model)*

- Type or handwrite the name and full address of the addressee in uppercase and lowercase letters.

- Center the address block on the envelope, top to bottom and left to right.

- Style a personal or confidential notation with an initial capital or in all capital letters, with or without underlining.

- Place the confidential notation about two line spaces below the return address.

- Style an attention line with all important words capitalized.

- Place the attention line in the lower left corner of the envelope or in another position left of the address block.

- Style mail instructions, such as SPECIAL DELIVERY, in all capital letters.

- Place the mail-instruction notice beneath the postage.

- Place account numbers (rare in this format) to the left of the address block.

## OCR Envelope Format *(see model)*

- Style the name and full address of the addressee in all capital letters.

- Omit punctuation except as required in an account number.

- Leave a minimum bottom margin of 5/8 inch and minimum side margins of 1/2 inch each.

- Begin the address block 2 3/4 inches from the bottom edge of the envelope.

- Style a personal or confidential notation in all capital letters, with or without underlining.

- Place the personal or confidential notation to the left of and two line spaces above the address block.

- Style an attention line in all capital letters.

- Place the attention line directly below the company name in the address block or left of the address block on any line above the second line from the bottom of the address.

- Style mail instructions, such as SPECIAL DELIVERY, in all capital letters.

- Place the mail instructions two to four line spaces below the postage.

- Place nonaddress data, such as an account number or date, immediately above the first line in the address block.

- Place barcodes (printed patterns of data that can be scanned and read by a computer) in the bottom 5/8 margin on the right bottom half of the envelope.

## OCR READ AREA AND BARCODE CLEAR ZONE

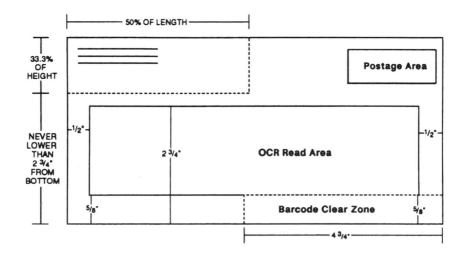

# HOW TO WRITE THE FIFTEEN PRINCIPAL PARTS OF A BUSINESS LETTER

Positioning the parts of a letter correctly on a page (format), described and illustrated in the first section of this chapter, is only part of the problem. Other questions must be answered, such as how to capitalize, spell, and punctuate each part. This section lists the important points of *style* to remember for each of the principal parts of a business letter. To see how the various elements are styled on the page, refer to the three letter models in the first section.

### *Date*

- When possible, date the letter the day it is dictated rather than the day it is typed.
- In business, use the traditional arrangement of data (month, day, year): *January 2, 1995.*
- In the military services, place the day first and omit the comma: *2 January 1995.*
- Spell out the month—*February* (not *Feb.* or *2*)—particularly in international correspondence since some countries treat the first number *(2-10-95)* as the day *(second day)* and others treat it as the month *(February)*.

### *Reference*

- When an incoming letter has a file reference, include the same reference in your letter when you reply.
- Capitalize the first word or each word of the reference, as preferred: *Your reference 12345; Your Reference 12345.*
- Abbreviate the word reference if desired: *Our ref. 54321; Our Ref. 54321.*

### *Personal or Confidential Notation*

- Use a personal or confidential notation when only the addressee or other designated persons should see the letter, not as an attention-getting device.

- Capitalize the first letter or write the entire word in all capital letters, as desired: *Personal; CONFIDENTIAL.*

- Underline the notation if desired, but avoid using both underlining *and* all capitals: <u>Personal</u>; *CONFIDEN-TIAL.*

*Inside Address*

- Spell and punctuate the data in the inside address exactly as the addressee styles it, for example, *National Company, Inc.; National Company Inc.;* or *National Co., Inc.*

- Use a post office box, if known, for postal mail (or both street address and post office box).

- Use a street address for private-courier package delivery since nonpostal mail cannot be delivered to a post office box number.

- Spell out the numerical names of streets when they are twelve or less: *41 West Twelfth Street; 41 West 13th Street.* But see the next point.

- As an alternative to the previous point, some authorities recommend that numerals be used for numbers above *nine: 41 West 12 Street.* When in doubt, follow the example of the post office in the particular city.

- Add *d, st,* or *th* to a street number only when it is part of the official street name: *101 North 76 Street; 101 North 76th Street.*

- Separate a house or building number from a street number with a space, a hyphen, and another space: *32 - 21 Street; 1017 - 101 Street.*

- Use numerals for all house or building numbers except one: *2 Westlake Boulevard; One Washington Street.*

- Spell out the names of cities unless an abbreviation is standard: *Portland; St. Louis.*

- Use official U.S. Postal Service abbreviations (see Chapter 5) for the spelling of U.S. states, territories, possessions, and Canadian provinces: *Miami, FL; Toronto, ON.*

- Precede a name with the appropriate title, such as *Dr., Mr., Ms.,* or *Miss.* (*Note: Ms.* is uncommon in other countries.)

- Do not use two titles or a title and academic degrees that mean the same thing, for example, *Dr. Helen Chaffe* (not *Dr. Helen Chaffe, M.D.*).

- Place a short business title on the same line as the name, but place a long title on the next line.

```
Mr. Sheldon McKay, Director

Mr. Sheldon McKay
Director of Advertising and Marketing
```

- Hyphenate titles only when the words represent a combination of two offices: *secretary-treasurer.*

- When an addressee has more than one title, use the highest office, such as President, unless you are writing to the person in another capacity, such as *Chairman, ABC Fundraising Campaign.*

- When both a department or division and a company name are used, place the company name first:

```
Ms. Lynda Schroeder
Quality Consultants, Inc.
Engineering Department
```

- When there is more than one addressee, place the name of the person of higher rank first, and if both are equal, place the names in alphabetical order:

```
Ms. Lynda Schroeder, President
Mr. Sheldon McKay, Treasurer

Mr. Sheldon McKay, Director
Ms. Lynda Schroeder, Director
```

- When one of the lines is unusually long, carry part of it
  over to the next line, and indent the carryover portion on
  the inside address (not on an OCR-style envelope):

```
Mr. Sheldon McKay
Vice President of Sales and
  Director of Marketing
Quality Consultants, Inc.
600 Spring Mill Road
Stanford, KY 40484
```

*Attention Line*

- When you want to be certain that a letter will be opened
  even if the intended recipient is absent when it arrives, (1)
  address the letter to the firm and put the intended recipient's name in an attention line or (2) address the letter to
  the intended recipient but include someone else's name in
  an attention line.
- Use the first option just described when you don't care
  who acts on the letter if the person named in the attention
  line is absent.

```
Quality Consultants, Inc.
1010 Sixth Avenue
New York, NY 10023

Attention Lynda Schroeder
```

- Use the second option just described when you want a *specific* individual to take action in the addressee's absence.

```
Ms. Lynda Schroeder
Quality Consultants, Inc.
1010 Sixth Avenue
New York, NY 10023


Attention Sheldon McKay
```

- Do not underscore the word *Attention* or use punctuation after it: *Attention Sheldon McKay.*

- Omit the person's title unless you do not know his or her first name: *Attention Lynda Schroeder* (not *Attention Ms. Schroeder,* unless the person's first name is unknown).

*Salutation*

- Capitalize each important word in the salutation of a full-block or modified-block letter.

- Capitalize a person's name or title: *Dear Ms. Watts; Dear Director; Dear Friends of Animals.*

- Address a businessperson by name, not position, when you use a personal or scholastic title: *Dear Mr. Henderson* (not *Dear Mr. Business Manager*).

- Address certain high-ranking government officials, religious dignitaries, and certain other prominent officials by title in a formal salutation: *Dear Mr. Speaker* (House of Representatives); *Very Reverend Monsignor.* (See the examples in the forms-of-address chart at the end of this chapter.)

- When a letter is addressed to a company in the full-block or modified-block format, and when it includes an attention line to an individual, use a general salutation to the company: *Ladies and Gentlemen,* not *Gentlemen* alone and not *Dear Western Manufacturing Company.*

- When a general letter in the full-block or modified-block format, such as a letter of recommendation, is not addressed to a person, job title (*Director of Marketing*), or company in general, and you don't know where the letter will go or who will read it, use a broad greeting and capitalize the first word only or each word, as preferred: *To whom it may concern; To Whom It May Concern.*

- Use the appropriate titles in salutations to professionals who are married: *Dear Dr. and Mrs. Marsh; Dear Drs. Marsh; Dear Dr. and Mr. Marsh.*

- When addressing two unmarried persons, use the same order in the salutation as that used in the inside address:

```
Mr. David G. Oliver
Ms. Ann Rader
AB Distributing
P.O. Box 0100
Portland, ME 04101

Dear Mr. Oliver and Ms. Rader:
```

- Use the addressee's first name without the title *Mr.* or *Ms.* when gender is unknown: *Dear A. J. Stevens; Dear Leslie Cramer.*

- Use *Ms.* in domestic correspondence to a woman unless you know that the woman prefers *Mrs.: Dear Ms. Gurstein.* But avoid using *Ms.* in international correspondence. (See the last section of this chapter for more about proper forms of address for women.)

*Subject*

- Use a subject line to summarize the content of the letter so that it is unnecessary to describe the content in the first paragraph.

- If the word *Subject* is included (it is frequently omitted), capitalize the first letter *(Subject)* or the entire word *(SUBJECT)* as preferred.

- Put a colon after the word *(Subject: SUBJECT:)*, but omit the colon if *In re* is used instead of *Subject.*

- Capitalize each important word of the topic or write the entire topic in all capitals, as desired: *Project X; PRO-JECT X; Subject: Project X; SUBJECT: Project X; SUB-JECT: PROJECT X.*

- Underline the subject if desired (usually, it is not under-lined): <u>Project X;</u> *Project X.*

*Body*

- Get to the point of the letter immediately in the first paragraph.

- Use all the requirements of professional writing pertinent to the different types of business documents: correct spelling, grammar, punctuation, word choice, and so on.

- Make use of format options such as itemized lists and extracts to simplify complex discussions.

- Use a brief concluding paragraph to summarize an important point(s) or to request one specific action.

- Do not give the reader alternatives from which to choose when you are requesting action.

- If the letter will not fit on one page, carry at least two lines of the body to another page.

- Begin the continued portion of the body on the next page two to three line spaces below the continuation-page heading:

```
Shari Norris
January 2, 1995
page two

carry at least two lines of the body to the
continuation page. The word continued need not be
placed on either page.

Shari Norris, January 2, 1995, page 2

carry at least two lines of the body to the
continuation page. The word continued need not be
placed on either page.
```

*Complimentary Close*

- Capitalize the first word of the complimentary close in the full-block and modified-block formats: *Sincerely yours; Best regards.*

- Place a comma after the last word of the close *(Cordially,)*.

- Position the close on the page so that it will fit on one line (flush left in the full-block format or slightly right of the page center in the modified-block format).

- Use warm, friendly closes in letters to friends and close associates: *Cordially; Regards; Best regards; Best wishes.*

- Use more formal closes with people you don't know well, with high-ranking officials, and with readers in other countries who may disapprove of too much familiarity: *Sincerely; Yours truly; Respectfully.*

*Signature*

- Sign a name exactly as it is typed (unless you are signing only your first name or a nickname); if the typed signature is *Robert A. Marshall,* the handwritten signature should not be *R. A. Marshall.*

- Omit the typed signature line if the sender's name is already printed on the letterhead.

- Include a handwritten signature even when the sender's name is printed on the letterhead.

- Use the title *Mr.* or *Ms.* in parentheses before a name only if gender would otherwise be unclear or if you need to let someone in another country, who is unfamiliar with the title *Ms.,* know that you want to be addressed by that title: *(Ms.) J. D. Bender; (Mr.) Leslie Farr.*

- Place the title *Mrs.* in parentheses before a woman's name if she prefers to be addressed as *Mrs.* rather than *Ms.: (Mrs.) Lisa Thurston.*

- Place business titles, degrees, and professional designations after a name: *Philip Vale, Manager; Jessica O'Neill, Ph.D.; Maxine McNeill CPS.* (*Note*: PSI® omits the comma before the designation *CPS.*)

- If you use the traditional style for a married or widowed woman in formal social situations, type *Mrs.* with her husband's full name, all enclosed in parentheses: *(Mrs. Jeffrey Sullivan).*

- Even when using the traditional style just described, the woman should sign the letter with her own first name and married last name: *Thelma Sullivan.*

- When using the modern style for a married or widowed woman in formal social situations, place *Mrs.* in parentheses before the woman's own first name and married last name: *(Mrs.) Thelma Sullivan.* But see the next point.

- When a married businesswoman prefers to be addressed as *Ms.* rather than *Mrs.* even in formal social situations, follow her preferences.

- For a divorced woman in formal social situations, use her own first name and the last name she has chosen, which may be her maiden name or her former husband's last name.

- Enclose *Mrs.* in parentheses before a divorced woman's name in formal social situations only if she prefers that title rather than *Ms.: Josephine Cabrera; (Mrs.) Josephine Cabrera.*

- When you sign your employer's name to a letter in his or her absence, (1) type the person's name and title as described earlier for a letter format, (2) handwrite the person's name in the signature space, and (3) add your own initials under the handwritten signature.

- When you sign a letter with your own name, put *"Secretary to . . ."* in the typed signature line (*Secretary to Mr. Warner*), and handwrite your own signature above it.

- When you write a letter for someone else and sign your own name rather than that person's name, type the other person's name in the signature line preceded by "For" (*For Mrs. Angela Sanders*), and handwrite your own name above it.

*Identification*

- Use identification initials if you need to know who dictated, signed, and transcribed a letter (usually, the person dictating and signing the letter are the same).

- Omit the identification initials from the original, if desired, although it is usually easier to include the same information on all copies.

- Place the signer's initials first, then those of the person dictating the letter (if different from the signer), and last those of the transcriber.

- Use lowercase initials for the transcriber and capital letters for the others: *AC:RM:fl.*

*Enclosure Notation*

- Use the enclosure notation to indicate that something else is being sent along with a letter.

- Spell out the word *Enclosure (or Enclosures)* or use the abbreviation *Enc. (or Encs.)* as preferred.

- If there is more than one enclosure, put the number of enclosures after the notation: *Encs. 2.*

- If enclosures are of special importance, identify them: *Enc. Certificate PD19-80765.*

- Place a colon after the abbreviation, if desired, when additional information follows: *Enc.: Check.*

*Mailing Notation*

- Use the mailing notation to specify a type of mail or transmission other than regular postal service: *By messenger.*

- Capitalize each important word in the notation beginning with *By: By UPS Next-Day Air.*

*Copy-Distribution Notation*

- Use the copy-distribution notation to list the names of people other than the addressee who will be receiving a copy of the letter.

- Use *Copy* or *c* for any type of copy, *c* or *cc* for a computer copy, and *fc* for a fax copy.

- Use *bc* for a blind copy (sent to someone without the addressee's knowledge).

- Place a blind-copy notation only on the file copies, never on the original: *bc: Irene Thomas.*

*Postscript*

- Use a postscript to make a comment unrelated to the subject of the letter.

- Do not use a postscript for afterthoughts or points that you forgot to put in the letter's body, both of which indicate lazy or careless composition.

- Begin the postscript with the capital letters *P.S.,* sometimes written without periods, followed by a colon and the comment.

- Conclude the postscript with the sender's initials: *P.S. Do you have Martin Sloane's address? I can't find it in our files. ACF*

## HOW TO WRITE THE EIGHT PRINCIPAL PARTS OF A STANDARD MEMO

The parts of a memo, like those of a letter, must not only be positioned correctly on the page (see the second section in this chapter), but they must also be spelled, capitalized, and punctuated correctly. This section lists the important points of style to remember for each of the principal parts of a memo.

*Guide Words*

- Since more than one style is acceptable for guide words such as *Date, To, From,* and *Subject,* use the style you select consistently for all of the guide words: bold, italic, or regular face (**Date;** *Date;* Date).

- Use an initial capital or all capital letters: *Date; DATE.*

- Spell out long guide words (*Reference; REFERENCE*) or abbreviate them (*Ref.; REF.*), as preferred.

- Use or omit the period after abbreviated guide words (*Attn.; ATTN*), as preferred.

- Use or omit the colon after each guide word (*Subject: SUBJECT*), as preferred.

## *Body*

- Follow the suggestions given in the previous section for writing a letter body.

- If the memo will not fit on one page (memo reports frequently run over one page), follow the guidelines given in the previous section for carrying the remaining portions of a letter body onto a continuation sheet.

## *Signature Initials*

- If no printed signature line appears on the stationery, you may (but need not) include the sender's initials after the body, as described earlier.

- Type or have the sender handwrite the signature initials in capital letters, closed, without periods.

## *Identification*

- Follow the instructions in the previous section for styling an identification line in a letter.

## *Enclosure Notation*

- Follow the instructions in the previous section for styling an enclosure notation in a letter.

## *Mailing Notation*

- Follow the instructions in the previous section for styling a mailing notation in a letter.

- Omit the notation on interoffice memos that are hand-delivered.

*Copy-Distribution Notation*

- Follow the instructions in the previous section for styling a copy-distribution notation in a letter.

- As an alternative to a copy notation, refer to the "Distribution" list described earlier.

*Postscript*

- Follow the instructions in the previous section for styling a postscript in a letter.

## FOUR COMMON SIZES OF LETTER AND MEMO STATIONERY

Ordering stationery is one of the many duties that secretaries handle. Most stationery is ordered in a 20- or 24-pound weight, which laser printers and copiers usually accommodate without problems. Although all offices require standard-size stationery, some executives also like to have smaller-size stationery for social-business messages, informal memos, and other uses. Nonstandard sizes may vary slightly depending on the supplier, but the following four sizes are widely available.

    1. *Standard letterhead paper.* 8 1/2 by 11 inches (routine and formal business correspondence)

    2. *Official or personal paper.* 8 by 10 1/2 inches (personal and social-business correspondence)

    3. *Executive or monarch paper.* 7 1/4 by 10 1/2 inches (personal and social-business correspondence)

    4. *Baronial paper.* 5 1/2 by 8 1/2 inches (personal correspondence, memos, miscellaneous use)

*Five Common Sizes of Envelopes*

    The secretary who orders paper will also order matching envelopes in a size to accommodate the paper when folded in thirds or in half. As is the case with the paper, envelope sizes may vary depending on the supplier, but most printers and office-supply stores can provide these five sizes.

1. *No. 10 envelope.* 4 1/8 by 9 1/2 inches (for standard letter-head, memo, personal, and other paper)

2. *No. 9 official envelope.* 3 7/8 by 8 7/8 inches (for standard letterhead, memo, official or personal, and other paper)

3. *No. 7 executive or monarch envelope.* 3 7/8 by 7 1/2 inches (for personal and social-business correspondence and other relatively small-size paper)

4. *No. 6 3/4 commercial envelope.* 3 5/8 by 6 1/2 (for memos, personal and social-business correspondence, and other relatively small-size paper)

5. *No. 5 (or 5 1/2) Baronial envelope.* 4 5/8 by 5 5/16 (for memos, personal and social-business correspondence, and other relatively small-size paper)

## GENERAL RULES FOR USING FORMS OF ADDRESS CORRECTLY

Secretaries who spend a substantial portion of each day preparing various forms of communication know how important it is to use the correct forms of address—both to avoid offending someone and to avoid the appearance of carelessness or ignorance. The correct form, however, depends on the addressee's gender, professional status, and familiarity with the sender. Although you would likely call a peer *Mary* or *Jim,* for example, you would more likely address the chairman of the board as *Mr., Ms.,* or *Dr. Samuelson.* In international correspondence, especially, it is important to use last names until asked to do otherwise. This section describes conventional rules for addressing business and social correspondence and provides a detailed chart about addressing governmental, judicial, military, religious, academic, and other officials.

*Titles and Names*

- Use the addressee's personal or scholastic title (*Mr., Ms., Mrs., Dr.*) both on the envelope and in the inside address and salutation (unless you are writing to a close associate and use only the first name in the salutation). But see the next point.

- Use scholastic degrees after the name, on the envelope and in the inside address, if you believe that the addressee prefers them over a title.

- When more than one degree is used, place the one pertaining to the person's profession first: *Professor Barry Brentmore, Sc.D., Ph.D.*

- If you are including degrees, omit the title preceding the name if the degrees refer to the same thing as the title: *Louise Tollelson, Sc.D.*, not *Dr. Louise Tollelson, Sc.D.*

- Use a colon after the person's name in the salutation of a business or social letter (use a comma in a personal letter).

- Place initials for military service, religious order, or professional designations after a name: *Captain Ann Severs, USA; Father Mark Cassell, S.J.; Mary Foster CPS.*

- Do not use a title before a name if you use *Esq.* after it for a prominent person: *Jane Whitmore, Esq.*

- In international correspondence, follow the addressing practices of the particular country.

- Do not use a job title such as *Manager* before the name of an addressee in the United States, but use such titles when appropriate in other countries: *Arch. [Architect] Leoni Andreotti.* (*Note*: In Germany, upper management and some other professional people are addressed by title only: *Herr Doktor.*)

- Follow the practice of stating the family name first in certain Asian countries: *Mr. Yasushi Mieno.*

- Notice that in some Asian countries businesspeople have adopted the Western style of placing the family name last: *Mr. Mieno Yasushi.*

*Men and Women*

- Use *Mr.* for a man, unless the person has a doctorate or other title such as *Dean: Mr. Charles Wallace; Dean Charles Wallace.*

- In business, use *Ms.* for a single woman in the United States, unless the person has a doctorate or other title such as *Reverend: Ms. Phyllis Snowden; The Reverend Phyllis Snowden.*

- In the modern style for formal social situations, use *Ms.* for a single woman in the United States.

- In the traditional style for formal social situations, use *Miss* for a single woman.

- In business, use *Ms.* for a married or widowed woman in the United States who is using her married name, unless the woman prefers *Mrs.* or unless the person has a doctorate or other title such as *Ambassador: Ms. Paula B. Daniels; Mrs. Paula B. Daniels; The Honorable Paula B. Daniels.*

- In business, use *Ms.* for a married or widowed woman in the United States who is using her maiden name, unless the person has a doctorate or other title such as *Captain: Ms. Paula Brighton; Captain Paula Brighton.*

- In the modern style for formal social situations, use a married or widowed woman's own first name (rather than her husband's first name) with *Ms., Mrs., Dr.,* or other title, such as *General: Mrs. Paula Daniels; General Paula Daniels.* See also the next point.

- In the traditional style for formal social situations, use *Mrs.* with the full name of a married or widowed woman's husband (*Mrs. John Daniels*). See also the previous point.

- In business, use *Ms.* for a divorced woman in the United States, unless the woman prefers *Mrs.* or has a doctorate or other title such as *Senator: Ms. Sheila Cartwright; Senator Sheila Cartwright.*

- In the modern style for formal social situations, use a divorced woman's own first name and the last name she has chosen with *Ms., Miss, Dr.,* or other title, such as *General: Ms. Paula Daniels.* See also the next point.

- In the traditional style for formal social situations, use a divorced woman's maiden name and former married name, but no first name, preceded by *Mrs.: Mrs. Davidson Russell.*

- When gender is unknown and when no doctorate or other title is available, use the person's first name or initials without a title: *Dear A. R. Schindler.*

## Two or More Persons

- When two or more unmarried people are being addressed in both social and business correspondence, list the names by rank or, if they have equal rank, in alphabetical order: *Dear Dr. Rollins and Mr. Jenson; Dear Mr. Jenson and Mr. Rollins.*

- In social situations, when a married couple have different titles, list the higher rank first: *Dr. and Mrs. Gerald C. Cooper; Drs. Gerald C. and Jean R. Cooper; Dr. Jean R. and Mr. Gerald C. Cooper.*

- When none of the situations just described applies, use the traditional social form for a married couple: *Mr. and Mrs. Gerald C. Cooper.*

## Organizations

- In the inside address and on the envelope, use the company's official name as stated on its letterhead: *Northern Manufacturing Co., Inc.*

- Use a general salutation (*Ladies and Gentlemen*) in the full-block and modified-block formats, as described earlier, when a letter is addressed to a firm rather than to a specific person or job title.

## CORRECT FORMS OF ADDRESS

### U.S. Government Officials

| Personage | Envelope and Inside Address (Add Org., City, State, Zip) | Formal Salutation | Informal Salutation | Formal Close | Informal Close | 1. Spoken Address 2. Informal Introduction of Reference |
|---|---|---|---|---|---|---|
| *The President* | The President The White House | Mr. President: | Dear Mr. President: | Respectfully yours, | Sincerely yours, | 1. Mr. President *or* Sir 2. Not introduced (The President) |
| *Former President of the United States*[1] | The Honorable William R. Blank (local address) | Sir: | Dear Mr. Blank: | Respectfully yours, | Sincerely yours, | 1. Mr. Blank *or* Sir 2. The Honorable John Blank |
| *The Vice President of the United States* | The Vice President United States Senate | Mr. Vice President: | Dear Mr. Vice President: | Very truly yours, | Sincerely yours, | 1. Mr. Vice President *or* Sir 2. The Vice President |
| *The Chief Justice of the United States Supreme Court* | The Chief Justice The Supreme Court | Sir: | Dear Chief Justice: *or* Dear Chief Justice Blank: | Very truly yours, | Sincerely yours, | 1. Chief Justice *or* Sir 2. The Chief Justice |
| *Associate Justice of the United States Supreme Court* | Justice Blank The Supreme Court | Sir: | Dear Justice Blank: | Very truly yours, | Sincerely yours, | 1. Justice Blank *or* Sir 2. Justice Blank |

*Note:* In this chart the form of address for a man is used throughout except where not applicable. To use the form of address for a woman in any of these positions, use the substitution *Madam* for *Sir* and *Mrs.*, *Miss*, or *Ms.* for *Mr.* Thus *Dear Madam*; *Mrs. Blank*; *Representative from New York*; *The Lieutenant Governor of Iowa*, *Miss Blank*; *The American Minister, Ms. Blank.* The *Mr.* preceding a title becomes *Madam.* Thus *Madam Secretary; Madam Ambassador.* Use *Esquire* or *Esq.* in addressing a man or woman where appropriate. This chart lists accepted options for correct forms such as spoken address and introductions. For a detailed listing with additional options, consult a current guide to social usage, such as *Protocol* (Devon Publishing, latest edition).
1. If a former president has a title, such as General of the Army, address him by it.

*Source:* Mary A. De Vries, *Professional Secretary's Encyclopedic Dictionary*, 5th ed. (Englewood Cliffs, NJ: Prentice Hall, 1994), pp. 200-221. Reprinted by permission of the publisher, Prentice Hall/A Division of Simon & Schuster.

## U.S. Government Officials *continued*

| Personage | Envelope and Inside Address (Add Org., City, State, Zip) | Formal Salutation | Informal Salutation | Formal Close | Informal Close | 1. Spoken Address 2. Informal Introduction of Reference |
|---|---|---|---|---|---|---|
| *Retired Justice of the United States Supreme Court* | The Honorable William R. Blank Chief Justice of the United States Supreme Court | Sir: | Dear Chief Justice Blank: | Very truly yours, | Sincerely yours, | 1. Chief Justice *or* Sir 2. Chief Justice Blank |
| *The Speaker of the House of Representatives* | The Honorable William R. Blank Speaker of the House of Representatives | Dear Mr. Speaker: | Dear Mr. Blank: | Very truly yours, | Sincerely yours, | 1. Mr. Speaker *or* Mr. Blank 2. The Speaker of the House of Representatives, Mr. Blank |
| *Former Speaker of the House of Representatives* | The Honorable William R. Blank (local address) | Sir: | Dear Mr. Blank: | Very truly yours, | Sincerely yours, | 1. Mr. Blank 2. Mr. Blank |
| *Cabinet Officers addressed as "Secretary"[2]* | The Honorable William R. Blank Secretary of State  If written from abroad: The Honorable William R. Blank Secretary of State of the United States of America | Dear Mr. Secretary: | Dear Mr. Blank: | Very truly yours, | Sincerely yours, | 1. Mr. Secretary *or* Mr. Blank 2. The Secretary of State, Mr. Blank |
| *Former Cabinet Officer* | The Honorable William R. Blank (local address) | Dear Mr. Blank: | Dear Mr. Blank: | Very truly yours, | Sincerely yours, | 1. Mr. Blank 2. Mr. Blank |

2. Titles for cabinet secretaries are Secretary of State; Secretary of the Treasury; Secretary of Defense; Secretary of Education; Secretary of Energy; Secretary of the Interior; Secretary of Agriculture; Secretary of Commerce; Secretary of Labor; Secretary of Health and Human Services; Secretary of Housing and Urban Development; Secretary of Transportation.

## U.S. Government Officials *continued*

| Personage | Envelope and Inside Address (Add Org., City, State, Zip) | Formal Salutation | Informal Salutation | Formal Close | Informal Close | 1. Spoken Address 2. Informal Introduction of Reference |
|---|---|---|---|---|---|---|
| *Postmaster General* | The Honorable William R. Blank Postmaster General | Dear Mr. Postmaster General: | Dear Mr. Blank: | Very truly yours, | Sincerely yours, | 1. Mr. Postmaster General *or* Mr. Blank 2. The Postmaster General, Mr. Blank |
| *The Attorney General* | The Honorable William R. Blank Attorney General of the United States | Dear Mr. Attorney General: | Dear Mr. Blank: | Very truly yours, | Sincerely yours, | 1. Mr. Blank 2. The Attorney General, Mr. Blank *or* Mr. Blank |
| *Under Secretary of a Department* | The Honorable William R. Blank Under Secretary of Labor | Dear Mr. Under Secretary: | Dear Mr. Blank: | Very truly yours, | Sincerely yours, | 1. Mr. Blank 2. Mr. Blank |
| *United States Senator* | The Honorable William R. Blank United States Senate | Sir: | Dear Senator Blank: | Very truly yours, | Sincerely yours, | 1. Senator Blank *or* Senator 2. Senator Blank |
| *Former Senator* | The Honorable William R. Blank (local address) | Dear Sir: | Dear Mr. Blank: | Very truly yours, | Sincerely yours, | 1. Senator Blank 2. The Honorable John Blank, former United States Senator from (state) |
| *Senator-elect* | The Honorable William R. Blank Senator-elect United States Senate | Dear Sir: | Dear Mr. Blank: | Very truly yours, | Sincerely yours, | 1. Mr. Blank 2. Mr. Blank |

## U.S. Government Officials *continued*

| Personage | Envelope and Inside Address (Add Org., City, State, Zip) | Formal Salutation | Informal Salutation | Formal Close | Informal Close | 1. Spoken Address 2. Informal Introduction of Reference |
|---|---|---|---|---|---|---|
| *Committee Chairman—United States Senate* | The Honorable William R. Blank, Chairman Committee on (name) United States Senate | Dear Mr. Chairman: | Dear Senator Blank: | Very truly yours, | Sincerely yours, | 1. Senator Blank *or* Senator 2. Senator Blank |
| *Subcommittee Chairman—United States Senate* | The Honorable William R. Blank, Chairman Subcommittee on (name) United States Senate | Dear Mr. Chairman: | Dear Senator Blank: | Very truly yours, | Sincerely yours, | 1. Senator Blank *or* Senator 2. Senator Blank |
| *United States Representative or Congressman*[3] | The Honorable William R. Blank House of Representatives *When away from Washington, D.C.:* The Honorable William R. Blank (local address) | Sir: | Dear Mr. Blank: | Very truly yours, | Sincerely yours, | 1. Mr. Blank 2. The Honorable Mr. Blank, Representative from (state) *or* Mr. Blank |
| *Former Representative* | The Honorable William R. Blank (local address) | Dear Sir: *or* Dear Mr. Blank: | Dear Mr. Blank: | Very truly yours, | Sincerely yours, | 1. Mr. Blank 2. Mr. Blank *or* The Honorable John Blank, former Representative from (state) |
| *Territorial Delegate* | The Honorable William R. Blank Delegate of (territory) House of Representatives | Dear Sir: *or* Dear Mr. Blank: | Dear Mr. Blank: | Very truly yours, | Sincerely yours, | 1. Mr. Blank 2. Mr. Blank |

3. The official title of a "congressman" or "congresswoman" is *Representative*. Senators are also congressmen or congresswomen.

## U.S. Government Officials *continued*

| Personage | Envelope and Inside Address (Add Org., City, State, Zip) | Formal Salutation | Informal Salutation | Formal Close | Informal Close | 1. Spoken Address 2. Informal Introduction of Reference |
|---|---|---|---|---|---|---|
| *Resident Commissioner* | The Honorable William R. Blank Resident Commissioner from (territory) House of Representatives | Dear Sir: *or* Dear Mr. Blank: | Dear Mr. Blank: | Very truly yours, | Sincerely yours, | 1. Mr. Blank 2. Mr. Blank |
| *Directors or Heads of Independent Federal Offices, Agencies, Commissions, Organizations, etc.* | The Honorable William R. Blank Director | Dear Mr. Director (etc): | Dear Mr. Blank: | Very truly yours, | Sincerely yours, | 1. Mr. Blank 2. Mr. Blank |
| *Other High Officials of the United States* | The Honorable William R. Blank Public Printer (etc.) | Dear Sir: *or* Dear Mr. Blank: | Dear Mr. Blank: | Very truly yours, | Sincerely yours, | 1. Mr. Blank 2. Mr. Blank |
| *Secretary to the President* | The Honorable William R. Blank Secretary to the President The White House | Dear Sir: *or* Dear Mr. Blank: | Dear Mr. Blank: | Very truly yours, | Sincerely yours, | 1. Mr. Blank 2. Mr. Blank |
| *Assistant Secretary to the President* | The Honorable William R. Blank Assistant Secretary to the President The White House | Dear Sir: *or* Dear Mr. Blank: | Dear Mr. Blank: | Very truly yours, | Sincerely yours, | 1. Mr. Blank 2. Mr. Blank |
| *Press Secretary to the President* | Mr. William R. Blank Press Secretary to the President The White House | Dear Sir: *or* Dear Mr. Blank: | Dear Mr. Blank: | Very truly yours, | Sincerely yours, | 1. Mr. Blank 2. Mr. Blank |

## State and Local Government Officials

| Personage | Envelope and Inside Address (Add Org., City, State, Zip) | Formal Salutation | Informal Salutation | Formal Close | Informal Close | 1. Spoken Address / 2. Informal Introduction of Reference |
|---|---|---|---|---|---|---|
| *Governor of a State or Territory*[1] | The Honorable William R. Blank Governor of (state) | Sir: | Dear Governor Blank: | Very truly yours, | Sincerely yours, | 1. Governor Blank *or* Governor 2. Governor Blank *or* The Governor |
| *Acting Governor of a State or Territory* | The Honorable William R. Blank Acting Governor of (state) | Sir: | Dear Mr. Blank: | Very truly yours, | Sincerely yours, | 1. Mr. Blank 2. Mr. Blank |
| *Lieutenant Governor* | The Honorable William R. Blank Lieutenant Governor of (state) | Sir: | Dear Mr. Blank: | Very truly yours, | Sincerely yours, | 1. Mr. Blank 2. Mr. Blank *or* The Honorable John Blank, Lieutenant Governor |
| *Secretary of State* | The Honorable William R. Blank Secretary of State of (state) | Dear Mr. Secretary: | Dear Mr. Blank: | Very truly yours, | Sincerely yours, | 1. Mr. Blank *or* Sir 2. Mr. Blank |
| *Attorney General* | The Honorable William R. Blank Attorney General State of (state) | Dear Mr Attorney General: | Dear Mr. Blank: | Very truly yours, | Sincerely yours, | 1. Mr. Attorney General *or* Mr. Blank 2. Mr. Blank |
| *President of the Senate of a State* | The Honorable William R. Blank President of the Senate of the State of (state) | Sir: | Dear Mr. Blank: | Very truly yours, | Sincerely yours, | 1. Mr. Blank 2. Mr. Blank |

1. The form of addressing governors varies in different states. The form given here is the one used in most states. In Massachusetts by law and in some other states by courtesy, the form is *His (Her) Excellency, the Governor of (state)*.

## State and Local Government Officials *continued*

| Personage | Envelope and Inside Address (Add Org., City, State, Zip) | Formal Salutation | Informal Salutation | Formal Close | Informal Close | 1. Spoken Address / 2. Informal Introduction of Reference |
|---|---|---|---|---|---|---|
| *Speaker of the Assembly or The House of Representatives*[2] | The Honorable William R. Blank<br>Speaker of the Assembly of the State of (state) | Sir: | Dear Mr. Blank: | Very truly yours, | Sincerely yours, | 1. Mr. Blank<br>2. The Speaker of the Assembly of the State of (state), Mr. Blank |
| *Treasurer, Auditor or Comptroller of a State* | The Honorable William R. Blank<br>Treasurer of (state) | Dear Sir: | Dear Mr. Blank: | Very truly yours, | Sincerely yours, | 1. Mr. Blank<br>2. Mr. Blank |
| *State Senator* | The Honorable William R. Blank<br>The Senate of (state) | Dear Sir: | Dear Senator Blank: | Very truly yours, | Sincerely yours, | 1. Mr. Blank<br>2. Mr. Blank<br>*or*<br>The Honorable John Blank, (state) State Senator |
| *State Representative, Assemblyman, or Delegate* | The Honorable William R. Blank<br>House of Delegates | Dear Sir: | Dear Mr. Blank: | Very truly yours, | Sincerely yours, | 1. Mr. Blank<br>2. Mr. Blank<br>*or*<br>Delegate Blank |
| *District Attorney* | The Honorable William R. Blank<br>District Attorney State of (state) | Dear Sir: | Dear Mr. Blank: | Very truly yours, | Sincerely yours, | 1. Mr. Blank<br>2. Mr. Blank |
| *Mayor of a city* | The Honorable William R. Blank<br>Mayor of (city) | Dear Sir: | Dear Mr. Mayor:<br>*or*<br>Dear Mayor Blank: | Very truly yours, | Sincerely yours, | 1. Mayor Blank<br>*or*<br>Mr. Mayor<br>*or*<br>Sir<br>2. Mayor Blank |

2. In most states the lower branch of the legislature is the House of Representatives. The exceptions to this are New York, California, Wisconsin, and Nevada, where it is known as the Assembly; Maryland, Virginia, and West Virginia—the House of Delegates; New Jersey—the House of General Assembly.

## State and Local Government Officials *continued*

| Personage | Envelope and Inside Address (Add Org., City, State, Zip) | Formal Salutation | Informal Salutation | Formal Close | Informal Close | 1. Spoken Address 2. Informal Introduction of Reference |
|---|---|---|---|---|---|---|
| *President of a Board of Commissioners* | The Honorable William R. Blank, President Board of Commissioners of the City of (city) | Dear Sir: | Dear Mr. Blank: | Very truly yours, | Sincerely yours, | 1. Mr. Blank 2. Mr. Blank |
| *City Attorney, City Counsel, Corporation Counsel* | The Honorable William R. Blank, City Attorney (etc.) | Dear Sir: | Dear Mr. Blank: | Very truly yours, | Sincerely yours, | 1. Mr. Blank 2. Mr. Blank |
| *Alderman, Alderwoman* | Alderman William R. Blank City Hall | Dear Sir: | Dear Mr. Blank: | Very truly yours, | Sincerely yours, | 1. Mr. Blank 2. Mr. Blank |

### Court Officials

| Personage | Envelope and Inside Address (Add Org., City, State, Zip) | Formal Salutation | Informal Salutation | Formal Close | Informal Close | 1. Spoken Address 2. Informal Introduction of Reference |
|---|---|---|---|---|---|---|
| *Chief Justice[1] of a State Supreme Court* | The Honorable William R. Blank Chief Justice Supreme Court of (state)[2] | Sir: | Dear Mr. Chief Justice: | Very truly yours, | Sincerely yours, | 1. Mr. Chief Justice *or* Sir 2. Chief Justice Blank *or* The Honorable John Blank, Chief Justice of the Supreme Court of the State of (state) |
| *Associate Justice of a State Supreme Court* | The Honorable William R. Blank Associate Justice Supreme Court of (state) | Sir: | Dear Justice Blank: | Very truly yours, | Sincerely yours, | 1. Justice Blank *or* Sir 2. Justice Blank |

1. If his or her official title is *Chief Judge* substitute *Chief Judge* for *Chief Justice*, but never use *Mr., Mrs., Miss,* or *Ms.* with *Chief Judge* or *Judge.*
2. Substitute here the appropriate name of the court. For example, the highest court in New York State is called the Court of Appeals.

## Court Officials *continued*

| Personage | Envelope and Inside Address (Add Org., City, State, Zip) | Formal Salutation | Informal Salutation | Formal Close | Informal Close | 1. Spoken Address 2. Informal Introduction of Reference |
|---|---|---|---|---|---|---|
| *Presiding Justice* | The Honorable William R. Blank Presiding Justice Appellate Division Supreme Court of (state) | Sir: | Dear Justice Blank: | Very truly yours, | Sincerely yours, | 1. Justice Blank *or* Sir 2. Justice Blank |
| *Judge of a Court*[3] | The Honorable William R. Blank Judge of the United States District Court for the Southern (etc.) District of (state) | Sir: | Dear Judge Blank: | Very truly yours, | Sincerely yours, | 1. Judge Blank 2. Judge Blank |
| *Clerk of a Court* | William R. Blank, Esq, Clerk of the Superior Court of (state) | Dear Sir: | Dear Mr. Blank: | Very truly yours, | Sincerely yours, | 1. Mr. Blank 2. Mr. Blank |

3. Not applicable to judges of the U.S. Supreme Court.

## U.S. Diplomatic Representatives

| Personage | Envelope and Inside Address (Add Org., City, State, Zip) | Formal Salutation | Informal Salutation | Formal Close | Informal Close | 1. Spoken Address 2. Informal Introduction of Reference |
|---|---|---|---|---|---|---|
| *American Ambassador*[1] | The Honorable William R. Blank The American Ambassador to (country) | Sir: | Dear Mr. Ambassador: *or* Dear Ambassador Blank: | Very truly yours, | Sincerely yours, | 1. Mr. Ambassador *or* Mr. Blank 2. The American Ambassador to (country) (The Ambassador or Mr. Blank) |

1. When an ambassador or minister is not at his or her post, the name of the country to which he or she is accredited must be added to the address, for example, *The American Ambassador to Great Britain*. If he or she holds military rank, the diplomatic complimentary title *The Honorable* should be omitted, thus *General William R. Blank, American Ambassador (or Minister)*.

## U.S. Diplomatic Representatives *continued*

| Personage | Envelope and Inside Address (Add Org., City, State, Zip) | Formal Salutation | Informal Salutation | Formal Close | Informal Close | 1. Spoken Address 2. Informal Introduction of Reference |
|---|---|---|---|---|---|---|
| American Minister (to Central or South America)[2] | The Honorable William R. Blank / The Minister of the United States of America | Sir: | Dear Mr. Minister: / or / Dear Minister Blank: | Very truly yours, | Sincerely yours, | 1. Mr. Minister / or / Mr. Blank / 2. The Minister of the United States of America, Mr. Blank (The Minister or Mr. Blank) |
| American Chargé d'Affaires, Consul General, Consul, or Vice Consul | William R. Blank, Esq. / Chargé d'Affaires ad interim of the United States of America | Sir: | Dear Mr. Blank: | Very truly yours, | Sincerely yours, | 1. Mr. Blank / 2. Mr. Blank |
| High Commissioner | The Honorable William R. Blank / United States High Commissioner for (country) | Sir: | Dear Mr. Blank: | Very truly yours, | Sincerely yours, | 1. Commissioner Blank / or / Mr. Blank / 2. Commissioner Blank / or / Mr. Blank |

2. With reference to ambassadors and ministers to Central or South American countries substitute *The Ambassador (or Minister) of the United States* for *American Ambassador or American Minister*.

### Foreign Officials and Representatives

| Personage | Envelope and Inside Address (Add Org., City, State, Zip) | Formal Salutation | Informal Salutation | Formal Close | Informal Close | 1. Spoken Address 2. Informal Introduction of Reference |
|---|---|---|---|---|---|---|
| Foreign Ambassador[1] in the United States | His Excellency[2] / Erik Rolf Blankson / Ambassador of (country) | Excellency: | Dear Mr. Ambassador: | Very truly yours, | Sincerely yours, | 1. Mr. Ambassador or Mr. Blankson / 2. The Ambassador of (country) (The Ambassador or Mr. Blankson) |

1. The correct title of all ambassadors and ministers of foreign countries is *Ambassador (Minister) of (name of country)*, with the exception of Great Britain. The adjective form is used with reference to representatives from Great Britain—*British Ambassador, British Minister*.
2. When the representative is British or a member of the British Commonwealth, it is customary to use *The Right Honorable* and *The Honorable* in addition to *His (Her) Excellency*, whenever appropriate.

## Foreign Officials and Representatives *continued*

| Personage | Envelope and Inside Address (Add Org., City, State, Zip) | Formal Salutation | Informal Salutation | Formal Close | Informal Close | 1. Spoken Address 2. Informal Introduction of Reference |
|---|---|---|---|---|---|---|
| *Foreign Minister*[3] *in the United States* | The Honorable George Macovescu Minister Embassy of (country) | Sir: | Dear Mr. Minister: *or* Dear Mr. Macovescu: | Very truly yours, | Sincerely yours, | 1. Mr. Minister *or* Mr. Macovescu 2. The Minister of (country) (The Minister or Mr. Macovescu) |
| *Foreign Diplomatic Representative with a Personal Title*[4] | His Excellency[5] Count Allesandro de Bianco Ambassador of (country) | Excellency: | Dear Mr. Ambassador: | Very truly yours, | Sincerely yours, | 1. Mr. Ambassador *or* Count Bianco 2. The Ambassador of (country) (The Ambassador or Count Bianco) |
| *Prime Minister* | His Excellency Christian Jawaharal Blank Prime Minister of (country) | Excellency: | Dear Mr. Prime Minister: | Respectfully yours, | Sincerely yours, | 1. Mr. Blank 2. Mr. Blank *or* The Prime Minister |
| *British Prime Minister* | The Right Honorable Godfrey Blanc, K.G., M.P. Prime Minister | Sir: | Dear Mr. Prime Minister: *or* Dear Mr. Blanc: | Respectfully yours, | Sincerely yours, | 1. Mr. Blanc 2. Mr. Blanc *or* The Prime Minister |
| *Canadian Prime Minister* | The Right Honorable Claude Louis St. Blanc, C.M.G. Prime Minister of Canada | Sir: | Dear Mr. Prime Minister: *or* Dear Mr. St. Blanc: | Respectfully yours, | Sincerely yours, | 1. Mr. St. Blanc 2. Mr. St. Blanc *or* The Prime Minister |

3. The correct title of all ambassadors and ministers of foreign countries is *Ambassador (Minister) of (name of country)*, with the exception of Great Britain. The adjective form is used with reference to representatives from Great Britain—*British Ambassador, British Minister.*

4. If the personal title is a royal title, such as *His (Her) Highness* or *Prince*, the diplomatic title *His (Her) Excellency* or *The Honorable* is omitted.

5. *Dr., Señor, Don,* and other titles of special courtesy in Spanish-speaking countries may be used with the diplomatic title *His (Her) Excellency* or *The Honorable.*

## Foreign Officials and Representatives *continued*

| Personage | Envelope and Inside Address (Add Org., City, State, Zip) | Formal Salutation | Informal Salutation | Formal Close | Informal Close | 1. Spoken Address 2. Informal Introduction of Reference |
|---|---|---|---|---|---|---|
| *President of a Republic* | His Excellency Juan Cuidad Blanco President of the Republic of (country) | Excellency: | Dear Mr. President: | Respectfully yours, | Sincerely yours, | 1. Your Excellency *or* Mr. President 2. The President of the Republic of (country) |
| *Premier* | His Excellency Charles Yves de Blanc Premier of the Republic of (country) | Excellency: | Dear Mr. Premier: | Respectfully yours, | Sincerely yours, | 1. Your Excellency *or* Mr. Premier 2. The Premier of the Republic of (country), Mr. de Blanc |
| *Foreign Chargé d'Affaires (de missif[6] in the United States* | Mr. Jan Gustaf Blanc Chargé d'Affaires of (country) | Sir: | Dear Mr. Blanc: | Very truly yours, | Sincerely yours, | 1. Sir *or* Mr. Blanc 2. The Chargé d'Affaires of (country), Mr. Blanc |
| *Foreign Chargé d'Affaires ad interim in the United States* | Mr. Edmund Blank Chargé d'Affaires ad interim[7] of (country) | Sir: | Dear Mr. Blank: | Very truly yours, | Sincerely yours, | 1. Sir *or* Mr. Blank 2. The Chargé d'Affaires ad interim of (country), Mr. Blank |

6. The full title is usually shortened to *Chargé d'Affaires.*
7. The words *ad interim* should not be omitted in the address.

### The Armed Forces/Army

| *General of the Army* | General of the Army William R. Blank, USA Department of the Army | Sir: | Dear General Blank: | Very truly yours, | Sincerely yours, | 1. General Blank 2. General Blank |
|---|---|---|---|---|---|---|

## The Armed Forces /Army continued

| Personage | Envelope and Inside Address (Add Org., City, State, Zip) | Formal Salutation | Informal Salutation | Formal Close | Informal Close | 1. Spoken Address 2. Informal Introduction of Reference |
|---|---|---|---|---|---|---|
| *General, Lieutenant General, Major General, Brigadier General* | General (etc.) William R. Blank, USA[1] | Sir: | Dear General (etc.) Blank: | Very truly yours, | Sincerely yours, | 1. General Blank 2. General Blank |
| *Colonel, Lieutenant Colonel* | Colonel (etc.) William R. Blank, USA | Dear Colonel (etc.) Blank: | Dear Colonel (etc.) Blank: | Very truly yours, | Sincerely yours, | 1. Colonel Blank 2. Colonel Blank |
| *Major* | Major William R. Blank, USA | Dear Major Blank: | Dear Major Blank: | Very truly yours, | Sincerely yours, | 1. Major Blank 2. Major Blank |
| *Captain* | Captain William R. Blank, USA | Dear Captain Blank: | Dear Captain Blank: | Very truly yours, | Sincerely yours, | 1. Captain Blank 2. Captain Blank |
| *First Lieutenant, Second Lieutenant* [2] | First (etc.) Lieutenant William R. Blank, USA | Dear Lieutenant Blank: | Dear Lieutenant Blank: | Very truly yours, | Sincerely yours, | 1. Lieutenant Blank 2. Lieutenant Blank |
| *Chief Warrant Officer, Warrant Officer* | Chief Warrant Officer (etc.) William R. Blank, USA | Dear Mr. Blank: | Dear Mr. Blank: | Very truly yours, | Sincerely yours, | 1. Mr. Blank 2. Mr. Blank |
| *Chaplain in the U.S. Army* [3] | Chaplain William R. Blank, Captain, USA | Dear Chaplain Blank: | Dear Chaplain Blank: | Very truly yours, | Sincerely yours, | 1. Chaplain Blank 2. Chaplain Blank |

*Note:* Although civilian writers traditionally spell out the rank for all branches of the service, military writers use abbreviations such as *CPT* for *Captain* and *1LT* for *First Lieutenant.*
1. *USA* indicates regular service; *USAR* signifies the reserve.
2. In all *official* correspondence, the full rank should be included in both the envelope and the inside address, but not in the salutation.
3. Roman Catholic chaplains and certain Anglican priests are introduced as *Chaplain Blank* but are spoken to and referred to as *Father Blank.*

## The Armed Forces/Navy

| | | | | | | |
|---|---|---|---|---|---|---|
| *Fleet Admiral* | Admiral William R. Blank, USN Chief of Naval Operations Department of the Navy | Sir: | Dear Admiral Blank: | Very truly yours, | Sincerely yours, | 1. Admiral Blank 2. Admiral Blank |

## The Armed Forces /Navy continued

| Personage | Envelope and Inside Address (Add Org., City, State, Zip) | Formal Salutation | Informal Salutation | Formal Close | Informal Close | 1. Spoken Address 2. Informal Introduction of Reference |
|---|---|---|---|---|---|---|
| *Admiral, Vice Admiral, Rear Admiral* | Admiral (etc.) William R. Blank, USN[1] | Sir: | Dear Admiral (etc.) Blank: | Very truly yours, | Sincerely yours, | 1. Admiral Blank 2. Admiral Blank |
| *Commodore, Captain, Commander, Lieutenant Commander* | Commodore (etc.) William R. Blank, USN | Dear Commodore (etc.) Blank: | Dear Commodore (etc.) Blank: | Very truly yours, | Sincerely yours, | 1. Commodore (etc.) Blank 2. Commodore (etc.) Blank |
| *Junior Officers: Lieutenant, Lieutenant Junior Grade, Ensign* | Lieutenant (etc.) William R. Blank, USN | Dear Mr. Blank: | Dear Mr. Blank: | Very truly yours, | Sincerely yours, | 1. Mr. Blank[2] 2. Lieutenant (etc.) Blank (Mr. Blank) |
| Chief Warrant Officer, Warrant Officer | Chief Warrant Officer (etc.) William R. Blank, USN | Dear Mr. Blank: | Dear Mr. Blank: | Very truly yours, | Sincerely yours, | 1. Mr. Blank 2. Mr. Blank |
| Chaplain | Chaplain William R. Blank, Captain, USN | Dear Chaplain Blank: | Dear Chaplain Blank: | Very truly yours, | Sincerely yours, | 1. Chaplain Blank 2. Captain Blank (Chaplain Blank) |

1. *USN* signifies regular service; *USNR* indicates the reserve.
2. Junior officers in the medical or dental corps are spoken to and referred to as *Dr.* but are introduced by their rank.

### The Armed Forces/Air Force

Air Force titles are the same as those in the army, except that *USAF* is used instead of *USA,* and *USAFR* is used to indicate the reserve.

### The Armed Forces/Marine Corps

Marine Corps titles are the same as those in the army, except that the top rank is *Commandant of the Marine Corps. USMC* indicates regular service; *USMCR* indicates the reserve.

### The Armed Forces/Coast Guard

Coast Guard titles are the same as those in the navy, except that the top rank is *Admiral. USCG* indicates regular service; *USCGP* indicates the reserve.

## Church Dignitaries/Catholic Faith

| Personage | Envelope and Inside Address (Add Org., City, State, Zip) | Formal Salutation | Informal Salutation | Formal Close | Informal Close | 1. Spoken Address 2. Informal Introduction of Reference |
|---|---|---|---|---|---|---|
| The Pope | His Holiness, The Pope or His Holiness, Pope (name) | Your Holiness: or Most Holy Father: | Always Formal | Respectfully yours, | Always Formal | 1. Your Holiness 2. Not introduced (His Holiness or The Pope) |
| Apostolic Pro-Nuncio | His Excellency The Most Reverend William R. Blank[1] Titular Archbishop of (place) The Apostolic Pro-Nuncio | Your Excellency: | Dear Archbishop Blank: | Respectfully yours, | Sincerely yours, | 1. Your Excellency 2. Not introduced (the Apostolic Delegate) |
| Cardinal in the United States | His Eminence William Cardinal Blank Archbishop of (place) | Your Eminence: | Dear Cardinal Blank: | Respectfully yours, | Sincerely yours, | 1. Your Eminence or Cardinal Blank 2. Not introduced (His Eminence or Cardinal Blank) |
| Bishop and Archbishop in the United States | The Most Reverend William R. Blank, D.D. Bishop (etc.) of (place) | Dear Bishop (etc); or Most Reverend Sir: | Dear Bishop (etc.) Blank: | Respectfully yours, | Sincerely yours, | 1. Bishop (Archbishop) Blank 2. Bishop (Archbishop) Blank |
| Bishop in England | The Right Reverend William R. Blank Bishop of (place) (local address) | Right Reverend Sir: | Dear Bishop: | Respectfully yours, | Sincerely yours, | 1. Bishop Blank 2. Bishop Blank |
| Abbot | The Right Reverend William R. Blank Abbot of (place) | Dear Father Abbot: | Dear Father Blank: | Respectfully yours, | Sincerely yours, | 1. Father Abbot 2. Father Blank |
| Monsignor (Lower Rank) | The Very Reverend[2] Monsignor William R. Blank | Very Reverend Monsignor: | Dear Monsignor Blank: | Respectfully yours, | Sincerely yours, | 1. Monsignor Blank 2. Monsignor Blank |

1. Sources differ on the use of *The* preceding a religious title. Some churches are no longer using *The*, whereas others retain it in the traditional style. Follow the style of the particular church.
2. Substitute *The Right Reverend* for *The Very Reverend* for a Higher Rank Monsignor.

## Church Dignitaries/Catholic Faith *continued*

| Personage | Envelope and Inside Address (Add Org., City, State, Zip) | Formal Salutation | Informal Salutation | Formal Close | Informal Close | 1. Spoken Address 2. Informal Introduction of Reference |
|---|---|---|---|---|---|---|
| *Superior of a Brotherhood and Priest*[3] | The Very Reverend William R. Blank, M.M. Director | Dear Father Superior: | Dear Father Superior: | Respectfully yours, | Sincerely yours, | 1. Father Blank 2. Father Blank |
| *Priest* | *With scholastic degree:* The Reverend William R. Blank, Ph.D. | Dear Dr. Blank: | Dear Dr. Blank: | Very truly yours, | Sincerely yours, | 1. Doctor (Father) Blank 2. Doctor (Father) Blank |
| | *Without scholastic degree (but member of religious order):* The Reverend William R. Blank, S.J.[4] | Dear Father Blank: | Dear Father Blank: | Very truly yours, | Sincerely yours, | 1. Father Blank 2. Father Blank |
| *Brother* | Brother John Blank | Dear Brother: | Dear Brother John: | Very truly yours, | Sincerely yours, | 1. Brother John 2. Brother John |
| *Mother Superior of a Sisterhood (Catholic or Protestant)*[5] | Mother Mary Blank, O.C.A. | Dear Mother Blank: | Dear Mother Blank: | Respectfully yours, | Sincerely yours, | 1. Reverend Mother 2. Reverend Mother |
| *Sister Superior* | Sister Mary Blank (order, if used)[6] | Dear Sister Blank: | Dear Sister Blank: | Respectfully yours, | Sincerely yours, | 1. Sister Blank *or* Sister Margaret 2. The Sister Superior *or* Sister Blank (Sister Margaret) |

3. The address for the superior of a Brotherhood depends on whether or not he is a priest or has a title other than a superior. Consult the *Official Catholic Directory.*
4. When the order is known, the initials immediately follow the person's name, preceded by a comma.
5. Many religious congregations no longer use the title *Superior.* The head of a congregation is known instead by another title such as *President.*
6. The address of the superior of a Sisterhood depends on the order to which she belongs. The abbreviation of the order is not always used. Consult the *Official Catholic Directory.*

## Church Dignitaries/Catholic Faith *continued*

| Personage | Envelope and Inside Address (Add Org., City, State, Zip) | Formal Salutation | Informal Salutation | Formal Close | Informal Close | 1. Spoken Address 2. Informal Introduction of Reference |
|---|---|---|---|---|---|---|
| Sister[7] | Sister Mary Blank | Dear Sister: *or* Dear Sister Blank: | Dear Sister Mary: | Very truly yours, | Sincerely yours, | 1. Sister Mary 2. Sister Mary |

7. Use the form of address preferred by the person if you know it. Some women religious prefer to be addressed as "Sister Blank" rather than "Sister Mary" in business situations, but others object to the use of the last name.

## Church Dignitaries/Jewish Faith

| Personage | Envelope and Inside Address (Add Org., City, State, Zip) | Formal Salutation | Informal Salutation | Formal Close | Informal Close | 1. Spoken Address 2. Informal Introduction of Reference |
|---|---|---|---|---|---|---|
| Rabbi | *With scholastic degree:* Rabbi William R. Blank, Ph.D. | Sir: | Dear Dr. Blank: *or* Dear Rabbi Blank: | Very truly yours, | Sincerely yours, | 1. Rabbi Blank *or* Dr. Blank 2. Rabbi Blank *or* Dr. Blank |
| | *Without scholastic degree:* Rabbi William R. Blank | Sir: | Dear Rabbi Blank: | Very truly yours, | Sincerely yours, | 1. Rabbi Blank 2. Rabbi Blank |

## Church Dignitaries/Protestant Faith

| Personage | Envelope and Inside Address (Add Org., City, State, Zip) | Formal Salutation | Informal Salutation | Formal Close | Informal Close | 1. Spoken Address 2. Informal Introduction of Reference |
|---|---|---|---|---|---|---|
| Archbishop (Anglican) | The Most Reverend Archbishop of (place) *or* The Most Reverend John Blank Archbishop of (place) | Your Grace: | Dear Archbishop Blank: | Respectfully yours, | Sincerely yours, | 1. Your Grace 2. Not introduced (His Grace or The Archbishop) |

## Church Dignitaries/Protestant Faith *continued*

| Personage | Envelope and Inside Address (Add Org., City, State, Zip) | Formal Salutation | Informal Salutation | Formal Close | Informal Close | 1. Spoken Address 2. Informal Introduction of Reference |
|---|---|---|---|---|---|---|
| *Presiding Bishop of the Protestant Episcopal Church in America* | The Right Reverend William R. Blank, D.D., L.L.D. Presiding Bishop of the Protestant Episcopal Church in America | Right Reverend Sir: | Dear Bishop Blank: | Respectfully yours, | Sincerely yours, | 1. Bishop Blank 2. Bishop Blank |
| *Anglican Bishop* | The Right Reverend John Blank The Lord Bishop of (place) | Right Reverend Sir: | Dear Bishop Blank: | Respectfully yours, | Sincerely yours, | 1. Bishop Blank 2. Bishop Blank |
| *Methodist Bishop* | The Reverend William R. Blank Methodist Bishop | Reverend Sir: *or* Dear Bishop Blank: | Dear Bishop Blank: | Respectfully yours, | Sincerely yours, | 1. Bishop Blank 2. Bishop Blank |
| *Protestant Episcopal Bishop* | The Right Reverend William R. Blank, D.D., L.L.D. Bishop of (place) | Right Reverend Sir: | Dear Bishop Blank: | Respectfully yours, | Sincerely yours, | 1. Bishop Blank 2. Bishop Blank |
| *Archdeacon* | The Venerable William R. Blank Archdeacon of (place) | Venerable Sir: | Dear Archdeacon Blank: | Respectfully yours, | Sincerely yours, | 1. Archdeacon Blank 2. Archdeacon Blank |
| *Dean*[1] | The Very Reverend William R. Blank, D.D. Dean of (place) | Very Reverend Sir: | Dear Dean Blank: | Respectfully yours, | Sincerely yours, | 1. Dean Blank *or* Dr. Blank 2. Dean Blank *or* Dr. Blank |
| *Canon* | The Reverend William R. Blank, D.D. Canon of (place) | Reverend Sir: | Dear Canon Blank: | Respectfully yours, | Sincerely yours, | 1. Canon Blank 2. Canon Blank |

1. Applies only to the head of a cathedral or of a theological seminary.

## Church Dignitaries/Protestant Faith *continued*

| Personage | Envelope and Inside Address (Add Org., City, State, Zip) | Formal Salutation | Informal Salutation | Formal Close | Informal Close | 1. Spoken Address 2. Informal Introduction of Reference |
|---|---|---|---|---|---|---|
| *Protestant Minister* | *With scholastic degree:* The Reverend William R. Blank, D.D., Litt.D. *or* The Reverend Dr. William R. Blank | Dear Dr. Blank: | Dear Dr. Blank: | Very truly yours, | Sincerely yours, | 1. Dr. Blank 2. Dr. Blank |
| | *Without scholastic degree:* The Reverend William R. Blank | Dear Mr. Blank: | Dear Mr. Blank: | Very truly yours, | Sincerely yours, | 1. Mr. Blank 2. Mr. Blank |
| *Episcopal Priest (High Church)* | *With scholastic degree:* The Reverend William R. Blank, D.D., Litt.D. *or* The Reverend Dr. William R. Blank | Dear Dr. Blank: | Dear Dr. Blank: | Very truly yours, | Sincerely yours, | 1. Dr. Blank 2. Dr. Blank |
| | *Without scholastic degree:* The Reverend William R. Blank | Dear Father Blank: *or* Dear Mr. Blank | Dear Father Blank: *or* Dear Mr. Blank: | Very truly yours, | Sincerely yours, | 1. Father Blank *or* Mr. Blank 2. Father Blank *or* Mr. Blank |

### College and University Officials

| Personage | Envelope and Inside Address | Formal Salutation | Informal Salutation | Formal Close | Informal Close | 1. Spoken Address 2. Informal Introduction |
|---|---|---|---|---|---|---|
| *President of a College or University* | *With scholastic degree:* Dr. William R. Blank *or* William R. Blank, L.L.D., Ph.D. President | Sir: | Dear Dr. Blank: | Very truly yours, | Sincerely yours, | 1. Dr. Blank 2. Dr. Blank |

College and University Officials *continued*

| Personage | Envelope and Inside Address (Add Org., City, State, Zip) | Formal Salutation | Informal Salutation | Formal Close | Informal Close | 1. Spoken Address 2. Informal Introduction of Reference |
|---|---|---|---|---|---|---|
| *President of a College or University* | *Without a scholastic degree:* Mr. William R. Blank President | Sir: | Dear President Blank: | Very truly yours, | Sincerely yours, | 1. Mr. Blank 2. Mr. Blank *or* Mr. Blank, President of the College |
| | *Catholic Priest:* The Reverend William R. Blank, S.J., D.D., Ph.D. President | Sir: | Dear Dr. Blank: | Very truly yours, | Sincerely yours, | 1. Doctor (Father) Blank 2. Doctor (Father) Blank |
| *University Chancellor* | Dr. William R. Blank Chancellor | Sir: | Dear Dr. Blank: | Very truly yours, | Sincerely yours, | 1. Dr. Blank 2. Dr. Blank |
| *Dean or Assistant Dean of a College or Graduate School* | Dean (Assistant Dean) William R. Blank School of Law | Dear Sir: *or* Dear Dean Blank: | Dear Dean Blank: | Very truly yours, | Sincerely yours, | 1. Dean (Assistant Dean) Blank *or* 2. Dean (Assistant Dean) Blank |
| | *With a scholastic degree:* Dr. William R. Blank Dean (Assistant Dean), School of Law | Dear Sir: *or* Dear Dean Blank: | Dear Dean Blank: | | | Dr. Blank, the Dean (Assistant Dean) School of Law |
| *Professor* | Professor William R. Blank | Dear Professor Blank: | Dear Professor Blank: | Very truly yours, | Sincerely yours, | 1. Professor (Dr.) Blank 2. Professor (Dr.) Blank |
| | *With a scholastic degree:* Dr. William R. Blank | Dear Dr. (or Professor) Blank: | Dear Dr. (or Professor) Blank: | | | |
| *Associate or Assistant Professor* | Mr. William R. Blank | Dear Professor Blank: | Dear Professor Blank: | Very truly yours, | Sincerely yours, | 1. Professor (Dr.) Blank 2. Professor (Dr.) Blank |
| | *With a scholastic degree:* Dr. William R. Blank Associate (Assistant) Professor | Dear Dr. (or Professor) Blank: | Dear Dr. (or Professor) Blank: | | | |

## College and University Officials continued

| Personage | Envelope and Inside Address (Add Org., City, State, Zip) | Formal Salutation | Informal Salutation | Formal Close | Informal Close | 1. Spoken Address / 2. Informal Introduction of Reference |
|---|---|---|---|---|---|---|
| Instructor | Mr. William R. Blank / *With a scholastic degree:* / Dr. William R. Blank | Dear Mr. Blank: / Dear Dr. Blank: | Dear Mr. Blank: / Dear Dr. Blank: | Very truly yours, | Sincerely yours, | 1. Mr. (Dr.) Blank / 2. Mr. (Dr.) Blank |
| Chaplain of a College or University | Chaplain William R. Blank / *With a scholastic degree:* / The Reverend William R. Blank, D.D. / Chaplain | Dear Chaplain Blank: / Dear Dr. Blank: | Dear Chaplain (Dr.) Blank: | Very truly yours, | Sincerely yours, | 1. Chaplain Blank / 2. Chaplain Blank / *or* / Dr. Blank |
| **United Nations Officials[1]** | | | | | | |
| Secretary General | His Excellency William R. Blank / Secretary General of the United Nations | Excellency[2] | Dear Mr. Secretary General: / *or* / Dear Mr. Blank: | Very truly yours, | Sincerely yours, | 1. Excellency / *or* / Mr. Secretary General / 2. The Secretary General of the United Nations, Mr. Blank |
| Under Secretary | The Honorable William R. Blank / Under Secretary of the United Nations / The Secretariat / United Nations | Sir: | Dear Mr. Under Secretary: / *or* / Dear Mr. Blank: | Very truly yours, | Sincerely yours, | 1. Mr. Blank / 2. Mr. Blank |

1. The six principal branches through which the United Nations functions are The General Assembly, The Security Council, The Economic and Social Council, The Trusteeship Council, The International Court of Justice, and The Secretariat.
2. An American citizen should never be addressed as "Excellency."

## United Nations Officials *continued*

| Personage | Envelope and Inside Address (Add Org., City, State, Zip) | Formal Salutation | Informal Salutation | Formal Close | Informal Close | 1. Spoken Address 2. Informal Introduction of Reference |
|---|---|---|---|---|---|---|
| *Foreign Representative (with ambassadorial rank)* | His Excellency William R. Blank Representative of (country) to the United Nations | Excellency: | Dear Mr. Ambassador: | Very truly yours, | Sincerely yours, | 1. Mr. Ambassador 2. Ambassador Blank *or* The Representative of (country) to the United Nations, Ambassador Blank |
| *United States Representative (with ambassadorial rank)* | The Honorable William R. Blank United States Representative to the United Nations | Sir: *or* Dear Mr. Ambassador: | Dear Mr. Ambassador: | Very truly yours, | Sincerely yours, | 1. Mr. Ambassador 2. Ambassador Blank *or* The United States Representative to the United Nations, Ambassador Blank |

# — 5 —
# ELECTRONIC AND CONVENTIONAL MAIL

## EFFECTIVE PROCEDURES FOR PROCESSING INCOMING MAIL

In a typical office, secretaries process a variety of incoming mail, including postal mail, private-courier mail, and one or more forms of electronic transmission, such as fax and E-mail. When the mail volume is heavy, an efficient routine is essential to avoid delays in processing, delays from procedures that are cumbersome and time consuming, and errors resulting from general confusion. The following tips will help you process your incoming electronic and conventional mail more efficiently.

- Check computer mailboxes, fax machines, and other electronic systems for incoming messages the first thing each morning and throughout the day.

- Process urgent messages immediately.

- Combine all routine printouts, private-courier packages, and other irregular deliveries with the incoming postal mail for processing together at one time.

- Follow your employer's instructions for processing and presentation of incoming mail at a particular time each day or more often during the day.

- Assemble the supplies you will need for mail processing: pens, pencils, yellow (or other) highlighter pen, self-sticking notes, date stamp, letter opener, paper clips, stapler, cellophane tape, and so on.

- Before opening the envelopes and packages, sort the mail into categories such as personal mail, faxes and E-mail printouts, postal and private-courier correspondence, invoices, advertising material, and newspapers and other printed material.

- Collect and deliver or forward the personal and confidential mail as well as mail intended for someone else.

- Readdress missent mail or write "Not at This Address" near the addressee data.

- If you accidentally open one of the personal or confidential pieces, immediately seal it with cellophane or other tape and write on the envelope an appropriate notation, such as "Opened in Error," with the date and your initials.

- If you have been asked to open personal and confidential mail, follow those instructions.

- Separate, open, and process telegrams, special delivery envelopes, express packages, and other urgent mail first.

- Using either a manual or automatic opener, tap the lower edge of the envelope to shake the contents away from the top edge being opened.

- Attach large enclosures in back of letters and small enclosures in front.

- Check for enclosures that are missing, and if any were omitted, make a notation on the letter and promptly notify the sender.

- Check whether the sender has a return address on the contents, and if there is none, staple or paper-clip the envelope or mailing label to the letter.

- Check whether incoming money matches the amount stated in the cover letter or invoice, and if it does not, make a note on the letter or invoice and promptly notify the sender.

- Keep envelopes with the postmark date when a letter is undated or when the postmark date is important for another reason.

- Stamp opened pieces with the date and time (if required).

- Sort the opened mail into material requiring your attention or your employer's attention and material to be routed to someone else.

- When practical, set up a folder for each category of mail (e.g., correspondence, invoices) where you can hold material until you are ready to present it or handle it yourself.

- Find out your employer's preference for keeping or disposing of unsolicited advertising material.

- Follow your employer's instructions regarding the highlighting of key points.

- Observe office restrictions about writing on incoming mail, and attach self-sticking notes or make a photocopy if writing on original material is prohibited.

- Follow company policy for noting retention periods or destruction dates on incoming mail.

- Assemble the mail in each category according to priority.

- If practical, place material to be presented to your employer in folders color-coded for different categories, with urgent material on top in each folder or with top-priority material in a separate folder.

- If it would help your employer reply to an incoming message, attach pertinent file material, such as a report, financial statement, or previous correspondence.

- Photocopy material that should be read by others, attach a routing slip, and send the photocopies to the other people, keeping the originals in the office.

- Use action-requested slips for routed mail: ( ) For your information ( ) For your action ( ) For your approval ( ) For your comments ( ) Please forward ( ) Please return ( ) Please review with me ( ) Please file ( ) Other _____.

- If a letter or package contains threatening information or if you believe it may contain dangerous material, immediately call company security, the police, or the Postal Inspection Service.

- If you are required to keep a mail record of all important pieces of mail received, fill out the record before routing any of the items.

- Set up a columnar form on the computer or use an accounting sheet with at least ten columns: *Date Received, Time Received, Date on Item, Sender's Name and Address, Name and Department of Recipient, Type of Mail* (e.g., *Fax*), *Description of Mail* (e.g., *meeting notice*), *To Whom Sent for Action, Type of Action Required, Follow-up Date.*

- When your employer or the intended recipient is absent, follow instructions concerning the person's preferred method for you to forward urgent material—fax, express mail, or other method.

## EFFECTIVE PROCEDURES FOR PROCESSING OUTGOING MAIL

The procedures for handling outgoing mail may vary more than those for handling incoming mail. In a small office, for example, the outgoing mail volume may be too small to justify the use of electronic mailing equipment, whereas in a large office having a large mail volume, an electronic scale, a postage meter, and other mail processing equipment may be essential. In either case, most secretaries will benefit from following some or all of the following procedures for processing the outgoing mail.

- In addition to using your computer spell-checker, manually proofread everything for format, punctuation and capitalization style, spelling, grammar and word usage, and overall accuracy and appearance.

- Follow your employer's preference in submitting material to be signed with or without envelopes attached.

- If you need not include envelopes or labels with material presented for signature, you can be preparing them while your employer is signing the material.

- Follow your employer's preference concerning the best time of day (or throughout the day) to submit outgoing mail for signing.

- If the signature location might be overlooked, attach a self-sticking note by the location as a reminder.

- If the volume of material to be signed is substantial, present it in one or more "To Be Signed" folders for checks, contracts, letters, and other documents.

- When something must be sent immediately and your employer is in another office, present the material for signing on a clipboard to provide a hard surface for writing.

- If you sign letters for your employer, follow the guidelines in Chapter 4.

- Before folding and inserting letters and other material, double-check that no signatures are missing.

- Follow office practice about whether to send a paper confirmation copy of an electronic transmission and whether the sender should initial the confirmation printout.

- Before sealing any envelopes, double-check that all enclosures have been included and that the letter or other document contains the appropriate enclosure notation.

- Attach small enclosures in front of a letter and large enclosures behind it. See also the next point.

- As an alternative, to avoid damage to automated mailing equipment from paper clips, insert enclosures in the fold of a letter or behind it without clips or staples.

- Insert loose items, such as coins, in a small envelope or tape them to a card.

- Before sealing envelopes or closing an electronic file, double-check that the appropriate file copies have been made and that electronic documents have been saved in the computer.

- If an outgoing mail record is required, set up a form in the computer or use a columnar accounting sheet with at least five headings, *Date Sent, Name and Address of Addressee, Type of Mail* (e.g., *E-Mail*), *Description of Mail* (e.g., *proposal*), *Follow-up Date.*

- Fill out the mail record before mail leaves the office.

- Prepare envelopes according to the addressing guidelines given in Chapter 4.

- Fold a standard letter or memo in thirds, and insert it in the envelope so that the text appears ready to read when removed.

- If paper clips are used to enclose other material with a letter, insert the folded material so that the clip falls at the bottom of the envelope to avoid damaging postal equipment.

- Fold a letter to be inserted in a window envelope with the inside address facing out. (*Note:* Forms and invoices often have corner marks to designate the space within which the address must be typed.)

- If your office does not have electronic equipment that seals as well as meters the mail, close envelopes and packages by sponge, mouth, tape, or staples.

- If your office does not use a postal meter or prepaid imprints (an authorized stamp printed on an envelope), maintain an accurate postage scale, a list of current postage rates, and a sufficient supply of stamps.

- Code the mail (individual pieces or bundles) as required so that the mail room can charge mail to the appropriate office account.

## TEN STEPS TO ENSURE THAT MAIL IS ADDRESSED PROPERLY

In many organizations, secretaries are responsible for ensuring that the mail is addressed properly. One of three things may happen when it isn't addressed properly: (1) it may be returned to the sender for a better address; (2) it may be redirected from one person or place to another in search of the correct destination; or (3) it may be processed more slowly. In any one of the three situations, the result is delayed delivery, which can create problems in conducting business on schedule. Since "time is money" in business, such delays can be costly. The following steps will help you avoid common addressing errors and omissions.

1. Style envelope and mailing label addresses in all capital letters, which can be scanned more accurately by automated equipment, without punctuation except as required to avoid misreading. See the model in Chapter 4.

2. Put address data in the order described in Chapter 4: account numbers, addressee's name, organization's name, attention line, street or postal box, room or suite number, and city, state, and ZIP Code.

3. Always use the two-letter abbreviation for states, territories, and Canadian provinces. See the list at the end of this chapter.

4. Use accepted abbreviations for other address data, such as *ST, HOSP,* and *UNIV.* See the list at the end of this chapter.

5. Use the complete street name (*1095 WESTCHESTER RD,* not *1095 WESTCHESTER*), including apartment, suite, room, building, or other numbers (if any).

6. Use the nine-digit ZIP Code when known (call your local post office for missing codes).

7. Be certain that your return address appears in the upper left corner of envelopes (see the illustration in Chapter 4), not on the back flap or perpendicular across the left edge.

8. Follow precise Postal Service specifications for location of barcodes, postage, and other parts of the envelope face. See the illustrations in Chapter 4.

9. Use a standard-size envelope (see Chapter 4), in a light color, without nonaddress printing such as advertising material, to reduce the chances of misreading the address data.

10. Keep your address lists current to prevent the wasted time and expense of returns and remailings (investigate Postal Service list-correction services).

## THE CHIEF DO'S AND DON'TS OF E-MAIL ETIQUETTE

E-mail users sometimes have less trouble learning how to *transmit* E-mail messages than how to compose them courteously and thoughtfully. Often this happens because senders fail to take into account the way that E-mail is read and the way that receivers respond to it. Also, the speed of E-mail transmissions can cause some people to forget that the content still requires planning and thought. The very nature of E-mail may mean that some readers won't want to receive lengthy or frivolous messages. Questions of courtesy, privacy, and legality are arising every day, in fact, and until E-mail protocol is firmly established, users should follow these simple guidelines.

- Follow any E-mail policies specified by your company.

- Don't allow the ease of transmission, including multiple simultaneous transmissions, to encourage you to send messages to people who may not need or want to receive them.

- Give people with whom you communicate regularly a list of codes you may use from time to time to designate emotions, such as *<k>* = *kidding*. (*Note*: Generally, avoid emotions in E-mail messages.)

- Avoid nonliteral expressions, such as sarcasm or irony, that could be misinterpreted, but if you must use them, add the appropriate codes after such expressions.

- Take the same care in the use of format, capitalization, punctuation, and grammar in E-mail messages that you would use in traditional letters and memos.

- Take the same care in selecting the right tone and degree of formality and familiarity in E-mail messages that you would use for traditional letters and memos.

- Do not respond by E-mail (or any other form of mail) to a letter or situation while you are angry or unhappy.

- Before you use E-mail abbreviations such as *BTW* (by the way) and *PLS* (please), be certain that the recipient understands them or that you have sent a list of abbreviations you sometimes use.

- Send short, single-subject messages that fit on one computer screen (send a new message for each new subject).

- Use specific, informative subject lines (*AVAILABLE LABEL DESIGNS: WHALES, FISH, PLANTS*) rather than general lines (*DESIGNS*).

- Use bullets, lists, and other formatting techniques to help the reader scan your message with ease.

- Remember that since E-mail messages may be seen by more people than the intended recipient, you should word comments so as not to embarrass yourself or the recipient.

- Remember also that nonserious messages may be printed out by the recipient (and distributed to others), creating a sense of formality and importance that you didn't intend.

- Forward a message that you receive in error with a cover note explaining what happened, or if you do not know the address, return the message to the sender with a cover letter.

- Be patient with contacts who may still be learning the rules of E-mail etiquette.

## SIXTEEN WAYS TO SAVE MONEY IN THE MAIL ROOM

Although the use of E-mail and faxes is moving some of the cost of mailing letters and packages out of the mail room and into the office, companies must regularly search for ways to save money on heavy volumes of postal and private-courier mail. Simple cost-saving measures are sometimes overlooked as employees continue to follow inefficient practices out of habit. Often a study of mail room activities will readily reveal weaknesses in operations that contribute to rising expenses. Here are sixteen ways to combat increasing expenses whether you do your own mailing from your office or work with a central mail room.

1. Be certain that everyone on your list needs to receive a copy of the mailing.

2. Regularly update your mailing list to eliminate unnecessary, obsolete, and inaccurate addresses.

3. Have an endorsement printed on envelopes that asks for address corrections (consult the post office for current costs).

4. If you send several postal or private-courier messages every couple of days to the same person, consider reducing the number of messages or combining several messages into one.

5. Use postcards rather than higher-cost letters when appropriate, such as for informal notes to field personnel.

6. Try to eliminate unnecessary enclosures or very heavy envelopes that add to the weight and cost of mailing.

7. Use routing slips when practical instead of mailing numerous identical copies to several people.

8. Consider sending microfilm or diskettes if continual postal or private-courier mailings of large reports and other documents are costly.

9. Compare the costs of fax and E-mail with the costs of express deliveries.

10. Consider bulk or presort postal mailings that have reduced rates (consult the post office for details).

11. Use modern electronic scales and check them regularly for accuracy.

12. Use the telephone for local contacts when practical.

13. Use only the service you need (e.g., do not pay for expensive express service if fax, E-mail, or regular first-class postal mail will arrive just as soon and cost less).

14. Keep your messages brief and to the point—wordiness and unnecessary comments cost more money in added paper weight and in extra electronic transmission time.

15. Guard against unauthorized use or theft of equipment and supplies.

16. Keep accurate records so that you can monitor usage (see the next section about security).

## A Checklist of Ways to Improve Mail Room Security

Mail room supplies and equipment must be protected from abuse the same as telephone, computer, and other supplies and equipment. Companies have reported unauthorized use of postage and other supplies as well as the theft of valuable equipment. Other security problems may be less obvious. Confidential mail, for example, may not be sufficiently protected, and computer passwords and other security devices may be ineffective. To help you improve your mail room security, the Postal Service offers this checklist (edited for inclusion here) for customers to use in spotting weaknesses in their current security systems.

( ) Mail room personnel screened

( ) Location of furniture and the mail flow organized for maximum security

( ) Access limited to authorized personnel

( ) Distribution delays eliminated

( ) Postage and meter protected from unauthorized use and theft

( ) High-value items locked overnight

( ) Accountable items verified and secured

( ) Registered, express, and insured services used properly

( ) Control of address labels maintained

( ) Labels securely fastened to mail items

( ) Postage strips overlap labels

( ) Labels and cartons marked so as not to identify valuable contents

( ) Return address included and duplicate copy put in carton

( ) Parcels packaged properly

( ) Containers and sacks used when possible

( ) Outgoing mail properly delivered into postal custody

( ) Employee parking separated from dock area

( ) Lost and rifled mail reported to post office

( ) Supervisor able to see all employees and work areas

( ) Contract delivery services screened

( ) Unnecessary stops by delivery vehicle eliminated

( ) Procedures established for handling unexplained or potentially dangerous packages

( ) Periodic testing done for loss and quality control

## FREQUENTLY USED CLASSES OF PRIVATE-COURIER AND POSTAL MAIL

Because such a large volume of mail is sent conventionally through the Postal Service or one of the private couriers, secretaries should periodically write to the various delivery organizations for up-to-date information on current services, rates, and regulations. A cost comparison should be made not only among the various delivery services but with different forms of electronic transmission, such as fax and E-mail. The specific services of private couriers vary from one organization to another. Even the same service may be described differently. One company, for example, may refer to *overnight express* while another company may call the same thing *next-day air*. The seven basic types of service offered by most major couriers are listed below, but individual companies may have numerous other variations or incidental services. On the other hand, bus companies, taxis, and other organizations that also deliver packages may have very few options. The classes of U.S. Postal Service mail have remained fairly constant over the years, but rates and regulations have changed from time to time. The *Domestic Mail Manual* and the *International Mail Manual*, available by subscription from the Superintendent of Documents, offer regular updates of the services listed in this section.

*Private-courier mail*

- Overnight service
- Second-day service
- Airport cargo service
- International air and sea transport service
- Custom services
- Hold-for-pickup service
- Collect-on-delivery service

*U.S. Postal Service Domestic Mail*

- *Express Mail:* Express Mail next-day/second-day services, same-day airport service, custom-designed service, and military service
- *First-class mail:* First class (up to 11 ounces), priority (over 11 ounces), postal cards and commercial postcards, and various mailings of five hundred or more pieces
- *Second-class mail:* second-class nonprofit, classroom, science-of-agriculture; second-class presort; second-class barcoded letters; and second-class barcoded flats
- *Third-class mail:* third-class nonprofit, barcoded flats, basic and 3/5 presort, carrier-route presort, walk-sequence presort, barcoded letters, machinable parcels, and destination entry discount mailings
- *Fourth-class mail:* fourth-class bound printed matter, special fourth class (e.g., books), fourth-class library rate, and fourth-class parcel post

*U.S. Postal Service International Mail*

- *Postal Union mail:* letters and cards (LC mail) and other articles (AO mail)

- *Parcel post:* CP *(colis postaux)* mail
- *Express Mail international service:* custom-designed service and on-demand service

## COMMON MAILING ABBREVIATIONS FOR PROPER ADDRESSING

Although you should not abbreviate place names and countries on a letter's inside address, you should use the two-letter abbreviation for states, territories, and Canadian provinces. On the envelope, the U.S. Postal Service prefers that you abbreviate as much as possible to condense the address within the designated machine-readable area (see the illustrations in Chapter 4). *The National Zip Code Directory,* available for public use in most post offices and in many library reference rooms, provides detailed lists of address abbreviations. This section has abbreviations for the most commonly used states, territories, Canadian provinces, countries, and streets and place names.

*States and Territories*

| States and Territories | Postal Abbrev. | States and Territories | Postal Abbrev. |
|---|---|---|---|
| Alabama | AL | Florida | FL |
| Alaska | AK | Georgia | GA |
| Arizona | AZ | Guam | GU |
| Arkansas | AR | Hawaii | HI |
| American Samoa | AS | Idaho | ID |
| California | CA | Illinois | IL |
| Colorado | CO | Indiana | IN |
| Connecticut | CT | Iowa | IA |
| Delaware | DE | Kansas | KS |
| District of Columbia | DC | Kentucky | KY |
| Federated States of Micronesia | FM | Louisiana | LA |
| | | Maine | ME |

| States and Territories | Postal Abbrev. | States and Territories | Postal Abbrev. |
|---|---|---|---|
| Marshall Islands | MH | Ohio | OH |
| Maryland | MD | Oklahoma | OK |
| Massachusetts | MA | Oregon | OR |
| Michigan | MI | Palau | PW |
| Minnesota | MN | Pennsylvania | PA |
| Mississippi | MS | Puerto Rico | PR |
| Missouri | MO | Rhode Island | RI |
| Montana | MT | South Carolina | SC |
| Nebraska | NE | South Dakota | SD |
| Nevada | NV | Tennessee | TN |
| New Hampshire | NH | Texas | TX |
| New Jersey | NJ | Utah | UT |
| New Mexico | NM | Vermont | VT |
| New York | NY | Virgin Islands | VI |
| North Carolina | NC | Virginia | VA |
| North Dakota | ND | Washington | WA |
| Northern Mariana Islands | MP | West Virginia | WV |
|  |  | Wisconsin | WI |
|  |  | Wyoming | WY |

## Canadian Provinces

| Province | Abbrev. | Province | Abbrev. |
|---|---|---|---|
| Alberta | AB | Northwest Territories | NT |
| British Columbia | BC | Nova Scotia | NS |
| Labrador | LB | Ontario | ON |
| Manitoba | MB | Prince Edward Island | PE |
| New Brunswick | NB | Quebec | PQ |
| Newfoundland | NF | Saskatchewan | SK |
|  |  | Yukon | YT |

### Streets and Place Names

| Word | Abbrev. | Word | Abbrev. |
|---|---|---|---|
| Academy | ACAD | City | CY |
| Air Force Base | AFB | Clear | CLR |
| Agency | AGNCY | Cliffs | CLFS |
| Airport | ARPRT | Club | CLB |
| Alley | ALY | College | CLG |
| Annex | ANX | Common | CMM |
| Arcade | ARC | Corner | COR |
| Arsenal | ARSL | Corners | CORS |
| Avenue | AVE | Course | CRSE |
| Bayou | BYU | Court | CT |
| Beach | BCH | Courts | CTS |
| Bend | BND | Cove | CV |
| Big | BG | Creek | CRK |
| Black | BLK | Crescent | CRES |
| Bluff | BLF | Crossing | XING |
| Bottom | BTM | Dale | DL |
| Boulevard | BLVD | Dam | DM |
| Branch | BR | Depot | DPO |
| Bridge | BRG | Divide | DV |
| Brook | BRK | Drive | DR |
| Burg | BG | East | E |
| Bypass | BYP | Estates | EST |
| Camp | CP | Expressway | EXPY |
| Canyon | CYN | Extension | EXT |
| Cape | CPE | Fall | FALL |
| Causeway | CSWY | Falls | FLS |
| Center | CTR | Farms | FRMS |
| Central | CTL | Ferry | FRY |
| Church | CHR | Field | FLD |
| Churches | CHRS | Fields | FLDS |
| Circle | CIR | Flats | FLT |

| Word | Abbrev. | Word | Abbrev. |
|------|---------|------|---------|
| Ford | FRD | Junction | JCT |
| Forest | FRST | Key | KY |
| Forge | FRG | Knolls | KNLS |
| Fork | FRK | Lake | LK |
| Forks | FRKS | Lakes | LKS |
| Fort | FT | Landing | LNDG |
| Fountain | FTN | Lane | LN |
| Freeway | FWY | Light | LGT |
| Gardens | GDNS | Little | LTL |
| Gateway | GTWY | Loaf | LF |
| Glen | GLN | Locks | LCKS |
| Grand | GRND | Lodge | LDG |
| Great | GR | Loop | LOOP |
| Green | GRN | Lower | LWR |
| Ground | GRD | Mall | MALL |
| Grove | GRV | Manor | MNR |
| Harbor | HBR | Meadows | MDWS |
| Haven | HVN | Memorial | MEM |
| Heights | HTS | Middle | MDL |
| High | HI | Mile | MLE |
| Highlands | HGLDS | Mill | ML |
| Highway | HWY | Mills | MLS |
| Hill | HL | Mines | MNS |
| Hills | HLS | Mission | MSN |
| Hollow | HOLW | Mound | MND |
| Hospital | HOSP | Mount | MT |
| Hot | H | Mountain | MTN |
| House | HSE | National | NAT |
| Inlet | INLT | Naval Air Station | NAS |
| Institute | INST | Neck | NCK |
| Island | IS | New | NW |
| Islands | IS | North | N |
| Isle | ISLE | Orchard | ORCH |

| Word | Abbrev. | Word | Abbrev. |
|------|---------|------|---------|
| Oval | OVAL | Santo | SN |
| Palms | PLMS | School | SCH |
| Park | PARK | Seminary | SMNRY |
| Parkway | PKY | Shoal | SHL |
| Pass | PASS | Shoals | SHLS |
| Path | PATH | Shore | SHR |
| Pike | PIKE | Shores | SHRS |
| Pillar | PLR | Siding | SDG |
| Pines | PNES | South | S |
| Place | PL | Space Flight Center | SFC |
| Plain | PLN | Speedway | SPDWY |
| Plains | PLNS | Spring | SPG |
| Plaza | PLZ | Springs | SPGS |
| Point | PT | Spur | SPUR |
| Port | PRT | Square | SQ |
| Prairie | PR | State | ST |
| Radial | RADL | Station | STA |
| Ranch | RNCH | Stream | STRM |
| Ranches | RNCHS | Street | ST |
| Rapids | RPDS | Sulphur | SLPHR |
| Resort | RESRT | Summit | SMT |
| Rest | RST | Switch | SWCH |
| Ridge | RDG | Tannery | TNRY |
| River | RIV | Tavern | TVRN |
| Road | RD | Terminal | TERM |
| Rock | RK | Terrace | TER |
| Row | ROW | Tower | TWR |
| Run | RUN | Town | TWN |
| Rural | R | Trace | TRCE |
| Saint | ST | Track | TRAK |
| Sainte | ST | Trafficway | TRFY |
| San | SN | Trail | TRL |
| Santa | SN | Trailer | TRLR |

| Word | Abbrev. | Word | Abbrev. |
|---|---|---|---|
| Tunnel | TUNL | Ville | VL |
| Turnpike | TPKE | Vista | VIS |
| Union | UN | Walk | WALK |
| University | UNIV | Water | WTR |
| Upper | UPR | Way | WAY |
| Valley | VLY | Wells | WLS |
| Viaduct | VIA | West | W |
| View | VW | White | WHT |
| Village | VLG | Works | WKS |
|  |  | Yards | YDS |

## Countries

| Country | Abbrev. | Country | Abbrev. |
|---|---|---|---|
| Afghanistan | Afghan. | Bolivia | Bol. |
| Albania | Alb. | Bosnia and Herzegovina | Bos. and Herz. |
| Algeria | Alg. |  |  |
| Andorra | And. | Botswana | Botswana, Bots. |
| Angola | Ang. | Brazil | Braz. |
| Antigua | Ant. | Brunei Darussalam | Brun. Dar. |
| Argentina | Argen. | Bulgaria | Bulg. |
| Armenia | Armen. | Burkina Faso | Burk. Fas. |
| Australia | Aust., Austl. | Burundi | Burun. |
| Austria | Aus. | Cambodia | Cambod. |
| Azerbaijan | Azer. | Cameroon | Cam. |
| Bahamas, The | Bah. | Canada | Can. |
| Bahrain | Bah. | Cape Verde | C.V., CV |
| Bangladesh | Bangla. | Central African Republic | C.A.R., CAR., C. Afr. Rep. |
| Barbados | Barb. |  |  |
| Belgium | Belg. | Chad | Chad |
| Belize | Bel. | Chile | Chile |
| Benin | Benin, Ben. | China | Chin. |
| Bhutan | Bhu. | Colombia | Col., Colom. |

| Country | Abbrev. | Country | Abbrev. |
|---------|---------|---------|---------|
| Comoros | Comoros, Com. | Guyana | Guy. |
| Congo | Congo, Cong. | Haiti | Haiti |
| Costa Rica | C.R., CR | Honduras | Hond. |
| Croatia | Croat. | Hungary | Hung. |
| Cuba | Cuba | Iceland | Ice. |
| Cyprus | Cyp. | India | Ind. |
| Czech Republic | Czech. Rep. | Indonesia | Indon. |
| Denmark | Den. | Iran | Ir. |
| Djibouti | Djib. | Iraq | Iraq |
| Dominica | Dom. | Ireland | Ir. |
| Dominican Republic | D.R., DR, Dom. Rep. | Israel | Isr. |
| | | Italy | It. |
| Ecuador | Ecua. | Ivory Coast | I.C., IC, Iv. Cst. |
| Egypt | Egyp. | | |
| El Salvador | El. Sal. | Jamaica | Jam. |
| Equatorial Guinea | E.G., EG, Eq. Guin. | Japan | Jap. |
| | | Jordan | Jord. |
| Eritrea | Erit. | Kazakhstan | Kazakh. |
| Estonia | Est. | Kenya | Ken. |
| Ethiopia | Eth. | Kiribati | Kir. |
| Fiji | Fiji | Korea, North | N. Kor. |
| Finland | Fin. | Korea, South | S. Kor. |
| France | Fr. | Kuwait | Kuw. |
| Gabon | Gab. | Kyrgyzstan | Kyrgyz. |
| Gambia, The | Gam. | Laos | Laos |
| Georgia | Georg. | Latvia | Lat. |
| Germany | Ger. | Lebanon | Leb. |
| Ghana | Ghana | Lesotho | Leso. |
| Greece | Greece | Liberia | Lib., Liberia |
| Grenada | Gren. | Libya | Lib. |
| Guatemala | Guat. | Liechtenstein | Liech. |
| Guinea | Guinea | Lithuania | Lith. |
| Guinea Bissau | Guinea-Bissau | Luxembourg | Lux. |

| Country | Abbrev. | Country | Abbrev. |
|---------|---------|---------|---------|
| Macedonia | Maced. | Philippines | Phil. |
| Madagascar | Madag. | Poland | Pol. |
| Malawi | Malawi, Mal. | Portugal | Port. |
| Malaysia | Mal. | Qatar | Qatar, Qa. |
| Maldives | Mald. | Romania | Rom. |
| Mali | Mali | Russia | Rus. |
| Malta | Mal. | Rwanda | Rwanda |
| Mauritania | Maurit. | Saint Lucia | S.L., SL, St. Lu. |
| Mauritius | Maur. | Saint Vincent and the Grenadines | St. V.&G., St. V&G |
| Mexico | Mex. | | |
| Micronesia | Micron. | San Marino | S.M., SM |
| Moldova | Mold. | São Tomé and Príncipe | São Tomé and Príncipe |
| Monaco | Mon. | | |
| Mongolia | Mong. | Saudi Arabia | S.A., SA |
| Morocco | Mor. | Senegal | Seneg. |
| Mozambique | Mozam. | Serbia | Serb. |
| Myanmar (Burma) | Myan. (Bur.) | Seychelles | Seychelles, Sey. |
| Namibia | Nam. | Sierra Leone | S.L., SL |
| Nauru | Nau. | Singapore | Sing. |
| Nepal | Nep. | Slovakia | Slovak. |
| Netherlands, The | Neth. | Slovenia | Slov. |
| New Zealand | N.Z., NZ | Solomon Islands | S.I., SI |
| Nicaragua | Nica. | Somalia | Som. |
| Niger | Nig. | South Africa | S.A., SA, S. Afr. |
| Nigeria | Nig. | | |
| Norway | Nor. | Spain | Sp. |
| Oman | Om. | Sri Lanka (Ceylon) | S.L., SL, Sri Lan. (Cey.) |
| Pakistan | Pak. | | |
| Panama | Pan. | Sudan | Sud. |
| Papua New Guinea | Pap. N.G., Pap. NG | Suriname | Suri. |
| | | Swaziland | Swaz. |
| Paraguay | Para. | Sweden | Swed. |
| Peru | Peru | Switzerland | Switz. |
| | | Syria | Syr. |

| Country | Abbrev. | Country | Abbrev. |
|---------|---------|---------|---------|
| Taiwan | Taiw. | United Arab Emirates | U.A.E., UAE |
| Tajikistan | Tajik. | United Kingdom | U.K., UK |
| Tanzania | Tanz. | Uruguay | Uru. |
| Thailand | Thai., Thail. | Uzbekistan | Uzbek. |
| Togo | To. | Vanuatu | Vanu. |
| Tonga | Ton. | Vatican City | V.C., VC |
| Trinidad and Tobago | Trin. and Tob. | Venezuela | Venez. |
| Tunisia | Tun. | Vietnam | Viet. |
| Turkey | Turk. | Western Samoa | W.S., WS |
| Turkmenistan | Turkmen. | Yemen | Yem. |
| Tuvalu | Tuv. | Zaïre | Zaï. |
| Uganda | Ugan. | Zambia | Zam. |
| Ukraine | Ukrain. | Zimbabwe | Zimb. |

# ─ 6 ─
# WORD PROCESSING

## THE EIGHT BASIC STEPS IN CREATING DOCUMENTS ELECTRONICALLY

Secretaries use computers and electronic typewriters to create documents. With electronic processing, tasks such as document creation can be completed faster and easier. One of the main benefits of electronic word processing is the ability to reformat quickly, but other important advantages are on-screen editing and spell-checking. In computer processing, such tasks are accomplished with applications software that directs the computer to carry out program instructions. Although the individual functions and capabilities may vary from one software program to another, the eight basic steps in creating documents electronically are the same.

1. *Loading the software.* Before document entry can begin, it is necessary to load the operating system software and then the word processing software.

2. *Formatting.* You can enter format specifications (e.g., margins, line spacing, paragraph indention, tab stops) immediately or later and can also revise them at any time.

3. *Input.* You can enter text before or after formatting; if it is entered after formatting, the document viewed on screen will closely resemble the final product.

4. *Editing.* You can correct and change the text as it is entered or after the full document has been entered; you can also revise it at a future date by retrieving the file.

5. *Saving.* You can save what you have entered periodically, either at your discretion or by using an automatic save feature to avoid losing your work through power failure or other problem.

6. *Spell-checking.* You can run the spell-check program periodically or just before making a printout, but keep in mind that spell-checkers cannot detect certain errors, such as a correctly spelled but inappropriate word.

7. *Printing.* After all text has been entered, the formatting completed, and preliminary corrections and changes made, you are ready to print out the document.

8. *Proofreading.* Since spell-checking programs do not guarantee complete accuracy, you should proofread the printout manually for additional errors and inconsistencies.

## IMPORTANT GUIDELINES FOR DRAFTING MANUSCRIPTS TO BE TYPESET

If your company does not have a desktop-publishing system, in most cases either you will use your word processing program to prepare finished documents, or you will prepare a manuscript draft to be sent to an outside typesetter and printer. Depending on the capabilities of the firm you use, you also may be able to submit a diskette rather than, or along with, a manuscript. Whether the final text is set from a diskette or rekeyed from a manuscript, your printout will be the compositor's guide to formatting and other matters. If you are not given specific instructions for manuscript or disk preparation, follow these general guidelines.

- Use 8 1/2- by 11-inch white, 20-pound bond paper.

- Use a laser or other quality-copy printer (or an electronic typewriter used as a printer) to prepare clear, easily readable copy.

- Use 5- to 6-inch lines, such as the default (preset) length in your word processing program.

- Double-space all manuscript copy.

- Indent paragraphs at least 1/2 inch.

- Place chapter titles, list titles, table titles, major headings, and subheadings where you want them to be on the printed page: centered, flush left, or indented the same as the paragraphs.

- Leave a margin of 1 to 1 1/2 inches on all sides, such as the default settings in your word processing program.

- Keep the length of pages as nearly uniform as possible, but carry headings or single lines that fall at the end of a page over to the next page.

- Indent extracts 1/2 to 1 inch, or the same as the amount of paragraph indention, from the left or from both the left and right margins.

- Prepare bottom-of-page footnotes double-spaced on a separate page, or put the notes in separate notes sections either at the ends of chapters or all at the end of the manuscript (endnotes) after the appendix.

- Prepare bibliographies and reference lists double-spaced in separate sections at the end of the manuscript just before the index.

- Indicate text cross-references to other parts of the manuscript as "see page 000," and after the document has been typeset, fill in the appropriate number while checking the page proofs.

- Write and circle special instructions to the typesetter or printer in the margins. But write instructions for camera-ready copy (to be photographed directly) on removable, self-sticking notes.

- Check the manuscript carefully for errors and inconsistencies before submitting it. (See Chapters 10–16 and the editing checklist later in this chapter.)

- Follow the guidelines in Chapter 13 for marking page proofs while proofreading.

- Make as many photocopies (or additional printouts) of the manuscript as required, but send the original, with your instructions, to the typesetter.

## HOW TO ORGANIZE THE SIXTEEN PRINCIPAL PARTS OF A BUSINESS REPORT

Although most informal reports are prepared as letters or memos, secretaries need to be familiar with long, formal reports. If you are required to prepare a more complex document, you will be expected either to follow the pattern of previous reports in your company or to follow the traditional organizational pattern of a formal report. A formal report may be single- or double-spaced, depending on the length. In either case, most long, formal reports will have some or all of the sixteen principal parts as listed here in their traditional order.

1. *Cover.* A separate cover or binder is common for very long, heavy reports, whereas the title page often doubles as the cover for a shorter report.

2. *Flyleaf.* The *flyleaf* is a blank page placed between the cover and the title page.

3. *Title page.* The title page, usually prepared with each line centered, may include the report title, to whom submitted, by whom submitted, and date submitted (see illustration on page 156).

4. *Letter of transmittal.* The letter of transmittal, prepared like other letters (see Chapter 4), briefly states the purpose, scope, and sources consulted and may include acknowledgments of help, authorizations or requests, and other comments.

5. *Table of contents.* The contents page lists all major headings and subheadings in the report (see illustration on page 157).

6. *List of illustrations and tables.* This list is formatted like the table of contents (see illustration), with figure captions and table titles combined in a single list or placed in separate lists.

7. *Abstract.* This condensed summary of the report, stating research results and conclusions, may be prepared in any appropriate format, such as a few paragraphs, a numbered list, or even hundreds of pages of commentary.

## TITLE PAGE

---

HOW TO PREPARE BUSINESS PLANS

Submitted to
Carol E. McNeil, General Manager
Peterson Manufacturing, Inc.
2160 Shoales Street
St. Louis, MO 63102

Submitted by
Martin A. Tipton
Director, Budget Office
Financial Consultants, Inc.
100 Roselle Drive
St. Louis, MO 63104
Phone: 314-555-6767
Fax: 314-555-6768

September 14, 1995

---

**TABLE OF CONTENTS**

---

Contents

Abstract........................................ vi

Introduction.....................................  1

I.   Preparing Business Plans....................  3

     Purpose.....................................  4
     Procedures..................................  5


II.  Management Plan.............................  6

     Duties and Responsibilities.................  7
     Policies and Practices......................  9
     Operational Summaries....................... 10


III. Financial Plan............................. 13

     Operating Conditions....................... 15
     Profit and Loss Projections................ 17
     Cash Flow Projections...................... 20


Conclusions and Recommendations.................. 22

Appendix:  Sample Forms.......................... 26

Notes............................................ 40

8. *Introduction.* The body of the report begins with one or more introductory paragraphs that tell the reader what the report will include and discuss.

9. *Background information.* Usually, a report must give the reader some historical data or other explanatory background information about the topic of the report.

10. *Data analysis.* The evaluation of the data collected for the report constitutes the main portion of the text discussion.

11. *Conclusions and recommendations.* This final section of the body, which may be detailed but is often brief, draws a conclusion from the foregoing evaluation and, if pertinent, makes appropriate recommendations.

12. *Appendix.* Supplementary supporting material (tables, charts, and other related information) collected in this final section is formatted the same as the preceding text.

13. *Notes.* If bottom-of-page footnotes or end-of-chapter notes sections are not desired, the notes may all be placed in a single concluding endnotes section.

14. *Glossary.* If a number of technical terms are used, they may be listed alphabetically and defined in dictionary style in a glossary near the end of the document.

15. *Bibliography.* A bibliography or reference list is an alphabetical list of references consulted or recommended (see the description of these lists later in this chapter).

16. *Index.* A very long report may have an index similar to the index in this book, prepared by using computer indexing software or by listing key terms and page numbers on index cards that can be alphabetized before entering items in the computer.

## HOW TO ORGANIZE THE EIGHT PRINCIPAL PARTS OF A BUSINESS PROPOSAL

Proposals in general vary greatly. Sometimes the funding organization provides very precise requirements for preparing the proposal and may, additionally, supply printed forms that must be filled in. Most business proposals, however, are prepared for associates or clients. In such cases, no firm rules exist, and the preparers try to develop an appropriate format, writing style, and organizational plan to present the proposed idea or project. The length of the proposal and the degree of formality desired will determine how long the proposal is and the type of organization of data that are needed. Here are eight principal parts that are appropriate for a semiformal or formal proposal.

1. *Introduction.* The introduction describes the proposing organization or person, including accomplishments and expertise, and lists previous funding sources and amounts.

2. *Problem.* This section describes in detail the problem that will be discussed and states how the proposing organization or person is qualified to address the problem.

3. *Objectives.* The objectives refer to the project goals, including the project's relation to other programs dealing with the same problem and how the proposed project will contribute to a long-range solution.

4. *Procedure.* This section explains how the proposed plan will be handled—steps involved, time required, techniques to be used, staff requirements, and so on.

5. *Evaluation.* The evaluation is an explanation of methods you will use to determine later if the proposed program has been successful.

6. *Personnel.* The proposal must list the job descriptions of the people who are involved, including board, committee, and other leadership positions.

7. *Budget.* All proposals must list anticipated expenses, including everything from rent to postage, and anticipated income, such as grants and contributions.

8. *Addenda.* Supporting material, such as staff biographies and press clippings of previous work, is usually collected at the end of the proposal.

## WHERE TO PLACE THE SEVEN PRINCIPAL PARTS OF A TABLE

Business documents frequently have supporting material, such as lists and tables. It is often left up to the secretary to format such

material properly. Sometimes an organization has a preferred format, and the specifications for it are stored in the computer. If you
don't have a style sheet or a file copy of previous tabular material to
follow, the guidelines given here will help you position the seven
principal parts of a table correctly.

1. *Table number.* Place the number on the line above the title or on
the same line, centered or flush left (see illustration on page 161), and number the tables consecutively throughout the document (e.g., Table 1, Table
2) or within each chapter (e.g., Table 1.1, Table 1.2, Table 2.1, Table 2.2).

2. *Table title.* Place the title on the line below the number or on
the same line (see illustration) and the subtitle, if any, following the
title after a colon or in parentheses on a separate line below the title;
capitalize each main word.

3. *Column heads.* Place heads above the columns, centered or
aligned at the left (see illustration), and capitalize main words. (*Note*:
The first column heading is singular; others may be singular or plural.)

4. *Stub.* The first (left-hand) column is a vertical list of items,
with subitems usually indented at least two spaces and the word
*Total* indented at least two more spaces than the preceding item;
capitalize only the first word in stub items.

5. *Body.* In the body, consisting of text or statistics (see illustration), figures are aligned at the decimal and dollar signs at the left.
(*Note*: When a column has the same types of figures, place a symbol
such as % only after the top figure.)

6. *Source note.* Place the source note (if any), which identifies
the source of data and gives proper copyright credit, immediately
after the table body (see illustration).

7. *Footnotes.* Place footnotes after the source note, with any
general note first (see illustration). (*Note:* Use a general note for
comments about the title or the overall table to avoid using a number, letter, or symbol with the table title.)

## COMMON STYLES FOR BASIC REFERENCE FORMS

Documents such as reports and proposals may require end-of-page
footnotes (or a separate notes section), bibliographies, or name-date

**TABLE FORMAT**

Table 6.1

Secretarial Enrollment in Four Courses,
ABC Secretarial School, 1992–1995

| Class | Enrollment (% of Total Class) | | | |
|---|---|---|---|---|
| | 1992 | 1993 | 1994 | 1995 |
| Word processing | 98% | 97% | 99% | 98% |
| Telecommunications | 64 | 72 | 69 | 78 |
| Accounting | 11[a] | 29 | 35 | 54 |
| Communications[b] | 76 | 81 | 87 | 92 |

*Source:* ABC Secretarial School, *Executive Bulletin 1* (December 1995): 9.

*Note:* The four courses selected for comparison are required courses at the ABC Secretarial School in Madison, Wisconsin.

a. Only 11 percent of the class enrolled in accounting in 1992 because previously this course was not available, and it was offered only after many enrollees had already prepared their programs.

b. The obvious increase in communications enrollment between 1992 and 1995 reflects the ongoing importance of communications in the secretarial profession.

reference lists. Although a standard format exists for each type of reference, the capitalization and punctuation style and the arrangement of data within entries may vary. Whatever style your organization prefers, apply it consistently to all entries. The following entries are examples of common note, bibliography, and reference-list styles. For more examples, consult a general style guide, such as *The Chicago Manual of Style*, or a business style guide, such as *The Prentice Hall Style Manual*.

*Note (Footnote) Style*

Notes are numbered or lettered consecutively. Symbols, such as asterisks and daggers, may be used when there are only a few notes. A corresponding number, letter, or symbol, as used in the note, must then be placed at the appropriate place in the text, typed as a superscript. Credit lines used with illustrations or to acknowledge a general contribution are usually prepared apart from the specific individual text notes. Those credit lines for illustrations are placed below the photographs or other figures: *Courtesy T. M. Hays.* Those acknowledging a general text contribution may appear at the bottom of the first page of the text that is involved: *Acknowledgment is made to T. M. Hays for the data on computers.*

1. Barry Ellis, The U.S. Postal Service, 6th ed. (New York: RST Press, 1995), 132.

2. Holly C. Brooks, Guide to Mailers, 3 vols. (Dayton: Beale-McKay, 1991), 3:17.

3. Jeffrey A. Samuelson, "Electronic Mail," in Computers Today, ed. Barbara Webster (San Francisco: College Press, 1992), 101–12.

4. M. J. Templeton, "Mailing Tips," Mail Standards, 18 February 1995, 63–64.

5. Daniel Sloane and Kim Brewer, "What Not to Do," Mail Journal 13 (June 1995): 10–11.

6. Daniel Sloane and Kim Brewer, "Mail Backlogs," Birmingham Post, 28 April 1993.

7. Anna Macready, "History of the Postal System" (M.A. thesis, University of Hawaii, 1990), 200–202.

8. Darlene Jefferson, Foreword to "Mail Processing at True," mimeographed (Dallas: True Industries, 1989), iv.

9. U.S. Congress, Senate, Committee on Ways and Means, <u>Hearings on Postal Regulations</u>, 100th Cong., 2d sess., 1982. Committee Print 29.

10. Aaron Schlemmer, Jr., proposals for Postal Annex, MS. 32, B. C. Sims Collection, Historical Library, Little Rock, Arkansas, n.d.

11. Ibid., 2.

12. Templeton, "Mailing Tips," 63; Sloane and Brewer, "What Not to Do," 12; idem, "Mail Backlogs."

*Bibliography Style*

Bibliographies are arranged alphabetically by author rather than consecutively like notes. If a bibliography does not contain all sources cited in the footnotes, it may be called *Select(ed) Bibliography*. Other common titles are *Works Cited* and *Works Consulted*.

Brooks, Holly C. <u>Guide to Mailers</u>. 3 vols. Dayton: Beale-McKay, 1991.

Ellis, Barry. <u>The U.S. Postal Service</u>, 6th ed. New York: RST Press, 1995.

Jefferson, Darlene. Foreword. "Mail Processing at True." Mimeographed. Dallas: True Industries, 1989.

Macready, Anna. "History of the Postal System." M.A. thesis, University of Hawaii, 1990.

Samuelson, Jeffrey A. "Electronic Mail." In <u>Computers Today</u>, edited by Barbara Webster, 101–21. San Francisco: College Press, 1992.

Schlemmer, Aaron, Jr. Proposals for Postal Annex. MS. 32, B. C. Sims Collection, Historical Library, Little Rock, Arkansas, n.d.

Sloane, Daniel, and Kim Brewer. "Mail Backlogs." <u>Birmingham Post</u>, 28 April 1993.

_____. "What Not to Do." <u>Mail Journal</u> 13 (June 1995): 10–21.

Templeton, M. J. "Mailing Tips." Mail Standards, 18 February 1995, 63–71.

U.S. Congress, Senate, Committee on Ways and Means. Hearings on Postal Regulations. 100th Cong., 2d sess., 1982. Committee Print 29.

*Reference-List Style*

Reference lists, like bibliographies, are arranged alphabetically by author, but the date is placed after the author's name. In the text, then, readers are directed to a particular entry by a citation of the name and date: *Brown 1994*. If the list has several *Browns*, the first initial should be included: *J. Brown 1994*. If *J. Brown* has two or more entries, they should be labeled *1994a, 1994b*, and so on.

Brooks, Holly C. 1991. Guide to Mailers. 3 vols. Dayton: Beale-McKay.

Ellis, Barry. 1995. The U.S. Postal Service, 6th ed. New York: RST Press.

Jefferson, Darlene. 1989. Foreword. "Mail Processing at True." Mimeographed. Dallas: True Industries.

Macready, Anna. 1990. "History of the Postal System." M.A. thesis, University of Hawaii.

Samuelson, Jeffrey A. 1992. "Electronic Mail." In Computer Today, edited by Barbara Webster, 101–21. San Francisco: College Press.

Schlemmer, Aaron, Jr. n.d. Proposals for Postal Annex. MS. 32, B. C. Sims Collection, Historical Library, Little Rock, Arkansas.

Sloane, Daniel, and Kim Brewer. 1993. "Mail Backlogs." Birmingham Post, 28 April.

_____. 1995. "What Not to Do." Mail Journal 13 (June): 10–22.

Templeton, M. J. 1995. "Mailing Tips." Mail Standards, 18 February, 63–74.

U.S. Congress, Senate, Committee on Ways and Means. 1982. Hearings on Postal Regulations. 100th Cong., 2d sess. Committee Print 29.

## An Easy Way to Review Your Work Using an Editing Checklist

Complex documents cannot simply be scanned quickly, like a brief memo or note. When you check a larger manuscript for errors, omissions, and inconsistencies, you need to scrutinize many points of formatting, style, grammar, and word choice. Often, because there are so many things to watch for, it is necessary to make several passes through the manuscript. Even then, it is easy to forget something. The following checklist is designed to help you check your drafts for completeness and correctness. If your document has additional aspects that should be checked, use the "Other" item at the conclusion to devise a checklist tailored especially to the type of work you do. (All of the items in the checklist are discussed in this book. Refer to the Table of Contents or the Index for individual topics.)

( ) The format is appropriate for the document.

( ) The format is consistent throughout the document.

( ) The title page, copyright page, contents page, preface, and other front-matter pages are complete.

( ) The front-matter pages are in the proper order.

( ) Each front-matter page is set up correctly.

( ) The opening text is appropriate for the document.

( ) The opening is well written and effectively leads the reader into the body of the document.

( ) The text sections or subdivisions are logical and represent a clear topical break or change.

( ) The sections or subdivisions are in the proper order to advance the subject.

( ) The heads and subheads are appropriate for the text that follows.

( ) The heads and subheads are well written and styled consistently throughout the document.

( ) The paragraphs are properly developed and are not overly long or short.

( ) The paragraphs have smooth and effective transitions from one to another.

( ) The sentences are well written and effective, with lead sentences opening each paragraph.

( ) Complicated points or long discussions have been simplified as lists or other easy-to-follow material.

( ) The conclusion is appropriate for the document.

( ) The conclusion is well written, is appropriately concise, and brings the reader to the desired conclusion.

( ) The appendixes, glossary, reference material, index, and other back-matter pages are complete.

( ) The back-matter pages are in the proper order.

( ) Each back-matter page is set up correctly.

( ) The illustrations (tables and figures) are appropriate and essential to the associated discussion, not merely cosmetic.

( ) The illustrations are set up properly and consistently.

( ) The illustrations are accurate, with statistical and other data verified.

( ) The illustrations are properly numbered and positioned appropriately in the manuscript.

( ) The footnotes (or notes section), bibliography, and reference lists are complete.

( ) The footnote (or notes), bibliography, and reference-list entries are in correct numerical or alphabetical order.

( ) The footnotes (or notes section), bibliography, and reference list are positioned properly in the manuscript.

( ) The footnote (or notes), bibliography, and reference-list entries are styled properly and consistently throughout.

( ) Punctuation is used correctly in the document.

( ) Punctuation is used consistently in the document.

( ) Terms, headings, and other material are capitalized correctly.

( ) The capitalization style is applied consistently throughout the document.

( ) The document has been spell-checked by computer and proofread manually for spelling errors and other problems.

( ) Words, terms, prefixes, and suffixes are spelled, punctuated, accented, capitalized, and generally treated consistently throughout the document.

( ) The correct grammar is used throughout the document.

( ) The choice of words is appropriate and effective for the discussion.

( ) The active voice is used whenever possible and appropriate.

( ) Nonessential information, irrelevancies, and wordiness have been deleted.

( ) Clichés have been deleted.

( ) Clear, specific words and terms have been substituted for vague, general expressions.

( ) Simple words and expressions have been substituted for complex, pretentious language.

( ) Jargon has been deleted or changed except as required for a technical discussion.

( ) Gobbledygook (incomprehensible jargon and other expressions) has been rewritten in clear, simple English.

( ) Euphemisms have been deleted or changed as appropriate.

( ) Clear, specific language has been substituted for trite expressions.

( ) Discriminatory language has been rephrased to avoid racial, sexual, age, and disability bias.

( ) Other _____

# COMMON BUSINESS APPLICATIONS FOR DESKTOP PUBLISHING (DTP)

Desktop publishing is a sophisticated form of word processing. The technology enables users to view pages on their computer screens as they will look when printed. But more than this is possible: with DTP you can generate different typefaces, set up multiple columns, and combine text and illustrations. Companies that have their own DTP equipment can produce a variety of material that otherwise would have to be typeset and printed by an outside establishment. Here are the most common business uses for DTP.

- Magazines
- In-house newsletters and bulletins
- Customer newsletters and bulletins
- Business forms, such as purchase orders, invoices, and job applications
- Equipment and software manuals and other instruction materials
- Training manuals
- Company brochures, ads, and annual reports
- Product brochures and ads
- Product price lists
- Sales kits
- Meeting programs and conference-registration kits
- Business reports and proposals
- Transparencies and slides

## THIRTEEN WAYS TO IMPROVE YOUR DTP DOCUMENTS

Secretaries who work for companies that use DTP need to have a strong working knowledge of design and of visual as well as verbal communication. Since DTP covers everything from a simple bulletin to a sophisticated glossy magazine, the particular techniques you use will depend on the complexity of the project you handle. In all cases, using DTP requires that you think about not only what a document says but how the information is presented. Here are thirteen ways to improve your DTP documents.

1. Use a clean, simple design, with generous white space in your layout to avoid a cluttered, crowded presentation.

2. Avoid hard-to-read lines of more than 60 to 65 characters or fewer than 20 to 25 characters.

3. Choose a basic, readable type style rather than a complete, ornate style, and avoid mixing numerous styles in the same document.

4. Choose a standard type size between 10 and 12 points (1 point = 1/72 inch) for the basic text.

5. Do not justify the right margin (all lines end at the same place) if it creates rivers of white space through the middle of the document.

6. Since DTP uses proportional type, leave only one character space rather than two after periods, colons, and other punctuation marks.

7. Use the solid, or closed, character (—) for a dash rather than two hyphens (--).

8. Avoid underlining and solid capitals for emphasis, instead making use of bold, italic, and different-size type.

9. Use bullets or other symbols with unnumbered lists to separate the entries more clearly.

10. Use photos, graphs, and charts only when they are essential to clarify or illuminate the text discussion.

11. Use clip art (standard drawings) or other decorative art sparingly to avoid a design that is cluttered, inconsistent, and unrelated to the text discussion.

12. Use horizontal and vertical rules in moderation to avoid a distracting blur of lines.

13. Use color, which is more expensive and time consuming, discriminately.

## SIMPLE PROCEDURES THAT WILL PROMOTE BETTER SCANNING RESULTS

Scanners, which convert typed or printed material into digital form that computers can use, are most common in offices that handle information-intensive projects. Already-prepared text and photographs can be placed on a scanner's surface and electronically inserted into a new document. Although most scanning software has less than 100 percent accuracy, the time saved in using it can be substantial, even with the required proofreading and correction of scanning errors. If you're having trouble scanning some material, however, review this list of procedures that will promote better scanning results.

- Clean up pages before inserting them in the scanner to avoid having marks, dust, and other blemishes accidentally be read as letters, numbers, or punctuation marks.

- Photocopy pages with folds or creases that sensitive equipment might misread as art or text.

- Photocopy faded originals to make them darker for more accurate scanning.

- Avoid writing on pages to be scanned since the scanner will read handwriting and creases along with the other material. (*Note:* Nonreproducible blue pencil may be invisible to your scanning equipment, but test it first.)

- Test-scan material to find the best resolution and other settings. (*Note:* Low-resolution and brighter settings pick up fewer stray marks and smudges; high-resolution settings may be better for highly detailed material.)

- Group similar-quality material together so that you can use the same settings without repeated changes.

- If you find that multiple-column pages are scanning as a single column, separate the columns and scan each column individually.

- Monitor sheet feeders that are used for large jobs to be certain the pages aren't sticking together, causing only the top sheet to be read.

- Be prepared to find and correct some misreads and nonsense characters even after taking all possible precautions.

# EFFECTIVE METHODS FOR HANDLING TRANSCRIPTION DUTIES MORE EFFICIENTLY

If you work for an executive who dictates correspondence and other documents by machine, transcribing by machine will be one of your regular duties. If an executive does not enunciate clearly or tends to forget to provide all the information you need, transcription can be a chore. But not all aspects of transcription need to be difficult. Experienced secretaries have learned that following a certain routine will eliminate many of the difficulties and will help them handle their transcription duties more efficiently.

- If you have a new system, read the instruction manual and become thoroughly familiar with the unit before you start typing.

- Clear your desk of unrelated material, and assemble the things you will need for transcription: stationery, envelopes, address lists, dictionary, files, and so on.

- Enter your name, identification number, and other information required in your office.

- Listen carefully to the dictation *before* starting to type, and review the instructions which may be at the beginning or end of a document.

- Make a note of missing information, and inquire about anything you need before you begin. (*Note:* If you can't locate the person who did the dictating, attach a self-sticking note to the printout for later clarification.)

- Transcribe the documents in order of importance or the order that the dictator has specified.

- Treat telephone-generated dictation the same as office-generated dictation.

- Follow standard procedures for editing documents on screen and using a spell-checker, but also proofread the printout manually.

- Submit transcribed documents for signing according to practices in your office.

- Label and store transcribed tapes or disks according to practices in your office.

## USEFUL HINTS FOR SELECTING THE RIGHT PAPER FOR BUSINESS DOCUMENTS

Secretaries are often responsible for ordering printer, copier, fax, and other paper for various uses in the office. You may have specific instructions about what to use for different types of documents (correspondence, reports, presentations, and so on), or you may be expected to use your best judgment. Printers have a variety of samples that you can examine and are happy to make recommendations about appropriateness, quality, cost, and other matters. Paper manufacturers can also advise you about the selections they offer. Here are common types of paper and typical applications.

- *Quality bond and cotton-content paper*. Correspondence, reports and proposals, contracts, deeds, bulletins, newsletters, meeting agendas and programs, and announcements

- *Cover stock*. Report and proposal covers, announcement cards, presentation materials, posters, business cards, and dividers for catalogs and manuals

- *Water- and stain-resistant paper and cover stock*. Charts, graphs, service manuals, price lists, and contracts and other legal documents

- *Perforated-forms paper*. Checks, invoices and statements, and requisitions and purchase orders

- *Parchment paper*. Certificates, awards, brochures, top-executive letterhead, and important reports or proposals

- *Label stock* (gummed and self-adhesive). Mailing labels, identification tags, price tags, and routing labels

- *Transparencies*. Text and graphs, charts, and other illustrations

- *Safety papers and check stock*. Documents read by optical scanners, stock certificates, and checks

## NINE THINGS YOU CAN DO TO PROTECT DISKETTES

Floppy disks (diskettes) are common temporary storage media for computer documents. Because they are so familiar and so common, however, they may be treated more casually than they should be. If a diskette copy is the only copy of a document, it is crucial that it be handled with the utmost care to keep the information intact. Whether you are using 3 1/2- or 5 1/4-inch diskettes, here are nine things you can do to prevent scrambled data or the complete loss of data.

1. Use and store diskettes only in a clean environment away from food, beverages, and cigarette smoke that could destroy many hours of work if they come in contact with a diskette.

2. Keep magnets, which can erase or scramble data, away from diskettes.

3. Never bend the flexible 5 1/4-inch diskettes since any crease may affect your disk drive's ability to read the surface.

4. Remove diskettes from the drive when they are not being used since a power surge or "spike," merely from turning the computer off and on, could scramble or destroy the information.

5. Store diskettes horizontally (no more than ten deep) or vertically but never at a slant, which could cause bending and the loss of information.

6. Never use paper clips or rubber bands to hold diskettes together since clips could act like a magnet and bands could bend the diskettes.

7. Insert and remove diskettes slowly and carefully to prevent misalignment or other damage that could affect the information.

8. Avoid touching the magnetic surface of a diskette since oil, dirt, or other contaminants could be transferred to the surface and destroy stored information.

9. Write your label before applying it to the diskette, and use a soft felt pen to add information to labels after you have applied them.

## CRUCIAL COMPUTER-SECURITY GUIDELINES FOR THE OFFICE

Secretaries and other employees need to be very familiar with their companies' policies concerning computer security. The three principal threats to both hardware and software are loss, damage, and unauthorized access to data. Regardless of whether a company has a sophisticated security system, each person who uses the hardware and software must assume responsibility for taking basic precautions. The following points are commonsense, but crucial, computer-security guidelines.

- Use containers for software and covers for hardware when they are not in use to prevent damage from dust, sprays, and other contaminants.

- Keep foods and beverages away from hardware and software.

- Never leave diskettes or tapes on your desk or in other obvious locations when you are unable to watch and protect them.

- Never write down log-on sequences, passwords, or other security codes that someone could read or remove.

- Strictly observe company instructions and requirements concerning the use and protection of passwords and other security measures.

- Log off your system, particularly if it is part of a local area network, before you leave the workstation even briefly, so that it will not be open to intruders.

- Use company- or office-authorization policies, furniture arrangements, and any other means to limit access to your workstation and diskette-storage area.

- Report security breaches (e.g., unauthorized access or use of passwords) immediately.

- Keep software and hardware out of locations with high or low temperatures and humidity as well as away from direct sunlight.

- When equipment must be moved, use the appropriate command to move the read/write heads to a position where they will not destroy data.

- Use adequate surge protectors to prevent power-surge damage, and unplug the equipment during severe power fluctuations and storms.

- Use disk-drive cleaners to remove dust, smoke, and other contaminants from the drives.

- Avoid needless trading of diskettes or use of outside diskettes that could be contaminated with a virus.

- Install an antiviral program and update it as new, more complete issues are available.

- Use only properly formatted diskettes in good condition that your system can accept.

- Back up files frequently to save data that might be lost on the hard disk.

- Check cables and electrical connections periodically. Correct loose or faulty connections and move cables that someone might trip over, causing personal injury as well as pulling over the equipment.

- Use properly grounded equipment.

- Replace the battery when an on-screen message alerts you that it is time.

- Consider purchasing a maintenance agreement for regular servicing if your equipment is used heavily.

- Start a user network directory for troubleshooting, and keep an 800 number/hotline file for emergencies.

## HOW TO USE ERGONOMICS TO PREVENT INJURIES IN THE OFFICE

Ergonomics is the science that considers human performance and well-being in relation to jobs, equipment, and the work environment. A source of major concern today is the computer workstation and the stresses and injuries that employees have experienced in it, from headaches and backaches to carpal tunnel syndrome (serious wrist and hand injury) and elbow tendinitis. In addition to taking very short breaks (even as brief as 10 seconds) frequently and doing relaxation and stretching exercises at your desk, you can take steps to adjust your workstation furniture and equipment to provide relief from repetitive-strain injuries, eyestrain, and other problems.

- Use a swivel chair that you can adjust (both seat and back) to a variety of seated postures.

- Add a lower-back pad to the chair for additional support if necessary.

- Tilt and adjust the keyboard so that it is at elbow height directly in front of you and tilted to match your forearm angle.

- Sit straight, and keep your feet flat on the floor (or use a foot rest), pointed toward the monitor, with your knees bent from 80 to 150 degrees, depending on comfort, and thighs parallel to the floor.

- Use an adjustable-height table, and position the chair and the work surface so that you need not lean forward or twist your upper body to reach supplies and equipment.

- Position the monitor so that your eyes are horizontal with the top of the screen, 13 to 24 inches away.

- Use a large enough screen so that characters will be readable without straining.

- Position the monitor to avoid window or artificial lighting glare, and adjust the brightness of the monitor or use an antiglare shield if illumination or glare is still creating a problem.

- Keep your elbows close to your sides and bent at a 90-degree angle.

- Use arm and wrist rests with your keyboard for pauses, but keep your hands suspended while typing the keys and touch lightly by keeping your wrists and fingers relaxed.

- Use a copy stand attached to your monitor or positioned the same height as the screen.

- Use printer enclosures to reduce the noise level during printouts.

- Use a telephone headset to help keep your head upright and your body straight.

# — 7 —
# INFORMATION PROCESSING
# AND ACCOUNTING

## THE THREE CRUCIAL COMPONENTS OF THE ACCOUNTING PROCESS

Information processing systems are designed to help people collect data needed to make decisions and to prepare important financial statements. Businesses of all sizes follow the same basic accounting process to collect and record the data. This process makes use of accounting journals and ledgers, maintained either manually or electronically. Here are the three crucial components of the accounting process and the function of each component.

1. *General and special journals.* These accounting records are used to record data obtained by analyzing individual transactions, such as the payment of rent or income from the sale of a copier.

2. *General ledger.* This accounting record contains a summary of the data recorded in the general and special journals, with each account (e.g., *office expenses, income from product sales*) summarized by itself on one or more pages.

3. *Subsidiary ledger.* This accounting record provides a detailed analysis of the balance that appears in a general ledger account, such as the *inventories* or *notes payable* account.

# BASIC RULES FOR USING DEBIT AND CREDIT ENTRIES IN BOOKKEEPING

Accounts have two columns—a debit (left) and a credit (right) column. In double-entry bookkeeping, amounts are entered in both columns for each transaction, and the total of all debit balances must therefore equal the total of all credit balances. When an amount is recorded in the debit column, it increases certain accounts and decreases others. The same principle applies when an amount is recorded in the credit column. Here are the two possibilities—an increase or a decrease in the account—for five general types of account. Notice in the first table that a credit entry in an asset account *decreases* the account, and in the second table that a debit entry in an asset account *increases* the account. (For detailed information on bookkeeping procedures, consult a modern secretarial or accounting handbook.)

*Transactions That Decrease Accounts*

| Type of Account | Type of Entry |
| --- | --- |
| Asset | Credit |
| Liability | Debit |
| Capital | Debit |
| Income | Debit |
| Expense | Credit |

*Transactions That Increase Accounts*

| Type of Account | Type of Entry |
| --- | --- |
| Asset | Debit |
| Liability | Credit |
| Capital | Credit |
| Income | Credit |
| Expense | Debit |

## THREE ESSENTIAL FINANCIAL STATEMENTS THAT YOU MAY NEED TO PREPARE

Secretaries may be required to set up three important financial statements, each of which provides a different type of financial information. Company management needs such information to make operating decisions, and organizations require it for other purposes, such as to process a loan request. If you are setting up any one of these three main reports, follow the format required by your employer. If the specifications are not stored in your computer, you can probably find copies of previous reports in the files. Each of the three types is also illustrated in this section.

1. *Balance sheet*. This statement reports a company's assets, liabilities, and owner's equity at any given time. (*Note*: The illustration here has a stacked format, but assets also may be listed in a left column and liabilities and owner's equity in a right column.)

2. *Income statement*. This statement, also known as the profit and loss (P & L) statement, reports sales less the cost of goods and services sold and other costs, resulting in a net profit or loss (see illustration).

3. *Statement of cash flows*. This statement, required by standards governing certified public accounts but not commonly used by persons in a company, provides sources and uses of cash for the same period covered by the income statement (see illustration).

## THE FIVE MAJOR COMPONENTS OF A SPREADSHEET

A *spreadsheet* is a worksheet that looks like an accounting ledger sheet. Arranged in a grid with columns and rows, the spreadsheet provides a place for amounts to be entered and calculations performed on them. Because spreadsheets have so many uses, they are commonplace in many offices, and secretaries working for executives who use them should become familiar with spreadsheet software. Here are the five major components of a spreadsheet.

# BALANCE SHEET

ABC Company, Inc.
Balance Sheet
December 31, 1995

### ASSETS

Current assets
| | | |
|---|---|---|
| Cash | | $ 20,000 |
| Marketable securities | | 18,000 |
| Accounts receivable, net | | 64,000 |
| Inventories | | 132,000 |
| Prepaid insurance | | 7,000 |
| Total current assets | | 241,000 |

Fixed assets
| | | |
|---|---|---|
| Land | $ 167,000 | |
| Buildings | 800,000 | |
| Furniture and fixtures | 64,000 | |
| Equipment | 201,000 | |
| | 1,232,000 | |
| Less accumulated deprec. | 696,000 | |
| Total fixed assets | | 536,000 |

Other assets
| | | |
|---|---|---|
| Long-term investments | 58,000 | |
| Long-term receivables | 12,000 | |
| Goodwill, net | 61,000 | |
| Other assets | 9,000 | |
| Total other assets | | 140,000 |

| | | |
|---|---|---|
| TOTAL ASSETS | | $917,000 |

### LIABILITIES & OWNER'S EQUITY

Current liabilities
| | | |
|---|---|---|
| Accounts payable | | $ 72,000 |
| Bank loan payable | | 100,000 |
| Accrued wages and salaries payable | | 10,000 |
| Current portion of mortgage payable | | 7,000 |
| Taxes payable | | 12,000 |
| Total current liabilities | | 201,000 |

Long-term liabilities
| | | |
|---|---|---|
| Mortgage payable | $300,000 | |
| Bonds payable | 107,000 | |
| Total long-term liabilities | | 407,000 |

| | | |
|---|---|---|
| Total liabilities | | 608,000 |

Owner's equity
| | | |
|---|---|---|
| Common stock | 200,000 | |
| Retained earnings | 109,000 | |
| Total owner's equity | | 309,000 |

| | | |
|---|---|---|
| TOTAL EQUITIES | | $917,000 |

# INCOME STATEMENT

National Industries, Inc.
Income Statement
for the Year Ending December 31, 1995

| | | |
|---|---|---|
| Gross sales | | $4,500,000 |
| Less sales returns, allow., and disc. | | 340,000 |
| Net sales | | 4,160,000 |
| Less cost of goods sold | | 2,399,000 |
| | | |
| Gross profit | | 1,761,000 |
| | | |
| Less operating expenses | | |
| Selling, gen., and admin. exp. | | |
| Insurance | $ 21,000 | |
| Office salaries | 490,000 | |
| Selling expense | 220,000 | |
| Heat, light, and power | 29,000 | |
| Advertising | 195,000 | |
| Telephone | 80,000 | |
| Office supplies | 30,000 | |
| Automobile expense | 35,000 | |
| Bad debt expense | 60,000 | |
| Travel expense | 201,000 | |
| Depreciation expense | 40,000 | |
| Miscellaneous expense | 60,000 | |
| Total selling, gen., and admin. expenses | | 1,461,000 |
| | | |
| Research and development costs | | 150,000 |
| Other operating expenses | | 19,000 |
| | | |
| Total operating expenses | | 1,630,000 |
| | | |
| Operating profit | | 131,000 |
| | | |
| Other income and expenses | | |
| Interest expense | 200,000 | |
| Interest income | (173,000) | |
| Miscellaneous income | ( 20,000) | |
| | | |
| Total other income and expenses | | 7,000 |
| | | |
| Profit before taxes | | 124,000 |
| Provision for corporate income taxes | | 45,000 |
| | | |
| Net income | | $ 79,000 |

## STATEMENT OF CASH FLOWS

Evans & Evans, Inc.
Statement of Cash Flows
for the Year Ending December 31, 1995

*Cash balance, January 1, 1995*                              -0-

Cash Flows Generated (Used)
from Operating Activities

| | | |
|---|---:|---:|
| Net income for the period | $149,000 | |
| Depreciation | 26,000 | |
| Decrease in marketable securities | 11,000 | |
| Increase in accounts receivable | (21,000) | |
| Decrease in inventories | 18,000 | |
| Increase in prepaid insurance | ( 4,000) | |
| Decrease in accounts payable | (29,000) | |
| Decrease in accrued salaries payable | ( 3,000) | |
| Decrease in taxes payable | ( 1,900) | |
| Cash flows generated from operating activities | | $ 109,100 |

Cash Flows Generated (Used)
from Financing Activities

| | | |
|---|---:|---:|
| Increase in mortgage payable, net of repayments | $ 80,000 | |
| Decrease in bonds payable | (65,000) | |
| Sale of common stock | (49,000) | |
| Cash flows generated from financing activities | | 64,000 |

Cash Flows Generated (Used)
from Investing Activities

| | | |
|---|---:|---:|
| Purchases of fixed assets | $(67,000) | |
| Purchases of long-term invest. | (52,000) | |
| Cash flows generated from investing activities | | (119,000) |
| Net cash generated (used) for the year ending December 31, 1995 | | $ 54,100 |
| *Cash balance, December 31, 1995* | | $ 54,100 |

1. *Columns and rows.* An individual spreadsheet always has a number of columns and rows arranged in a grid, although the maximum number of columns and rows, or *parameters,* may vary. For example,

|   | A | B | C | D |
|---|---|---|---|---|
|   | **A** | **B** | **C** | **D** |
| 1 | DEPT | OFFICE EXPENSE | SELLING EXPENSE | PRODUCTION EXPENSE |
| 2 |   |   |   |   |
| 3 | SALES | 234 | 1914 | 23 |

2. *Cells and addresses.* A *cell* is the point where a vertical column and a horizontal row intersect. The *cell address* is usually the column *letter* and row *number* (e.g., D3), by which each cell is identified by the computer.

3. *Cell reference.* The *cell reference*, the cell address of the highlighted cursor block (e.g., *C3: 1914*), usually found on the top line of the screen, tells you where you are (cell address) in the spreadsheet. (*Note*: The *active cell* is any cell on which the cursor block is located.)

4. *Labels.* A *label,* the heading that describes the entries made in the columns and rows (e.g., *PRODUCTION EXPENSE*), is similar to a table head (see Chapter 6).

5. *Values.* A value is any amount that is entered in any column or row of the spreadsheet.

## SEVEN COMMANDS YOU CAN USE TO MANIPULATE DATA WITH SPREADSHEET SOFTWARE

Your employer may use spreadsheets for various reasons. Spreadsheet software will help an executive make decisions by working out different "what if" scenarios; for example, if I do this, what will be the result? Or if I do that, what will be the result? Since a spreadsheet is a decision-support tool, and the software is capable of performing all basic mathematical operations on any cell that you specify, it can be used in a variety of tasks, from budgeting to project planning and scheduling to making sales projections. Most spreadsheets have seven basic commands that you can use to manipulate data.

1. *Load.* The *load* command enables you to retrieve a spreadsheet from a disk so that you can begin, view, edit, or reformat it.

2. *Move.* The *move* command enables you to move a group or range of cells.

3. *Copy.* The *copy* command enables you to copy a group or range of cells from one part of the spreadsheet and "paste" or insert them in another part, leaving the original range of cells in place.

4. *Insert.* The *insert* command enables you to insert rows or columns anywhere in the spreadsheet.

5. *Delete.* The *delete* command enables you to delete rows or columns or a block of rows and columns anywhere in the spreadsheet.

6. *Save.* The *save* command enables you to store a spreadsheet in a diskette or hard-disk file.

7. *Print.* The *print* command enables you to print on paper the entire spreadsheet or any portion that you designate.

## THE FOUR MAJOR COMPONENTS OF A DATABASE

A *database* is a collection of information stored manually or electronically. The principal use of the term is in reference to an electronic program that allows you to manipulate the collection of data in a variety of ways. Secretaries frequently must set up, maintain, and use databases, such as an address file, and therefore should understand the basic anatomy of a database. The following list identifies the four major components of a typical database.

1. *Data file.* A *file,* or *data file*, is a collection of records on a particular subject, such as a complete address book.

2. *Record.* A *record* is all of the data used in any entry of a data file, such as someone's name and address.

3. *Field.* A *field* refers to each individual category of information in a particular record, such as the ZIP Code in someone's address.

4. *Field name.* A *field name* is the title or heading used to identify a list of fields, such as the heading "City" or "State" in an address list.

# FIVE WAYS YOU CAN PROCESS INFORMATION WITH DATABASE SOFTWARE

Three types of data can be stored in a database: alphabetic data, numeric data, and alphanumeric data. Most businesses organize data into computer files, with each file consisting of several different fields (see previous section). Each field, in turn, is then identified as an alphabetic field, numeric field, or alphanumeric field. In an address file, the name of the city would be an alphabetic field, the ZIP Code a numeric field, and an account number such as 4907C an alphanumeric field. To manipulate such data, you will rely largely on the following five database software features.

1. *Sort.* The *sort* feature enables you to arrange data in a desired order, such as alphabetically (e.g., selecting a field such as "state" and telling the program to sort all entries by the field *STATE* in alphabetic order).

2. *Select.* The *select* feature, sometimes called "get" or "search," enables you to select a group of records according to some criteria that you specify (e.g., doing a search for all persons who have the ZIP Code *09854*).

3. *Format.* The *format* feature is used to set up the record structure (e.g., How may fields will a record have? How wide will a field, or column, be?).

4. *Input.* The *input* feature is used to enter the data in the fields that you formatted. (*Note*: The program will also have some editing commands you can use to correct data that you have entered in case of error.)

5. *Proofreading.* Applications programs usually have a proofreading feature used to check material on screen before saving it, printing it, or exiting the program.

# THE FOUR PRINCIPAL TYPES OF STORAGE MEDIA USED IN AN OFFICE

After you have finished working on a document, it has to be saved somewhere. Ensuring that data are stored on the proper medium and retained for the required period is a principal duty for most secretaries. Often the medium used depends on the type of record—active or inactive—and available space, as well as any retention policies that affect the type of storage used. Here are the four principal types of storage media used in an office.

1. *Paper media.* Paper copies are the principal storage medium in many offices, with files kept in conventional cabinets, on shelves, in trays, and in other various containers.

2. *Magnetic media.* Computer diskettes, hard disks, and tapes are also important storage media in many offices, and hard-disk files may be backed up on removable diskettes or tapes, which then are usually placed in small containers for permanent storage.

3. *Microimage media.* Microforms (microfilm rolls and flat forms), which store data in greatly reduced form, are used when massive amounts of data are placed into long-term storage.

4. *Optical-memory media.* Optical media (e.g., CD-ROM) are used to store vast quantities of computerized data as well as paper or other records that can be scanned into an optical-memory system, with data stored on disks, tapes, or cards.

# USEFUL TIPS FOR FILING INFORMATION ELECTRONICALLY

The data that you process must be stored, as described in the previous section. To store documents with your computer, you must use the *SAVE* command to file it on a hard disk or on a diskette or tape. But other factors must be considered, such as whether it is destined for active or inactive storage, how much room you have on your hard disk, whether an appropriate directory already exists for it, and so on. The following tips may make your electronic filing a little easier.

- Select a file name when you begin creating a document, even if you may rename it later, so that you can exit the program quickly. (*Note*: With some programs, a file must be named before you can save it.)

- Use directories to increase your file-naming capacity, since you can use the same file name for numerous documents as long as each one appears in a different directory.

- Use generic file names, such as *SCHEDULE.DOC*, for easy recognition if you plan to use the same name in more than one directory.

- Use numerous subdirectories, and keep each one small so that it will be easier to handle in the same way that an uncrowded file folder is easier to use.

- Use the *RENAME* command either to change the name in the original subdirectory or to move a file to another subdirectory by also renaming the subdirectory.

- Use file extensions to designate storage, if they are not needed for other purposes (e.g., *.CUR* or *.ACT* might mean a current or active hard-disk file).

- Use file extensions to designate file categories, such as *.RPT* (report) and *.LTR* (letter), and revise the extension when appropriate (e.g., to designate inactive storage).

- To make more room on your hard disk, regularly transfer inactive files into storage on removable diskettes or tape.

- To save hard-disk space, use archiving programs that reduce files with the same extension (e.g., *.LTR*) to a smaller size so that you can store a group of reduced files as one large file (e.g., *LETTERS.ARC*).

- Establish a regular schedule and procedure for purging outdated files from a hard disk.

- When you create a document, if possible provide a date when the file will no longer be needed or need no longer be active.

- If you principally use disk storage, don't try to save setup time by typing a brief memo on a typewriter since it will then have to be stored apart from the other correspondence on disk.

- Use antiviral programs and dust- and contaminant-free locations to protect your storage media.

- Use an appropriate security system to protect your storage media from theft and unauthorized access.

## USEFUL TIPS FOR FILING INFORMATION MANUALLY

In many offices, electronic storage has not replaced the paper files, and paper storage, in fact, continues to increase every year. Secretaries who must deal with massive amounts of paper are always searching for ways to make conventional data storage easier and more manageable. Here are some tips that filing experts recommend to help you cope with expanding paper files.

- Use an appropriate alphabetic or numeric filing system for the type and amount of information you handle.

- Contact the Association of Records Managers and Administrators (ARMA), 4200 Somerset, Prairie Village, Kansas 66208, for up-to-date information on different systems if you are planning a change.

- Contact office-supply stores and software vendors for information on the latest systems, equipment, and computer aids used in paper filing.

- Conduct a records and equipment inventory periodically to use in evaluating the proper use and the efficiency of your system and to determine any needed improvements.

- Use modern, timesaving supplies, such as pressure-sensitive and continuous-feed labels.

- File regularly, every day or twice weekly if possible, to prevent filing overloads.

- Label folders, separators, and file drawers and containers with simple headings and clear typing or printing.

- If the same document is stored electronically and on paper, use the same file name in both cases or include a cross-reference sheet or cross-index entry.

- Open an additional folder rather than overcrowd an existing folder, but be certain that a new file is needed before opening a completely new subject or numeric folder.

- Leave four to six inches of space in a file drawer to permit easy insertion and removal of folders.

- Keep an up-to-date cross-index of names or subjects if you use a numeric system.

- Use the computer to assist your paper filing, such as in maintaining cross-indexes, automating records-management programs, and using barcodes (printed patterns that a computer can scan and read) on file containers to track and manage files.

- Use color coding to help locate material more easily and to spot misfiles at a glance.

- Clean out unnecessary duplicates of documents, and use cross-reference sheets instead.

- Transfer inactive files to permanent storage (e.g., microfilm) periodically.

- Follow your company's records-retention requirements concerning length of retention, type of storage, and authorized destruction of certain material.

- Establish a policy and procedure for handling borrowed files—time allowed, authorization, tracking system, and so on.

- Use *Out* guides and cards/sheets to keep track of removed material. (*Note*: Usually, secretaries insert a guide only for authorized removal outside the office.)

- Print the file name in the upper right corner of all documents to be filed. (*Note*: If your employer does not permit writing on documents, attach a small slip of paper.)

- Staple, rather than paper-clip, papers that need to be kept together.

- Repair torn or otherwise damaged pages before filing.

- Appoint one person to be responsible for overseeing the filing system to ensure control, authorized access, and consistency in maintenance.

# —8—
# MEETINGS

## A MEETING-PREPARATION CHECKLIST TO MAKE YOUR JOB EASIER

Secretaries regularly help their employers prepare meetings of all kinds and sizes, from a small office conference to a large outside convention. The task involves strong organizational skills and an ability to handle extensive details. The larger the meeting, the more important these attributes become. A large meeting, in fact, may require many additional skills and abilities, such as coordination among other meeting planners and supervisory skills for the assistants who handle some of the routine tasks. Many questions have to be answered during meeting preparation, but the most important one may be: Where do I start? A checklist such as the following can be invaluable not only in getting started but in monitoring adherence to your meeting schedule.

( ) Purpose of meeting confirmed

( ) Meeting theme selected

( ) Meeting date and time selected

( ) Site (city and hotel or other facility) selected

( ) Meeting committees (finance, program, and so on) appointed

( ) Speakers selected and invitations to speak prepared and mailed

( ) Speakers confirmed for program

( ) Meeting-room reservations made

( ) Meals arranged: ( ) breakfasts, ( ) lunches, ( ) dinners, ( ) refreshment breaks and cocktails

( ) Entertainment arranged

( ) Tours and other events arranged for attendees, spouses and companions, and other guests

( ) Ground transportation (buses, courtesy cars, and so on) arranged

( ) Exhibit and display facilities arranged

( ) Announcement, program, registration packet, and other materials drafted

( ) Announcement, program, registration packet, and other materials printed

( ) Announcement, program, registration packet, and other materials mailed

( ) Press releases and other notices prepared and mailed

( ) Registration-desk supplies (name tags, premiums, and so on) ordered

( ) Equipment-rental and -delivery arrangements made for presentations, displays, and so on

( ) Equipment-operator arrangements made

( ) Agenda topics requested from officers and committee members

( ) Agenda prepared and mailed

( ) Travel (car, train, plane) arrangements made for employer and other office personnel

( ) Hotel-room reservations made for employer and other office personnel

( ) Meeting folders prepared for employer to take to meeting

( ) Supplies (stationery, diskettes, and so on) collected for employer to take to meeting

( ) Minute book, resolution forms, rules of order, and other necessary meeting material collected

( ) Arrangements made for delivery of meeting-room supplies (pencils, pads, water glasses, and so on)

( ) Meeting rooms inspected for coat closets, temperature, lighting, seating, acoustics, sound systems, and so on

( ) Message (telephone, fax, and so on) arrangements made for secretary, executive, and meeting attendees

( ) Procedures in place for postmeeting cleanup, bill paying, and so on

## A DOZEN USEFUL TIPS FOR PREPARING EFFECTIVE PRESENTATIONS

If an executive in your office makes presentations, you may help prepare them or may even be responsible for certain aspects, such as design and layout. Regardless of the extent of your involvement, you will share the presenter's interest in creating a professional, effective presentation that will make both the executive and the company look good. In some cases, the presentation may cause your employer either to win or lose an important contract. Here are a dozen tips for preparing successful presentations.

1. Identify your company name on cover and title pages and, if desired, on all pages.

2. Personalize presentations being sent to various executives by using the executive's name on the copy he or she receives.

3. Select the best type of visual—slides, flip charts, overhead transparencies, posters, and so on—for the audience, message, room size, and seating arrangement.

4. Keep the organizational plan, format, and design simple and consistent, with each visual making a single point and containing only one illustration.

5. Remember that since the first visual makes the initial impression and sets the tone for the rest of the presentation, it should be used to capture the interest of the audience immediately.

6. Use short words and simple English (no jargon) in a bold face with uppercase and lowercase letters, rather than all capital letters, to emphasize important points.

7. Use bulleted points, rather than complete sentences, with short lines of about six words each and no more than about six lines per visual.

8. Use visuals to amplify and enhance, but not to duplicate, the speaker's comments.

9. Use large (14-point or more) readable type fonts, such as Times Roman, with plenty of white space so that everyone can easily see the presentation. (*Note:* Letters projected on a screen should be 3 inches high.)

10. Use graphics software imaginatively to add flip charts, slides, overheads, or anything else that will enhance and enliven the presentation.

11. Use a single color for the background, a contrasting color for the key points, and no more than three additional colors for any illustration (or no more than three colors for *everything*).

12. Have more than one person proofread the presentation, which must be 100 percent accurate, with each person reading it more than once.

## MEETING-ATTENDANCE STRATEGIES THAT WILL BOOST YOUR BENEFITS

The better you prepare yourself for meetings and the more professionally that you conduct yourself at them, the greater your benefits will be. Unfortunately, not everyone goes to a meeting armed with a list of strategies to accomplish this. Many people simply show up and respond to events as they occur. Passive attendees—no matter how large or small the meeting—miss important opportunities to make contacts, discover new techniques, and demonstrate their interest and capabilities. Here are some strategies that will boost your benefits at a meeting.

- Go to the meeting with the attitude that you intend to gain something useful from it.

- Learn as much as possible in advance about the meeting site (useful things to see and do, appropriate places to meet someone with whom you want to talk, and so on).

- Make appointments in advance with people you want to consult.

- Carry an appointment book for scheduling other appointments during the meeting or for future contacts you want to schedule.

- Develop an advance list of ideas and problems that you would like to explore with others.

- Stand or sit where you can meet and talk with numerous attendees and others during refreshment breaks and free periods.

- Carry your own business cards, and collect those of others for your address list, making appropriate notations about the people directly on their cards.

- Sit where you can make eye and verbal contact with the speaker or meeting chair during the session.

- Take notes using traditional shorthand, speed writing, or another rapid or abbreviated form of writing so that you can devote most of your time to participating in discussions.

- Segregate session notes, ideas and tips that you glean from other attendees, address lists, and appointments.

- Maximize your visibility (introduce yourself to speakers and other important guests, offer to help presenters, and so on).

- Don't be afraid to speak up during sessions, whether it be to ask a question or make a comment.

- Be willing to share your knowledge and exchange information with others.

- Adopt a positive attitude of being for something rather than only against something.

- Develop a sense of humor to deflect unwanted or disagreeable comments and situations.

- Watch your body language (see Chapter 1) so that you will appear poised and confident.

- Use correct grammar (see Chapter 10), with strong, active verbs, and speak slowly and clearly.

- Try to get enough rest each night so that you will be alert and prepared the following day.

## FOUR PRINCIPAL TELECONFERENCING METHODS

A *teleconference* is a meeting conducted by two or more persons in different locations. It could be as simple as a telephone connection or as complex as a full-motion video transmission. Depending on the type of activity in your office and the size of your company, you may be involved in one of the following four teleconferencing methods, or a combination or variation thereof, that may be used to conduct meetings long distance.

1. *Audioconference.* The *audioconference* is a voice-only meeting conducted over the telephone, with conference calls arranged through the long-distance operator and charged like any other person-to-person call.

2. *Audiographic conference.* The *audiographic conference* adds forms of graphics or visual transmission (e.g., electronic blackboard) to voice communication.

3. *Computer-document conference.* The *computer-document conference* is a nonvoice, visual-only electronic meeting, with participants using a computer network to connect their computers so that they can simultaneously work on the same document on screen.

4. *Videoconference.* The *videoconference,* the most sophisticated type of electronic meeting, connects participants in different locations who can both see and hear one another, using anything from speakerphones to elaborate television cameras.

# A DOZEN ESSENTIAL STEPS IN ARRANGING A TELECONFERENCE

As more and more executives use teleconferences to save time and travel costs, secretaries will play an increasing role in arranging this type of meeting. The simpler forms of conferencing, such as an audioconference, can be arranged in a relatively short time on relatively short notice. The more complex forms, however, such as a two-way videoconference, usually require advance room and equipment reservations. Here are twelve steps you need to keep in mind when arranging a teleconference.

1. Call several teleconferencing services (check the Yellow Pages) for cost estimates, stating the meeting date, beginning and closing times, expected number of participants, and their telephone numbers and location.

2. Send meeting notices with the preliminary agenda giving the conference date, name of moderator or chair, start-to-finish times, and special preparation required of participants.

3. Prepare a clear, concise agenda (see the next section), and enclose it with the meeting notice (described in item 2).

4. Make room and equipment reservations for complex video meetings one or more weeks in advance (ask about this when you get cost estimates).

5. Verify the participants' telephone numbers, and contact each one or the leader at each site to be certain that everyone will be available.

6. Ask participants to arrive a half hour early so that the meeting can begin on time.

7. Call the long-distance conference operator a few days before a conference-call meeting to verify the setup if more than ten locations are involved.

8. Make arrangements to tape the program for the company files and for later evaluation or review.

9. Be certain that everyone has any necessary equipment, such as a calculator, and a copy of any material required for reference during the meeting.

10. Send speakers information about the audience, and, if appropriate, send participants information about the speakers.

11. Check all teleconference rooms before the meeting for equipment availability and setup (microphones, VCRs, televisions, projectors, screens, bulletin boards, and so on), lighting, acoustics, and ventilation.

12. Check with equipment operators before the meeting to ensure that they will be on time.

## KEY AGENDA TOPICS AND HOW TO ORGANIZE THEM

Those who conduct meetings need an organized list of topics to guide the proceedings. Such an outline of items to be introduced, discussed, and acted upon is the *agenda*. Secretaries usually keep a current meeting file between meetings from which agenda topics can be drawn. In addition, officers, and sometimes all attendees, are asked if they have suggestions for agenda topics. From these and other sources, enough topics can be collected to prepare a tentative agenda to be sent to each prospective attendee and appropriate personnel. On the day of the meeting, or the day before, a final agenda that includes any changes or additions should be typed and placed at each attendee's chair in the meeting room. Although the specific topics and order of topics may vary as desired or as required by the organization's bylaws, the following items and order are common.

1. Call to order

2. Announcement of quorum

3. Introduction of guests

4. Reading and approval of previous meeting's minutes

5. Treasurer's report

6. Committee reports

7. Other reports

8. Nominations and elections (*Note:* In some organizations, this item follows "New Business.")

9. Old business

10. New business

11. Committee appointments

12. Announcements

13. Miscellaneous

14. Adjournment

## TIMESAVING SUGGESTIONS FOR TAKING THE MEETING MINUTES

Taking the meeting minutes is an important responsibility. The minutes of a formal meeting constitute a legal record that must be accurate, unbiased, and complete. To ensure that nothing is missed, most people in charge of taking the minutes also tape-record the proceedings to back up their handwritten notes. If you are asked to take the minutes, review copies from previous meetings before you start. Notice the order of topics, the names of regular participants, the amount of detail used, and other characteristics. Here are some additional suggestions that may simplify your work.

- Prepare a seating chart before the meeting to help you identify those who speak during the proceedings (ask for help in identifying people if necessary).

- Make a list of attendees, including late arrivals and early departures.

- Take with you a copy of the agenda, financial reports, and any other material that might be discussed or referred to during the meeting.

- Have several pens and pencils available so that you don't run out in the middle of an important discussion.

- Use shorthand, speed writing, or any other method of quick note taking that is effective.

- Use timesaving fill-in forms to record resolutions, amendments, and other material that must be recorded verbatim. (*Note:* Keep a record of people's names whether or not you use them in the minutes.)

```
Motion #1:_____

Proposed by:_____

Seconded by:_____

For:_____ Against:_____
```

- Choose words judiciously when describing emotional situations (e.g., a shouting match laced with expletives might be described [if described at all] as an "intense" discussion).

- Don't be afraid to signal the chair that you need to get clarification of a name or statement.

- Don't hesitate to ask for further assistance both during and after the meeting if you believe you missed something or are not certain about your facts.

- Review your notes and the taped version as soon as possible after the meeting while names and events are still fresh in your mind and in the minds of those for whom you may have further questions.

## IMPORTANT GUIDELINES FOR PREPARING THE MINUTES PROPERLY

Secretaries usually prepare a draft of the minutes for approval before submitting the final copy. Depending on your office practices concerning draft material, this preliminary version should be triple- or double-spaced. Otherwise, the format should be the same as that used for the final copy. After all necessary changes and corrections have been made, prepare the final version according to the requirements of your organization (refer to previous minutes), or if none exists, follow these guidelines (see also the examples of the first and second pages of minutes).

- Single-space the text if the minutes exceed one page, with a blank line space between paragraphs and at least one blank line space before and after subheads.

## FIRST PAGE OF MINUTES

---

BRENTWOOD COMMUNITY LEAGUE

Board of Directors
Regular Meeting
February 6, 1995


CALL TO ORDER

A regular meeting of the Board of Directors
of the Brentwood Community League was called to
order at 10:30 a.m., February 6, 1995, at the
headquarters of the League, 640 Prospect Street,
Des Plaines, IL 60017. The presiding officer was
John Chilton. A quorum was present, including the
following:

        John Chilton (president)
        Mary Daniels (vice president)
        Cindy Hall (secretary)
        Tim Winneta (treasurer)
        Barry Fines (director)
        Jeanette Medi (director)

Director Ken Stahlings, who was absent, voted
by proxy.


MINUTES

The secretary, Cindy Hall, read the minutes
of the January 6, 1995, meeting, and they were
approved as read.

---

## SECOND PAGE OF MINUTES

---

MINUTES, February 6, 1995                         page 2

FINANCES

The treasurer, Tim Winneta, presented a financial statement showing a checking balance on December 31, 1994, of $2,697.87 and a savings balance of $31,544.91 (copy attached). The treasurer's report was approved as read.

COMMITTEE REPORTS

Jeanette Medi, chair of the Activities Committee, reported that the next special event to be sponsored by the League is the community Business Fair to be held in October. Details will be available at the March 6 meeting.

NEW BUSINESS

Mary Daniels moved that Barry Fines be appointed to investigate the establishment of a scholarship fund. The motion was seconded, and, after Barry agreed to serve, it passed unanimously.

ADJOURNMENT

There being no further business, the meeting adjourned at 11:55 a.m.

---

Secretary                    President

---

- Use uniform margins of about 1 1/2 inches all around and allow more for the left margin if the minutes will be bound on that side.

- Indent paragraphs about 1/2 inch or type all of them flush left, as preferred.

- Center the heading, with the organization's name in all capitals, and specify the type of meeting and date.

- In the first paragraph state the date, time, place, presiding officer, and type of meeting and whether a quorum was present.

- List the attendees under the first paragraph if the meeting was relatively small (e.g., one or two dozen people), and list those voting by proxy in the next paragraph.

- Use left-margin subheadings (shown here) or above-paragraph subheadings (see the first-page model) that follow the topic items and order of the agenda.

```
MINUTES   The secretary, Cindy Hall, read
          the minutes of the August 16,
          1995, meeting, and they were
          approved as read.
```

- Format a resolution like an indented, blocked quotation (extract), with a blank line space above and below the resolution text.

- Capitalize *WHEREAS* and *RESOLVED,* and capitalize *That* when it follows *RESOLVED.*

```
RESOLVED That Edwin Barstrom receive the
association's highest commendation for his
thirty years' volunteer service in support
of community goals and ideals.
```

- Capitalize general references to the governing board or body for whom the minutes are being written (*the Board of Directors; the Corporation*).

- Follow the recommendations in other chapters of this book for proper grammar (Chapter 10), spelling (Chapter 11), punctuation (Chapter 12), and correct word choice (Chapters 14 and 15).

- State the time of adjournment and the date for the next meeting (if it will not be a regularly scheduled meeting) in the last paragraph.

- Add two lines at the bottom of the page for the secretary (left side) and chair (right side) to sign the document.

- Attach pertinent documents referred to in the body of the minutes, such as a treasurer's report.

- Add key topics to the general index to all minutes (if any)

## Twenty-eight Basic Parliamentary Motions and What They Mean

Whether you are attending a meeting, conducting one, or taking the minutes, you need to know something about motions. Also referred to as *questions,* motions are proposals made at a semi-formal or formal meeting, such as a directors' or stockholders' meeting, for consideration and action. They enable participants to discuss common interests and decide what to do in an orderly manner, and they give presiding officers a means by which to guide the proceedings. Most motions must be seconded by another person before they can be put to a vote. (The three that need no second are the call to order, an objection to considering a question, and the call for orders of the day.) The twenty-eight motions listed here are based on those originally developed by H. M. Robert in the late 1800s and published in numerous editions of *Robert's Rules of Order* since then.

1. *Adjourn.* This motion is made to dismiss an organized meeting (assembly): "I move that we adjourn."

2. *Fix the time to which to adjourn.* This motion is made to set the time, or the time, date, and place, of a future meeting: "I move that when we adjourn, we adjourn to meet at . . . on . . . in . . . ."

3. *Amend.* This motion is made to change or revise something: "I move that we amend the motion by striking out the words . . . and inserting the words . . . ."

4. *Amend an amendment.* This motion is made to change or revise an existing amendment: "I move that we amend the amendment by deleting the words . . . ."

5. *Amend the rules.* This motion is made to change or revise the rules of order currently in force at a meeting: "I move that we amend the third rule in the Rules of Order by . . . ."

6. *Appeal relating to decorum.* This statement is made to question or object to something pertaining to indecorum, transgression of the rules of speaking, or priority of business: "I appeal from the decision of the chair."

7. *Appeal relating to other matters.* This statement is made in the same way as an appeal relating to decorum to question or object to something other than matters of decorum: "I appeal from the decision of the chair."

8. *Call (a member) to order.* This statement may be made by a member to point out the violation of another member, or it may be made by the chair to instruct a member to conform to the rules: *Member:* "I rise to a point of order . . . ." *Chair:* "I call the member to order . . . ."

9. *Close debate.* This motion is made to bring discussion of the current motion to a close: "I move that we close debate on the motion to . . . and that we vote immediately on the pending question."

10. *Commit or refer.* This motion is made to assign some task to a few members, such as a committee: "I move that the matter of . . . be referred to a committee of . . . to be appointed by the chair."

11. *Extend the limits of debate.* This motion is made to allow discussion to continue beyond the established limits on debate in regard to the number or length of speeches: "I move that we increase the number of speeches allowed to . . . and that the time for each speech be increased to . . . minutes."

12. *Lay on the table.* This motion is made to put business aside temporarily and hold it for later discussion: "I move that . . . be laid on the table [be tabled]."

13. *Limit debate*. This motion is made to limit the number of speakers allowed and the time each may speak: "I move that we limit debate to . . . members, with . . . people on each side of the issue and . . . minutes for each person."

14. *Object to consideration of a question*. This motion is made to discourage discussion that is thought to be irrelevant, unprofitable, or contentious: "I object to the consideration of the question."

15. *Call for orders of the day*. This motion is made to force the assembly to return to its scheduled program when the attendees digress: "I call for the orders of the day."

16. *Postpone to a certain time*. This motion is made to set a later time when a particular subject must then be considered: "I move that . . . be postponed to . . . ".

17. *Postpone indefinitely*. This motion is made by members opposing a current motion to force it open to debate: "I move that . . . be postponed indefinitely."

18. *Call for the previous question*. This motion, the title of which is somewhat misleading, is made to bring debate on the current motion to a close and order an immediate vote on it: "I call for [or move] the previous question."

19. *Questions of privilege*. This statement is made to get the attention of the chair immediately, to ask the chair a question, or to make some other point that can't wait: "I rise to a question of privilege."

20. *Read a paper*. This motion is made to request that a paper be read before the assembly votes on it: "I move that . . . be permitted to read . . . ".

21. *Reconsider a question*. This motion is made to bring back before the assembly a matter that was discussed earlier (it must be made on the day of or after the original vote by someone who voted on the prevailing side): "I move that we reconsider the vote on . . . ".

22. *Request to continue speaking after indecorum*. This motion is made to get the assembly's permission to continue a discussion after being called to order for making improper remarks: "I move that . . . be allowed to continue speaking."

23. *Rescind.* This motion is made to annul a previous action when it is too late to use the motion to reconsider a question: "I move that the motion to . . . adopted on . . . be rescinded."

24. *Create a special order.* This motion is made to suspend all rules that might interfere with considering a question at its specified time: "I move that . . . be made a special order for 11:30 A.M."

25. *Suspend the rules.* This motion is made to enable an assembly to act on something that otherwise would be prohibited by the rules: "I move that we suspend the rules that interfere with . . . ."

26. *Take from the table.* This motion is made to bring back to the floor a matter that was previously tabled: "I move that the motion . . . be taken from the table."

27. *Take up a question out of order.* This motion is made along with the motion to suspend the rules to make it possible to discuss something out of order: "I move that we suspend the rules and take up the matter of . . . at this time."

28. *Withdraw a motion.* This motion is made to remove a current motion from further consideration or from a vote on it: "I withdraw my motion to . . . ."

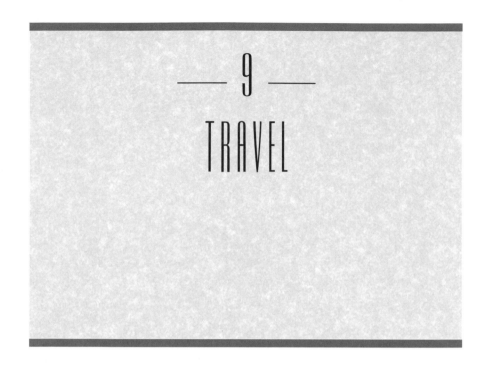

## A USEFUL CHECKLIST TO HELP YOU SELECT THE BEST POSSIBLE TRAVEL AGENT

A travel agent is one of a secretary's best friends. Although it is possible to find travel information and make reservations on your own—by telephone, through an on-line computer service, or in person—it takes time to do so, time that a secretary often does not have. Travel agents—both from outside agencies and in-house travel offices—are experts in the field who can save you time and money. They can rapidly cut through the maze of travel information to find what you want. They can not only make arrangements to fit your needs and budget but can also do many other travel-related tasks, such as plan itineraries, guide you through Customs, figure out foreign exchange, and issue tickets and boarding passes. Even though secretaries usually prefer to work with a travel agent, selecting the right one may not be easy. Here is a checklist designed to help you find the best possible travel agent for you and your employer.

( ) The agent is experienced, and the agency has been in business for several years.

( ) The agent is a Certified Travel Counselor (CTC) graduate.

( ) The agency is a member of the American Society of Travel Agents (ASTA) or Association of Retail Travel Agents (ARTA).

( ) The agency displays the seals of the Air Traffic Conference (ATC) or International Air Transport Association (IATA).

( ) The Better Business Bureau and local Chamber of Commerce have no record of a complaint filed against the agent or agency.

( ) The agent and agency compare favorably in price and services with at least three others that I have investigated.

( ) Friends and business associates whom I trust have recommended the agent and agency.

( ) The agency does a major portion of its work for business travelers.

( ) The agent has personally visited many of the cities and countries to which my employer travels.

( ) The agent is someone with whom I am comfortable and who seems to appreciate our company's travel needs and budget.

( ) The agency is in a convenient location and has hours that are convenient.

( ) The agent, the staff, or a hotline/800 number is available to handle emergency requests 24 hours a day.

( ) The agency is willing to accept new clients.

## Two Dozen Domestic Trip-Preparation Guidelines

Secretaries usually make all or part of the business travel arrangements for their employers. Although a travel agent can assume much of the burden of checking schedules and timetables as well as making the reservations, many other steps, such as making financial arrangements, are also involved in a business trip. Knowing a traveler's preferences and expectations will help; in fact, if you maintain a traveler's preference profile (e.g., preferred hotel accommodations, rental-car requirements), you will be better equipped to make travel plans on short notice. Here are two dozen guidelines for planning a domestic trip. (See also the suggestions later in this chapter for planning an international trip.)

1. Get complete travel information (e.g., schedules, fares, and so on) from your company travel office or the outside agency your employer uses.

2. Use your on-line travel database or request information by fax or telephone.

3. Prepare and submit a *preliminary* travel schedule (e.g., times, route, carriers) to your employer for consideration and recommended changes.

4. Upon approval of the preliminary schedule, ask the travel agent to make the desired transportation and hotel reservations.

5. Check that tickets have been issued by the agent, have been sent to your office, or will be available for pickup at the airline counter before departure.

6. Prepare and submit to your employer the final itinerary (e.g., departure and arrival cities and times, carriers, ground transportation), or submit the one prepared by the travel agent.

7. Prepare and submit to your employer a travel appointment schedule (e.g., contact's name and address, type of meeting).

8. Collect files, correspondence, and any information that your employer will need. (*Note:* When practical, make photocopies and leave the originals in the office.)

9. Collect equipment and supplies, such as a notebook computer and letterhead stationery, that your employer will need.

10. Prepare any identification tags that are needed, and submit baggage instructions to your employer.

11. Help your employer make financial arrangements, including company travel advances, traveler's checks, and letters of credit.

12. Verify for accuracy and submit tickets and hotel confirmations to your employer.

13. Check weather predictions, and submit wardrobe reminders, such as rain gear or formal attire, to your employer.

14. Make a copy of the travel itinerary and appointment schedule for your employer's family.

15. Remind your employer to order and take along any necessary medication and prescriptions.

16. Remind your employer to make any necessary insurance or security provisions (see the next section about travel security).

17. Submit a telephone-address list of banks and other establishments that your employer might require while traveling in other cities.

18. Check if the hotels offer computer, fax, and other on-site business services or where such services might be available in the city.

19. Check if the hotels will provide VCRs in the rooms for use with business tapes, exercise videos, or other tapes your employer may want to take along or rent.

20. Check if the air or rail transportation being used includes airfone or railfone service.

21. Make any additional reservations your employer requests, such as dining-room or theater-ticket reservations.

22. Ask whether any incoming communications are expected that you should fax or mail to your employer during the trip.

23. If your employer will have free time while traveling, collect information on sightseeing opportunities at each stopover.

24. If you must cancel any part or all of the arrangements, do so immediately by telephone and follow up with a confirmation copy by fax or mail.

## A VALUABLE COLLECTION OF TRAVEL-SAFETY TIPS

Travelers who are in unfamiliar places are especially vulnerable to assault, theft, and other misfortunes. In some cities, the threat is especially serious, and international travelers often have additional concerns about terrorism and other militant activities in certain countries. However, both domestic and international travelers can take a variety of preventive measures to avoid unnecessary exposure to the dangers associated with travel. Here are commonsense but often overlooked precautions that you and your employer should observe while traveling.

*Before You Leave*

- Review your homeowner's insurance, and add coverage if necessary to cover property you intend to take with you.
- Check with your travel agent about travel insurance to cover luggage and personal property and to protect you if you must cancel the trip.
- Leave a vacation "hold" for your mail at the post office (or have someone pick it up) so that it doesn't pile up at your residence.
- Arrange for a housesitter, or use timers on lights and a radio or television in your residence, with times staggered as though someone were at home.
- Give a set of your house keys to a neighbor or friend you can trust, and ask the person occasionally to park in your driveway, mow the lawn, and so on.
- Make photocopies of important documents (e.g., passport), leaving a copy in the office and one with your family and packing one copy in a suitcase apart from the originals.
- Prepare a list of information about your traveler's checks (e.g., serial numbers, denominations), leaving a copy in the office (if the checks were paid for by the company) and one with your family and packing one copy in a suitcase apart from the checks.
- Prepare an inventory of everything you plan to take along in case your luggage is lost and you must file a claim, leaving a copy in the office and one with your family.
- Take only the credit cards you need, prepare a list of their account numbers and 800 numbers to call if any are lost or stolen, and keep the list in a secure place apart from the cards.

- Register valuables, such as cameras and jewelry, with Customs before you leave to confirm the free entry of your own property when you return.

- Carry a list of emergency contacts (doctors and others), and ask the travel agent about country or worldwide networks or numbers of individuals to call for assistance.

- Collect supplies (stationery, etc.), separating important material (e.g., files, passport) to be hand-carried.

- Use your office address for identification purposes (e.g., luggage, hotel), placing your name and address inside each piece as well as on the outer tag.

- Avoid expensive luggage that would attract thieves, and use combination locks and luggage tags that conceal your name and address.

- Prepay as much as possible or use credit cards while traveling so that you need only take along a limited amount of cash, such as up to $200.

- If you use credit cards, destroy any copies of charge receipts that someone could retrieve from a wastebasket.

- Ask your travel agent or hotel personnel about local problems in the places you intend to visit, such as unsafe areas to walk or nearby street-gang activities.

- Call the State Department in Washington, D.C., for the latest advisories on high-risk areas in other countries.

*At the Hotel*

- Stay at hotels that have a good safety record (ask your travel agent), offering not only secure doors (e.g., deadbolts, chain locks, peepholes) but also valet parking.

- Avoid hotels that indiscreetly call out your room number to bellhops or other personnel (ask immediately upon registering that this not be done).

- Request a hotel room between the second and seventh floors part-way down the hall from the elevator, but not by a fire escape or at the far end of a hall.

- Memorize the number of doors between your room and the nearest exit (in case of blackouts or fire).
- Register with only your last name and first initial to avoid revealing your gender, marital status, or professional status.
- Check your hotel room completely for security problems (e.g., windows, door locks) before the person escorting you and your luggage leaves.
- Check that balcony doors in your hotel room lock properly.
- Take along portable door-locking devices to use in addition to each door's chain lock and deadbolt.
- Arrange to have your hotel room made up during breakfast, and thereafter hang a "Do Not Disturb" sign on the door.
- Turn on the television or a radio when you leave to make it appear as though the room is occupied.
- Keep your room key with you at all times, but do not leave it lying on a counter or restaurant table or hold it for everyone to see your room number while you are in the lobby or elevator.
- Do not open the door of your hotel room unless you know who is there or have called the front desk to confirm any hotel-staff visit.
- Entertain clients in the lobby or a restaurant, not in your room.
- Leave the hall door open when room service delivers a tray, and keep inner doors closed so that no one will see that you are alone.
- Refuse to accept suspicious or unexpected packages.
- Study maps and guidebooks in the privacy of your room, not in a restaurant, in the lobby, or on a street corner, so that you can give the appearance that you know where you are going at all times.

*In Transit*

- Travel on carriers that have a good safety record.

- Ask your travel agent about dates and times, as well as places, that are generally safer than others.

- Be certain that you receive a claim check for each piece of luggage you check.

- Read all emergency instructions, and check transportation carriers and hotels for the nearest exits.

- Park your rental or other car only in secure, well-lit areas.

- Never enter a car without checking the back seat where someone might be hiding.

- Avoid leaving objects in a car, but if you must do so, lock them in the trunk and take the key with you.

- Avoid using "gypsy" taxis, which are often unlicensed and unregulated and may pick up more than one person per cab.

- Be wary of street vendors whose purpose may be to distract you while someone else robs you.

- Don't offer to transport packages or bags of strangers or friends, unless you are positive that nothing illegal is inside.

- Avoid carrying a small case or pocketbook (unless it is hidden under your clothing), but if it is necessary to do so, use a shoulder bag and hold the bag tightly in front of you.

- Stay away from the curbside where a thief on a motorcycle could snatch a bag and speed away.

- Never leave luggage or other articles unattended.

- Carry your wallet in a front pocket, and wrap it with a rubber band so that a thief cannot easily slide it out of the pocket.

- Carry your passport with you in an inaccessible or hidden pocket or in a hidden money belt, and never leave it lying on a counter or table.

- Keep a low profile, avoiding the use of conspicuous manners and conversation, equipment such as binoculars that marks you as a tourist, or clothing that suggests you are wealthy or a stranger.

- Wear inexpensive jewelry, and use hidden pockets or money belts for extra cash and other valuables.

- At stopovers, keep valuables (e.g., cash, jewelry, computer diskettes) in a hotel safe or a safe-deposit box at a bank.

- Register with the consular officer in the U.S. Embassy immediately upon arrival in a high-risk area.

- Report losses or assaults immediately to the police and other appropriate authorities.

- Keep a copy of any police report for your insurance claim.

## IMPORTANT INTERNATIONAL TRIP-PREPARATION GUIDELINES

In the current global marketplace, more and more secretaries not only make international travel arrangements but also travel to other countries along with their employers. Trip preparation for international travel is much more elaborate than it is for domestic travel. Most of the suggestions given earlier in this chapter for arranging a domestic trip also apply to arranging a foreign trip, but numerous additional factors must be considered when dealing with different governments, different laws, and different social and business customs. For international trips, the following guidelines should be added to the list of steps described earlier in this chapter for domestic trips.

1. Collect current economic, social, legal, and other information on each country from the appropriate government sources (e.g., State Department), U.S. and foreign embassies and consulates (see the list later in this chapter), libraries, bookstores, and so on.

2. Prepare a list of key phrases (e.g., "What time is it?") in the language of each country.

3. If your employer plans to do business with certain countries, consider taking language courses and an international communication course.

4. Have business cards printed on both sides, with the reverse side in the language of the country being visited. (*Note:* On that side, avoid abbreviations, such as *Ave.* for *Avenue* and *E.* for *East.*)

5. Study the rules of etiquette for each country (e.g., guide-books, government or embassy information), which may differ from the rules in the United States.

6. Write for Customs regulations before departure if anyone plans to shop in other countries.

7. When you are ready to return, pack all receipts in one envelope and all purchases in one suitcase to expedite entry.

8. Get an extra copy of an up-to-date guide to international dialing codes that can be taken on the trip (leave your desk copy in the office).

9. Call the international department of your firm's bank to get current exchange rates just before leaving.

10. Ask your travel agent or the appropriate foreign embassy or consulate about admission (entry) requirements for the country to be visited.

11. Apply for the necessary passports, visas, tourist cards, and other documents in sufficient time.

12. Ask a travel agent or embassy for details about special regulations or requirements that the country has established for business/commercial travelers (e.g., bringing in electronic equipment).

13. Contact the American Automobile Association or the American Automobile Alliance for applications for an international driving permit (ask your travel agent for details and current addresses).

14. Ask your travel agent for a list of immunizations required for the countries being visited.

15. Contact the federal Centers for Disease Control and Prevention in Atlanta for current advisories about health problems (e.g., diseases, drinking water) in other countries.

16. See your personal or company doctor for the necessary inoculations according to the time required before entry, and ask for a prescription to accompany any medication that contains narcotics.

17. Compile a list of desirable and undesirable foods and beverages for coping with jet lag and movement through time zones (ask your doctor or check your library for suggestions).

18. Ask your long-distance carrier for an international calling card that can be used with direct-dial as well as operator-assisted service.

19. Make arrangements for outside interpreters or translators before leaving, if a trained employee is not available. (*Note:* Contact embassies or the American Translators Association in Ossining, New York, for suggestions.)

20. Take along small amounts of foreign currency for tips, taxis, and other small purchases.

21. Exchange currency only at banks and other authorized places to avoid violating local currency laws. (*Note:* Banks generally offer better rates than hotels and other sources, and the risk of being cheated is far less.)

22. Remember when planning a wardrobe for the trip that the seasons are reversed in Southern Hemisphere countries and weather and climate differ from one country or region to another.

23. Check whether the foreign hotels provide fax or telex service and whether computers, VCRs, and other required equipment are provided.

24. Draft an announcement of the proposed visit (e.g., dates, host company) for international publications headquartered in the cities being visited, unless your employer wants to avoid publicity for security reasons.

25. Send a copy of the itinerary and other pertinent information (e.g., purpose of the trip) to the International Trade Division, Department of Commerce, Washington, D.C., in time for the department to advise its foreign offices.

26. Ask the Dun & Bradstreet credit service, if your firm is a subscriber, for authorization to call on its foreign offices in case credit information is needed while traveling.

27. Draft letters for your employer's signature to be sent to banks and other businesses to ask them for letters of introduction to their international offices.

28. Draft letters for your employer's signature announcing the travel plans to the host companies, stating dates of the visit and expected temporary address while there.

29. Remind your employer to get a letter of authorization from your firm's president or other person who has authorized him or her to represent the company.

30. Contact secretaries in the firms being visited, and arrange for all secretaries to help any visiting executives. (*Note:* You can offer to help through the National Council for International Visitors, Washington, D.C.)

31. Use international associations such as PSI®, the Internet, and other networks for exchanging information.

## A SIMPLE GUIDE TO CALCULATING TIME AROUND THE WORLD

Travelers often pass through different time zones, and it is necessary to compute time differentials while traveling throughout the world. Chapter 3 has a detailed chart that shows what the time is at a particular hour in selected cities across the globe. There, for example, you can see that when it is 7:00 P.M. in New York City, it is 8 P.M. in Buenos Aires, midnight in London, and 5:30 A.M. the next day in New Delhi. The following list enables a traveler to determine time in various cities of the world by adding or subtracting a constant amount from current eastern standard time. For example, if you were leaving New York City at 9 A.M. eastern standard time destined for Bonn, Germany, and you wanted to know what time it would be in Bonn at that moment, you would add 6 hours, which means that it would be 3 P.M. in Bonn. However, if you were leaving Bonn for New York City at 3 P.M., you would *subtract* 6 hours; it would therefore be 9 A.M. in New York City. (Adjust all time figures in the following list as needed if you know that a form of daylight savings time applies at the departure or destination location.)

| City | Time Difference |
| --- | --- |
| Buenos Aires, Argentina | +2 |
| Sydney, Australia | +15 |
| Vienna, Austria | +6 |
| Brussels, Belgium | +6 |

| City | Time Difference |
|---|---|
| La Paz, Bolivia | +1 |
| Rio de Janeiro, Brazil | +2 |
| Ottawa, Ontario, Canada | -0- |
| Santiago, Chile | +1 |
| Beijing, China | +13 |
| Bogotá, Colombia | -0- |
| Prague, Czech Republic | +6 |
| Copenhagen, Denmark | +6 |
| Quito, Ecuador | -0- |
| Cairo, Egypt | +7 |
| London, England | +5 |
| Addis Ababa, Ethiopia | +8 |
| Helsinki, Finland | +7 |
| Paris, France | +6 |
| Tbilisi, Georgia | +8 |
| Bonn, Germany | +6 |
| Accra, Ghana | +5 |
| Athens, Greece | +7 |
| Guatemala City, Guatemala | -1 |
| Budapest, Hungary | +6 |
| New Delhi, India | +10 1/2 |
| Jakarta, Indonesia | +12 |
| Dublin, Ireland | +5 |
| Jerusalem, Israel | +7 |
| Rome, Italy | +6 |
| Tokyo, Japan | +14 |
| Amman, Jordan | +7 |
| Nairobi, Kenya | +8 |
| Seoul, South Korea | +14 |
| Kuala Lumpur, Malaysia | +13 |
| Mexico City, Mexico | -1 |
| Casablanca, Morocco | +5 |
| Amsterdam, The Netherlands | +6 |

| City | Time Difference |
|---|---|
| Auckland, New Zealand | +17 |
| Lagos, Nigeria | +6 |
| Oslo, Norway | +6 |
| Lahore, Pakistan | +10 |
| Asunción, Paraguay | +2 |
| Lima, Peru | -0- |
| Manila, Philippines | +13 |
| Warsaw, Poland | +6 |
| Lisbon, Portugual | +5 |
| Moscow, Russia | +8 |
| Riyadh, Saudi Arabia | +8 |
| Belgrade, Serbia (Yugoslavia) | +6 |
| Singapore, Singapore | +13 |
| Johannesburg, South Africa | +7 |
| Madrid, Spain | +6 |
| Kotte, Sri Lanka | +10 1/2 |
| Stockholm, Sweden | +6 |
| Geneva, Switzerland | +6 |
| Taipei, Taiwan | +13 |
| Bangkok, Thailand | +12 |
| Tunis, Tunisia | +6 |
| Istanbul, Turkey | +7 |
| Entebbe, Uganda | +8 |
| Kiev, Ukraine | +8 |
| Montevideo, Uruguay | +2 |
| Caracas, Venezuela | +1 |
| Hanoi, Vietnam | +12 |
| Amran, Yemen | +8 |
| Harare, Zimbabwe | +7 |

## CURRENCIES USED IN THE MAJOR COUNTRIES OF THE WORLD

Business travelers in other countries who exchange their own currencies for those of the countries being visited should learn the basic unit, such as *dollar,* and the fractional unit (if any), such as *cent,* of each country. Travel guides, almanacs, and other reference books, such as the *MRI Bankers' Guide to Foreign Currency* (Monetary Research International), contain such information. Contact banks for recent changes in currency, especially by newly formed countries, and for up-to-the-minute exchange rates. The following list gives the basic and fractional currency units for all major countries of the world.

*Afghanistan:* afghani (Af) = 100 puls

*Albania:* lek (L) = 100 quintars

*Algeria:* Algerian dinar (DA) = 100 centimes

*Andorra:* French franc (F) = 100 centimes; Spanish peseta (Pta) = 100 céntimos

*Angola:* kwanza (Kz) = 100 kwei

*Antigua* and *Barbuda:* East Caribbean dollar (EC$) = 100 cents

*Argentina:* peso (ARP) = 100 centavos

*Armenia:* ruble (R) = 100 kopeks

*Australia:* Australian dollar ($A) = 100 cents

*Austria:* Austrian schilling (S) = 100 groschen

*Azerbaijan:* manat (N.A.) = 10 rubles

*The Bahamas:* Bahamian dollar (B$) = 100 cents

*Bahrain:* Bahraini dinar (BD) = 1,000 fils

*Bangladesh:* taka (Tk) = 100 paise

*Barbados:* Barbadian dollar (Bds$) = 100 cents

*Belarus:* rubel (N.A.) = 10 Russian rubles

*Belgium:* Belgian franc (BF) = 100 centimes

*Belize:* Belizean dollar (Bz$) = 100 cents

*Benin:* CFA franc (CFAF) = 100 centimes

*Bhutan:* ngultrum (Nu) = 100 chetrum

*Bolivia:* boliviano ($B) = 100 centavos

*Bosnia* and *Herzegovina:* dinar (D) = 100 paras

*Botswana:* pula (P) = 100 thebe

*Brazil:* cruzeiro (Cr$) = 100 centavos

*Brunei Darussalam:* Bruneian dollar (B$) = 100 cents

*Bulgaria:* lev (Lv) = 100 stotinki

*Burkina Faso:* CFA franc (CFAF) = 100 centimes

*Burundi:* Burundi franc (BFu) = 100 centimes

*Cambodia:* riel (CR) = 100 sen

*Cameroon:* CFA franc (CFAF) = 100 centimes

*Canada:* Canadian dollar (Can$) = 100 cents

*Cape Verde:* Cape Verdean escudo (CVEsc) = 100 centavos

*Central African Republic:* CFA franc (CFAF) = 100 centimes

*Chad:* CFA franc (CFAF) = 100 centimes

*Chile:* Chilean peso (Ch$) = 100 centavos

*China:* yuan (¥) = 10 jiao

*Colombia:* Colombian peso (Col$) = 100 centavos

*Comoros:* Comoran franc (CFAF) = 100 centimes

*Congo:* CFA franc (CFA Fr) = 100 centimes

*Costa Rica:* Costa Rican colón (C) = 100 centimos

*Croatia:* Croatian dinar (CD) = 100 paras

*Cuba:* Cuban peso (Cu$) = 100 centavos

*Cyprus:* Cypriot pound (£C) = 100 cents

*Czech Republic:* koruna (Kc) = 100 haleru

*Denmark:* Danish krone (DKr) = 100 øre

*Djibouti:* Djiboutian franc (DF) = 100 centimes

*Dominica:* East Caribbean dollar (EC$) = 100 cents

*Dominican Republic:* Dominica peso (RD$) = 100 centavos

*Ecuador:* sucre (S/) = 100 centavos

*Egypt:* Egyptian pound (£E) = 100 piasters

*El Salvador:* Salvadoran colón (C$) = 100 centavos

*Equatorial Guinea:* CFA franc (CFAF) = 100 centimes

*Eritrea:* N.A.

*Estonia:* Estonian kroon (EEK) = 100 (N.A.)

*Ethiopia:* birr (Br) = 100 cents

*Fiji:* Fijian dollar (F$) = 100 cents

*Finland:* markkaa (FMk) = 100 pennia

*France:* franc (F) = 100 centimes

*Gabon:* CFA franc (CFAF) = 100 centimes

*The Gambia:* dalasi (D) = 100 bututs

*Georgia:* Russian ruble (R) = 100 kopeks (lari to be introduced)

*Germany:* deutsche mark (DM) = 100 pfennige

*Ghana:* cedi (C) = 100 pesewas

*Greece:* drachma (Dr) = 100 lepta

*Grenada:* East Caribbean dollar (EC$) = 100 cents

*Guatemala:* quetzal (Q) = 100 centavos

*Guinea:* Guinean franc (FG) = 100 centimes

*Guinea-Bissau:* Guinea-Bissauan peso (PG) = 100 centavos

*Guyana:* Guyanese dollar (G$) = 100 cents

*Haiti:* gourde (G) = 100 centimes

*Honduras:* lempira (L)= 100 centavos

*Hungary:* forint (Ft) = 100 fillér

*Iceland:* Icelandic krona (IKr) = 100 aurar

*India:* Indian rupee (Re) = 100 paise

*Indonesia:* Indonesian rupiah (Rp) = 100 sen (sen discontinued)

*Iran:* Iranian rial (IR) = 10 tomans

*Iraq:* Iraqi dinar (ID) = 1,000 fils

*Ireland:* Irish pound (£IR) = 100 pence

*Israel:* new Israeli shekel (NIS) = 100 new agorot (sing. agora)

*Italy:* Italian lira (Lit) = 100 centesimi

*Ivory Coast:* CFA franc (CFAF) = 100 centimes

*Jamaica:* Jamaican dollar (J$) = 100 cents

*Japan:* yen (¥) = 100 sen

*Jordan:* Jordanian dinar (JD) = 1,000 fils

*Kazakhstan:* Russian ruble (R) = 100 kopeks

*Kenya:* Kenyan shilling (KSh) = 100 cents

*Kiribati:* Australian dollar ($A) = 100 cents

*Korea (North):* North Korean won (Wn) = 100 chon

*Korea (South):* South Korean won (W) = 10 chon (theoretical)

*Kuwait:* Kuwaiti dinar (KD) = 1,000 fils

*Kyrgyzstan (Kirghizia):* som (new currency)

*Laos:* new kip (KK) = 100 at

*Latvia:* lat = 100 N.A.

*Lebanon:* Lebanese pound (£L) = 100 piasters

*Lesotho:* loti (L) = 100 lisente

*Liberia:* Liberian dollar (L$) = 100 cents

*Libya:* Libyan dinar (LD) = 1,000 dirhams

*Liechtenstein:* Swiss franc (SsF) = 100 centimes

*Lithuania:* talonas, to be replaced with litas

*Luxembourg:* Luxembourg franc (LuxF) = 100 centimes

*Macedonia:* denar (N.A.) = 100 N.A.

*Madagascar:* Malagasy franc (FMG) = 100 centimes

*Malawi:* Malawian kwacha (MK) = 100 tambala

*Malaysia:* ringgit (M$) = 100 sen

*Maldives:* rufiyaa (Rf) = 100 laaris

*Mali:* CFA franc (CFAF) = 100 centimes

*Malta:* Maltese lira (LM) = 100 cents

*Marshall Islands:* U.S. dollar (US$) = 100 cents

*Mauritania:* ouguiya (UM) = 5 khoums

*Mauritius:* Mauritian rupee (MauR) = 100 cents

*Mexico:* Mexican peso (Mex$) = 100 centavos

*Micronesia:* U.S. dollar (US$) = 100 cents

*Moldova:* Russian ruble (R) = 100 kopeks (lei to be introduced)

*Monaco:* French franc (F) = 100 centimes

*Mongolia:* tughrik (Tug) = 100 mongos

*Morocco:* Moroccan dirham (DH) = 100 centimes

*Mozambique:* metical (Mt) = 100 centavos

*Myanmar (Burma):* kyak (K) = 100 pyas

*Namibia:* South African rand (R) = 100 cents

*Nauru:* Australian dollar ($A) = 100 cents

*Nepal:* Nepalese rupee (NR) = 100 paisa

*The Netherlands:* guilder, gulden, or florin (f.) = 100 cents

*New Zealand:* New Zealand dollar (NZ$) = 100 cents

*Nicaragua:* córdoba (C$) = 100 centavos

*Niger:* CFA franc (CFAF) = 100 centimes

*Nigeria:* naira (N) = 100 kobo

*Norway:* Norwegian krone (NKr) = 100 øre

*Oman:* Omani rial (RO) = 1,000 baiza

*Pakistan:* Pakistan rupee (PRe) = 100 paisa

*Panama:* balboa (B) = 100 centesimos

*Papua New Guinea:* kina (K) = 100 toea

*Paraguay:* guaraní (G) = 100 centimos

*Peru:* nuevo sol (S/.) = 100 centavos

*Philippines:* Philippine peso (P) = 100 centavos

*Poland:* zloty (Zl) = 100 groszy

*Portugal:* Portuguese escudo (Esc) = 100 centavos

*Qatar:* Qatari riyal (QR) = 100 dirhams

*Romania:* leu (L) = 100 bani

*Russia:* ruble (R) = 100 kopeks

*Rwanda:* Rwandan franc (RF) = 100 centimes

*Saint Kitts* and *Nevis:* East Caribbean dollar (EC$) = 100 cents

*Saint Lucia:* East Caribbean dollar (EC$) = 100 cents

*Saint Vincent* and the *Grenadines:* East Caribbean dollar (EC$) = 100 cents

*San Marino:* Italian lira (L) = 100 centesimi; also national coins

*São Tomé* and *Príncipe:* dobra (Db) = 100 centimos

*Saudi Arabia:* Saudi rial (SR) = 100 halalas

*Senegal:* CFA franc (CFAF) = 100 centimes

*Serbia* and *Montenegro:* Yugoslav new dinar (YD) = 100 paras

*Seychelles:* Seychelles rupee (SRe) = 100 cents

*Sierra Leone:* leone (Le) = 100 cents

*Singapore:* Singapore dollar (S$) = 100 cents

*Slovakia:* koruna (Kc) = 100 haleru

*Slovenia:* tolar (SIT) = 100 N.A.

*Solomon Islands:* Solomon Islands dollar (SI$) = 100 cents

*Somalia:* Somali shilling (So.Sh.) = 100 centesimi

*South Africa:* rand (R) = 100 cents

*Spain:* peseta (Pta) = 100 centimos

*Sri Lanka:* Sri Lankan rupee (SLRe) = 100 cents

*Sudan:* Sudanese pound (£Sd) = 100 piasters

*Suriname:* Surinamese guilder, gulden, or florin (Sf.) = 100 cents

*Swaziland:* lilangeni (E) = 100 cents

*Sweden:* Swedish krona (SKr) = 100 öre

*Switzerland:* Swiss franc (SwF) = 100 centimes

*Syria:* Syrian pound (£S) = 100 piasters

*Taiwan:* New Taiwan dollar (NT$) = 100 cents

*Tajikistan:* Russian ruble (R) = 100 kopeks

*Tanzania:* Tanzanian shilling (TSh) = 100 cents

*Thailand:* baht (B) = 100 satang

*Togo:* CFA franc (CFAF) = 100 centimes

*Tonga:* pa'anga (T$) = 100 seniti

*Trinidad* and *Tobago:* Trinidad and Tobago dollar (TT$) = 100 cents

*Tunisia:* Tunisian dinar (TD) = 1,000 millimes

*Turkey:* Turkish lira (TL) = 100 kurus

*Turkmenistan:* Russian ruble (R) = 100 kopeks (manat to be introduced)

*Tuvalu:* Australian dollar ($A) = 100 cents or Tuvaluan dollar ($T) = 100 cents

*Uganda:* Uganda shilling (USh) = 100 cents

*Ukraine:* karbovanet (hryvnya to be introduced)

*United Arab Emirates:* Emirian dirham (Dh) = 100 fils

*United Kingdom:* pound sterling (£) = 100 pence

*Uruguay:* Uruguayan nuevo peso (N$Ur) = 100 centésimos

*Uzbekistan:* Russian ruble (R) = 100 kopeks

*Vanuatu:* vatu (VT) = 100 centimes

*Vatican City:* Vatican lira (VLit) = 100 centesimi

*Venezuela:* bolívar (Bs) = 100 centimos

*Vietnam:* new dong (D) = 100 xu

*Western Samoa:* tala (WS$) = 100 sene

*Yemen:* North Yemeni rial (YR) = 100 fils; South Yemeni dinar (YD) = 1,000 fils; Yemeni rial (new currency)

*Zaïre:* zaïre (Z) = 100 makuta

*Zambia:* Zambian kwacha (ZK) = 100 ngwee

*Zimbabwe:* Zimbabwe dollar (Z$) = 100 cents

## U.S. EMBASSIES IN OTHER COUNTRIES

One of the best sources of up-to-date and reliable information is the U.S. embassy. An embassy can provide important information before a traveler leaves home and can be very helpful after he or she arrives in the foreign country. Since addresses change from time to time, secretaries should periodically update the following list of embassy locations in other countries. If your employer does a lot of business in other countries, consider subscribing to *Key Officers of Foreign Service Posts*, available from the Superintendent of Documents, U.S. Government Printing Office, in Washington, D.C., for regular updates.

*Afghanistan:* Ansari Wat, Wazir Akbar Khan Mina, Kabul.

*Albania:* Rruga Labinoti 103, Room 2921, Tirane.

*Algeria:* 4 Chemin Cheikh Bachir El-Ibrahimi, Algiers.

*Antigua* and *Barbuda:* Queen Elizabeth Highway, Saint John's, Antigua.

*Argentina:* 4300 Colombia, 1425 Buenos Aires.

*Armenia:* 18 Gen Bagramian, Yerevan.

*Australia:* Moonah Place, Yarralumla, Canberra, Australian Capital Territory 2600.

*Austria:* Chancery: Boltzmanngasse 16, A-1091. Unit 27937, Vienna.

*Azerbaijan:* Hotel Intourist, Baku.

*The Bahamas:* Mosmar Building, Queen Street, Nassau.

*Bahrain:* Road 3119 (next to Alahli Sports Club), Zinj District, Manama.

*Bangladesh:* Diplomatic Enclave, Madani Avenue, Baridhara, Dhaka.

*Barbados:* Canadian Imperial Bank of Commerce Building, Broad Street, Bridgetown.

*Belarus:* Starovilenskaya 46, Minsk.

*Belgium:* 27 Boulevard du Régent, Brussels.

*Belize, C.A.:* Gabourel Lane and Hutson Street, Belize City.

*Benin:* Rue Caporal Anani Bernard, Cotonou.

*Bermuda:* U.S. Consulate General, Crown Hill, 16 Middle Road, Devonshire, Hamilton.

*Bolivia:* Banco Popular del Perú Building, corner of Calle Mercado and Colón, La Paz.

*Botswana:* P.O. Box 90, Gaborone.

*Brazil:* Avenida das Nações, Lote 3, Brasilia DF.

*Brunei:* 3rd Floor, Teck Guan Plaza, Jalan Sultan, Bandar Seri Begawan.

*Bulgaria:* 1 Alexander Stamboliski Boulevard, Sofia, Unit 25402.

*Burkina Faso:* Avenue Raoul Follerau, Ouagadougou.

*Burundi:* Avenue des Etats-Unis, Bujumbura.

*Cambodia:* U.S. Mission: 27 EO Street 240, Phnom Penh.

*Cameroon:* Rue Nachtigal, Yaoundé.

*Canada:* 100 Wellington Street, Ottawa, Ontario, K1P 5T1.

*Cape Verde:* Rua Hoji Ya Yenda 81, Praia.

*Central African Republic:* Avenue David Dacko, Bangui.

*Chad:* Avenue Félix Eboué, N'Djaména.

*Chile:* Codina Building, 1343 Agustinas, Santiago.

*China:* Xiu Shui Bei Jie 3, Beijing.

*Colombia:* Calle 38, No. 8-61, Bogotá.

*Comoros:* P.O. Box 1318, Moroni.

*Congo:* Avenue Amílcar Cabral, Brazzaville.

*Costa Rica:* Pavas Road, San Jose.

*Croatia:* Andrije Hebranga 2, Zagreb.

*Cuba:* U.S. Interests Section, USINT, c/o Swiss Embassy, Calzada entre L y M, Vedado Seccion, Havana.

*Cyprus:* corner of Dositheos Street and Therissos Street, Nicosia.

*Czech Republic:* Trziste 15, 125 48, Prague 1.

*Denmark:* Dag Hammarskjølds Allé 24, 2100 Copenhagen Ø.

*Djibouti:* Plateau du Serpent, Boulevard Marechal Joffre.

*Dominican Republic:* corner of Calle César Nicolás Pensón and Calle Leopoldo Navarro, Santo Domingo.

*Ecuador:* Avenida 12 de Octubre and Avenida Patria, Quito.

*Egypt:* Lazougi Street, Garden City, Cairo.

*El Salvador:* Final Boulevard, Station Antigua Cuscatlan, San Salvador.

*Equatorial Guinea:* Calle de Los Ministros, Malabo.

*Estonia:* Kentmanni 20, Tallin EE 0001.

*Ethiopia:* Entoto Street, Addis Ababa.

*Fiji:* 31 Loftus Street, Suva.

*Finland:* Itäinen Puistotie 14A, SF-00140, Helsinki.

*France:* 2 Avenue Gabriel, 75382 Paris Cedex 08, Unit 21551.

*Gabon:* Boulevard de la Mer, Libreville.

*The Gambia:* Pipeline Road (Kairaba Avenue), Fajara, Banjul.

*Georgia:* 25 Antoneli Street, Tbilisi.

*Germany:* Deichmanns Avenue, 5300 Bonn 2, Unit 21701.

*Ghana:* Ring Road East, East of Danquah Circle, Accra.

*Greece:* 91 Vasilissis Sofias Boulevard, 10160 Athens.

*Grenada:* Ross Point Inn, Saint George's.

*Guatemala:* 7-01 Avenida de la Reforma, Zone 10, Guatemala City.

*Guinea:* 2nd Boulevard and 9th Avenue, Conakry.

*Guinea-Bissau:* 17 Avenida Domingos Ramos, Bissau.

*Guyana:* 99-100 Young and Duke Streets, Georgetown.

*Haiti:* Boulevard Harry Truman, Port-au-Prince.

*Honduras, C.A.:* Avenida La Paz, Tegucigalpa.

*Hong Kong:* General Consulate of the United States of America, 26 Garden Road.

*Hungary:* V. Szabadsag Ter 12, Budapest.

*Iceland:* Laufasvegur 21, Box 40, Reykjavik.

*India:* Shanti Path, Chanakyapuri 110021, New Delhi.

*Indonesia:* Medan Merdeka Selatan 5, Jakarta.

*Iraq:* Masbah Quarter (opposite Foreign Ministry Club), Baghdad.

*Ireland:* 42 Elgin Road, Ballsbridge, Dublin.

*Israel:* 71 Hayarkon Street, Tel Aviv.

*Italy:* Via Veneto 119/A, 00187, Rome.

*Ivory Coast:* 5 Rue Jesse Owens, Abidjan.

*Jamaica:* Mutual Life Center, 3rd Floor, 2 Oxford Road, Kingston.

*Japan:* 10-5, Akasaka 1-chome, Minato-ku (107), Tokyo.

*Jordan:* Jebel Amman, Amman.

*Kazakhstan:* Furumanova 99/97, Almaty.

*Kenya:* corner of Moi Avenue and Haile Selassie Avenue, Nairobi.

*Korea, South:* 82 Sejong-Ro, Chongro-ku, Seoul, AM EMB, Unit 15550.

*Kuwait:* Bneid al-Gar (opposite Kuwait International Hotel), Kuwait City.

*Kyrgyzstan (Kirghiza):* Erkindik Prospekt 66, Bishkek (temporary address).

*Laos:* Rue Bartholonie, Vientiane.

*Latvia:* Raina Boulevard 7, Riga 226050.

*Lebanon:* P.O. Box 70-840, Antelias, Beirut.

*Lesotho:* P.O. Box 333, Maseru 100.

*Liberia:* 111 United Nations Drive, Monrovia.

*Lithuania:* Akmenu 6, Vilnius 232600.

*Luxembourg:* 22 Boulevard Emmanuel-Servais, 2535 Luxembourg City.

*Madagascar:* 14 and 16 Rue Rainitovo, Antsahavola, Antananarivo.

*Malawi:* P.O. Box 30016, Lilongwe.

*Malaysia:* 376 Jalan Tun Razak, 50400 Kuala Lumpur.

*Mali:* Rue Rochester NY and Rue Mohamed V, Bamako.

*Malta:* 2nd Floor, Development House, Saint Anne Street, Floriana, Valletta.

*Marshall Islands:* P.O. Box 1379, Majuro.

*Mauritania:* B.P. 222, Nouakchott.

*Mauritius:* 4th Floor, Rogers House, John Kennedy Street, Port Louis.

*Mexico:* Paseo de la Reforma 305, 06500 Mexico, D.F.

*Micronesia:* P.O. Box 1286, Pohnpei 96941.

*Moldova:* Strada Alexei Mateevich 103, Chisinau.

*Mongolia:* Ulaanbaatar, c/o American Embassy Beijing, Micro Region II, Big Rind Road; PSC 461, Box 300, FPO AP 96521-0002.

*Morocco:* 2 Avenue de Marrakech, Rabat.

*Mozambique:* Avenida Kenneth Kuanda, 193 Maputo.

*Myanmar (Burma):* 581 Merchant Street, Yangon (Rangoon).

*Namibia:* Ausplan Building, 14 Lossen Street, Windhoek.

*Nepal:* Pani Pokhari, Kathmandu.

*The Netherlands:* Lange Voorhout 102, The Hague.

*New Zealand:* 29 Fitzherbert Terrace, Thorndon, Wellington.

*Nicaragua:* Kilometer 4.5 Carretera Sur, Managua.

*Niger:* Avenue des Ambassades, Niamey.

*Nigeria:* 2 Eleke Crescent, Lagos.

*Norway:* Drammensveien 18, 0244, Oslo 2.

*Oman:* P.O. Box 50202 Madinat Qaboos, Muscat.

*Pakistan:* Diplomatic Enclave, Ramna 5, Islamabad.

*Panama:* Avenida Balboa and Calle 38, Apartado 6959, Panama City 5.

*Papua New Guinea:* Armit Street, Port Moresby.

*Paraguay:* 1776 Avenida Mariscal Lopez, Asunción.

*Peru:* corner of Avenida Inca Garcilaso de la Vega and Avenida Espana, Lima.

*Philippines:* 1201 Roxas Boulevard, Manila.

*Poland:* Aleja Ujazdowskie 29/31, Warsaw.

*Portugal:* Avenida das Forças Armadas, 1600 Lisbon.

*Qatar:* 149 Ali Bin Ahmed Street, Farig Bin Omran, Doha.

*Romania:* Strada Tudor Arghezi 7-9, Bucharest.

*Russia:* Ulitsa Chaykovskogo 19/21/23, Moscow.

*Rwanda:* Boulevard de la Révolution, Kigali.

*Saudi Arabia:* Collector Road M, Diplomatic Quarter, Riyadh.

*Senegal:* Avenue Jean XXIII at the corner of Avenue Kleber, Dakar.

*Serbia* and *Montenegro:* American Embassy, Box 5070, Unit 25402, APO AE 09213-5070.

*Seychelles:* Victoria House, 4th Floor, Victoria.

*Sierra Leone:* Walpole and Siaka Stevens Street, Freetown.

*Singapore:* 30 Hill Street, Singapore City 0617.

*Slovakia:* Hviczdoslavovo Namestie 4, 81102 Bratislava.

*Slovenia:* P.O. Box 254, Cankarjeva 11, 61000 Ljubljana.

*Solomon Islands:* Mud Alley, Honiara.

*South Africa:* Thibault House, 225 Pretorius Street, Pretoria.

*Spain:* Serrano 75, 28006 Madrid.

*Sri Lanka:* 210 Galle Road, Colombo 3.

*Sudan:* Shar'ia Ali Abdul Latif, Khartoum.

*Suriname:* Dr. Sophie Redmondstraat 129, Paramaribo.

*Swaziland:* Central Bank Building, Warner Street, Mbabane.

*Sweden:* Standvägen 101, S-115 89 Stockholm.

*Switzerland:* Jubilaeumstrasse 93, 3005 Bern.

*Syria:* Abu Rumaneh, Al-Mansur Street, No. 2, Damascus.

*Tajikistan:* 39 Ainii Street, Dushanbe (temporary address).

*Tanzania:* 36 Laibon Road (off Bagamoyo Road), Dar es Salaam.

*Thailand:* 95 Wireless Road, Bangkok.

*Togo:* Rue Pelletier Caventou and Rue Vauban, Lomé.

*Trinidad* and *Tobago:* 15 Queen's Park West, Port-of-Spain.

*Tunisia:* 144 Avenue de la Liberté, 1002 Tunis-Belvédèri.

*Turkey:* 110 Ataturk Boulevard, Ankara.

*Turkmenistan:* Yubilenaya Hotel, Ashgabata (Ashkhabad).

*Uganda:* Parliament Avenue, Kampala.

*Ukraine:* 10 Vul. Yuri Kotsyubinskovo, 252053 Kiev 53.

*United Arab Emirates:* Al-Sudan Street, Abu Dhabi.

*United Kingdom:* 24/31 Grosvenor Square, London, W.1A1AE.

*Uruguay:* Lauro Muller 1776, Montevideo.

*Uzbekistan:* 55 Chelanzanskaya, Tashkent.

*Vatican City:* Villino Pacelli, Via Aurelia 294, 00165 Rome.

*Venezuela:* Avenida Francisco de Miranda and Avenida Principal de la Floresta, Caracas.

*Vietnam:* U.S. Liaison Officer; Hanoi (USLO), 7 Lang Ha, Ba Dinh District.

*Western Samoa:* P.O. Box 3430, Apia.

*Yemen:* Dhahr Himyar Zone, Sheraton Hotel District, Sanaa.

*Zaïre:* 310 Avenue des Aviateurs, Kinshasa.

*Zambia:* corner of Independence Avenue and United Nations Avenue, Lusaka.

*Zimbabwe:* 172 Herbert Chitapo Avenue, Harare.

## FOREIGN EMBASSIES IN THE UNITED STATES

If you need to know something about social, economic, legal, or other matters in another country, you may be able to find an accurate and up-to-date source in the embassy of the country located in the United States. Perhaps you need to know how to address someone (for example, the personal or professional title to use or whether to place the family name first or last), or you may want to check whether a certain gift would be appropriate to give the host in another country. Usually, the staff at a foreign embassy can provide all such answers. The following list contains the addresses of all important foreign embassies in the United States. Since most are located in Washington, D.C., only the ZIP Code is given after the street for Washington addresses.

*Afghanistan:* 2341 Wyoming Avenue, N.W., 20008.

*Albania:* 1511 K Street, N.W., 20036.

*Algeria:* 2118 Kalorama Road, N.W., 20008.

*Antigua* and *Barbuda:* 3400 International Drive, N.W., 20008.

*Argentina:* 1600 New Hampshire Avenue, N.W., 20009.

*Armenia:* 122 C Street, N.W., 20001.

*Australia:* 1601 Massachusetts Avenue, N.W., 20036.

*Austria:* 3524 International Court, N.W., 20008.

*Azerbaijan:* 1615 L Street, N.W., 20036.

*The Bahamas:* 2220 Massachusetts Avenue, N.W., 20008.

*Bahrain:* 3502 International Drive, N.W., 20008.

*Bangladesh:* 2201 Wisconsin Avenue, N.W., 20007.

*Barbados:* 2144 Wyoming Avenue, N.W., 20008.

*Belarus:* 1511 K Street, N.W., 20036.

*Belgium:* 3330 Garfield Street, N.W., 20008.

*Belize:* 2535 Massachusetts Avenue, N.W., 20008.

*Benin:* 2737 Cathedral Avenue, N.W., 20008.

*Bolivia:* 3014 Massachusetts Avenue, N.W., 20008.

*Botswana:* 3400 International Drive, N.W., 20008.

*Brazil:* 3006 Massachusetts Avenue, N.W., 20008.

*Brunei:* 2600 Virginia Avenue, N.W., 20037.

*Bulgaria:* 1621 22nd Street, N.W., 20008.

*Burkina Faso:* 2340 Massachusetts Avenue, N.W., 20008.

*Burundi:* 2233 Wisconsin Avenue, N.W., 20007.

*Cameroon:* 2349 Massachusetts Avenue, N.W., 20008.

*Canada:* 501 Pennsylvania Avenue, N.W., 20001.

*Cape Verde:* 3415 Massachusetts Avenue, N.W., 20007.

*Central African Republic:* 1618 22nd Street, N.W., 20008.

*Chad:* 2002 R Street, N.W., 20009.

*Chile:* 1732 Massachusetts Avenue, N.W., 20036.

*China:* 2300 Connecticut Avenue, N.W., 20008.

*Colombia:* 2118 Leroy Place, N.W., 20008.

*Comoros:* 336 East 45 Street, New York, NY 10017 (temporary address).

*Congo:* 4891 Colorado Avenue, N.W., 20011.

*Costa Rica:* 1825 Connecticut Avenue, N.W., 20009.

*Croatia:* 2356 Massachusetts Avenue, N.W., 20036.

*Cuba:* 2630 and 2639 16th Street, N.W., U.S. Interests Section, Swiss Embassy, 20009.

*Cyprus:* 2211 R Street, N.W., 20008.

*Czech Republic:* 3900 Spring of Freedom Street, N.W., 20008.

*Denmark:* 3200 Whitehaven Street, N.W., 20008.

*Djibouti:* 1156 15th Street, N.W., 20005.

*Dominican Republic:* 1715 22nd Street, N.W., 20008.

*Ecuador:* 2535 15th Street, N.W., 20009.

*Egypt:* 2310 Decatur Place, N.W., 20008.

*El Salvador:* 2308 California Street, N.W., 20008.

*Equatorial Guinea:* 57 Magnolia Avenue, Mount Vernon, NY 10553 (temporary address).

*Estonia:* 630 Fifth Avenue, New York, NY 10111 (temporary address).

*Ethiopia:* 2134 Kalorama Road, N.W., 20008.

*Fiji:* 2233 Wisconsin Avenue, N.W., 20007.

*Finland:* 3216 New Mexico Avenue, N.W., 20016.

*France:* 4101 Reservoir Road, N.W., 20007.

*Gabon:* 2034 20th Street, N.W., 20009.

*The Gambia:* 1030 15th Street, N.W., 20005.

*Germany:* 4645 Reservoir Road, N.W., 20007.

*Ghana:* 3512 International Drive, N.W., 20008.

*Greece:* 2221 Massachusetts Avenue, N.W., 20008.

*Grenada:* 1701 New Hampshire Avenue, N.W., 20009.

*Guatemala:* 2220 R Street, N.W., 20008.

*Guinea:* 2112 Leroy Place, N.W., 20008.

*Guinea-Bissau:* 918 16th Street, N.W., 20006.

*Guyana:* 2490 Tracy Place, N.W., 20008.

*Haiti:* 2311 Massachusetts Avenue, N.W., 20008.

*Honduras:* 3007 Tilden Street, N.W., 20008.

*Hungary:* 3910 Shoemaker Street, N.W., 20008.

*Iceland:* 2022 Connecticut Avenue, N.W., 20008.

*India:* 2107 Massachusetts Avenue, N.W., 20008.

*Indonesia:* 2020 Massachusetts Avenue, N.W., 20036.

*Iran:* Iranian Interests Section, 2209 Wisconsin Avenue, N.W., 20007.

*Iraq:* Iraqi Interests Section, 1801 P Street, N.W., 20036.

*Ireland:* 2234 Massachusetts Avenue, N.W., 20008.

*Israel:* 3514 International Drive, N.W., 20008.

*Italy:* 1601 Fuller Street, N.W., 20009.

*Ivory Coast:* 2424 Massachusetts Avenue, N.W., 20008.

*Jamaica:* 1850 K Street, N.W., 20006.

*Japan:* 2520 Massachusetts Avenue, N.W., 20008.

*Jordan:* 3504 International Drive, N.W., 20008.

*Kazakhstan:* 3421 Massachusetts Avenue, N.W., 20007.

*Kenya:* 2249 R Street, N.W., 20008.

*Korea, South:* 2370 Massachusetts Avenue, N.W., 20008.

*Kuwait:* 2940 Tilden Street, N.W., 20008.

*Kyrgyzstan (Kirghizia):* 1511 K Street, N.W., 20036.

*Laos:* 2222 S Street, N.W., 20008.

*Latvia:* 4325 17th Street, N.W., 20011.

*Lebanon:* 2560 28th Street, N.W., 20008.

*Lesotho:* 2511 Massachusetts Avenue, N.W., 20008.

*Liberia:* 5201 16th Street, N.W., 20011.

*Lithuania:* 2622 16th Street, N.W., 20009.

*Luxembourg:* 2200 Massachusetts Avenue, N.W., 20008.

*Madagascar:* 2374 Massachusetts Avenue, N.W., 20008.

*Malawi:* 2408 Massachusetts Avenue, N.W., 20008.

*Malaysia:* 2401 Massachusetts Avenue, N.W., 20008.

*Mali:* 2130 R Street, N.W., 20008.

*Malta:* 2017 Connecticut Avenue, N.W., 20008.

*Marshall Islands:* 2433 Massachusetts Avenue, N.W., 20008.

*Mauritania:* 2129 Leroy Place, N.W., 20008.

*Mauritius:* 4301 Connecticut Avenue, N.W., 20008.

*Mexico:* 1911 Pennsylvania Avenue, N.W., 20006.

*Micronesia:* 1725 N Street, N.W., 20036.

*Morocco:* 1601 21st Street, N.W., 20009.

*Myanmar (Burma):* 2300 S Street, N.W., 20008.

*Namibia:* 1605 New Hampshire Avenue, N.W., 20009.

*Nepal:* 2131 Leroy Place, N.W., 20008.

*The Netherlands:* 4200 Linnean Avenue, N.W., 20008.

*New Zealand:* 37 Observatory Circle, N.W., 20008.

*Nicaragua:* 1627 New Hampshire Avenue, N.W., 20009.

*Niger:* 2204 R Street, N.W., 20008.

*Nigeria:* 2201 M Street, N.W., 20037.

*Norway:* 2720 34th Street, N.W., 20008.

*Oman:* 2342 Massachusetts Avenue, N.W., 20008.

*Pakistan:* 2315 Massachusetts Avenue, N.W., 20008.

*Panama:* 2862 McGill Terrace, N.W., 20008.

*Papua New Guinea:* 1615 New Hampshire Avenue, N.W., 20009.

*Paraguay:* 2400 Massachusetts Avenue, N.W., 20008.

*Peru:* 1700 Massachusetts Avenue, N.W., 20036.

*Philippines:* 1617 Massachusetts Avenue, N.W., 20036.

*Poland:* 2640 16th Street, N.W., 20009.

*Portugal:* 2125 Kalorama Road, N.W., 20008.

*Qatar:* 600 New Hampshire Avenue, N.W., 20037.

*Romania:* 1607 23rd Street, N.W., 20008.

*Russia:* 1125 16th Street, N.W., 20036.

*Rwanda:* 1714 New Hampshire Avenue, N.W., 20009.

*São Tomé* and *Príncipe:* 801 Second Avenue, New York, NY 10017 (temporary address).

*Saudi Arabia:* 601 New Hampshire Avenue, N.W., 20037.

*Senegal:* 2112 Wyoming Avenue, N.W., 20008.

*Seychelles:* 820 Second Avenue, New York, NY 10017 (temporary address).

*Sierra Leone:* 1701 19th Street, N.W., 20009.

*Singapore:* 1824 R Street, N.W., 20009.

*Slovakia:* 3900 Spring of Freedom Street, N.W., 20008.

*Slovenia:* 1300 19th Street, N.W., 20036 (temporary address).

*Somalia:* 600 New Hampshire Avenue, N.W., 20037.

*South Africa:* 3051 Massachusetts Avenue, N.W., 20008.

*Spain:* 2700 15th Street, N.W., 20009.

*Sri Lanka:* 2148 Wyoming Avenue, N.W., 20008.

*Sudan:* 2210 Massachusetts Avenue, N.W., 20008.

*Suriname:* 4301 Connecticut Avenue, N.W., 20008.

*Swaziland:* 3400 International Drive, N.W., 20008.

*Sweden:* 600 New Hampshire Avenue, N.W., 20037.

*Switzerland:* 2900 Cathedral Avenue, N.W., 20008.

*Syria:* 2215 Wyoming Avenue, N.W., 20008.

*Tanzania:* 2139 R Street, N.W., 20008.

*Thailand:* 2300 Kalorama Road, N.W., 20008.

*Togo:* 2208 Massachusetts Avenue, N.W., 20008.

*Trinidad* and *Tobago:* 1708 Massachusetts Avenue, N.W., 20036.

*Tunisia:* 1515 Massachusetts Avenue, N.W., 20005.

*Turkey:* 1714 Massachusetts Avenue, N.W., 20036.

*Uganda:* 5909 16th Street, N.W., 20011.

*Ukraine:* 3350 M Street, N.W., 20007.

*United Arab Emirates:* 600 New Hampshire Avenue, N.W., 20037.

*United Kingdom:* 3100 Massachusetts Avenue, N.W., 20008.

*Uruguay:* 1918 F Street, N.W., 20006.

*Uzbekistan:* 200 Pennsylvania Avenue, N.W., 20006.

*Venezuela:* 1099 30th Street, N.W., 20007.

*Vietnam:* Liaison Officer, 1233 20th Street, N.W., Suite 501, 20036.

*Western Samoa:* 1155 15th Street, N.W., 20005 (temporary address).

*Yemen:* 600 New Hampshire Avenue, N.W., 20037.

*Zaïre:* 1800 New Hampshire Avenue, N.W., 20009.

*Zambia:* 2419 Massachusetts Avenue, N.W., 20008.

*Zimbabwe:* 1608 New Hampshire Avenue, N.W., 20009.

# PART TWO

# LANGUAGE SKILLS

# GRAMMAR

## THE EIGHT PARTS OF SPEECH THAT YOU USE EVERY DAY

Office professionals who are concerned about their language skills must have a basic understanding of the parts of speech that they use every day. The parts of speech (adjective, adverb, conjunction, interjection, noun, preposition, pronoun, and verb) describe the grammatical function of words as used in a particular context.

1. *Adjective.* A word that modifies (describes or limits) a noun or pronoun: *busy* office, *two* secretaries. Different types of adjectives (e.g., adjective pronoun) are defined in the next section.

2. *Adverb.* A word that modifies a verb (*eagerly* complied), an adjective (*very* hopeful candidate), another adverb (*exceptionally* well planned), or a clause or sentence (*Unfortunately*, the company lost money). The relative adverb is defined in the next section.

3. *Conjunction.* A word that connects or shows the relationship between other words, phrases, clauses, or sentences: John *and* Nancy will coauthor the report. See also the lists of coordinate, subordinate, and correlative conjunctions later in this chapter.

4. *Interjection.* A word expressing sudden or strong feeling: *Oh! Great!*

5. *Noun.* A word that names a person (*Helen*), place (*Los Angeles*), thing (*car*), idea (*proposition*), action (*visit*), or quality (*perfection*). Different types of nouns (e.g., collective noun) are defined in the next section.

6. *Preposition.* A word that shows the relationship between its object and an antecedent: The manager *went* [antecedent] *to* [preposition] the *convention* [object of the preposition *to*]. See also the forthcoming list of prepositions and prepositional phrases and the definitions of prepositional phrases and phrasal prepositions in the next section.

7. *Pronoun.* A word that takes the place of a noun: *We* [Sam and Lois] would like to put the matter to a vote. The seven classes of pronouns are defined in the next section.

8. *Verb.* A word that expresses action (*call*) or state of being (*appear*). Different types of verbs (e.g., auxiliary) are defined in the next section.

## THE MOST IMPORTANT GRAMMATICAL TERMS

Correct grammar is an essential component of effective communication, the goal of every office professional. The following list contains dozens of important grammatical terms, as well as cross-references to other sections where additional terms are defined. These terms are used to describe how words must be properly combined to form intelligent, understandable sentences in business communication.

*Active voice.* A verb that indicates that the subject of a sentence is performing the action: I *developed* the new system.

*Adjective.* See the definition in the previous section. See also ADJECTIVE PRONOUN, PREDICATE ADJECTIVE, and RELATIVE ADJECTIVE.

*Adjective pronoun.* A pronoun that modifies a noun: *Most* [adjective pronoun] *businesspeople* [noun] participate in regular meetings. It includes DEMONSTRATIVE, RELATIVE, and all INDEFINITE PRONOUNS, except *none, another, any, both, each, either, neither, one, other, some, such.*

*Adverb.* See the definition in the previous section. See also RELATIVE ADVERB.

*Antecedent.* The noun or pronoun to which another pronoun refers: *Mr. Wyatt* [noun] is always at *his* [pronoun] desk by 8 A.M.

*Appositive.* A word or words that identify or explain another word or words: Anne Simmons, *advertising manager*, will make the presentation.

*Article.* The adjectives *a* and *an* (indefinite articles) and *the* (definite article): *The* report is due Friday.

*Auxiliary verb.* A linking verb (e.g., *be, must*) used with a principal verb that together forms a verb phrase: He *should* [auxiliary] *think* [principal] before he speaks.

*Case.* The relationship of a noun or pronoun to other words in a sentence. See NOMINATIVE CASE, OBJECTIVE CASE, and POSSESSIVE CASE.

*Collective noun.* A noun (e.g., *family, committee*) that denotes a group or collection of objects: The *members* will elect a new board in January.

*Common noun.* A noun (e.g., *bus, book*) that denotes a class of persons, places, or things: The *secretary* has two assistants.

*Comparative degree.* A form of adverb or adjective used to compare two persons or things: Our dot-matrix printer is *faster* than our laser printer, but it is *less* reliable than our laser printer.

*Comparison.* The form of an adjective or adverb used to show the degree of comparison. See COMPARATIVE DEGREE and SUPERLATIVE DEGREE.

*Complement.* A word or words that complete the meaning of a verb: The power surge caused the *damage*.

*Compound predicate.* The part of a sentence consisting of two or more connected verbs or verb phrases: He *researched* and *wrote* the article.

*Compound sentence.* Two or more independent clauses that are connected: She consulted an attorney, and on October 1 she filed a complaint.

*Compound subject.* The part of a sentence consisting of two or more words joined by *and, or,* or *nor:* The *secretary* and the *supervisor* agreed that the deadline was unrealistic.

*Compound term.* Two or more words expressing a single idea that are written together as one word, joined by a hyphen, or written as separate words: *Businesspeople* are always concerned with effective communication.

*Conjunction.* See the definition in the previous section. See also COORDINATE CONJUNCTION, CORRELATIVE CONJUNCTION, and SUBORDINATE CONJUNCTION.

*Coordinate conjunction.* A conjunction (e.g., *or, but*) that connects words, phrases, or clauses of equal value or rank: Mr. Hill *and* Mr. Lewis will develop a program.

*Correlative conjunction.* A conjunction used in pairs or a series: The manager *not only* is a good speaker *but also* is a skilled writer.

*Dangling modifier.* A word or words that do not refer to or modify another word: *After filing* [dangling] the claim, the matter was closed. *Better: After filing* the claim, *the director* said the matter was closed.

*Demonstrative pronoun.* A pronoun (e.g., *that, those*) that may stand alone or refer to an antecedent [noun] directly or demonstratively: *This* [pronoun] *computer* [noun] has expanded memory.

*Dependent (subordinate) clause.* A group of words in a sentence consisting of a subject and predicate that alone does not express a complete thought: The cabinet *that has a lock on it* is available only to authorized personnel.

*Direct object.* A noun or noun equivalent receiving a verb's action and often answering the question *what* or *whom* after the verb: The secretary purchased [*what?*] the *supplies.*

*Expletive.* An introductory word (e.g., *it, there*) occupying the position of the subject while the actual subject comes after the verb: *There* are two ways that we can approach this problem. *Better:* We can approach this problem in two ways.

*Gerund.* A verb form ending in *-ing* used as a noun; it may be a SUBJECT, a DIRECT OBJECT, an object of a preposition (see the previous section), a subjective COMPLEMENT, or an APPOSITIVE: Writing [subject] is a form of therapy for him.

*Imperative mood.* An expression that states a command, wish, or something similar: *Run* off three copies when you're finished typing.

*Indefinite pronoun.* A pronoun (e.g., *all, something*) that stands for an object generally or indefinitely: *Few* of us will succeed on luck alone.

*Indicative mood.* An expression that states or questions a fact: This *is* your notebook. *Is* this your notebook?

*Indirect object.* A noun or noun equivalent that usually indicates to whom or for whom something is done; it may precede the direct object: The secretary gave her *boss* [indirect object] the *message* [direct object].

*Infinitive.* A verb form used as a noun, an adjective, or an adverb; the verb (e.g., *go*) is usually preceded by *to:* The staff wants *to go* to the convention.

*Interjection.* See the definition in the preceding section.

*Interrogative pronoun.* A pronoun (e.g., *whose, which*) that asks a question: *Who* will volunteer for the assignment?

*Intransitive verb.* A verb that has no object: He *works* rapidly.

*Irregular verb.* A verb that forms the past and past participle in different ways (e.g., *blow, blew, blown*). See the list later in this chapter.

*Misplaced modifier.* A modifier positioned in a sentence where it seems to modify the wrong word: He *only* [misplaced] ordered the computer paper. *Better:* He ordered *only* the computer paper.

*Modifier.* A word or group of words restricting or qualifying the meaning of another word. See the definitions of adjectives and adverbs in the previous section.

*Mood.* The form of a verb used to show the attitude of a speaker or writer. See IMPERATIVE MOOD, INDICATIVE MOOD, and SUBJUNCTIVE MOOD.

*Nominative case.* The CASE of a subject or a predicate noun: The *instructor* [subject] is a *physicist* [predicate noun].

*Nonrestrictive clause.* A subordinate clause, usually set off with commas, that is not essential to the meaning of a sentence: The new policy, *which is difficult to understand,* will take effect in January.

*Noun.* See the definition in the previous section. See also COLLECTIVE NOUN, COMMON NOUN, and PROPER NOUN.

*Objective case.* The CASE of a DIRECT OBJECT, an INDIRECT OBJECT, or the object of a preposition (see the previous section): The regional manager sent *him* [indirect object of *sent*] the *proposal* [direct object of *sent*] to submit to the *general manager* [object of preposition *to*].

*Participle.* A verb form used as an adjective or a predicate adjective; the present participle ends in *-ing:* The *increasing* work load is causing numerous delays.

*Passive voice.* A verb indicating that the subject is receiving an action: The new system *was developed* by me.

*Person.* A term used to identify the person speaking *(I),* spoken to *(you),* or spoken of *(he, she, it, they, we):* I [first person] have to leave. *You* [second person] have to leave. *He* [third person] has to leave.

*Personal pronoun.* A pronoun (e.g., *you, she*) indicating whether reference is to the person speaking, spoken to, or spoken of. See PERSON.

*Phrasal preposition.* Two or more words (e.g., *along with*) regarded as a single preposition. See examples in the next section.

*Possessive case.* The CASE that shows possession: The *secretary's* previous employer asked her to return to the company.

*Predicate.* The part of a sentence containing a verb and other words that makes a statement about the subject: The fax machine *will transmit wide documents.*

*Predicate adjective.* An adjective following an AUXILIARY VERB: The president *is* [auxiliary verb] *well known* [predicate adjective] in the industry.

*Preposition.* See the definition in the previous section. See also PREPOSITIONAL PHRASE and PHRASAL PREPOSITION.

*Prepositional phrase.* A preposition, its object, and any modifiers of the object: He is the owner *of the new computer service.*

*Pronoun.* See the definition in the previous section. See also ADJECTIVE PRONOUN, DEMONSTRATIVE PRONOUN, INDEFINITE PRONOUN, INTERROGATIVE PRONOUN, PERSONAL PRONOUN, REFLEXIVE OR INTENSIVE PRONOUN, and RELATIVE PRONOUN.

*Proper noun.* A word or words (e.g., *Newsweek, John Jones*) that name a particular person, place, or thing: Both *Arabic* and *French* are spoken in *Tunisia.*

*Reflexive* or *intensive pronoun.* A pronoun (e.g., *himself, themselves*) formed by adding *-self* or *-selves* to a PERSONAL or INDEFINITE PRONOUN: I will handle it *myself.*

*Relative adjective.* A relative pronoun (e.g., *who, what*) used as an adjective: The sales manager is the one *whose* hours are the most flexible.

*Relative adverb.* An adverb (e.g., *where, why*) referring to an antecedent in the main clause but modifying a word in the subordinate clause: The president scheduled a meeting for Tuesday *when* a majority would be able to attend.

*Relative pronoun.* A pronoun (e.g., *who, which*) relating an antecedent to a dependent or qualifying clause: It is the *public contact* [antecedent] *that* [relative pronoun] makes secretarial work interesting.

*Restrictive clause.* A subordinate clause that is essential to a sentence's meaning and should not be set off with commas: The computer *with two disk drives* has been moved to another office.

*Subject.* The part of a sentence about which a statement is made in the PREDICATE: *The department manager* expects the machine to be on-line by the end of the day.

*Subjunctive mood.* An expression of an action or state of being as desired, doubtful, or contrary to fact: I wish she *were* in charge.

*Subordinate conjunction.* A conjunction (e.g., *as, unless*) connecting a subordinate clause to the principal clause in a sentence: *I will let you know* [principal clause] *when* [subordinate conjunction] the supplies arrive.

*Superlative degree.* A form of adverb or adjective used to compare more than two persons or things and formed by adding *-est* to a word or by placing *most* or *least* before the word: Our dot-matrix printer is the *fastest* of our three printers, but our laser printer is the *most* reliable.

*Tense.* The form of a verb that indicates the time of an action or state of being. The six tenses of a verb are defined later in this chapter.

*Transitive verb.* A verb that has an object: They *prepared* [transitive verb] a new *statement* [object].

*Verb.* See the definition in the previous section. See also AUXILIARY VERB, INTRANSITIVE VERB, IRREGULAR VERB, and TRANSITIVE VERB.

*Verbal.* A verb form used as another part of speech. See GERUND, INFINITIVE, and PARTICIPLE.

*Voice.* The form of a verb indicating whether a subject is the doer or receiver of an action. See ACTIVE VOICE and PASSIVE VOICE.


# THE MOST FAMILIAR PREPOSITIONS IN THE ENGLISH LANGUAGE

Prepositions abound in both business writing and speech, and the English language has more than 150 common prepositions and phrasal (compound) prepositions. The following list contains the most familiar of them, although many of these words also function as other parts of speech. *Around,* for example, may be used as an adjective or adverb as well as a preposition. Consult a dictionary for further information on correct usage.


*Prepositions*

| | | |
|---|---|---|
| aboard | among(st) | beneath |
| about | around | beside(s) |
| above | aslant | between |
| across | at | betwixt |
| after | athwart | beyond |
| against | barring | but |
| along | before | by |
| alongside | behind | concerning |
| amid(st) | below | considering |

| despite | off | through |
|---|---|---|
| down | on | throughout |
| during | onto (or on to) | till |
| ere | opposite | to |
| except(ing) | out | touching |
| for | outside | toward(s) |
| from | over | under |
| in | past | underneath |
| inside | pending | until (*or* till) |
| into | per | unto |
| like | regarding | up |
| mid | respecting | upon |
| midst | round | via |
| near | save | with |
| notwithstanding | saving | within |
| of | since | without |

### *Phrasal Prepositions*

| according to | by dint of | from over |
|---|---|---|
| ahead of | by means of | from under |
| along with | by reason of | in accordance with |
| alongside of | by virtue of | in addition to |
| apart from | by way of | in apposition with |
| as against | contrary to | in back of |
| as between | due to | in behalf of |
| as compared with | except for | in case of |
| as for | exclusive of | inclusive of |
| aside from | for the sake of | in comparison to |
| astern of | from above | in comparison with |
| as to | from among | in compliance with |
| as well as | from behind | in consequence of |
| away from | from beneath | in consideration of |
| because of | from between | in default of |

| | | |
|---|---|---|
| independently of | instead of | relative to |
| in front of | in view of | round about |
| in lieu of | on account of | up to |
| in opposition to | on behalf of | with a view to |
| in place of | opposite to | without regard to |
| in preference to | out of | with reference to |
| in reference to | outside of | with regard to |
| in regard to | over | with respect to |
| in respect to | owing to | with the intention of |
| inside of | regardless of | with the view of |
| in spite of | relating to | |

## A SAMPLER OF COMMON COORDINATE, SUBORDINATE, AND CORRELATIVE CONJUNCTIONS

The three types of conjunctions described in the second section of this chapter are included in this list of nearly a hundred common conjunctions. Some of the words, however, also function as other parts of speech. *Since,* for example, is also used as an adverb and a preposition. Consult a dictionary for further information.

| | | |
|---|---|---|
| after | before | in case |
| also | both | inasmuch as |
| although | both . . . and | in order that |
| although . . . yet | but | in spite of |
| and | but that | in that |
| as | either | lest |
| as . . . as | either . . . or | neither |
| as if | even if | neither . . . nor |
| as long as | except for | nevertheless |
| as often as | for the purpose of | nor |
| as . . . so | how | not only . . . but also |
| as soon as | however | notwithstanding |
| as though | if | now . . . now |
| because | if . . . then | now that |

| | | |
|---|---|---|
| now . . . then | therefore | wherefore |
| only | though | wherein |
| or | though . . . yet | whereof |
| provided | till | whereupon |
| provided that | unless | wherever |
| save | until | whether |
| seeing | what | whether . . . or |
| since | whatever | which |
| so | when | whichever |
| so . . . as | whence | while |
| so . . . as (that) | whenever | whither |
| so that | where | who |
| still | whereas | whoever |
| such . . . as (that) | whereas . . . therefore | why |
| than | whereat | with a view to |
| that | whereby | without |
| then | wherever | yet |

## THE PRESENT, PAST, AND PAST PARTICIPLE OF MORE THAN ONE HUNDRED COMMON IRREGULAR VERBS

Regular verbs are easily recognized since both the past and the past participle tenses are formed by adding -*d* or -*ed: call, called, had called.* But irregular verbs form the past tense and past participle in different ways. This list provides the forms for more than one hundred common irregular verbs. (*Note:* In using the past participle, place *have, has,* or *had* before the form listed here.)

| *Present* | *Past* | *Past Participle* |
|---|---|---|
| abide | abided/abode | abided/abode |
| awake | awaked/awoke | awaked/awoke |
| arise | arose | arisen |
| be (am) | was | been |
| bear | bore | borne |
| beat | beat | beaten/beat |

| *Present* | *Past* | *Past Participle* |
|---|---|---|
| become | became | become |
| begin | began | begun |
| behold | beheld | beheld |
| bid (*offer to buy*) | bid | bid |
| bid (*command*) | bade | bidden/bid |
| bind | bound | bound |
| bite | bit | bitten |
| bleed | bled | bled |
| blow | blew | blown |
| break | broke | broken |
| breed | bred | bred |
| bring | brought | brought |
| broadcast | broadcast/broadcasted | broadcast/broadcasted |
| build | built | built |
| burst | burst | burst |
| buy | bought | bought |
| cast | cast | cast |
| catch | caught | caught |
| choose | chose | chosen |
| cleave | cleft/clove/cleaved | cleft/cloven |
| cling | clung | clung |
| come | came | come |
| cost | cost | cost |
| creep | crept | crept |
| cut | cut | cut |
| deal | dealt | dealt |
| do | did | done |
| draw | drew | drawn |
| drink | drank | drunk |
| drive | drove | driven |
| eat | ate | eaten |
| fall | fell | fallen |
| feed | fed | fed |

| Present | Past | Past Participle |
|---|---|---|
| feel | felt | felt |
| fight | fought | fought |
| find | found | found |
| flee | fled | fled |
| fling | flung | flung |
| fly | flew | flown |
| forbid | forbade | forbidden |
| forget | forgot | forgotten |
| forsake | forsook | forsaken |
| freeze | froze | frozen |
| get | got | got/gotten |
| give | gave | given |
| go | went | gone |
| grind | ground | ground |
| grow | grew | grown |
| hang (*a picture*) | hung | hung |
| have | had | had |
| hide | hid | hidden |
| hit | hit | hit |
| hold | held | held |
| hurt | hurt | hurt |
| keep | kept | kept |
| know | knew | known |
| lay (*place or put*) | laid | laid |
| lead | led | led |
| leave | left | left |
| lend | lent | lent |
| let | let | let |
| lie (*recline*) | lay | lain |
| lose | lost | lost |
| make | made | made |
| mean | meant | meant |
| meet | met | met |

| *Present* | *Past* | *Past Participle* |
|---|---|---|
| mistake | mistook | mistaken |
| pay | paid | paid |
| put | put | put |
| read | read | read |
| rid | rid | rid |
| ride | rode | ridden |
| ring | rang | rung |
| rise | rose | risen |
| run | ran | run |
| say | said | said |
| see | saw | seen |
| seek | sought | sought |
| sell | sold | sold |
| send | sent | sent |
| set | set | set |
| shake | shook | shaken |
| shed | shed | shed |
| shine (*give light*) | shone | shone |
| shoot | shot | shot |
| show | showed | shown/showed |
| shrink | shrank/shrunk | shrunk/shrunken |
| shut | shut | shut |
| sing | sang | sung |
| sink | sank | sunk |
| sit | sat | sat |
| sleep | slept | slept |
| slide | slid | slid |
| sling | slung | slung |
| speak | spoke | spoken |
| speed | sped | sped |
| spend | spent | spent |
| spill | spilt/spilled | spilled |
| spin | spun | spun |

| Present | Past | Past Participle |
|---------|------|-----------------|
| spit | spat | spat |
| split | split | split |
| spread | spread | spread |
| spring | sprang/sprung | sprung |
| stand | stood | stood |
| steal | stole | stolen |
| stick | stuck | stuck |
| sting | stung | stung |
| stink | stank | stunk |
| strike | struck | struck/stricken |
| string | strung | strung |
| strive | strove | striven |
| swear | swore | sworn |
| sweep | swept | swept |
| swim | swam | swum |
| take | took | taken |
| teach | taught | taught |
| tear | tore | torn |
| tell | told | told |
| think | thought | thought |
| thrive | throve/thrived | thrived/thriven |
| throw | threw | thrown |
| thrust | thrust | thrust |
| tread | trod | trodden |
| understand | understood | understood |
| wake | waked/woke | waked |
| wear | wore | worn |
| weave | wove | woven |
| weep | wept | wept |
| win | won | won |
| wind | wound | wound |
| wring | wrung | wrung |
| write | wrote | written |

# THE SIX VERB TENSES THAT DENOTE TIME

The particular verb tense that you use tells readers and listeners when the action takes place. In addition to the three basic time divisions of past, present, and future, there are three other tenses that describe when an act may be completed: present perfect, past perfect, and future perfect.

1. *Present.* The present tense refers to something occurring now or to something that is generally true: He *speaks* clearly. To form the progressive present, add a form of the verb *to be*: He *is speaking* clearly.

2. *Present perfect.* The present perfect tense refers to something either completed at the time it is mentioned or continuing into the present and is formed by combining the past participle of the main verb with *has* or *have:* I *have called* that number many times.

3. *Past.* The past tense refers to something already completed: He *arrived* yesterday.

4. *Past perfect.* The past perfect tense refers to something completed before a specific time in the past and is formed by combining the past participle of the main verb with *had:* By the end of the day, he *had reached* the same conclusion.

5. *Future.* The future tense refers to something that will happen at a future time and is formed by combining the main verb with *shall* or *will:* He *will decide* after hearing both sides of the issue.

6. *Future perfect.* The future perfect tense refers to something that will be completed at a specific time in the future and is formed by combining the past participle of the main verb with *shall have* or *will have*: By Friday, she *will have finished* the essay.

# A GUIDE TO THE NOUNS AND ADJECTIVES THAT DENOTE NATIONALITY AROUND THE WORLD

For businesspeople involved in international trade, using the correct nouns and adjectives denoting nationality is mandatory to avoid offending someone in another country. A *Filipino* (noun), for example, is part of *Philippine* (adjective) society. The following list gives the common form for major countries around the world.

| Country | Noun | Adjective |
|---|---|---|
| Afghanistan | Afghan(s) | Afghan |
| Albania | Albanian(s) | Albanian |
| Algeria | Algerian(s) | Algerian |
| Andorra | Andorran(s) | Andorran |
| Angola | Angolan(s) | Angolan |
| Antigua and Barbuda | Antiguan(s) | Antiguan |
| Argentina | Argentine(s) | Argentine |
| Armenia | Armenian(s) | Armenian |
| Australia | Australian(s) | Australian |
| Austria | Austrian(s) | Austrian |
| Azerbaijan | Azerbaijani(s) *or* Azeri(s) | Azerbaijani |
| Bahamas | Bahamian(s) | Bahamian |
| Bahrain | Bahraini(s) | Bahraini |
| Bangladesh | Bangladeshi(s) | Bangladesh |
| Barbados | Barbadian(s) | Barbadian |
| Belarus | Belorussian(s) | Belorussian |
| Belgium | Belgian(s) | Belgian |
| Belize | Belizean(s) | Belizean |
| Benin | Beninese | Beninese |
| Bhutan | Bhutanese | Bhutanese |
| Bolivia | Bolivian(s) | Bolivian |
| Bosnia-Herzegovenia | Bosnian(s) | Bosnian |
| Botswana | Motswana *(sing.)* Batswana *(pl.)* | Batswana or Botswanan |
| Brazil | Brazilian(s) | Brazilian |
| Brunei | Bruneian(s) | Bruneian |
| Bulgaria | Bulgarian(s) | Bulgarian |
| Burkina Faso | Burkinabe | Burkinabe |
| Burundi | Burundian(s) | Burundi |
| Cambodia (Kampuchea) | Cambodian(s) (Kampuchean[s]) | Cambodian (Kampuchean) |
| Cameroon | Cameroonian(s) | Cameroonian |
| Canada | Canadian(s) | Canadian |

| Country | Noun | Adjective |
|---|---|---|
| Cape Verde | Cape Verdean(s) | Cape Verdean |
| Central African Republic | Central African(s) | Central African |
| Chad | Chadian(s) | Chadian |
| Chile | Chilean(s) | Chilean |
| China | Chinese | Chinese |
| Colombia | Colombian(s) | Colombian |
| Comoros | Comoran(s) | Comoran |
| Congo | Congolese | Congolese or Congo |
| Costa Rica | Costa Rican(s) | Costa Rican |
| Croatia | Croatian(s) | Croatian |
| Cuba | Cuban(s) | Cuban |
| Cyprus | Cypriot(s) | Cypriot |
| Czech Republic | Czech(s) | Czech |
| Denmark | Dane(s) | Danish |
| Djibouti | Djiboutian | Djiboutian |
| Dominica | Dominican(s) | Dominican |
| Dominican Republic | Dominican(s) | Dominican |
| Ecuador | Ecuadorian(s) | Ecuadorian |
| Egypt | Egyptian(s) | Egyptian |
| El Salvador | Salvadoran(s) | Salvadoran |
| Equatorial Guinea | Equatorial Guinean(s) | Equatorial Guinean |
| Eritrea | Eritrean(s) | Eritrean |
| Estonia | Estonian(s) | Estonian |
| Ethiopia | Ethiopian(s) | Ethiopian |
| Fiji | Fijian(s) | Fijian |
| Finland | Finn(s) | Finnish |
| France | Frenchman, Frenchwoman | French |
| Gabon | Gabonese | Gabonese |
| The Gambia | Gambian(s) | Gambian |
| Georgia | Georgian(s) | Georgian |

| Country | Noun | Adjective |
|---|---|---|
| Germany | German(s) | German |
| Ghana | Ghanaian | Ghanaian |
| Greece | Greek(s) | Greek |
| Grenada | Grenadian(s) | Grenadian |
| Guatemala | Guatemalan(s) | Guatemalan |
| Guinea | Guinean(s) | Guinean |
| Guinea-Bissau | Guinea-Bissauan(s) | Guinea-Bissauan |
| Guyana | Guyanese | Guyanese |
| Haiti | Haitian(s) | Haitian |
| Honduras | Honduran(s) | Honduran |
| Hungary | Hungarian(s) | Hungarian |
| Iceland | Icelander(s) | Icelandic |
| India | Indian(s) | Indian |
| Indonesia | Indonesian(s) | Indonesian |
| Iran | Iranian(s) | Iranian |
| Iraq | Iraqi(s) | Iraqi |
| Ireland | Irishman, Irishwoman *(sing.),* Irish *(pl.)* | Irish |
| Israel | Israeli(s) | Israeli |
| Italy | Italian(s) | Italian |
| Ivory Coast (Côte d'Ivoire) | Ivorian(s) | Ivorian |
| Jamaica | Jamaican(s) | Jamaican |
| Japan | Japanese | Japanese |
| Jordan | Jordanian(s) | Jordanian |
| Kazakhstan | Kazakh(s) | Kazakh |
| Kenya | Kenyan(s) | Kenyan |
| Kiribati | Kiribatian(s) | Kiribati |
| Korea, North | Korean(s) | Korean |
| Korea, South | Korean(s) | Korean |
| Kuwait | Kuwaiti(s) | Kuwaiti |
| Kyrgyzstan (Kirghizia) | Kyrgyz (Kirghiz) | Kyrgyz (Kirghiz) |

| Country | Noun | Adjective |
|---|---|---|
| Laos | Lao | Laotian or Lao |
| Latvia | Latvian(s) | Latvian |
| Lebanon | Lebanese | Lebanese |
| Lesotho | Mosotho (*sing.*), Basotho (*pl.*) | Basotho |
| Liberia | Liberian(s) | Liberian |
| Libya | Libyan(s) | Libyan |
| Liechtenstein | Liechtensteiner(s) | Liechtenstein |
| Lithuania | Lithuanian(s) | Lithuanian |
| Luxembourg | Luxembourger(s) | Luxembourg |
| Macedonia | Macedonian(s) | Macedonian |
| Madagascar | Malagasy | Malagasy |
| Malawi | Malawian(s) | Malawian |
| Malaysia | Malaysian(s) | Malaysian |
| Maldives | Maldivian(s) | Maldivian |
| Mali | Malian(s) | Malian |
| Malta | Maltese | Maltese |
| Marshall Islands | Marshallese | Marshallese |
| Mauritania | Mauritanian(s) | Mauritanian |
| Mauritius | Mauritian(s) | Mauritian |
| Mexico | Mexican(s) | Mexican |
| Micronesia | Micronesian(s) | Micronesian |
| Moldova | Moldovian(s) | Moldovian |
| Monaco | Monacan(s) *or* Monegasque(s) | Monacan *or* Monegasque |
| Mongolia | Mongolian(s) | Mongolian |
| Morocco | Moroccan(s) | Moroccan |
| Mozambique | Mozambican(s) | Mozambican |
| Myanmar (Burma) | Burmese | Burmese |
| Namibia | Namibian(s) | Namibian |
| Nauru | Nauruan(s) | Nauruan |
| Nepal | Nepalese | Nepalese |

| Country | Noun | Adjective |
|---|---|---|
| The Netherlands | Dutchman, Dutchwoman | Dutch |
| New Zealand | New Zealander(s) | New Zealand |
| Nicaragua | Nicaraguan(s) | Nicaraguan |
| Niger | Nigerian(s) | Nigerian |
| Nigeria | Nigerian(s) | Nigerian |
| Norway | Norwegian(s) | Norwegian |
| Oman | Omani(s) | Omani |
| Pakistan | Pakistani(s) | Pakistani |
| Panama | Panamanian(s) | Panamanian |
| Papua New Guinea | Papua New Guinean(s) | Papua New Guinean |
| Paraguay | Paraguayan(s) | Paraguayan |
| Peru | Peruvian(s) | Peruvian |
| Philippines | Filipino(s) | Philippine |
| Poland | Pole(s) | Polish |
| Portugal | Portuguese | Portuguese |
| Qatar | Qatari(s) | Qatari |
| Romania | Romanian(s) | Romanian |
| Russia | Russian(s) | Russian |
| Rwanda | Rwandan(s) | Rwandan |
| Saint Kitts and Nevis | Kittsian(s), Nevisian(s) | Kittsian, Nevisian |
| Saint Lucia | St. Lucian(s) | St. Lucian |
| Saint Vincent and the Grenadines | St. Vincentian(s) *or* Vincentian(s) | St. Vincentian *or* Vincentian |
| San Marino | Sanmarinese | Sanmarinese |
| São Tomé and Principe | São Toméan(s) | São Toméan |
| Saudi Arabia | Saudi(s) | Saudi *or* Saudi Arabian |
| Senegal | Senegalese | Senegalese |
| Serbia | Serb(s) | Serbian |
| Seychelles | Seychellois | Seychelles |
| Sierra Leone | Sierra Leonean(s) | Sierra Leonean |

| Country | Noun | Adjective |
|---------|------|-----------|
| Singapore | Singaporean(s) | Singapore |
| Slovakia | Slovak(s) | Slovak |
| Slovenia | Slovene(s) | Slovene |
| Solomon Islands | Solomon Islander(s) | Solomon Islander |
| Somalia | Somali(s) | Somali |
| South Africa | South African(s) | South African |
| Spain | Spaniard(s) | Spanish |
| Sri Lanka | Sri Lankan(s) | Sri Lankan |
| Sudan | Sudanese | Sudanese |
| Suriname | Surinamer(s) | Surinamese |
| Swaziland | Swazi(s) | Swazi |
| Sweden | Swede(s) | Swedish |
| Switzerland | Swiss | Swiss |
| Syria | Syrian(s) | Syrian |
| Taiwan | Chinese | Chinese |
| Tajikistan | Tajik(s) | Tajik |
| Tanzania | Tanzanian(s) | Tanzanian |
| Thailand | Thai | Thai |
| Togo | Togolese | Togolese |
| Tonga | Tongan(s) | Tongan |
| Trinidad and Tobago | Trinidadian(s), Tobagonian(s) | Trinidadian, Tobagonian |
| Tunisia | Tunisian(s) | Tunisian |
| Turkey | Turk(s) | Turkish |
| Turkmenistan | Turkmen | Turkmen |
| Tuvalu | Tuvaluan(s) | Tuvaluan |
| Uganda | Ugandan(s) | Ugandan |
| Ukraine | Ukrainian(s) | Ukrainian |
| United Arab Emirian(s) | Emirian(s) | Emirates |
| United Kingdom | Briton(s), British (*collective pl.*) | British |
| Uruguay | Uruguayan(s) | Uruguayan |

| Country | Noun | Adjective |
|---|---|---|
| Uzbekistan | Uzbek(s) | Uzbek |
| Vanuatu | Vanuatuan(s) | Vanuatuan |
| Venezuela | Venezuelan(s) | Venezuelan |
| Vietnam | Vietnamese | Vietnamese |
| Western Samoa | Western Samoan(s) | Western Samoan |
| Yemen | Yemini(s) | Yemeni |
| Zaïre | Zaïrian(s) | Zaïrian |
| Zambia | Zambian(s) | Zambian |
| Zimbabwe | Zimbabwean(s) | Zimbabwean |

# SPELLING

## ONE THOUSAND MOST OFTEN MISSPELLED WORDS

Office professionals who communicate daily in writing want their messages to appear professional and intelligent. Misspelled words mar this appearance and suggest that the writer is either careless or ignorant. Yet even the most competent businesspeople misspell certain words—sometimes repeatedly. A word with a different meaning may sound the same as the word you meant to use (see the list of homophones in Chapter 15). Sometimes words are not spelled precisely as they sound. There are many reasons why words are misspelled, and often the safest course is to check questionable words in a dictionary rather than risk an incorrect assumption. The following list contains one thousand words that businesspeople frequently misspell.

| | | |
|---|---|---|
| abhorrence | accessible | accordance |
| absence | accessory | accrued |
| absurd | accidentally | accumulate |
| accede | accommodate | accuracy |
| accept | accompanied | accustom |
| acceptance | accompanying | achieved |

achievement
acknowledgment
acquaintance
acquainted
acquiesce
acquire
acquitted
across
adapt
address
adequate
adjustment
admirable
advantageous
advertisement
advertising
advisable
advise
adviser
advisory
aerogramme *or*
  aerogram
affect
affects
affidavit
affluent
aggravate
agreeable
aisle
allotment
allotted
allowable
allowance
all right

almost
already
altar
alter
altogether
aluminum
alumnus
amateur
ambassador
amendment
among
amortize
analogous
analysis
analyze
angel
angle
announce
announcement
annoyance
annual
antecedent
anticipate
anxiety
anxious
apocalypse
apologize
apparatus
apparel
apparent
appearance
appliance
applicable
applicant

appointment
appraisal
appreciable
appropriate
approximate
archaeology
archetype
archipelago
architect
archive
arctic
argument
arrangement
article
ascend
ascertain
assassin
assessment
assignment
assistance
associate
assured
attendance
attention
attorneys
auditor
authorize
auxiliary
available
awkward
baccalaureate
bachelor
bankruptcy
barbarous

bargain

baroque

barren

basis

beggar

beginning

believe

believing

beneficial

beneficiary

benefited

binary

biscuit

bloc *(political)*

bologna

bookkeeper

bouillon

boundary

boutonniere

brilliant

brochure

bruised

budget

bulletin

buoy

buoyant

bureau

business

businessperson

busy

caddie *(golf)*

caddy *(tea)*

cafeteria

calendar

campaign

canceled *or* cancelled

cancellation

candidate

cannot

capital

capitol *(building)*

career

carriage

casualty

catalog *or* catalogue

catechism

catsup

Caucasian

cellar

cemetery

chancellor

changeable

changing

characteristic

chauffeur

chlorophyll

choice

choose

cigarette

cinnamon

circuit

circumstances

client

clientele

clique

coalesce

coarse

coconut

codicil

collar

collateral

colloquial

colonel

column

coming

commission

commitment

committed

committee

commodity

comparable

comparative

comparatively

comparison

compel

compelled

competent

competitor

complement

compliment

compromise

concede

conceivable

conceive

concern

concession

concurred

conference

confident

confidential

configuration

congratulate

connoisseur

conscience

conscientious

conscious

consensus

consequence

consignment

consistent

consonant

contemptible

continuous

controlling

controversy

convenience

convenient

cordially

corporation

correspondence

correspondents

council

councilor *or* councillor
  *(council member)*

counsel

counselor *or*
  counsellor *(legal)*

courteous

courtesy

coverage

credibility

creditor

crescendo

criticism

criticize

cruelty

cryptic

curiosity

current

curriculum

cursor

customer

cyanide

database *or* data base

dealt

debater

debtor

dcceitful

deceive

decide

decision

deducible

deductible

defendant

defense

deference

deferred

deficient

deficit

definite

definitely

delegate

delicatessen

demagogue

dependent

depositor

depreciation

derivative

descendant

describe

description

desirable

desktop publishing

desperate

destructible

deteriorate

develop

development

device

devise

diagnostic

dialog *or* dialogue

diaphragm

diarrhea

dictionary

dietitian

difference

different

dilemma

director

disappear

disappoint

disastrous

discipline

discourse

discrepancy

disk

disparate

dissatisfied

dissipate

drought

drudgery

dungeon

dying

dyeing
eagerly
ecclesiastical
economical
ecstasy
edible
edition
effect
effects
efficiency
efficient
effluent
eighth
eligible
eliminate
eloquent
embarrass
emergency
eminent
emphasis
emphasize
employee
enclose
encumbrance
endeavor
endorse
endorsement
enemy
enterprise
enthusiasm
envelope
environment
equaled
equipment

equipped
equivalent
especially
essence
essential
esthetic
etiquette
euphoria
exaggerate
exceed
excel
excellence
excellent
except
excessive
exercise
exhaust
exhibit
exhilarate
existence
expedite
expenditure
expense
experience
explanation
extension
extraordinary
extremely
facilities
familiar
familiarize
fantasy
fascinate
favorable

favorite
feasible
February
fetus
fiery
finally
financial
financially
financier
flaunt
flow chart *or* flowchart
forbade
forcible
foreign
foremost
forfeit
formally
formerly
fortuitous
forty
forward
fourth
frantically
fraudulent
freight
friend
fulfill
fulfillment
fungus
furthermore
gage
gaily
gallant
gasoline

gauge
generally
genius
genuine
glamour *or* glamor
goddess
good-bye *or* good-by
gourmet
government
governor
grammar
grandeur
grateful
grief
grievance
grievous
gruesome
guarantee
guerilla
guidance
guitar
gypsy
hallelujah
handkerchief
handled
harangue
harass
hardware
hazardous
height
heinous
hemorrhage
hesitancy
hesitant

hesitate
heterogeneous
heterogenous
hiccup
hindrance
homogeneous
homogenous
hoping
horrible
hosiery
humorous
hundredths
hurriedly
hygienic
hyperbole
hypocrisy
icicle
identical
idiosyncrasy
idyll *or* idyl
ignorant
illegible
imaginary
imitation
imitative
immediately
immigration
imminent
imperative
imperiled
impossible
impromptu
inasmuch as
inaugurate

incarcerate
incidentally
inconvenience
incredible
incredulous
incurred
indebtedness
independence
independent
indict
indigestible
indispensable
individual
induce
inducement
industrious
inevitable
infinite
influential
initial
innocence
inquiry
insignia
installment
instance
integral
intellectual
intelligence
intelligible
intention
intentionally
intercede
interest
interface

interrupted
intervene
inventory
investor
irrelevant
irresistible
itemized
itinerary
itself
jeopardize
jeopardy
jewelry
judge
judgment
juggle
justifiable
khaki
kindergarten
kleptomaniac
knapsack
knead
knell
knotty
knowledge
knowledgeable
knuckle
kosher
Ku Klux Klan
laboratory
landlord
larynx
legible
legitimate
leisure

lenient
length
letterhead
liable
liaison
library
license
licorice
lightning
likable
likelihood
likely
literature
livelihood
llama
loneliness
loose
lose
lying
lymph
magazine
maintain
maintenance
management
manual
manufacturer
manuscript
marital
marriage
Massachusetts
material
materiel
mathematics
maximum

meager
medical
medicine
medieval
megabyte
memorandum
menus
merchandise
messenger
microprocessor
mileage
miniature
minimum
miscellaneous
mischievous
misspell
Mississippi
moccasin
modernize
momentous
monochrome
monolog *or* monologue
morale
mortgage
murmur
muscle
mustache
necessary
negligible
negotiate
neighborhood
neither
nestle
nevertheless

niece

niche

nickel

nil

ninetieth

ninety

ninth

nobody

no one

noticeable

notoriety

nowadays

nuclear

nucleus

oblige

oblivious

obstacle

occasion

occasionally

occupant

occur

occurred

occurrence

occurring

offense

offering

official

omission

omit

omitted

operate

opinion

opportunity

optimistic

ordinary

organization

organize

original

outrageous

overdue

overrun

pageant

paid

pajamas

pamphlet

pantomime

paradigm

parallel

parliament

partial

participant

particularly

pastime

patronage

peculiar

perceive

percent

peremptory

periphery

permanent

permissible

permitted

perseverance

persistent

personal

personnel

perspiration

persuade

phase

physician

physically

picnic

picnicking

piece

planning

pleasant

pleasure

plebiscite

plow

politician

portentous

possess

possession

possibly

practical

practically

practice

prairie

precede

precedence

precision

preferable

preference

preferred

prejudice

preliminary

premium

preparation

presence

prevalent

previous

price list

primitive

principal *(n., adj.)*

principle *(n.)*

privilege

probably

procedure

proceed

prodigy

professor

programmer

prominent

promissory

pronunciation

propeller

prophecy

prophesy

prosecute

protocol

pseudonym

psyche

psychiatrist

psychology

ptomaine

pumpkin

purchase

pursue

quantity

quay

questionnaire

queue

quiet

quite

quixotic

quiz

quizzes

raccoon

realize

really

reasonable

recede

receipt

receive

recently

recipe

recognize

recognized

recommend

reconnaissance

recurrence

refer

referee

reference

referred

referring

region

registrar

regrettable

reign

reimburse

relieve

religious

remember

reminisce

remittance

renewal

repeat

repetition

representative

respectively

requirement

reservoir

residual

resistance

respectfully

response

responsible

responsibility

restaurant

reticence

retractable

retrieve

rhetoric

rheumatism

rhythm

ridiculous

route

saccharin

safety

sacrifice

sacrilegious

salable *or* saleable

salary

salmon

sarcasm

satisfactory

savior *or* saviour

scarcely

scenery

scepter

schedule

schism

science

scythe
secede
secession
secretary
securities
seized
semantic
sensible
sentinel
separate
sequence
sequential
sergeant
several
severely
serviceable
shepherd
shipment
shipping
shone
shown
shriek
siege
significant
similar
simile
simultaneous
sincerity
smolder
solemn
soliloquy
someone
somewhat
sophomore

specimen
speech
specialize
spell checker *or*
 spell-checker
stationary
stationery
statistics
strenuous
strictly
studying
suave
submitted
subpoena
subscriber
substantial
succeed
successful
sufficient
suffrage
summarize
superintendent
supersede
supervisor
suppress
surprise
survey
sustainable
syllable
syllabus
symmetrical
symmetry
synchronize
tariff

telecommunications
temperament
temperature
temporary
tendency
terrestrial
theater
their
there
thesaurus
thorough
thousandth
throughout
tied
time-sharing
too
tournament
toward
tragedy
tranquility
transfer
transferred
trauma
treacherous
treasurer
tremendous
tried
trivial
truly
twelfth
tying
typeface
typical
typing

| | | |
|---|---|---|
| tyranny | vicinity | worthwhile |
| ultimately | victory | wreck |
| unanimous | vigilance | wrestle |
| underrate | villain | writing |
| undoubtedly | visible | written |
| unfortunately | vitiate | yacht |
| universally | vivacious | yaw |
| unnecessary | volatile | yea |
| until | volume | yearn |
| unusual | voluntary | yeoman |
| urgent | volunteer | yield |
| usable | warehouse | yoke |
| usage | weather | yolk |
| usually | Wednesday | your |
| vacancy | weird | you're |
| vaccination | whether | zebra |
| vacuum | wholesale | zephyr |
| valuable | wholly | zero |
| various | who's | zigzag |
| vector | whose | zinc |
| vehicle | wintry | zodiac |
| vendor | wiry | zombie *or* zombi |
| vengeance | withhold | |

# HOW TO USE FAMILIAR PREFIXES IN BUSINESS WRITING

Prefixes, such as *non-* and *pro-,* are affixes to the beginning of a word that change the meaning of the original word. To spell words with prefixes correctly, follow a few simple rules, and consult a dictionary when in doubt. Refer to the next section for examples of common prefixes.

Write most prefixes and the original word closed, without a space or hyphen: *nonessential; semiautomatic.*

Hyphenate a prefix that precedes a proper noun: *pro-American; anti-CIA* (but: *transatlantic*).

Hyphenate a prefix when a double vowel is created that might be difficult to read: *anti-intelligence; extra-astrological.*

Hyphenate a prefix when you intentionally want to indicate a different meaning: *re-form* (to form again).

Retain the initial *s* of the original word when adding the prefixes *dis-* and *mis-: misspell; dissatisfy.*

Hyphenate the prefixes *ex-* and *self-: ex-senator; self-confident* (but: *selfsame*).

## ONE HUNDRED COMMON PREFIXES

The following list of one hundred common prefixes illustrates how affixes are added to original word forms following the rules presented in the previous section. Although many of the prefixes in this list are well established in the English language, they have Latin and Greek origins.

*a-* (on; toward): *a*cross

*ab-* (away; from): *ab*normal

*acro-* (height; summit): *acro*phobia

*ad-* (to; for): *ad*join

*after-* (after): *after*math

*allo-* (divergence): *allo*graph

*ambi-* (bath; around): *ambi*valence

*ante-* (before): *ante*room

*anthropo-* (man; human): *anthropo*morphous

*anti-* (opposed to): *anti*business

*aqua-* (water; liquid): *aqua*naut

*audio-* (sound; hearing): *audio*tape

*auto-* (from within; self): *auto*matic

*baro-* (weight; pressure): *baro*graph

*be-* (on all sides): *be*labor

*bene-* (well; well being): *bene*ficial

*bi-* (two): *bi*centennial

*bio-* (living organism): *bio*graphy

*by-* (out of the way): *by*pass

*centi-* (one hundredth): *centi*gram

*chrono-* (time): *chrono*meter

*circum-* (around): *circum*vent

*co-* (with; together; jointly): *co*operate

*com-* (with; together): *com*promise

*con-* (with; together): *con*fide

*contra-* (against): *contra*dict

*counter-* (contrary): *counter*act

*de-* (reversal; removal): *de*fraud

*deci-* (one-tenth): *deci*meter

*deka-* (ten): *deka*liter

*di-* (two): *di*meter

*dia-* (across; apart): *dia*gram

*dis-* (negation; reversal): *dis*charge

*duo-* (two): *duo*poly

*ecto-* (outside): *ecto*plasm

*endo-* (within): *endo*metrium

*epi-* (over; above): *epi*dural

*equi-* (equality): *equi*librium

*eu-* (good; well): *eu*phoria

*ex-* (out of; former): *ex*-president

*extra-* (outside; except; beyond): *extra*territorial

*extro-* (outward): *extro*version

*fore-* (before in time): *fore*cast

*geo-* (earth): *geo*centric

*hecto-* (one hundred): *hecto*liter

*hemi-* (half): *hemi*cycle

*hemo-* (blood): *hemo*phobia

*hyper-* (over; above; beyond): *hyper*critical

*hypo-* (beneath; under): *hypo*tension

*il-* (not): *il*legal

*im-* (not): *im*mobile

*in-* (not): *in*valid

*infra-* (below; within): *infra*red

*inter-* (between; among): *inter*act

*intra-* (within): *intra*mural

*intro-* (inside): *intro*spection

*ir-* (not): *ir*refutable

*juxta-* (beside): *juxta*position

*kilo-* (thousand): *kilo*meter

*litho-* (stone): *litho*sphere

*macro-* (large): *macro*cosm

*mal-* (bad; ugly; wrongly): *mal*distribution

*male-* (bad; ugly; wrong): *male*ficience

*micro-* (small): *micro*computer

*mid-* (middle): *mid*most

*milli-* (one-thousandth): *milli*meter

*mini-* (miniature): *mini*cam

*mis-* (wrong): *mis*management

*mono-* (single): *mono*poly

*morpho-* (shape; structure): *morpho*sis

*multi-* (many): *multi*lateral

*neo-* (new; recent): *neo*type

*non-* (not): *non*compliant

*ob-* (against): *ob*scure

*off-* (off; unusual): *off*set

*out-* (outside): *out*look

*over-* (above): *over*come

*pan-* (all): *pan*acea

*para-* (beside): *para*meter

*patho-* (disease; suffering): *patho*genic

*per-* (through; by; away): *per*cent

*peri-* (around): *peri*pheral

*photo-* (light): *photo*copy

*poly-* (many): *poly*centric

*post-* (after): *post*date

*pre-* (before): *pre*cede

*pseudo-* (false): *pseudo*morph

*re-* (back; again): *re*confirm

*retro-* (backward): *retro*active

*semi-* (half): *semi*formal

*sub-* (under; inferior): *sub*contract

*super-* (over; above): *super*script

*supra-* (above; transcending): *supra*liminal

*syn-* (with): *syn*chronize

*theo-* (god; gods): *theo*cracy

*trans-* (across): *trans*continental

*ultra-* (beyond): *ultra*modern

*un-* (not): *un*acceptable

*under-* (below): *under*productive

*up-* (up): *up*grade

## HOW TO USE FAMILIAR SUFFIXES IN BUSINESS WRITING

Suffixes, such as *-ment* and *-able,* are affixes to the end of a word that change the meaning of the original word. The rules for the spelling of suffixes are much more complex than those for prefixes, as is evident from the following list. Although the rules given here apply in most cases, numerous exceptions also exist, and it is important to consult a dictionary when in doubt. Refer to the next section for examples of common suffixes.

### Words That Double the Final Consonant

Usually, you should double the final consonant before adding *y* or a word ending starting with a vowel when a one-syllable word ends with one vowel followed by one consonant: *drop/dropped; ship/shipped.*

Usually, you should double the final consonant before adding a word ending starting with a vowel when a multisyllable word ends with one vowel followed by one consonant and the accent falls on the *last* syllable: *begin/beginning; regret/regrettable.*

Often, you should not double the final consonant before adding a word ending starting with a vowel when a multisyllable word ends with one vowel followed by one consonant and the accent falls on the *first* syllable: *offer/offering; transfer/transferable.*

### Words That Do Not Double the Final Consonant

Usually, you should not double the final consonant before adding a word ending starting with a consonant when a one-syllable word ends with one vowel followed by one consonant: *glad/gladly; ship/shipment.*

Usually, you should not double the final consonant before adding a word ending starting with a vowel when a multisyllable word ends with one vowel followed by a consonant: *benefit/benefiting; cancel/canceled.*

Usually, you should not double the final consonant before adding a word ending starting with a vowel or consonant when a multisyllable word ends with more than one vowel followed by a consonant: *deceit/deceitful; chief/chiefly.*

Usually, you should not double the final consonant before adding any type of word ending when either a single or a multisyllable word ends with more than one consonant: *hand/handful; return/returned.*

### Words Ending in -al

When you change an adjective ending in *-al* to an adverb ending in *-ly,* you should not drop letters from or add them to the original word: *accidental/accidentally; real/really.*

### Words Ending in -ance, -ancy, and -ant

Although no clear-cut rule exists for the use of words ending in *-ance, -ancy,* and *-ant,* these endings are sometimes used in words that have a *c* that sounds like *k* or a *g* that has a hard sound: *significance/significant; extravagance(-ancy)/extravagant.*

### Words Ending in -ary and -ery

Although hundreds of words end in *-ary* (*contemporary; solitary*), few English words end in *-ery: stationery; monastery.*

### Words Ending in -ation

When you change a noun ending in *-ation* to an adjective ending in *-able,* you should substitute *-able* for *-ation* without adding or dropping any other letters: *application/applicable; communication/communicable.*

### Words Ending in -ce or -ge

Usually, when a word ends in *-ce* or *-ge,* you should keep the *e* before adding a word ending that starts with *a* or *o,* but you should drop it before word endings beginning with *i: change/changeable; deduce/deducible.*

### Words Ending in -cede, -ceed, and -sede

In this category, one word ends in *-sede (supersede),* three words in *-ceed (exceed; proceed;* and *succeed*), and the rest in *-cede: concede; precede.*

### Words Ending in Silent e

Usually, when a word ends with a silent *e,* you should drop the *e* before adding a word ending starting with a vowel or before adding *y: propose/proposition; sale/salable; ease/easy.*

Usually, when a word ends with a silent *e,* you should keep the *e* before adding a word ending that begins with a consonant unless another vowel precedes the final silent *e: care/careless; argue/argument.*

### Words Ending in -ence, -ency, and -ent

Although no clear-cut rule exists for the use of words ending in *-ence, -ency,* and *-ent,* these endings are sometimes used in words that have a *c* that sounds like *s* or a *g* that sounds like *j: convalesce/convalescent (-ence); intelligence/ intelligent.*

### Words Ending in -ible

Often, the letters *ss* precede the word ending *-ible,* but no clear-cut rule exists: *accessible; permissible.*

When you substitute the word ending *-ible* for the ending *-ion,* you should not drop or add any other letters in the original word: *destruction/destructible; perception/perceptible.*

When the original word ends with a soft *c* or *g* sound, you should use the word ending *-ible* rather than *-able: deduce/ deducible; intelligence/intelligible.*

### Words Ending in -ic

When a word ends in *-ic,* you should add a *k* before any word ending that starts with *e, i,* or *y: picnic/picnicked; traffic/trafficking; panic/panicky.*

### Words Ending in -ie

Usually, when a word ends in *-ie,* you should change *-ie* to *y* before adding *-ing: lie/lying; tie/tying.*

### Words Ending in -ise, -ize, and -yze

Although most of the words in this category end in *-ize* and only a few in *-yze,* no rule exists for usage (consult a dictionary when in doubt): *advertise; criticize; analyze.*

*Words Ending in y*

Usually, when a word ends with a consonant and is followed by *y*, you should change the *y* to *i* before adding any word ending except one that starts with *i* or that consists of *-ship, -like, lady-*, and *baby-: accompany/accompaniment; easy/easier; lady/ladylike.*

Usually, when a word ends with a vowel followed by *y*, you should keep the *y* before adding any word ending: *employ/employment; replay/replaying.*

# ONE HUNDRED COMMON SUFFIXES

The following list of one hundred common suffixes illustrates how affixes are added to original word forms following the rules presented in the previous section. (*Note:* Some suffixes can be added to the original form without altering it; in other cases, one or more letters must be changed.) Although many of the suffixes in this list are well established in the English language, they have Latin and Greek origins.

*-able* (capable of): present*able*

*-aceous* (organism): seb*aceous*

*-acity* (quality or state of): ver*acity*

*-age* (result): dam*age*

*-agogue* (leader; inciter): ped*agogue*

*-an* (belonging to): Americ*an*

*-ance* (state of; action): resist*ance*

*-ancy* (state of; action): compli*ancy*

*-ant* (causing; being): repent*ant*

*-arch* (ruler; leadership): patri*arch*

*-archy* (rule; government): mon*archy*

*-arium* (place; housing): aqu*arium*

*-cade* (procession): ar*cade*

*-chrome* (color): poly*chrome*

*-cide* (killer): homi*cide*

*-coccus* (berry-shaped microorganism): strepto*coccus*

*-cracy* (government): theo*cracy*

*-cy* (state of being): priva*cy*

*-dom* (condition): star*dom*

*-ed* (having): wholehearted*

*-eer* (one concerned with): pion*eer*

*-en* (consisting of): wood*en*

*-ence* (state of): compet*ence*

*-ent* (state of): complac*ent*

*-er* (performer of action): work*er*

*-esce* (become): acqui*esce*

*-ese* (relating to): Chin*ese*

*-est* (most): farth*est*

*-fer* (agency; bearing): aqui*fer*

*-ferous* (bearing): coni*ferous*

*-fuge* (driving away from): vermi*fuge*

*-ful* (full of): plenti*ful*

*-fy* (form; make): modi*fy*

*-gamous* (marrying): poly*gamous*

*-gamy* (marriage): mono*gamy*

*-genesis* (birth): abio*genesis*

*-gnosis* (knowledge; recognition): pro*gnosis*

*-gram* (written material): aero*gram*

*-graph* (written material): tele*graph*

*-hood* (condition): false*hood*

*-ial* (pertaining to): dictator*ial*

*-ian* (of; resembling): Oregon*ian*

*-ible* (capable of): reduc*ible*

*-ic(s)* (pertaining to): metaphor*ic*

*-ine* (of; resembling): can*ine*

*-ing* (to form present participle): comput*ing*

*-ion* (act: process): organiza*tion*

*-ish* (of; like): sheep*ish*

*-ism* (system): social*ism*

*-ist* (agent; doer): public*ist*

*-ite* (native of; follower): urban*ite*

*-ity* (condition; degree): public*ity*

*-ive* (tending toward): mot*ive*

*-ize* (cause to be; render): capital*ize*

*-kinesis* (division; movement): photo*kinesis*

*-lepsy* (fit; seizure): narco*lepsy*

*-less* (without): help*less*

*-like* (resembling): business*like*

*-ling* (characterized by): earth*ling*

*-lith* (stone): xeno*lith*

*-lithic* (stone): mono*lithic*

*-logical* (adjective form of -logy): patho*logical*

*-logy* (study of): metho*dology*

*-ly* (like; characterized by): annual*ly*

*-mancy* (divination): geo*mancy*

*-mania* (exaggerated enthusiasm): pyro*mania*

*-ment* (act; process): govern*ment*

*-meter* (measuring device): chrono*meter*

*-metry* (science of measuring): geo*metry*

*-most* (most): inner*most*

*-ness* (state; quality): light*ness*

*-nomy* (body of knowledge): astro*nomy*

*-oid* (resembling): cellul*oid*

*-opsy* (examining): aut*opsy*

*-or* (performer of action): audit*or*

*-ory* (place for; something used as): reposit*ory*

*-osis* (abnormal condition): symbi*osis*

*-ous* (characterized by): advantage*ous*

*-petal* (moving toward): basi*petal*

*-phony* (sound): tele*phony*

*-plastic* (forming; growing): cyto*plastic*

*-proof* (able to resist): fire*proof*

*-sect* (cut; divide): dis*sect*

*-ship* (state; condition): town*ship*

*-some* (characterized by): tire*some*

*-sphere* (shape of sphere): atmo*sphere*

*-stat* (regulating device): rheo*stat*

*-stead* (place): in*stead*

*-tion* (act; process): affirma*tion*

*-tomy* (cutting): ana*tomy*

*-tor* (doer): edi*tor*

*-tude* (state of being): grati*tude*

*-ule* (small): minisc*ule*

*-ure* (act; process): press*ure*

*-urgy* (technology; working at): crystall*urgy*

*-ward* (direction): back*ward*

*-ways* (manage; direction): no*ways*

*-wide* (extent): state*wide*

*-work* (product; production): office*work*

*-worthy* (characterized by): credit*worthy*

## THE PREFERRED SPELLING OF COMMON COMPOUND TERMS

*Compound* terms consist of two or more words that are combined or used together to form a new word or to modify another word. Whether the new form should be written open as separate words,

with a hyphen between the words, or closed as a single word
depends on the style that you adopt. Although authorities may dis-
agree about the preferred spelling, the following rules are regularly
followed in business writing.

*Open Compounds*

Write a compound open when the words in it are capitalized:
*North American* continent.

Write a compound open when it consists of a foreign phrase: *a
la carte* order.

Write a compound open when it consists of a scientific term:
*propanoic acid* solution.

Write a compound open when a number is combined with a
possessive noun: *two weeks'* pay.

Write an adverb-adjective compound open when it follows the
noun it modifies: a recommendation that is *well received.*

Write a well-known compound open both before and after the
noun it modifies: *public relations* program.

Write most compound titles open: *surgeon general.*

Write a compound suggesting relationships open: *mother figure.*

Write a coined or temporary compound containing the word
*master* open: *master painter* (but: *masterpiece*).

Write a compound with *quasi-* used as a noun open: *quasi corporation.*

Write a compound open when it consists of two adverbs and an
adjective: *very well received* recommendation.

Write an adverb-adjective compound open when the adverb
ends in *-ly: highly prized* award.

Write a compound color term open when the first element
modifies the second: *bluish* grey.

Write most object-gerund compounds open: *Problem solving* is
a principal concern of management.

*Closed Compounds*

Write a compound closed when the words have been tradition-ally combined to form a particular term: *footnote.*

Write certain verb-preposition compounds closed: *backup* (but: *follow-up*).

Write most compounds with prefixes closed except before a proper noun (*pro-Republican*) or when a double vowel that is hard to read is created (*anti-intelligence*): *ultramodern.*

Write most compounds with suffixes closed: *nationwide.*

Write a compound describing relationships with the prefix *grand-* closed: *grandfather.*

Write a compound with the suffix *-like* closed except when it forms three *l's* (*bell-like*): *childlike.*

Write a compound with the word *one* closed (*anyone*) except when a different meaning is intended (*any one* of the three possibil-ities): *someone.*

*Hyphenated Compounds*

Hyphenate a compound that consists of nouns of equal value or when a person or thing has the characteristics of both nouns: the *sec-retary-treasurer.*

Hyphenate most compounds that have the prefixes *all-*, *cross-*, *ex-*, *self-*, and *quasi-* (when used in an adjective compound [*quasi-public corporation*]): *all-important.*

Hyphenate a compound when it is necessary to indicate a dif-ferent meaning: *re-create* (create again).

Hyphenate a compound before a noun except as noted in the rules for open compounds: *four-day* workshop.

Hyphenate a compound with the word *great-* that indicates relationship: *great-grandfather.*

Hyphenate a compound with the preposition *in* when it indi-cates a relationship or is used in a name description: *brother-in-law, stick-in-the-mud.*

Hyphenate the compound numbers *twenty-one* through *ninety-nine: sixty-six.*

Hyphenate a compound that designates a fraction except when either the numerator or denominator already has a hyphen (*nine twenty-seconds*): *two-tenths.*

Hyphenate a compound that designates a time period when it precedes a noun: *twentieth-century* technology.

## THREE HUNDRED COMMON COMPOUND TERMS

Although this list indicates an accepted way of spelling common compound terms, you should follow the style preferred by your organization and the style source, such as a dictionary or style manual, that you regularly use. Most of the terms in this list are given in their noun forms unless another part of speech is indicated.

| | | |
|---|---|---|
| aforementioned *(adj.)* | audiovisual *(adj.)* | bookkeeping |
| after-hours *(adj.)* | backup | bookkeeper |
| afterthought | ball bearing | bookmaker |
| air-condition *(v.)* | ballpark *or* ball park | bookseller |
| air conditioner | ballplayer | bookstore |
| airspace | ball-point *(adj.)* | bottom-line *(adj.)* |
| airtight *(adj.)* | bankbook | boxcar |
| all-around *(adj.)* | beforehand *(adj., adv.)* | box office |
| all-important *(adj.)* | billboard | brainpower |
| all right *(adv.)* | birthplace | brainstorm |
| all-time *(adj.)* | blue book *or* bluebook | brain trust |
| anti-intellectual *(adj.)* | blue-collar *(adj.)* | brainwash *(v.)* |
| antiwar *(adj.)* | blueprint | break-in |
| anyhow *(adv.)* | blue ribbon | breakout |
| anyplace *(adv.)* | boardinghouse | breakthrough |
| anything *(pron.)* | bondholder | breakup |
| attorney general | bookcase | briefcase |
| audiofrequency | bookend *or* book end | broadcast |

buildup
built-in *(adj.)*
burnout
businessperson
buttonhole
by-election
bylaw
byline
bypass
by-product
cardboard
card-carrying *(adj.)*
carryall
carryover
caseload
case study
casework
cashbook
castoff
catchword
catlike *(adj.)*
checkbook
check-in
checklist
check mark
checkout
checkpoint
checkup
city-state
class-conscious *(adj.)*
classmate
classroom
clean-cut *(adj.)*
cleanup

clear-cut
clearing house *or* clearinghouse
clipboard
closeout
close-up
coauthor
coed
coeducation
coexist *(v.)*
comeback
common-law *(adj.)*
common sense
consciousness-raising
co-op
co-opt *(v.)*
copyedit *(v.)*
copywriter
costar
cost-effective *(adj.)*
countdown
court-martial
courtroom
courtyard
crackdown
crack-up
cross-examine *(v.)*
cross-index *(v.)*
crossover
cross-reference
crossroad
cross section
day care
day labor

daytime
deadline
diehard *(adj.)*
direct-action *(adj.)*
double-check *(v.)*
double-cross *(v.)*
double entry
double-space *(v.)*
downplay *(v.)*
downtime
downtown
dry-clean *(v.)*
dry cleaner
dry goods
everybody *(pron.)*
everything *(pron.)*
everywhere *(adv.)*
ex officio *(adj., adv.)*
ex-president
extracurricular *(adj.)*
eyewitness
fair-weather *(adj.)*
farfetched *(adj.)*
filmmaker
filmstrip
fingertip
fireproof *(adj.)*
fire station
first aid
first-rate *(adj.)*
foolproof *(adj.)*
foothold
freelance *or* free lance
freeliving *(adj.)*

free trade

free will

ghostwriter

good-bye *(interj.)*

goodwill

groundwork

half-hour

halftime

halfway *(adj.)*

handbook

handmade *(adj.)*

headline

high rise

high tech *(adj.)*

holdover

holdup

horsepower

inasmuch as *(adv.)*

insofar as *(adv.)*

interrelate *(v.)*

jet lag

job lot

keystroke

labor intensive *(adj.)*

labor saving *(adj.)*

landholder

landowner

lawmaker

layoff

layout

lead time

letterhead

lifeline

life-style

lightweight *(adj.)*

lineup

looseleaf *(adj.)*

loudspeaker

lowdown

markdown

marketplace

moreover *(adv.)*

nation-state

nationwide *(adj., adv.)*

nearby *(adj., adv.)*

network

nevertheless *(adv.)*

newfound *(adj.)*

newscast

newsstand

newsworthy *(adj.)*

nonessential *(adj.)*

nonetheless *(adv.)*

no nonsense *(adj.)*

nonprofit *(adj.)*

no one *(pron.)*

notebook

noteworthy *(adj.)*

notwithstanding *(prep.)*

nowadays *(adv.)*

odd lot

offhand *(adj., adv.)*

officeholder

offset

one-half

on-line *(adj.)*

out of date *(adj.)*

overall *(adj.)*

overrate *(v.)*

paperwork

passbook

passerby

payroll

percent

pipeline

postmark

postmaster

postwar *(adj.)*

preeminent *(adj.)*

president-elect

prodemocratic *(adj.)*

proofread *(v.)*

pseudointellectual

pushbutton *(adj.)*

put-down

putoff

put-on

readout

recap *(v.)*

rewrite *(v.)*

rollback

roundup

rundown

salesclerk

salesperson

schoolteacher

self-concern

semiconscious *(adj.)*

sendoff

send-up

setback

setup

shortcut

short-term *(adj.)*

showdown

sideline

standby

stand-in

statewide *(adj.)*

stockbroker

stock market

stockpile *(v.)*

stopgap

subcommittee

subdivision

takeoff

takeout *(adj.)*

takeover

taxpayer

textbook

thereafter *(adv.)*

throwback

tie-in

tie-up

timecard

timesaving *(adj.)*

timetable

titleholder

trade-in

trademark

trade-off

transcontinental *(adj.)*

turnover

twofold *(adj.)*

underrate *(v.)*

underway *(adj., adv.)*

vice president

viewpoint

wavelength

wildlife

windup

workday

work force

work load

yearbook

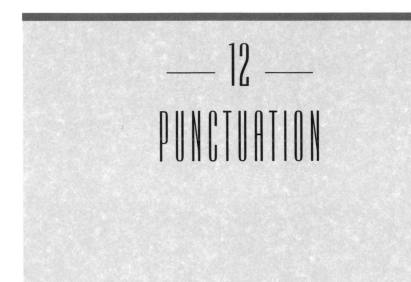

# PUNCTUATION

## GENERAL RULES TO HELP YOU USE THE PRINCIPAL MARKS OF PUNCTUATION CORRECTLY

Punctuation marks are like road signs that tell you when to pause, slow down, stop, change direction, and generally maneuver the roadway without making a mistake. We all need the same type of assistance when we read something, for without punctuation, a written message might appear confusing and misleading. Readers in other countries, for whom English is not the primary language, especially need this type of guidance. But the wrong punctuation or misplaced punctuation can be just as much of a problem as missing punctuation. Therefore, it is especially important that the following punctuation marks be used appropriately. When a passage is still confusing in spite of correct punctuation, it probably needs rewriting as well as repunctuating.

### Apostrophe (')

Use the apostrophe to indicate the possessive case of nouns: *Helen's* computer; *John's* office. But do not use it to indicate the possessive case of pronouns: *theirs; its.*

296

Use the apostrophe to indicate a contraction or omitted letters: *can't; nat'l.*

Use the apostrophe to indicate the plural of numbers, letters, and symbols when it might be confusing to use an *s* alone: *6's* and *7's; a's* and *b's; #'s.*

Use an apostrophe to indicate that a word is being referred to as a word, without regard to its meaning: I heard three *yes's* in the crowd.

Use an apostrophe to indicate the plural of an abbreviation: *abc's.*

### *Brackets [ ]*

Use brackets to indicate mistakes in quoted matter: The clack [sic] stopped at midnight.

Use brackets to enclose parenthetical comments within material that is already enclosed in parentheses: (Referrals [*specialist or hospital*] will continue according to the patient's needs or preference.)

Use brackets to indicate certain comments in manuscript copy that are not to be typeset: [*Insert illustration 12 about here.*]

### *Colon (:)*

Use a colon after a word, phrase, or sentence that introduces special material, such as a list: The chapter has three main parts: (1) . . . , (2) . . . , and (3) . . . .

Do not use a colon after a form of the verb *to be*: The three main parts of the chapter *are* (1) . . . , (2) . . . , and (3) . . . .

Use a colon to indicate a pause between two closely related sentences: The sales manager had only one objective: He wanted to break all previous sales records. (*Note:* The first word in the second sentence may or may not be capitalized as preferred.)

Use a colon after the state in footnotes and other reference material: Adam Kline, *Secretarial Skills* (New York: New York Publishing Co., 1994).

Use a colon after the date in periodical references: Michele Spencer, "Becoming a Secretary," *Secretary's News* 113, no. 2 (1995): 21–24.

Use a colon between the verse and chapter designations of biblical references: *Matthew 6:15.*

Use a colon after the salutation in a business letter: *Dear Mr. Daton:.*

Use a colon to indicate clock time: *11:45 A.M.*

Use a colon to indicate a ratio: *5:1.*

*Comma (,)*

Use a comma to separate most main clauses joined by a conjunction: I understand your reason for requesting a budget increase, but we won't have sufficient funds this quarter.

Omit the comma, if desired, between clauses when they are very short and closely connected in thought: He agreed but she didn't.

Use a comma to set off a nonessential clause that is not required for meaning and could be omitted: The new fax, *which I really like*, is easy to program.

Do not separate a participle from the noun it modifies when the noun alone is not the subject: The board *having heard all sides*, the suggestion was rejected. *Better:* Having heard all sides, the board rejected the suggestion.

Use commas around an appositive: The secretary in the Personnel Office, *Pamela Thorpe*, can give you a supply of application forms.

Do not use commas to set off one noun that modifies another: Her *daughter Sherri* is working in the same office.

Use commas around a state when both city and state are given: The headquarters office in *Birmingham, Alabama*, is hosting the Chinese press.

Use commas to separate the year from the month and day in a date: The article is due on *February 1, 1995*, or sooner.

Omit the comma if only the month and year are given: The article is due in *February 1995* or sooner.

Use a comma after certain introductory words, such as *however, for example*, and words ending in *-ly: Incidentally,* the supply of diskettes is running low.

Omit the comma after very short introductory words: *Thus* we should reexamine that policy.

Use a comma to indicate that words have been omitted: The sales guide covers all fifty states; the resource guide, twenty states.

Use a comma before *Inc., Sr.,* and *Jr.* when that is the organization's or person's preferred style: R. W. Maxwell, *Inc.;* John Harper, *Sr.*

Use a comma to designate thousands in amounts: *$20,192.*

Do not use commas in page numbers, street numbers, ZIP Codes, and similar numerical designations: *page 1401; 2659 Hudson Street; Princeton, NJ 08540.*

Use commas to set off parenthetical and transitional words: *In fact,* I don't even have the requisition.

Omit the comma if the connection with parenthetical and transitional words is close and smooth enough not to require a pause: That copier has a sorter and *therefore* is much better for complex collating jobs.

Use commas to set off direct quotations: "We need to test the machine further," he said, "and not be in such a rush to introduce it."

Use commas to separate words and phrases in a series: The company has offices in *Los Angeles, Chicago, and Detroit.*

Do not use a comma to separate two parallel constructions joined by a conjunction: The total is equal to the price of the merchandise plus (1) postage and handling *and* (2) replacement insurance.

### Dash (—)

Use a dash to set off explanatory or parenthetical clauses: The voice-mail system—*also known as "voice messaging"*—has a few glitches that we are working hard to eliminate. (*Note:* Avoid excessive use of the dash.)

Use a dash to indicate abrupt changes in the continuity of expression: He said that he would meet us in the dining room—or did he say in the lobby?

Use a dash to set off a comment repeated for emphasis: This is the *kind of service* that customers notice—*the kind of service* that makes a company look good.

Use a dash after a summary series of words or phrases: Putting a smile in your voice, maintaining a friendly but professional tone, and using positive words—these techniques will all help you improve your telecommunications skills.

*Ellipsis Points (. . .)*

Use three consecutive periods, with a space before and after each period, in quoted material to show words omitted from the beginning or middle of a sentence: "Diskettes are in ASCII format . . . to simplify searching."

Use four consecutive periods, with no space before the first but space before and after the other three periods (unless a quotation mark follows the final period) in quoted material, to show words omitted at the end of or paragraphs omitted after a sentence: "The session will begin on Tuesday. . . . But if enrollment doesn't increase, we may have to cancel it. . . . Let us hope that will not be necessary. . . ."

As an alternative to the preceding point, use three to five periods centered on a line alone, with a blank line space before and after, to indicate missing paragraphs after a sentence.

Use four consecutive periods, as just described, to indicate that words at the end of one sentence and the beginning of the next sentence are missing: "The session will begin on Tuesday. . . . if enrollment doesn't increase, we may have to cancel it. . . ."

Use leaders, a row of periods, to lead a reader's eye across a page to related information: *Total* . . . . . . . . . . . . . . *$4,765.89.*

*Exclamation Point (!)*

Use an exclamation point after an expression of strong emotion: The customer's claim is *outrageous!* I'm absolutely *appalled!* (*Note*: Avoid excessive use of the exclamation point.)

Use an exclamation point after words of exclamation: *Oh! Stop!*

Use an exclamation point in sales and advertising material for emphasis: *Clearance Sale!*

Use an exclamation point to suggest satire or irony: Wouldn't it be *cute* if we all caught the flu at the same time! (*Note*: Avoid this usage in international correspondence since readers in other countries may not understand or may take an expression literally.)

### Hyphen (-)

Use a hyphen to connect the parts of compound terms when they are not written as separate words or as one word: *cross-reference; right-of-way.*

Use a hyphen after certain prefixes: *pro-American; re-form* (to form again).

Use a hyphen in compound adjectives that precede a noun: *high-pressure* salesperson; *error-free* letter.

Use a suspended hyphen in a series of compound adjectives: *3- by 5-inch card; three- to four-part report.*

Use a hyphen to break a long word at the end of a line: *education.*

Use a hyphen to indicate time spans: *1995-96.* But do not use a hyphen with the words *from* or *between:* not *from* 1995-96 (*from* 1995 *to* 1996); not *between* 1995-96 (*between* 1995 *and* 1996).

Use a hyphen to indicate nouns of equal weight: *owner-operator; manager-director.*

### Parentheses ( )

Use parentheses to set off expressions that are outside the general sentence structure and could be omitted: Include a completed order form (*with name and address corrections*), even if you also send a purchase order.

Notice in the preceding example that no punctuation was placed *within* the parentheses but would have been included if the expression had been set apart from the sentence: Include a completed order form, even if you also send a purchase order. (*Include name and address corrections.*)

Use parentheses to enclose figures to clarify amounts: *Eight Thousand Seven Hundred Fifty Dollars ($8,750).*

Use parentheses to enclose numbers representing a list sequence: You may *(1)* enclose a check, *(2)* charge the amount to your VISA or MasterCard, or *(3)* order on your customer account to be billed later.

Use parentheses in question-and-answer material and to indicate action without dialogue: Q. (*by Ms. Langstrom*) Can you identify this photo? (*Holds a photo for witness to see.*)

Use double or single parentheses in outlines:

(1) Parentheses

    (a) Double

    (b) Single

1) Parentheses

    a) Double

    b) Single

*Period (.)*

Use a period to conclude a declarative sentence (We sent the notice early this week.) or an imperative sentence: Send the notice early this week.

Use a period after initials in a name or abbreviations of names. But do not use a period after a single letter designating a name: *Mr. X; J. T. Winslow; Jas. Winslow.*

Use a period after certain abbreviations except abbreviations that have become known as words in themselves: *Sc.D.; ibid.* (*Note*: Many abbreviations are written without periods: *sec'y; phone*; *CNN news.*)

Use a period after numbers or letters in outlines when they are not enclosed in parentheses:

A. Periods

    1. After numbers

    2. After letters

*Question Mark (?)*

Use a question mark after a direct question: Do you know who is in charge of purchasing?

Change the question mark to a period after an indirect question: Mr. Lyons asked me who is in charge of purchasing. Would you please hand me the almanac.

Use a question mark in parentheses after a fact or statement to indicate that you are uncertain about its accuracy: The company was formed on December 17(?), 1989.

Use a question mark after each question in a series when each is set apart for emphasis and each begins with a capital letter: What is the best way to approach an irate customer? To discipline a troublesome employee? To prevent computer security breaches?

### *Quotation Marks (' ")*

Use quotation marks to enclose the exact words of a speaker or writer: "We still have some work to do," said Noreen Wilson, director of public relations. But she indicated that the results would be "worth waiting for."

Omit the quotation marks in dialogue that opens with the person's name: *MR. BLAKE: I have no knowledge of that.*

Use quotation marks only at the beginning of each paragraph when quoted material consists of two or more paragraphs, placing the concluding quotation marks only at the end of the last paragraph.

Use single quotation marks within double marks when a quoted passage contains a quotation from another source: "According to J. M. Foster, 'the system is being deployed nationally.'"

Place periods and commas inside the quotation marks: "Yes," he said, "we should finish on time."

Place colons and semicolons outside the quotation marks: The news report said that "legally, they can't refuse"; however, their legal team hopes to find a loophole.

Place exclamation points and question marks inside or outside depending on whether they are part of the quoted material: Who distributes "Module A: Support Group"? "Let's do it!" they shouted.

Change single quotation marks to double when a quoted passage is set as an extract, since beginning and ending double quotation marks are omitted in displayed material:

According to J. M. Foster, "The system is being deployed nationally." But another company spokesperson contradicted that statement.

Use quotation marks to enclose a word or words that are defined (but italics are more common for this purpose): "Fermium" [or *Fermium*] is an artificially produced radioactive metallic element.

Use quotation marks to enclose a word or words the first time the word is used in a special sense and it is necessary to alert the reader to this (usually, it is clear without the marks): I don't place much stock in "hemline" market moves.

Use quotation marks to designate the titles of articles, chapters, unpublished works, short poems, songs, and television and radio episodes: "Liquid Theories" (article); "Punctuation" (chapter); "A Study of Isolationism in the Fourteenth Century" (thesis); "Summer" (short poem); "Star-Spangled Banner" (song); "Murphy Brown" (television series).

Do not use quotation marks (or italics) with the following: the Bible, names of its books (Psalms), or other parts (Old Testament); movements of a symphony, concerto, or other long or numbered composition (Symphony no. 5 in C Minor); parts of poems or plays (Scene 1); book series titles (Studies in Chemical Reactions) or editions (Third Edition); common book titles (Appendix); notices (No Parking); and mottoes (Ever Faithful).

Omit the quotation marks and italicize titles of books, periodicals, brochures, pamphlets, operas, paintings, plays, movies, and long poems. (*Note*: These titles are commonly underlined in manuscript copy when an italic face is not available.)


*Semicolon (;)*

Use a semicolon to separate compound sentences when a comma and conjunction are not used: A *heuristic* method of problem solving involves intelligent trial and error; an *algorithmic* solution is a clearly specified procedure guaranteed to give the correct answer.

Use a semicolon to separate clauses when at least one is already punctuated with one or more commas: We're aware of the additional value that consumers give to a commodity; for example, you can charge more for beverages at the beach because beachgoers will pay for the convenience of having beverages readily available.

Use a semicolon to separate items in a series that already contains commas. See the example in the section about the comma.

Use a semicolon before an adverb that functions like a conjunction when it is helpful for clarity or smoothness: A danger sign is notice to stay away or proceed with caution; *similarly,* a work-in-process sign is usually notice to stay away until the work is done.

Omit the comma after an adverb that functions like a conjunction if it will not affect clarity or smoothness: The papers require a third-party witness; *therefore* we haven't yet signed them.

### Virgule (also: Solidus; Slash) (/)

Use a virgule to indicate a fraction: *2/3.*

Use a virgule to write or type an identification number that contains a slash: *M/R-9000.*

Use a virgule in certain abbreviations: *B/L* (bill of lading); *o/o* (order of).

Use a virgule to indicate *per* in abbreviations: *rev./min.* (revolutions per minute). (*Note*: Such abbreviations should be spelled out in general business correspondence and other communications.)

Use a virgule to indicate time spans: *1995/96.* (*Note*: The hyphen is more common in this case.)

Use a virgule to indicate nouns of equal weight: *owner/operator; manager/director.* (*Note*: The hyphen is more common in this case.)

Use a virgule to separate lines of poetry run into the text, with a space on each side of the virgule: The afternoon pales / Before the deadly dark of night.

### The Nine Basic Diacritical Marks

*Diacritics* are marks added to a letter to indicate a particular phonetic value or to distinguish words that would otherwise appear the same, such as *resume* (start again) and *résumé* (condensed statement). Here are the nine basic diacritical marks.

1. acute accent (é)

2. grave accent (è)

3. circumflex (ô)

4. tilde (ñ)

5. macron (ō)

6. breve (ŭ)

7. haček (č)

8. diaeresis (ö)

9. cedilla (ç)

# 13

# PROOFREADING

## STANDARD PROOFREADER MARKS TO USE IN CORRECTING AND EDITING DOCUMENTS

Standard signs and symbols, such as those provided here, that are recognized and used by editors, typesetters, and printers should also be used by secretaries. When everyone uses the same markings, misunderstandings and confusion are less likely. Whether your organization has an in-house desktop-publishing department or uses an outside printer and typesetter, follow the example of the page of corrected proof illustrated here. Notice the following:

- Because the typeset copy is single-spaced, most of the proofreaders' marks are placed in the *margins*.

- With a double-spaced draft, there is usually sufficient room to make most corrections *within* the typed copy, between the lines.

## PROOFREADERS' MARKS

| | | | |
|---|---|---|---|
| ∧ | Make correction indicated in margin. | ⫽⫽⫽ | Hair space letters. |
| *Stet* | Retain crossed-out word or letter; let it stand. | *wf.* | Wrong font; change to proper font. |
| *Stet* | Retain words under which dots appear; write "Stet" in margin. | *Qu?* | Is this right? |
| | | *lc* | Set in lowercase (small letters). |
| X | Appears battered; examine. | *sc.* | Set in small capitals. |
| = | Straighten lines. | *Caps* | Set in capitals. |
| ✓✓✓ | Unevenly spaced; correct spacing. | *c+sc* | Set in caps and small caps. |
| ‖ | Line up; i.e., make lines even with other matter. | *rom.* | Change to roman. |
| *run in* | Make no break in the reading; no paragraph. | *ital.* | Change to italic. |
| *no ¶* | No paragraph; sometimes written "run in." | ≡ | Under letter or word means caps. |
| *Out-see copy* | Here is an omission; see copy. | — | Under letter or word means small caps. |
| ¶ | Make a paragraph here. | — | Under letter or word means italic. |
| *tr* | Transpose words or letters as indicated. | ∿ | Under letter or word means boldface. |
| *d* | Take out matter indicated; delete. | ∧ | Insert comma. |
| *ℑ* | Take out character indicated and close up. | ⫯ | Insert semicolon. |
| *ø* | Line drawn through a cap means lower case. | ⫶ | Insert colon. |
| *ꝺ* | Upside down; reverse. | ⊙ | Insert period. |
| ⊂ | Close up; no space. | /?/ | Insert interrogation mark. |
| # | Insert a space here. | /!/ | Insert exclamation mark. |
| ⊥ | Push down this space. | ⫽ | Insert hyphen. |
| ⸦ | Indent line one em. | ⩙ | Insert apostrophe. |
| [ | Move this to the left. | ⩙⩛ | Insert quotation marks. |
| ] | Move this to the right. | ⩘ | Insert superior letter or figure. |
| ⌐ | Raise to proper position. | ⩗ | Insert inferior letter or figure. |
| ⌐ | Lower to proper position. | —/— | One-em dash. |
| | | ⧧ | Two-em parallel dash. |
| | | ⊙ | Spell out. |

## HOW TO CORRECT PROOF

It does not appear that the earliest printers had any method of correcting errors before the form was on the press. The learned learned correctors of the first two centuries of printing were not proofreaders in our sense; they were rather what we should term office editors. Their labors were chiefly to see that the proof corresponded to the copy, but that the printed page was correct in its latinity; that the words were there, and that the sense was right. They cared but little about orthography, bad letters, or purely printers' errors, and when the text seemed to them wrong they consulted fresh authorities or altered it on their own responsibility. Good proofs, in the modern sense, were impossible until professional readers were employed, men who had first a printer's education, and then spent many years in the correction of proof. The orthography of English, which for the past century has undergone little change, was very fluctuating until after the publication of Johnson's Dictionary, and capitals, which have been used with considerable regularity for the past 80 years, were previously used on the miss or hit plan. The approach to regularity, so far as we have, may be attributed to the growth of a class of professional proofreaders, and it is to them that we owe the correctness of modern printing. More errors have been found in the Bible than in any other one work. For many generations it was frequently the case that Bibles were brought out stealthily, from fear of governmental interference. They were frequently printed from imperfect texts, and were often modified to meet the views of those who publised them. The story is related that a certain woman in Germany, who was the wife of a printer, and had become disgusted with the continual assertion of the superiority of man over woman which she had heard, hurried into the composing room while her husband was at supper and altered a sentence in the Bible, which he was printing, so that it read Narr instead of Herr, thus making the verse read "And he shall be thy fool" instead of "And he shall be thy lord." The word not was omitted by Barker, the king's printer in England in 1632, in printing the seventh commandment. He was fined £3,000 on this account.

*Source:* Mary A. DeVries, *Professional Secretary's Encyclopedic Dictionary,* 5th ed. (Englewood Cliffs, N.J.: Prentice Hall, 1994), p. 277. Reprinted by permission of the publisher, Prentice Hall/A Division of Simon & Schuster.

# TWO DOZEN COMMON ERRORS THAT EXPERT PROOFREADERS FIND

Secretaries must become expert proofreaders to do accurate work. Letters, reports, and other material must be error-free, and no spell-checker will find every possible error in a document. It is up to the secretary—after spell-checking the material—to reread it against the original material to look not only for typos but also for missing words, misplaced punctuation, grammatical errors, improper formatting, and other problems. Here are two dozen common errors that the experts look for.

1. Transposition of letters, such as *si* instead of *is.*

2. Missing letters, such as *th[a]t,* or extra letters, such as *mis[s]take.*

3. Inconsistency in spelling, such as spelling out *percent* part of the time and using the sign % the rest of the time.

4. Incorrect word division, such as *que-stions* instead of *questions.*

5. Incorrect insertion of space in the middle of a word that should not have a space, such as *proof reading* rather than *proofreading.*

6. Failure to capitalize the first word in a sentence or proper nouns, such as *WordPerfect.*

7. Failure to lowercase common nouns and other words that should begin with a small letter, such as *the department.*

8. Inconsistency in the use of italics, such as italicizing words being defined in some cases *(telecommuting)* and using roman type and quotation marks in other cases ("telecommuting").

9. Inconsistency in treatment of numbers, such as spelling out large round numbers *(seven hundred)* in some paragraphs and using numerals for them in other paragraphs *(700).*

10. Incorrect grammar, such as using an adjective *(slow)* when an adverb *(slowly)* is intended: "He worked *slowly* [not the adjective *slow*]."

11. Incorrect word usage, such as using the noun *principle* (doctrine) when the adjective *principal* (chief) is meant: "The *principal* [not the noun *principle*] objection concerns employee turnover."

12. Failure to space between words, after a period or other punctuation, and after numbers, bullets, and other symbols.

13. Incorrect addition, subtraction, multiplication, or division of numbers.

14. Omission of punctuation, such as a missing comma in dollar amounts and other numbers of *one thousand* or more (*$3,492*, not *$3492*).

15. Misaligned decimals, dollar signs, or other material in columns and tabulations.

16. Misuse of parentheses instead of brackets to insert personal remarks in quoted material: "The new policy directive [1994-95] was just released," according to the press release.

17. Inconsistency in formatting, such as indenting a list on one page and typing it flush left on another page.

18. Inconsistency in paragraph indention both in indenting some paragraphs and not others and in indenting some paragraphs a different amount than the others are indented.

19. Inconsistency in use and format of subheads, such as sometimes centering a first-level head and other times positioning it flush left or sometimes using roman numerals alone *(I)* and other times using words (*Promising Techniques*).

20. Clumsy or incorrect order of sentences or paragraphs.

21. Failure to break up very long sentences or paragraphs into two or more smaller units.

22. Missing or incorrect titles in tables or captions in figures.

23. References to people by last name and title (*Mr. Jones*) in some cases, by last name only (*Jones*) in other cases, and by first name only (*Dave*) in still other cases.

24. Sexism in referring to men by title and last name (*Mr. Blakely*) and women by first name only (*Paula*) or referring to *men* and *girls* rather than *men* and *women*.

# — 14 —
# USEFUL LANGUAGE

## THREE HUNDRED POSITIVE WORDS THAT WILL HELP YOU INFLUENCE PEOPLE

Skilled writers and speakers weave an abundant supply of positive words through their messages, even when they must deliver bad news or criticism. Rather than say, "You're still making *mistakes*," they would be more likely to say, "Your work is *improving* every day; with a little more practice, it will be *perfect.*" Some words, such as *assure, fine, important,* and *thanks,* tend to make us feel good, relieve our anxiety, increase our self-esteem, or motivate us to do better. Often, they are essential to create a favorable impression, such as in writing a letter of recommendation. This list of three hundred positive words, when used in the right context, will help you to influence people successfully and positively in your written and spoken communication.

312

able

absolutely

accommodate

admire(able)

advantage

agree(able)

aid

alleviate

amicable

anticipate

apprcciate(ation)

approve(al)

assist

assure

bargain

basic

beautiful

benefit

boundless

brilliant

capable

care(free)(ful)(ing)

certain

cheerful

clear(ly)

commend(able)

common

compassion(ate)

compatible

competent(ly)

compliment(ary)

concur

confident

congratulate(ation)

conscientious

considerate

cooperate(ation)(ative)

courteous(esy)

creative

declare

dedicate(ation)

definite

delight(ful)

demonstrate

depend(able)

desire(able)

determine(d)

develop(ment)

direct

distinct

eager

easy

effective

cfficie111

elate(d)

encourage(ment)

energetic

enhance(ment)

enjoy(able)

enrich(ed)

enthuse(iasm)(iastic)

entrust

establish

excellent

exceptional

excite(ing)(ment)

explore

express

extraordinary

facilitate

faithful

favor(able)

feasible

fervent

fine

first

flair

fluent

foremost

fortify(tude)

fortunate

forward

free(dom)

fresh

friend(ly)

fulfill

future

generous

gentle(ness)

genuine

glamor(ous)

glorious

goal

good

grateful

great

greet(ings)

growth

guarantee

handle

handsome

happy(ily)

harmonious
help(ful)
hero(ine)
high
honest(y)
honor(able)
hope(ful)
humor(ous)
idea
ideal
imaginative
impetus
important
improve(ment)
incentive
increase
infallible
infinite
influence
ingenious
initiative
integrity
intelligence(gent)
invaluable
invincible
joy(ful)(ous)
jubilant
kind(ness)
lasting
legitimate
liberal
liberate
liberty
lifelong

like(able)
live(ly)
longevity
love(ly)
loyal(ty)
luck(y)
lucrative
lustrous
luxury(ious)
magical
magnanimous
magnetic
magnificence(cent)
magnitude
majesty(ic)
major
manage(able)
markedly
marvel(ous)
massive
masterful
matchless
mellow
merit(orious)
meticulous
miracle
modern
momentous
motivation
moving
multiply
mutual
natural
necessary

negotiate(tion)
notable
numerous
nurture
nutrient
objective
oblige
obtain
offer
often
onward
open door
opportune(ity)
optimism
orderly
original
palatable
palatial
particular
patronage
payment
peace(ful)
perfect(ly)
permanent
perpetual
persevere
persistence
personality
pertinent
play
pleasant
please
pleasure
plenty(iful)

| | | |
|---|---|---|
| plus | salute | superlative |
| popular(ity) | sanction | support(ive) |
| positive | sane | supreme |
| premium | satisfaction(ory) | sure(ly) |
| prestige | satisfy | surmount(able) |
| pretty | save(ing) | surpass |
| produce | scientific | sustain(ing) |
| productive | secure(ity) | sweet |
| proficient | sensitive | sympathy(etic) |
| progress(ive) | serve(ice) | tempt(ing) |
| promise | shield | terrific |
| prompt(ly) | shine | thank(s) |
| propitious | significant | thank you |
| prove | smile | therapy(eutic) |
| quick(ly) | smooth | thorough |
| reasonable | solid | thoughtful |
| recommend | soothing | timely |
| regular(ity) | sparkling | together(ness) |
| reliable | special | total |
| remarkable | spectacular | tranquil(ity) |
| repay | splendid | transform |
| reputable | spontaneous | tremendous |
| respect(ful) | standard | trust(worthy) |
| responsible | staunch | uncommon |
| rest(ful) | steady | understand(able)(ing) |
| revenue | strength | undoubtedly |
| revitalize | stupendous | unforgettable |
| revive | substantiate | unique |
| reward | subtle | unlimited |
| right | success(ful) | well |
| safe(ty) | superb | well being |
| salutary | superior(ity) | wonder(ful) |

# TWO HUNDRED FIFTY ACTION WORDS THAT WILL MAKE YOUR MESSAGES MORE FORCEFUL

Secretaries and other office professionals need to convey their opinions, proposals, instructions, and other comments effectively. If a statement in a letter, résumé, or other important document is weak and bland, it may not be taken seriously or even noticed. Persuasion becomes easier when an idea is presented with confident, forceful words. When you want your message to be productive, use the following action words to help you create the right impression and make the desired impact on the receivers.

| | | |
|---|---|---|
| accelerate | budget | decide |
| accept | build | declare |
| accommodate | clarify | delegate |
| accompany | command | deliver |
| achieve | compare | demonstrate |
| acquire | compel | depend |
| act | compete | describe |
| administer | complete | design |
| advise | compose | detail |
| affect | conceive | determine |
| agree | concur | develop |
| allot | conduct | devise |
| analyze | construct | direct |
| appear | consume | discover |
| appreciate | control | discuss |
| approve | convert | display |
| arrange | cooperate | distribute |
| aspire | coordinate | double |
| assemble | correlate | earn |
| assist | correspond | educate |
| begin | create | effect |
| believe | deal | eliminate |
| benefit | debate | emphasize |

| | | |
|---|---|---|
| enact | imagine | market |
| encourage | implement | master |
| endorse | improve | mediate |
| energize | improvise | merit |
| engineer | increase | monitor |
| enhance | indict | motivate |
| establish | induce | negotiate |
| evaluate | influence | nominate |
| exceed | infuse | normalize |
| excel | initiate | obtain |
| exhibit | innovate | officiate |
| expand | inspire | operate |
| expedite | install | order |
| experience | instruct | organize |
| explain | insure | orient |
| facilitate | integrate | originate |
| finalize | intensify | overcome |
| finance | intercede | participate |
| form | interpret | pay |
| formalize | invent | perceive |
| formulate | judge | perfect |
| found | justify | perform |
| fulfill | key | persuade |
| gauge | keynote | pilot |
| generate | know | pinpoint |
| govern | last | pioneer |
| graduate | launch | place |
| handle | lead | plan |
| head | license | please |
| help | like | possess |
| hire | locate | practice |
| honor | maintain | praise |
| hope | manage | prepare |
| hurry | manufacture | preside |

procure

produce

profess

progress

promote

prompt

propel

propose

prove

provide

pursue

realize

reason

recede

receive

recognize

recommend

reconcile

reduce

refer

regulate

reign

reinforce

relate

relieve

reorganize

repeat

report

research

revamp

review

revise

route

satisfy

save

schedule

secure

seem

seize

sense

serve

service

show

simplify

solve

spark

stabilize

stimulate

streamline

structure

study

substantiate

succeed

supersede

supervise

support

suppress

surprise

teach

tend

think

tie

tolerate

train

transfer

transform

treble

try

turn

understand

unify

use

vacate

value

verify

vitiate

win

wrestle

write

# EXAMPLES OF TRANSITION WORDS AND PHRASES TO HELP YOUR WRITING FLOW SMOOTHLY

If your messages or your employer's messages sound abrupt and choppy, you may need to make greater use of transition words and phrases. Notice how stiff and awkward this comment sounds: "Most compounds are written solid or with a hyphen. They should be written open, as separate words, in certain cases." To make one sentence flow more smoothly into another, add a transition word: "Most compounds are written solid or with a hyphen; *however,* they should be written open, as separate words, in certain cases." The following list contains examples of transition words and phrases that you can draw on to make your writing flow more smoothly.

| | | |
|---|---|---|
| accordingly | eventually | in contrast |
| after all | evidently | in fact |
| afterwards | finally | in like manner |
| again | first (second, etc.) | in other words |
| also | for | in short |
| although | forasmuch as | in sum(mary) |
| and then | for example | in the meantime |
| and yet | for instance | later |
| anyhow | for this purpose | likewise |
| as a result | for this reason | meanwhile |
| at any rate | furthermore | moreover |
| at last | hence | namely |
| at length | however | naturally |
| at the same time | immediately | nevertheless |
| because | in addition | next |
| besides | in any case | no doubt |
| but | in any event | notwithstanding |
| clearly | inasmuch as | obviously |
| consequently | in brief | on account of |
| doubtless | in comparison | on the contrary |
| equally important | in conclusion | on the other hand |

| on the whole | soon | thus |
|---|---|---|
| otherwise | still | to be sure |
| perhaps | that is | to(ward) this end |
| possibly | then | whence |
| rather | thence | wherefore |
| similarly | therefore | yet |
| since | thereupon | |

# 15

# TROUBLESOME LANGUAGE

## STILTED EXPRESSIONS THAT SHOULD NEVER BE USED IN YOUR MESSAGES

Stilted expressions such as *recent date* were once common and considered a sign of appropriate formality and good taste. Today they are considered stiff and old-fashioned. Although most of the expressions in the following list went out of fashion several decades ago, some businesspeople continue to use them. But they are contrary to the aim of most writers to be casual and friendly as well as clear and precise. Even in international correspondence, where more formality is required, these expressions should be avoided.

**acknowledge receipt of**. Use *We received. Avoid:* This is to *acknowledge receipt* of your letter of June 6. *Better: We received* your letter of June 6.

**advise**. Use only to indicate actual advice or information: I would *advise* him not to sign the contract. Otherwise, use *say* or *tell*—or nothing. *Avoid:* We wish to *advise* that your order was shipped May 17, 1996. *Better:* Your order was shipped May 17, 1996.

**as per; per**. Used correctly with the Latin words *per annum* and *per diem*. Otherwise, *a, according to,* and so on are preferred. *Avoid:* Five dollars *per* yard. *Better:* Five dollars *a* yard. *Avoid: Per* our contract. *Better:* According to our contract.

**ascertain**. A more pompous way of saying *find out. Avoid:* Can you *ascertain* the reason for the delay? *Better:* Can you *find out* the reason for the delay?

**at all times**. Use *always. Avoid:* We are happy to hear from you *at all times. Better:* We are *always* happy to hear from you.

**at this time**. Use *at present, now, currently,* or *temporarily. Avoid:* We are out of fax paper *at this time. Better:* The fax paper is *temporarily* out of stock.

**at your convenience; at an early date**. Be specific. *Avoid:* Please let us know *at your convenience. Better:* Please let us know by July 9, 1996.

**consummate**. A more pretentious word for *complete. Avoid:* After we consummate the agreement . . . . *Better:* After we *complete* the agreement . . . .

**contents carefully noted**. Rephrase. *Avoid:* We received your letter and *contents carefully noted. Better:* The suggestion in your letter of April 3 has been carefully studied.

**duly**. Omit. *Avoid:* Your letter has been *duly* forwarded to our West Coast office. *Better:* We have sent your letter to our West Coast office.

**enclosed please find**. Rephrase. *Avoid: Enclosed please find* a copy of our September statement. *Better: We are enclosing* a copy of our September statement. *Or: Here is* a copy of our September statement.

**encounter difficulty**. A pompous substitute for *have trouble. Avoid:* You may *encounter difficulty* finding volunteers. *Better:* You may *have trouble* finding volunteers.

**enlighten**. A pretentious substitute for *tell. Avoid:* He will *enlighten* you about it. *Better:* He will *tell* you about it.

**forward**. Do not use for *send. Avoid:* Please *forward* the package to my office. *Better:* Please *send* the package to my office.

**give consideration to**. A pompous substitute for *consider.* *Avoid:* We will *give consideration to* the various options at the next board meeting. *Better:* We will *consider* the various options at the next board meeting.

**have before me**. Rephrase. *Avoid:* I *have before me* your memo of the 2nd. *Better: In answer* (or *reply*) to your memo of March 13 . . . . *Or:* Thank you for your memo of March 13.

**hereto**. Omit. *Avoid:* We are attaching *hereto* a copy of our report. *Better:* We are attaching a copy of our report.

**herewith**. Omit. *Avoid:* We enclose *herewith* a copy of the program. *Better:* Here is a copy of our program.

**I wish to bring to your attention that**. Omit. *Avoid: I wish to bring to your attention that* the third item is missing. *Better:* The third item is missing.

**in re**. Use *regarding, concerning,* or *about. Avoid: In re* our decision at the last meeting . . . . *Better: Regarding* our decision at the last meeting . . . .

**in the event that**. Use *if* or *in case. Avoid: In the event* that you are in the city next week . . . . *Better: If* you are in the city next week . . . .

**initiate**. A pompous substitute for *start* or *begin. Avoid:* They want to *initiate* work tomorrow. *Better:* They want to *start* work tomorrow.

**inquire**. A pompous substitute for *ask. Avoid:* May I *inquire* how soon we may begin? *Better:* May I *ask* how soon we may begin? *Or:* How soon may we begin?

**it is requested that**. Use *please. Avoid: It is requested that* you attend the presentation on Friday. *Better: Please* attend the presentation on Friday.

**line**. Use *merchandise* or *line of goods* when referring to products. *Avoid:* Our sales representative will be happy to show you our *line. Better:* Our sales representative will be happy to show you our *merchandise* (or *line of goods*).

**our Mr. Jones**. Use *our representative Mr. Jones* or just *Mr. Jones. Avoid: Our Mr. Jones* will call on you next Monday, November 6. *Better: Our representative Mr. Jones* will call on you next Monday, November 6.

**procure**. Use *get. Avoid:* Did she *procure* the supplies? *Better:* Did she *get* the supplies?

**pursuant to your request**. A pompous substitute for *as you requested. Avoid: Pursuant to your request*, we are sending your order by overnight express. *Better: As you requested*, we are sending your order by overnight express.

**recent date**. Be precise. *Avoid:* Your letter of *recent date. Better:* Your letter of August 22.

**render**. Use *do* or *offer. Avoid:* We would like to *render* our advice. *Better:* We would like to *offer* our advice.

**same**. Use *it, they,* or *them. Avoid:* Your order of the 9th received. Will ship *same* on the 14th. *Better:* Thank you for your order of May 9. We expect to ship *it* to you by the 14th of this month.

**state**. Use *say, tell,* or *let you know. Avoid:* We wish to *state . . . . Better:* We are happy to *let you know . . . .*

**take pleasure**. Use *are pleased, are happy,* or *are glad. Avoid:* We *take pleasure* in announcing the appointment of John Mason as chairman of the Finance Committee. *Better:* We *are pleased* to announce the appointment of John Mason as chairman of the Finance Committee.

**thanking you in advance**. Use *thank you, thank you very much*, or *thank you for your help. Avoid: Thanking you in advance* for the favor, I remain, yours faithfully. *Better: Thank you for* your help.

**the undersigned**. A pompous substitute for *I. Avoid: The undersigned* will deliver the keynote address. *Better: I* will deliver the keynote address.

**under separate cover**. Be specific. *Avoid:* We are sending you *under separate cover* a copy of our annual report. *Better:* We are sending you *by priority mail* a copy of our annual report.

**valued**. Omit. *Avoid:* We appreciate your *valued* order. *Better:* We appreciate your order.

**we regret to say**. Use *We are sorry that. Avoid: We regret to say* that the two-ring binder is no longer available. *Better: We are sorry that* the two-ring binder is no longer available.

**wish to say; wish to state; would say**. Omit. *Avoid:* Referring to your memo of the 2nd, we *wish to say* that we will mail your refund on October 11. *Better:* In answer to your memo of October 2, we will send your refund on October 11.

## EXAMPLES OF REDUNDANT EXPRESSIONS AND THE PREFERRED SHORTENED FORMS

The most effective communication is usually concise and direct. Extra words tend to take the edge off clear, simple expressions and slow the pace of reading for the recipient. Although repetition is used by advertising writers and others to imprint messages on a reader's mind, superfluous words are rarely helpful in other cases. This list has examples of wordy expressions and the preferred shortened forms.

*absolutely essential:* essential

*accordingly:* so

*accounted for by:* due to *or* caused by

*a certain person:* a person

*a check in the amount of:* a check for

*add the point that:* add that

*advance warning:* warning

*advise and inform:* advise *or* inform

*a great deal of:* much

*a great many:* many

*all of the:* all

*along the line of:* like *or* in

*a majority of:* most

*an example of this is the fact that:* for example

*another aspect of the situation to be considered is:* as for

*a number of:* about; numerous

*appraise and determine:* appraise *or* determine

*are engaged in:* are *or* are in

*are not in a position to:* cannot

*are of the opinion that:* think that

*arrange to send:* send

*as regards:* for *or* about

*as related to:* for *or* about

*as to:* about

*at a later date:* later

*at a meeting held in:* at a meeting in

*at a time when:* when

*at the hour of:* at

*at the present writing:* now

*at this point in time:* now

*based on the fact that:* because

*be in possession of:* have

*be of the opinion that:* believe

*bright and shiny:* bright *or* shiny

*bulk of:* most

*by means of this:* by this

*chief protagonist:* protagonist

*close proximity to:* close, proximity, *or* near to

*collect together:* collect

*color of blue:* blue

*completely unanimous:* unanimous

*complete monopoly:* monopoly

*concerning the nature of:* about

*conditions that exist in:* conditions in

*concensus of opinion/agreement:* concensus

*cooperate together:* cooperate

*deeds and actions:* deeds *or* actions

*demand and insist:* demand *or* insist

*depreciate in value:* depreciate

*depressed socioeconomic area:* slum

*due to the fact that:* because

*during the course of:* during

*during the time that:* while

*during the year of:* during

*each and every:* each *or* every

*eliminate completely:* eliminate

*except in a small number of cases:* usually

*exhibit a tendency to:* tend to

*few in number:* few

*final conclusion:* conclusion *or* end

*first and foremost:* first *or* foremost

*first began:* began

*for the purpose of:* for *or* to

*for the reason that:* because

*from the point of view of:* for

*future plans:* plans

*future prospect:* prospect

*green in color:* green

*had occasion to be:* was

*have an input into:* contribute to

*help and assist:* help *or* assist

*hopes and aspirations:* hopes *or* aspirations

*if at all possible:* if possible

*immediately and at once:* immediately

*in about three days' time:* in about three days

*in advance of:* before

*inasmuch as:* because; as

*in both of them:* in both *or* in them

*in case:* if

*in case of:* if

*in close proximity:* near

*in favor of:* for *or* to

*in light of the fact that:* because

*in many cases:* often

*in many instances:* often

*in order to:* to

*in rare cases:* rarely

*in reference to:* about

*in regard to:* about

*in relation with:* with

*inside of:* inside

*in spite of the fact that:* although

*in terms of:* in *or* for

*in the case of:* regarding

*in the case that:* if *or* when

*in the city of:* in

*in the course of:* during

*in the event that:* if

*in the field of:* in

*in the first place:* first

*in the majority of instances:* usually

*in the matter of:* about

*in the nature of:* like

*in the neighborhood of:* about

*in the normal course of our procedure:* normally

*in the not-too-distant future:* soon

*in the opinion of this writer:* in my opinion *or* I believe

*in the vicinity of:* near

*in view of the fact that:* therefore; because

*involve the necessity of:* require

*is defined as:* is

*is dependent on:* depends on

*is indicative of:* indicates

*it is clear that:* therefore *or* clearly

*it is observed that: omit*

*it is often the case that:* often *or* frequently

*it is our conclusion in light of investigation:* we conclude that

*it should be noted that the:* the

*it stands to reason: omit*

*it was noted that if:* if

*it would not be unreasonable to assume:* I assume

*large in number:* many

*large in size:* large

*leaving out of consideration:* disregarding

*make an examination of:* examine

*many in number:* many

*may possibly:* may

*mental attitude:* attitude

*month of January:* January

*mutual compromise:* compromise

*not of a high order of accuracy:* inaccurate

*notwithstanding the fact that:* although

*obligation and responsibility:* obligation *or* responsibility

*of considerable magnitude:* big, large, *or* great

*of very minor importance:* unimportant

*on account of the conditions described:* because of the conditions

*on account of the fact that:* because

*on a few occasions:* occasionally

*one or another reason:* some reason

*on the grounds that:* because

*on the order of:* about

*out of:* of

*outside of:* outside

*owing to the fact that:* since *or* because

*perform an analysis of:* analyze

*perhaps it may be that you:* perhaps or it may be that *or* you may

*personal friend:* friend

*positive growth:* growth

*prior to:* before

*proceed to investigate:* investigate

*prompt and speedy:* prompt, quick, *or* speedy

*put in an appearance:* appeared; came

*refer to as:* call

*refuse and decline:* refuse *or* decline

*relative to this:* about this

*renovate like new:* renovate

*resultant effect:* effect

*right and proper:* right *or* proper

*round in shape:* round

*short minute:* minute *or* moment

*sincere and good wishes:* sincere *or* good wishes

*small in number:* few

*small in size:* small

*solid facts:* facts

*someone or other:* someone

*some reason or another:* some reason

*spell out in detail:* spell out *or* detail

*subsequent to:* after

*successful triumph:* triumph

*take into consideration:* consider

*taking this factor into consideration, it is apparent that:* therefore; therefore it seems

*temporary reprieve:* reprieve

*the color of yellow:* yellow

*the data show that we can:* we can

*the existence of:* avoid

*the fact that he had arrived:* his arrival

*the foregoing:* the; this; that; these; those

*the fullest possible:* most; completely; fully

*the only difference being that:* except

*the question as to whether:* whether

*there are not very many:* few are

*the sum of five dollars:* five dollars

*the year of 19XX:* 19XX

*tire and fatigue:* tire

*to be sure:* avoid

*to summarize the above:* in sum *or* in summary

*true facts:* facts

*uniform and invariable:* uniform

*unjust and unfair:* unjust *or* unfair

*variously different:* different

*within the realm of possibility:* possible; possibly

*with reference to:* about

*with the exception of:* except

*with the result that:* so that

*with this in mind, it is clear that:* therefore; clearly

# NEGATIVE WORDS THAT MAY MAKE YOU SOUND PESSIMISTIC OR RUDE

Some words have the potential for making you sound pessimistic or rude when used in certain contexts. If, for example, you were writing a letter of criticism or complaint to an employee, using words such as *stupid, meddle*, or *weak* might fan the flames of discontent and anger or humiliate an employee to the point of lowering his or her productivity. Some words, such as *apparently,* seem innocent enough until you use them in a passage with a negative tone (*Apparently*, you haven't finished yet) or a pessimistic tone (*Apparently*, this isn't going to work), where they tend to emphasize the negativity or pessimism. If you're looking for a favorable or positive response to comments, words that have a negative potential should be avoided or used judiciously. This list has words that, in certain contexts, could give a reader the impression that you're pessimistic or rude.

| | | |
|---|---|---|
| abandon(ed) | anger | butt out |
| abhor | anguish | calamity |
| abolish | antagonize(d) | callous |
| abominable | anxiety | cancel(ed) |
| abrasive | apathy | capitalist |
| abscond | apology | careless(ness) |
| absurd | apparently | censure |
| abuse(d) | appease(d) | chaos |
| accident | argue(d) | cheap |
| acrimony | arrogant | claim(ed) |
| admonish | assume(d) | clash |
| adversity | aversion | collapse |
| affected | bad | collusion |
| afraid | banal | commonplace |
| alarm | bankrupt | Communist |
| alibi | beware | complain |
| allege(d) | bias(ed) | complaint |
| altercation | blame(d) | contaminate(d) |
| ambiguous | bleak | contempt |

contend(ed)

control

crisis

crocked

cruel

damage(d)

deadlock

deceive(d)

deception

decline

defeat

defy(ied)

demagogue

demand(ed)

dense

deny(ied)

deplore(d)

deprive(d)

desert

despise

destroy(ed)

dictator

disadvantage

disaster

discredit

dismal

dispute

dominate(d)

dread

drunk

dumb

evict

exaggerate

extravagant

fail(ure)

fall

false(ly)

fatal

fault

fear

fiasco

flagrant

flat

flimsy

forsake

foul

gloss over

gratuitous

grave

grief

hamper

hapless

harass(ed)

hardship

hate(d)

hazy

hinder

hogwash

hurt(ful)

idiot

ignoble

ignorant

ignore(d)

illiterate

imitation

immature

impasse

impede

implicate

impossible

improvident

inadequate

incompetent

indulge

insidious

insist(ed)

insolvent

in vain

invalid

irritate

liable

liar

lie(d)

long winded

lose

ludicrous

meager

meddle(d)

mediocre

menial

misfortune

misinform(ed)

misrepresent(ed)

muddle

mundane

must

naive

negate

neglect(ed)(ful)

negligence

nullify

obligated

| | | |
|---|---|---|
| oblique | ruthless | timid |
| obscure | sarcastic | tolerable |
| obstinate | senseless | troublesome |
| obstruct(ion)(ist) | shameful | ugly |
| one-sided | shirk | unfair |
| opinionate(d) | shortsighted | unfortunate |
| overbearing | shrink | unnerve |
| oversight | sketchy | unsuccessful |
| partisan | slack | untimely |
| perhaps | slow | useless |
| pernicious | split hairs | usurp |
| pessimist(ic) | squander(ed) | verbiage |
| plausible | stagnant | victim |
| precipitate | standstill | wanton |
| predatory | stereotype | waste(ful) |
| prejudice(d) | straggling | weak(ness) |
| premature | stubborn | worry |
| pretentious | stunt(ed) | wrong(ful) |
| quibble | stupid | you claim |
| radical | superficial | you misrepresented |
| recalcitrant | superfluous | you must |
| repulsive | taint(ed) | your carelessness |
| rude | tamper | |
| ruin | tardy | |

## A GUIDE TO HOMOPHONES THAT OFTEN CAUSE PROBLEMS

The confusion created by *homophones* (words that sound the same but are spelled differently and have different meanings) may cause a writer to misspell a word or pick the wrong word. Sometimes writers know better but in haste make a mistake, and their spell-check programs won't detect a correctly spelled but incorrectly used word. At other times writers simply may not realize that they're using the wrong word. Secretaries need to be alert to this common problem not only in their own writing but also in their employer's writing. This list contains some of the most troublesome homophones.

*accept:* to take without protest
*except:* to omit something

*acclamation:* loud, enthusiastic expression of approval, praise, or assent
*acclimation:* physiological adjustment to environmental change

*adherence:* steady or faithful attachment or observance
*adherents:* those who adhere to or follow

*affect.* influence
*effect:* result; to accomplish

*aid:* help
*aide:* assistant

*air:* atmosphere
*err:* to make a mistake
*heir:* one who inherits something

*aisle:* passageway between seats
*isle:* small island

*all ready:* everyone or thing is ready
*already:* by this time; soon

*all together:* everyone together
*altogether:* in total; entirely

*allude:* refer indirectly
*elude:* evade

*allusion:* indirect reference
*illusion:* something misleading

*altar:* a place of worship, ritual, or sacrifice
*alter:* to change

*amend:* to improve
*emend:* to correct text

*annunciate:* to announce
*enunciate:* be articulate

*ante:* poker stake
*anti:* against

*arc:* part of a curve
*ark:* a boat or ship

*area:* portion of space
*aria:* a melody or tune

*ascent:* climb; upward slope
*assent:* concur

*assay:* examination of characteristics
*essay:* short literary composition

*auger:* boring tool
*augur:* to predict

*axes:* cutting tool
*axis* (pl. *axes*): straight reference line

*basal:* fundamental
*basil:* herb

*berth:* sleeping accommodation; dock or mooring
*birth:* act of being born

*bite:* to seize with teeth
*byte:* a measurable number of consecutive binary digits usually
    operated on as a unit

*born:* brought forth by; deriving from
*borne:* endured or tolerated

*bouillon:* broth
*bullion:* metal in bars or ingots

*cache:* hiding place
*cash:* money

*calendar:* tabular register of days
*calender:* to press; a machine for calendering

*canvas:* woven cloth; to cover with canvas
*canvass:* personally solicit votes or opinion; discuss

*capital:* seat of government; stock of accumulated goods
*capitol:* building in which state legislative body meets
*Capitol:* building in which U.S. Congress meets

*cast:* to throw; to mold; group of actors
*caste:* social division or class

*censer:* vessel for burning incense
*censor:* person who studies something and deletes unauthorized material

*cent:* monetary unit
*scent:* odor

*cite:* mention or quote
*site:* location

*complacence:* secure self-satisfaction
*complaisance:* pleasing, ingratiating deportment

*complement:* something that supplements, completes; the act of complementing
*compliment:* to offer praise or commendation

*comptroller:* public official who audits and approves expenditures
*controller:* someone or something that controls

*consonance:* harmony of parts
*consonants:* speech sounds

*coop:* small cage
*co-op:* group or cooperative

*council:* deliberative body
*counsel:* advice, deliberation; lawyer or consultant

*curser:* one who curses
*cursor:* something moved over a surface such as a video display screen

*depravation:* corruption
*deprivation:* being deprived of something; removal from office

*descent:* moving downward
*dissent:* differ in opinion

*deviser:* one who plans or designs
*devisor:* person who bequeaths property
*divisor:* number by which dividend is divided

*die:* expire
*dye:* to color; coloring matter

*discreet:* tactful; prudent
*discrete:* constituting a separate entity

*eaves:* roof overhang
*eves:* evenings

*elicit:* draw forth or bring out
*illicit:* unlawful

*epic:* greater or more than usual; heroic
*epoch:* memorable event or date; event marking a new beginning

*exercise:* bringing into play; carrying out terms or duties; bodily activity
*exorcise:* expel by adjuration

*fir:* evergreen tree
*fur:* hair on mammals; dressed pelt

*florescence:* state or period of flourishing
*fluorescence:* emission of or property of emitting electromagnetic radiation

*flu:* influenza
*flue:* enclosed passageway or channel for directing a current

*forward:* in advance of something; moving ahead
*foreword:* prefatory comments

*fort:* fortified place
*forte:* strong point; loudly

*forth:* onward
*fourth:* number 4 in a series

*gaff:* spear or hook; gimmick
*gaffe:* social or diplomatic blunder

*gel:* jelly; gelatin
*jell:* take shape or become cohesive

*gild:* cover with gold
*guild:* association of persons with like interests

*gorilla:* anthropoid ape
*guerilla:* someone who practices irregular warfare

*hangar:* place for aircraft storage and repair
*hanger:* device on which to hang things

*heroin:* narcotic
*heroine:* principal female character in literary or dramatic work

*hoard:* accumulate
*horde:* loosely organized group

*immanent:* inherent
*imminent:* ready to take place

*indiscreet:* imprudent
*indiscrete:* not separated

*intercession:* medication
*intersession:* period between terms or meetings

*laches:* negligence; undue delay
*latches:* fastening devices

*leach:* pass out or through by percolation
*leech:* carnivorous or blood-sucking worm

*lean:* move from vertical position; with reduced fat; rawboned
*lien:* charge on property to satisfy a debt

*magnate:* someone of distinction
*magnet:* something that attracts

*medal:* inscribed metal award
*metal:* a substance

*millenary:* group of one thousand things
*millinery:* women's apparel for the head

*moral:* ethical; conforming to that which is right
*morel:* edible fungus

*naval:* relating to ships or shipping
*navel:* central depression in the abdomen where the umbilical
   cord was attached

*outcast:* regarded with contempt
*outcaste:* removed from a caste

*overdo:* do too much
*overdue:* past due

*palate:* roof of mouth
*palette:* board on which to mix paints
*pallet:* straw mattress; portable platform

*parlay:* increase the value
*parley:* discussion

*penance:* contrition for sin
*pennants:* flags

*pollan:* white fish
*pollen:* microspores in seed plant

*populace:* total number of people; common people
*populous:* numerous

*principal:* chief; most important
*principle:* fundamental law or doctrine

*rack:* framework or stand; acute suffering
*wrack:* to ruin; wreckage

*raise:* lift up
*raze:* destroy

*recite:* repeat
*resite:* build on a new site

*reign:* monarch's rule
*rein:* line for directing an animal

*retch:* try to vomit
*wretch:* miserable person

*saccharin:* crystalline compound used as artificial
   sweetener
*saccharine:* overly sweet or sentimental

*sailer:* ship
*sailor:* crew member on ship

*sisal:* strong white fiber
*sisel:* ground squirrel

*shear:* cut or dip
*sheer:* thin or transparent; unqualified; steep

*sleight:* deceitful craftiness; skill
*slight:* slim or delicate; meager

*stationary:* immobile; static
*stationery:* writing paper

*straight:* without curves, bends, and so on
*strait:* narrow passageway connecting bodies of water; junc-
   ture; difficulty

*tach:* tachometer
*tack:* nail

*tartar:* substance from juice of grapes; incrustation on
  teeth
*tarter:* sharper in taste

*taught:* instructed
*taut:* pulled tight

*terrain:* geographical area
*terrane:* area where particular rocks are evident

*tic:* twitch of muscles
*tick:* blood-sucking arachnid

*triptik:* roadmaps
*triptych:* three pictures side by side

*undo:* cancel; unfasten; destroy
*undue:* inappropriate

*unwanted:* not wanted
*unwonted:* unusual

*vail:* to let fall or lower, often as a show of respect
*vale:* valley
*veil:* cloth covering; something that obscures

*veracious:* truthful
*voracious:* ravenous

*viscous:* sticky
*viscus:* body organ

*wain:* farm vehicle
*wane:* dwindle

*waive:* voluntarily relinquish
*wave:* hand motion; liquid swell; successive curves

*whirl:* rotate rapidly
*whorl:* part of weaving or spinning machinery; swirled
  shape

# DISCRIMINATORY LANGUAGE THAT COULD GET YOU IN TROUBLE

Businesspeople usually try to eliminate discriminatory language from their messages. Although discrimination may take many forms, three of the most prevalent in business are sexism, racism, and bias against the disabled. Even though discriminatory language may be unintentional, it can insult or humiliate someone, and the goodwill of the company can quickly be damaged. Most people now know certain rules, for example, such as the one that in letters styled with a salutation they should use a general company salutation (*Ladies and Gentlemen*) instead of a male-oriented salutation (*Gentlemen*). But they may not realize that other terms, such as *disadvantaged minority,* are offensive or that some, such as *poetess,* are old-fashioned. Here are some terms that could get you in trouble along with the more acceptable substitutes.

*adman/advertising man/adwoman/advertising woman:* ad(vertising) agent; ad(vertising) writer; advertising representative

*administratrix:* administrator

*advance man:* advance agent

*adventuress:* adventurer

*airman:* aviator; flier; pilot

*alderman/alderwoman:* alderperson; member of the town board; town board member

*alumna(e)/alumnus/alumni:* former student; graduate

*ambassadress:* ambassador

*anchorman/anchorwoman:* anchor; anchorperson

*assemblyman/assemblywoman:* assembly member

*authoress:* author

*average man:* average person

*aviatrix:* aviator; pilot

*bachelor:* single person

*bachelor's degree:* baccalaureate

*bandmaster:* band conductor; band leader

*barmaid/barman:* bartender

*beachboy:* beach attendant

*bellboy/bellman:* bell captain; bellhop

*benefactress:* benefactor

*black worker/black scientist/black teacher/and so on:* worker; scientist; teacher; and so on

*bondsman/bondswoman:* bonder; bondsperson; guarantor; surety

*bowman:* archer

*brotherhood:* association; organization; union

*busboy/busgirl:* busperson

*businessman/businesswoman:* businessperson; executive

*busman:* bus driver

*cameraman/camerawoman:* camera operator; photographer; videographer

*cattleman:* cattle owner; cattle rancher

*chairman/chairwoman:* chair; chairperson; moderator; presiding officer

*checkout boy/checkout girl:* checker

*checkroom boy/checkroom girl:* checkroom attendant

*choirmaster:* choir director

*churchman/churchwoman:* church member

*city father:* city official; city founder

*cleaning lady/cleaning man:* cleaner; domestic worker; janitor

*clergyman/clergywoman:* clergy member; cleric

*comedienne:* comedian; humorist

*common man:* average person; ordinary person; common person

*congressman/congresswoman:* member of Congress; representative; senator *councilman/councilwoman:* council member; councilor

*countryman/countrywoman:* citizen; compatriot

*craftsman/craftswoman:* crafter; craftsperson; handcrafter; craftsworker

*crewman:* crew member

*crippled:* disabled

*deaf and dumb:* speech and hearing disabled; speech and hearing impaired

*delivery boy/delivery girl/delivery man/delivery woman:* delivery person

*directress:* director

*disadvantaged minority:* African-American; Asian; Mexican-American; and so on, heritage

*divorce/divorcee:* single

*elder statesman:* elder statesperson

*everyman:* average person; typical person; ordinary person

*executrix:* executor; personal representative

*fatherland/motherland:* homeland

*fellow countryman:* citizen; compatriot

*fiance/fiancee:* betrothed

*fireman:* firefighter

*fit:* seizure

*forefather:* founder; ancestor; forerunner

*foreman:* manager; supervisor

*founding father:* founder; pioneer; colonist

*garbageman:* garbage collector; sanitation worker

*gentleman/gentlewoman:* aristocrat; courteous person; gentleperson

*gentleman's agreement:* informal agreement; your word; handshake

*Girl Friday/Man Friday:* aide; assistant; right arm

*handyman:* handyperson; odd-jobber

*he/him/his:* he or she; him or her; his or hers (*or rewrite to use* they) *head master/head mistress:* director; head; principal

*hostess:* host

*househusband/housewife:* homemaker

*husband/wife:* spouse

*insane:* emotionally or mentally disabled

*insurance man/insurance woman:* insurance agent

*jack of all trades:* handyperson; person of all trades

*Jewess:* Jew

*journeyman:* apprentice

*lady:* aristocrat; courteous person; gentleperson

*ladylike:* courteous; proper; well bred

*Lady Luck:* luck

*landlady/landlord:* landowner; manager; property owner

*layman:* layperson

*maid:* domestic; servant

*maiden voyage:* first voyage; initial voyage

*mailman:* mail carrier; postal carrier

*maintenance man:* maintenance person; maintenance engineer

*manageress:* manager

*manhood/womanhood:* adulthood

*man-hour:* hour; person-hour; work-hour

*mankind:* civilization; humankind; people; society

*manmade:* artificial; constructed; handmade; machine-made synthetic

*manpower:* personnel; work force

*manservant:* servant

*man-sized:* large; voracious

*masseur/masseuse:* massager; massage therapist

*master bedroom:* principal bedroom; main bedroom

*masterful:* authoritative; excellent; skillful

*master key:* common key

*mastermind:* creator; originator; innovator; to plan; to direct

*master/mistress:* head; leader; owner; ruler; superior; teacher

*master of ceremonies/mistress of ceremonies:* host

*masterpiece:* great piece; great work; great creation

*master plan:* model plan; prototype

*mayoress:* mayor

*men and girls:* men and women

*middleman:* intermediary; jobber; middleperson; wholesaler

*millionairess:* millionaire

*Miss/Mrs.:* Ms.

*Mother Earth:* Earth

*motherland:* homeland

*Mother Nature:* nature

*Negress:* African-American woman; black woman

*newsman/newswoman:* editor; newscaster; reporter; news writer

*office boy/office girl:* office employee; office helper; office worker

*pageboy/pagegirl:* page

*paperboy/papergirl:* paper carrier

*patrolman/patrolwoman:* patrol officer; police officer

*poetess:* poet

*policeman/policewoman:* police officer

*postmaster/postmistress:* head of the Post Office; postal chief; postal director

*priestess:* priest

*proprietress:* proprietor

*repairman:* repairperson; repairer

*retarded/semiretarded:* learning disabled; slow learner

*rewrite man:* rewriter

*saleslady/salesman:* sales clerk; salesperson

*schoolmarm/schoolmaster:* educator; principal; teacher

*sculptress:* sculptor

*seaman:* sailor

*serviceman/servicewoman:* repairer; service representative

*she/her/hers:* she or he; her or him; hers or his (*or rewrite to use* they)

*spokesman/spokeswoman:* representative; spokesperson

*sportsmanship:* fair play

*starlet:* actor; aspiring star

*statesman/stateswoman:* statesperson

*steward/stewardess:* flight attendant

*tailoress:* tailor

*testatrix:* testator

*weathergirl/weatherman:* weathercaster; weather reporter

*widow/widower:* surviving spouse

*wives/husbands:* spouses

*workman:* worker

*workmen's compensation:* worker's compensation

*yes man:* yes person

# A COLLECTION OF CLICHES THAT WILL MAKE YOU SOUND OUT OF DATE

Although cliches are common in everyday conversation, they should be avoided in business speech and writing. Many of these overworked, tired expressions are vague and wordy. A more concise and precise wording will sound more professional and is less likely to be misunderstood. People in other countries, in fact, who tend to interpret everything literally, are frequently puzzled and confused by this type of language. Writers and speakers who use cliches tend to sound unimaginative and dull, which is the opposite of the image a professional wants to project. Here are examples of cliches that secretaries should rephrase with clear, understandable English.

*ace in the hole:* an advantage kept in reserve for use at a strategic time.

*acid test:* severe or crucial test.

*actions speak louder than words:* What you do is more important than what you say.

*across the board:* encompassing everything.

*add insult to injury:* to be unkind to someone who has already been hurt.

*all Greek to me:* incomprehensible.

*all in a day's work:* a routine matter.

*all in the same boat:* all sharing some experience.

*all things to all people:* try to please everyone.

*all thumbs:* awkward.

*all wet:* wrong.

*alpha and omega:* beginning and end.

*and I don't mean maybe:* I'm serious.

*apple of his eye:* something or someone who is cherished.

*arm's length:* intentionally kept at a distance.

*as fate would have it:* as it happened.

*as the crow flies:* by the shortest route.

*at one's fingertips:* readily available.

*at this point in time:* now.

*avoid like the plague:* avoid at all costs.

*ax to grind:* something to achieve.

*babe in the woods:* innocent.

*backhanded compliment:* one that seems to be a criticism.

*back to square one:* starting over.

*back to the drawing board:* return to redesign something.

*back to the wall:* in a desperate position.

*bad blood:* ill feeling between people.

*bag of tricks:* all available resources.

*bark up the wrong tree:* pursue the wrong thing.

*bear the brunt:* assume the burden or responsibility.

*beat a dead horse:* belabor an issue that is no longer of interest.

*beat around the bush:* be indirect.

*beat the rap:* escape punishment.

*be buffaloed:* puzzled, thwarted.

*bed of roses:* soft, desirable situation.

*beg the question:* accept as fact something not yet proven.

*bend someone's ear:* tell someone something.

*benefit of the doubt:* favorable decision even though the evidence may not support it.

*beside the point:* irrelevant.

*better late than never:* excuse for being late.

*better safe than sorry:* excuse for caution.

*betwixt and between:* neither one thing nor another; unsettled.

*bide time:* wait for an opportunity.

*big shot:* someone who is important.

*bird in the hand is worth two in the bush:* What you already have is worth more than the prospect of more later.

*bird's-eye view:* broad view.

*bite off more than you can chew:* undertake more than you can handle.

*bite the bullet:* prepare for a difficult task.

*blaze a trail:* lead the way in a new venture.

*blessing in disguise:* misfortune that turns out to be beneficial.

*blow hot and cold:* be inconsistent.

*blow off steam:* vent anger or frustration.

*bolt from the blue:* a surprise.

*bone of contention:* matter of dispute.

*both feet on the ground:* practical.

*bottom line:* net result.

*break the ice:* overcome awkward silence.

*bright and early:* early; ahead of time.

*bum's rush:* undignified ejection or rejection.

*burden of proof:* need to prove an assertion.

*burn candle at both ends:* to use one's resources and energies to excess.

*burn the midnight oil:* work late.

*bury the hatchet:* settle a dispute.

*business as usual:* continuing in the face of difficulty; doing the same thing in the same way.

*butter up:* flatter.

*by and large:* overall; on the whole.

*by leaps and bounds:* quickly.

*by the same token:* for the same reason.

*by word of mouth:* dissemination of information by speech rather than by writing.

*call a halt:* discontinue activity, usually temporarily.

*call into question:* challenge.

*call someone's bluff:* challenge to prove something.

*can't see beyond the end of nose:* can't see beyond the immediate problem.

*captain of industry:* leader in business community.

*cardinal sin:* major offense.

*cast aspersions:* make a damaging charge.

*cast the first stone:* be the first to criticize.

*catbird seat:* position of advantage.

*catch more flies with honey than vinegar:* accomplish more by being nice than by being unpleasant.

*change of heart:* reversal of opinion.

*checkered career:* record of successes and failure.

*chew out:* reprimand.

*chicken out:* lose nerve.

*child's play:* very easy.

*chips are down:* situation is unfavorable.

*clean as a whistle:* neat; clean; pure.

*clear the air:* be candid; remove complications.

*climb the wall:* to be so restless as to need action or relief.

*close shave:* narrow escape.

*close shop:* stop work for the day.

*cold feet:* fearful; doubtful

*cold turkey:* abruptly.

*conventional wisdom:* generally accepted ideas.

*cool as a cucumber:* calm.

*cream of the crop:* the best of a group.

*cross bridge when you come to it:* deal with a problem later.

*cry wolf:* sound a false alarm.

*cut and dried:* routine.

*cut and run:* leave quickly.

*dead letter:* something or someone that no longer is important.

*dead to rights:* certain; without possibility of error.

*deep-six:* discard.

*die is cast:* decision has been made.

*does my heart good:* pleases me.

*dog eat dog:* ruthless.

*dot the i's and cross the t's:* be thorough.

*down and out:* in poor financial, social, or physical condition.

*draw the line at:* refuse to cross a boundary.

*drop in the bucket:* insignificant amount.

*dyed in the wool:* ingrained.

*eagle eye:* sharp watch or examination.

*easy as pie:* pleasantly uncomplicated.

*egg on face:* embarrassment.

*eleventh hour:* latest possible time.

*entertain high hopes:* have high expectations.

*every man has his price:* There is a limit to everyone's principles.

*explore every avenue:* be diligent and resourceful in seeking a solution.

*face the music:* confront something unpleasant.

*fair shake:* fair treatment.

*fall by the wayside:* drop or lose.

*far cry:* long distance.

*fat cat:* wealthy person.

*feel the pinch:* suffer from adverse conditions.

*few and far between:* infrequent.

*fight tooth and nail:* fight or work hard.

*finishing touch:* final details or work.

*first magnitude:* prominent.

*fly in the ointment:* obstacle.

*food for thought:* something to consider.

*foot-in-mouth disease:* habit of saying the wrong thing.

*force to be reckoned with:* something of significance that must be dealt with.

*for the birds:* worthless.

*from A to Z:* from beginning to end.

*from the word go:* from the beginning.

*get a handle on:* find a way to cope with.

*get down to brass tacks:* deal with essentials of something.

*get sacked:* be fired.

*get to bottom of:* find the underlying reason.

*go for broke:* risk everything.

*go haywire:* go wrong.

*going in circles:* not accomplishing anything.

*gum up the works:* spoil an undertaking.

*half the battle:* a lot accomplished.

*handwriting on wall:* something bad about to happen.

*hang in balance:* be undecided.

*hard and fast:* rigid.

*have bone to pick:* have an issue to discuss or argue.

*hell to pay:* severe consequences.

*hit nail on the head:* reach right conclusion.

*hold forth:* discuss at length

*holding the bag:* left with a responsibility.

*hue and cry:* uproar.

*if worse comes to worst:* if things get really bad.

*in a nutshell:* briefly.

*in a word:* briefly.

*in hot water:* in trouble.

*ins and outs:* ramifications or changes.

*in the long run:* over a long period.

*jaundiced eye:* prejudiced view.

*John Hancock:* signature.

*keep ball rolling:* sustain something.

*keep head above water:* stay solvent.

*kill two birds with one stone:* achieve two objectives with a single effort.

*know the ropes:* know how to do something.

*lay cards on table:* be candid.

*leave no stone unturned:* be thorough.

*leave out in cold:* exclude.

*let chips fall where they may:* Don't worry about the consequences.

*let sleeping dogs lie:* don't stir up trouble.

*letter-perfect:* perfect.

*live and learn:* profit from mistakes.

*lock, stock, and barrel:* everything.

*long shot:* something with little chance of success.

*lost cause:* hopeless effort.

*make no bones about it:* be direct.

*make or break:* succeed or fail.

*moment of truth:* severe test; time for a decision.

*month of Sundays:* long time.

*more than one bargained for:* beyond what one expected.

*muddy the water:* confuse things.

*neither rhyme nor reason:* senseless.

*net result:* outcome.

*nose to the grindstone:* hard at work.

*no skin off my nose:* no concern of mine.

*not able to make heads or tails out of it:* can't make sense out of it.

*off and running:* on the way.

*off the beaten track:* isolated; inaccessible.

*off the deep end:* rashly or emotionally.

*on the fence:* neutral; undecided.

*on the go:* busy; moving quickly.

*on the tip of one's tongue:* on the verge of remembering.

*open and aboveboard:* fair.

*open book:* transparent.

*open question:* undecided issue.

*out on a limb:* in a dangerous position.

*over a barrel:* at a disadvantage.

*pack it in:* quit.

*paper over:* conceal.

*pave the way:* prepare for.

*pay through the nose:* be charged an exorbitant price.

*peter out:* fade away.

*plain as day:* obvious.

*play cards right:* make good decisions.

*play with fire:* invite trouble.

*point of no return:* too late to change something.

*pull it off:* succeed.

*put all eggs in one basket:* rely on one thing.

*put best foot forward:* show best image of self.

*put cart before horse:* take steps in illogical order.

*put foot down:* take a firm stand.

*put good face on it:* make a bad situation seem better.

*put money on the line:* back up opinions with investment.

*put on back burner:* postpone.

*rack one's brain:* strain to think of something.

*rank and file:* ordinary people.

*read between the lines:* determine what is really meant by what is written.

*read something into it:* assume something more than was said or done.

*red-letter day:* important day.

*rings a bell:* sounds familiar.

*roll with punches:* adjust.

*rubber check:* a check returned for insufficient funds.

*rule of thumb:* general guide.

*run its course:* go to completion.

*run off at the mouth:* talk excessively.

*run of the mill:* ordinary; usual.

*save face:* avoid embarrassment.

*second to none:* the best.

*see eye to eye:* agree.

*see red:* become angry.

*seize the bull by horns:* take bold action under difficult circumstances.

*separate men from boys:* reveal who is tough and mature.

*ship of state:* nation.

*short end of stick:* at a disadvantage.

*shot in the dark:* conjecture.

*sight unseen:* without inspection.

*sit tight:* wait.

*skate on thin ice:* risk danger.

*soft soap:* flattery.

*sound as a dollar:* reliable.

*sour grapes:* negative attitude; a claim that something unattainable wouldn't be desirable anyway.

*split hairs:* argue over fine points.

*stem the tide:* stop or change something.

*string along:* deceive.

*take by storm:* gain sudden acceptance.

*take with a grain of salt:* be skeptical.

*talk it up:* promote.

*that's the way the ball bounces:* That is how things usually occur.

*thorn in side:* annoyance.

*throw light on:* clarify.

*tip of iceberg:* only a small part of something.

*too good to be true:* not likely.

*turn the tide:* change things.

*up to snuff:* equal to a certain level of quality.

*walk on eggs:* proceed warily.

*wave of the future:* significant trend.

*whole ball of wax:* entire situation.

*whole new ball game:* a new or different situation.

*whys and wherefores:* questions and answers.

*with flying colors:* with success.

*wreak havoc:* destroy.

## EXAMPLES OF JARGON THAT SHOULD NOT BE USED OUTSIDE THE WORKPLACE

Jargon is specialized language pertaining to one or more trades or professions. Members of a trade or profession use it as a form of shorthand to facilitate communication. It's shorter to say *interface,* for example, than to say *connection of machines.* This type of usage is common and proper. But problems occur when the terminology is used loosely in other contexts: "We need to *interface* [meet] to discuss it." Secretaries can help their employers by checking messages for technical language that is misused in general communication or in international correspondence where it may not be understood. Such language should be replaced with clear, ordinary English. This list has examples of jargon that some businesspeople overuse and use improperly in nontechnical contexts.

*abort:* discontinue

*accessorize:* provide with accessories

*across the board:* in each office, department, and so on

*advance planning:* planning

*after market:* after something has been sold or purchased

*angel:* someone who backs or invests in something

*appearance money:* thinly disguised bribe

*at liberty:* out of work

*ax:* end; stop before completion

*baby legs:* low tripod

*back burner:* set aside and awaiting later attention

*back to back:* one thing immediately following another

*bag:* get; successfully acquire something

*balloon payment:* lump sum payable at end of loan

*ballpark figure:* estimate

*bear:* someone who believes prices will fall

*bottom line:* actual cost or price

*bounce around:* consider

*budgetwise:* in regard to the budget

*bull:* someone who believes prices will rise

*bumping:* downgrading; eliminating

*cap:* set a limit to

*causative factor:* cause

*change agent:* someone who takes steps to change things

*comeback:* successful return

*contact:* telephone; write; and so on

*cover-up:* an attempt to hide the truth

*credibility gap:* inability to believe something

*crossover:* activity in more than one area

*cross talk:* unwanted breakthrough in a program

*dead end:* no outlet, exit, or opportunity

*debug:* find and correct errors

*down time:* idle period created through an error or while awaiting repair or servicing

*end user:* a customer or client

*eta:* estimated time of arrival

*expertise:* special knowledge

*eyes only:* confidential

*fallout:* consequences

*finalize:* end; finish

*first generation:* earliest technology or equipment

*flap:* disturbance

*flipflop:* change views to opposite position

*flop:* failure

*frame of reference:* viewpoint; theory

*free ride:* benefiting without paying or contributing

*freeze:* stop and hold something at its present position

*game plan:* plan; approach

*graveyard shift:* from midnight to early morning

*gut feeling:* instinctive belief

*hammer out:* prepare; write; and so on

*handyman special:* a house needing repair

*hardball:* tough approach

*high tech:* advanced technology

*hype:* promote through exaggerated claims

*inaugurate:* begin

*infrastructure:* underlying foundation or basic framework

*in-house:* within the company

*input:* ideas; comments; information provided to a person or machine

*interface:* connection

*kick around:* discuss

*kill:* terminate; end; stop

*knockout:* exceptionally appealing

*know the ropes:* know the procedure

*log in:* gain access to a computer by using a password

*long haul:* long term; until completion

*man-hours:* hours worked

*markup:* increase in price

*Mickey Mouse:* petty; unnecessary

*moot point:* debatable or hypothetical point

*muzzle:* keep quiet; stop from commenting

*nitpick:* focus on minor points

*off the record:* confidentially

*on the fence:* unable to decide

*operative:* defining; determining; important

*OPM financing:* using other people's money

*optimize:* enhance; improve; increase

*optimum:* most

*option:* right to; alternative

*output:* what is produced

*overkill:* too much

*paradigm:* archetype; model; outline; pattern

*parameter:* boundary; constraint; guideline

*phase:* part; stage

*prioritize:* list by priority or in order of importance

*prior to:* before

*promo:* advertising to sell something or promote someone

*rap:* blame

*red ink:* financial loss

*rep:* representative

*responsive:* sensitive; responding

*rollback:* a return to lower prices

*rollover:* reinvestment

*sacred cow:* too important to change

*scenario:* estimate; event; situation

*screamer:* a persistently complaining customer

*smart money:* those who know best

*stonewall:* be inflexible; adamant

*systematize:* arrange according to a plan; put in order

*time frame:* time

*top of the line:* leading product; best product

*turnover:* change in personnel or products, with new ones coming in and previous ones going out

*update:* bring up to date

*upgrade:* to move up or improve

*viable:* capable of working or developing

*window:* opening in idea, attitude, and so on; opportunity

*workup:* routine diagnostic procedures

## THREE HUNDRED COMMONLY MISUSED WORDS

Misused words can lead to misunderstandings. Sometimes the words are used interchangeably by American businesspeople, but the subtle differences can create the wrong impression, particularly for readers in other countries who translate everything literally. *Acknowledge* and *admit,* for example, are loosely used to mean the same thing. But *admit* suggests that you *had* to concede something or possibly were previously wrong. Careful writers and speakers therefore choose their words carefully with the precise, literal meaning in mind. This list, completely revised and updated from a dictionary of misused words in *Guide to Better Business Writing* (New Century, 1981), contains three hundred of the most often abused terms.

*ability, capacity*

*Ability* means "the physical or mental power to do something": A DTP operator should have the *ability* to handle matters of design and layout.

*Capacity* means "a physical measure of content" (*capacity* of two tons) or "the power to absorb or learn something": She has the *capacity* to benefit from this experience.

*about, around, round*

*About* means "in the area" (*about* here), "nearly or approximately" (*about* three months), "almost" (*about* done). Do not use *at* with *about* (not *at about* the same time), and do not use *about* unnecessarily (not *about* two to three months).

*Around* is often used in place of *about* (stop *around* 8 o'clock), although grammatical authorities discourage this habit. It is used informally to describe "here and there" (walk *around*). But that usage should be avoided in international correspondence.

*Round* is a colloquial substitute for *about:* Let's meet *round* noon. That usage should also be avoided in international correspondence.

### abridged, unabridged

*Abridged* means "reduced, shortened": an *abridged* dictionary.

*Unabridged* means "not reduced or shortened; complete": an *unabridged* dictionary.

### accept, except

*Accept* means "to receive, to take; to agree with, to say yes": The manager decided to *accept* the proposal.

*Except,* as a verb, means "to make an exception of; to omit or exclude": We may *except* any late registrations. As a preposition, *except* means "other than": They all wanted to go *except* Jim.

### acknowledge, admit

*Acknowledge* means "to concede; to grant; to say that something is true": He wrote to *acknowledge* the rumor.

*Admit* also means "to concede or to say something is true" but is used more often to suggest a change in position or to suggest the involvement of wrongdoing, force, or pressure: The treasurer should *admit* that the use of funds was improper.

### adapt, adept, adopt

*Adapt* means "to change something for one's own purpose; to adjust": The programmer *adapted* the old program to our new format.

*Adept* means "proficient; skilled": He is *adept* in math.

*Adopt* means "to accept something without changing it": They will *adopt* the proposal.

### adverse, averse

*Adverse* means "opposed; strongly disinclined": She was *adverse* to the new policy.

*Averse* means "reluctant; having a distaste for": He is *averse* to taking more classes.

### advice, advise

*Advice,* a noun, means "a recommendation or suggestion": Our *advice* is to order the set rather than single items.

*Advise,* a verb, means "to counsel, to give advice": They *advise* us to apply early. *Advise* is often misused in business correspondence for *tell* or *say.*

### affect, effect

*Affect,* a verb, means "to influence": The longer hours may *affect* productivity.

*Effect,* as a noun, means "a result": The *effect* was to increase sales. As a verb, it means "to bring about": The ruling may *effect* a lower employee turnover.

### afflict, inflict

*Afflict* means "to distress; to trouble; to injure": Carpal tunnel syndrome *afflicts* many secretaries.

*Inflict* means "to impose; to cause to be endured": She should not *inflict* negative ideas on others.

### aid, assist, help

*Aid* means "to provide relief or assistance" and suggests incapacity or helplessness on the part of the recipient: The Red Cross provided *aid* to the flood victims.

*Assist* means "to support or aid" and suggests a secondary role: I will *assist* the manager at the conference.

*Help* means "to assist; to promote; to relieve; to benefit," and suggests steps toward some end: They will *help* set up the new library.

### aim, intend

*Aim* refers to a matter of positioning (take *aim*) or means "to try": I *aim* to achieve our goal.

*Intend* means "to plan on; to design": The delegation *intends* to complete its work in Japan this week.

### all ready, already

*All ready*, an adjectival phrase, means "completely ready": The shop will open when they are *all ready*.

*Already,* an adverb, means "previously": The office was *already* closed.

### all together, altogether

*All together* refers to everyone in the same place: We were *all together* for the Christmas party.

*Altogether* means "wholly; completely; all told": *Altogether,* they exceeded expectations.

*Completely* is preferred by some grammatical authorities in reference to "wholly."

### alter, change

*Alter* means "to make different without changing into something else": He plans to *alter* the last clause.

*Change* also means "to make different" but is not restricted in the sense that *alter* is: We want to *change* the decor of the reception room.

### amend, emend

*Amend* means "to improve; to make right": He hopes to *amend* the declaration.

*Emend* means "to correct; to alter": He took time to *emend* the erroneous paragraph.

### among, between

*Among* refers to the relationship of more than two things: The exchange of ideas *among* the attendees was helpful.

*Between* refers to the relationship of two things or more than two things if each one is individually related to the others: The exchange of ideas *between* Mr. Smith and the other members was useful.

### anxious, eager

*Anxious* refers to uneasiness or worry: He was *anxious* to know the decision.

*Eager* suggests earnest desire or anticipation: We are *eager* to begin.

### apt, liable, likely

*Apt* means "fit" (*apt* in debating) or "inclined to do something": *apt* to resign.

*Liable* means "obligated by law; responsible": The company is *liable* for the commitments of its employees.

*Likely* means "probable": An increase in interest rates is *likely*.

### as, since

*As* is a less effective conjunction than *since,* but it has other uses in the English language: preposition, adverb, and pronoun.

*Since* or *because* is a more effective conjunction than *as: Since* we have no other alternative, let's do it now.

### as . . . as, so . . . as

*As . . . as* is preferred for positive expressions: This book is *as* good *as* the others.

*So . . . as* is often preferred for negative expressions: Her typing is not *so* good *as* her other skills.

### as if, as though, like

*As if* is less formal than *as though*: He paused *as if* he were uncertain about something.

*As though* is used in the same sense, and like *as if*, it is followed by a verb in the subjunctive mood: She responded *as though* she were personally involved.

*Like* is widely used and misused in informal writing and conversation (*like* I said), but grammatical authorities recommend that it be used as a preposition and with a noun or pronoun that is not followed by a verb: The secretary writes *like* a pro.

### assure, ensure, insure

*Assure* means "to guarantee" and is used only in reference to persons: I *assure* you that we will comply.

*Ensure,* a less common variation of *insure* in the United States but favored in Britain, means "to make certain": The filing requirement will *ensure* that only qualified persons apply.

*Insure,* the usual American spelling of *ensure,* also means "to make certain; to guard against risk or loss": This policy will *insure* continued success.

### a while, awhile

*A while*, a noun phrase, refers to a period or interval: If you want to wait for *a while*, I can make the copies now.

*Awhile,* an adverb, means "for a short period or interval": The secretary decided to type *awhile* before doing the filing. Do not use *for* with *awhile* (not *for awhile*) since *for* is implied.

### balance, remainder

*Balance* refers to equality of totals (*balance* the budget) or to bookkeeping (the *balance* in his account).

*Remainder* should be used in all other instances to mean "what is left over": The first batch of programs is in the mail, and the *remainder* will be mailed tomorrow.

### barely, hardly, scarcely

*Barely* means "meagerly; narrowly": The computer could *barely* fit in my small car.

*Hardly* suggests "difficulty": He could *hardly* control the car at that speed.

*Scarcely* means "by a narrow margin" and suggests something hard to believe: She *scarcely* won the election.

Do not use a negative with these terms since each already has a negative quality (not *not barely, not hardly, not scarcely*).

### because, due to, owing to

*Because* should be used with nonlinking verbs: The plans were omitted *because* of an oversight.

*Due to* means "caused by" and may follow a linking verb: The poor turnout was *due to* the weather.

*Due to* is often used by careless business writers as a wordy substitute for *since* or *because.*

*Owing to* is primarily used as a compound preposition: The bill will be reenacted *owing to* his persistent strategy.

### begin, commence

*Begin* means "to start; to cause something to come into being": It's time to *begin. Begin* is preferred over *commence* in most business communication.

*Commence* means the same thing but should be reserved for legal or other formal writing.

### beside, besides

*Beside,* a preposition, means "next to": I stopped *beside* the statue.

*Besides,* most commonly used as an adverb, means "in addition to" (another form *besides* this one) or "moreover": *Besides,* she enjoys the work. However, *besides* should be avoided in international correspondence.

### bilateral, unilateral

*Bilateral* means "affecting two sides": The *bilateral* treaty was signed yesterday.

*Unilateral* means "affecting one side; undertaken by one party": His *unilateral* decision was unpopular.

### can, may

*Can* refers to ability: You *can* do it.

*May* refers to permission: *May* we leave early today?

### candid, frank

*Candid* means "open; straightforward": Their discussion was *candid.*

*Frank* means the same thing but suggests an outspoken, possibly less tactful remark: The two directors had a *frank* exchange of views.

### canvas, canvass

*Canvas,* a noun, means "a closely woven cloth": The cover was made of *canvas.*

*Canvass,* a verb, means "to solicit votes or opinions": The marketing department will *canvass* prospective customers.

### capital, capitol

*Capital* means "a stock or value of goods": They are in need of *capital.* It also means "the city that is the seat of government": Mexico City is the *capital* of Mexico.

*Capitol* refers to a state building. It is always capitalized in reference to the seat of the U.S. Congress: the *Capitol* in Washington, D.C.

### censor, censure

*Censor* means "to examine for possible deletions": The director will *censor* all films.

*Censure* means "to condemn; to blame": The president intends to *censure* the press coverage.

### client, customer, patron

*Client* refers to someone who consults a professional person: ABC Company is our main *client.*

*Customer* refers to someone who purchases a commodity or service: We have many *customers* for our products on the West Coast.

*Patron* has the same meaning as *customer* but also refers to someone who supports someone or something: The princess is a *patron* of the arts.

### close, near

*Close* means "very near" (*close* contest) or "intimate": *close* friend.

*Near* means "closely related" (*near* neighbors) and is sometimes used casually to mean "narrow margin" (a *near* victory). The last usage is not recommended.

### close, shut

*Close* means "to prevent passage to or from": They will have to *close* the highway.

*Shut,* which has the same meaning as *close,* is more emphatic. It also means "to suspend operations": He *shut* down the printing press.

### common, mutual

*Common* refers to something belonging equally to or shared equally by two or more: The employees use a *common* coat room.

*Mutual* means "having the same relationship each to the other or directed and received in equal amount": The secretary and his boss had a *mutual* respect for each other.

*comparatively, relatively*

*Comparatively* refers to a degree of comparison (We have a *comparatively* mild winter this year.) but is often used incorrectly when no comparison with another factor is involved.

*Relatively* refers to the state of something in relation to something else: The scanner is *relatively* easy to use. *Relatively* is overused by many business writers.

*compare, contrast*

*Compare* means "to examine for difference or similarity, mostly similarity." *Compare* is followed by *with* when similarities or differences of two like things are examined: You can *compare* my record with his. But when examining unlike things, *compare* is followed by *to:* She *compared* the "information highway" *to* a "spider web."

*Contrast* means "to show only differences." The noun form of *contrast* is followed by *to:* The new software, in *contrast to* the earlier versions, has a large thesaurus. But the verb *contrast* is usually followed by *with:* The new software *contrasts* markedly *with* the earlier versions.

*complement, compliment*

*Complement* means "to complete": The telephone survey *complements* the marketing study.

*Compliment* means "to flatter or praise": She received a nice *compliment* from her boss.

*complementary, supplementary*

*Complementary* means "completing to make up the whole": The word processing and data processing operations are *complementary*.

*Supplementary* means "added to something": The rider is *supplementary* to the basic policy.

*compose, comprise*

Compose means "to make up by combining": Four offices *compose* the department. *Or:* The department is *composed* of four offices. A general rule is that the parts (four offices) *compose* the whole (the department).

*Comprise* means "to include": The department *comprises* fifty-six employees. A general rule is that the whole (the department) *comprises* the parts (fifty-six employees).

### concept, idea, notion

*Concept* refers to a general idea based on specifics: The book explores the *concept* of top-down management.

*Idea* refers to a plan, a thought, or a representation: The program emphasizes his *idea* of self-initiative.

*Notion* suggests an inconclusive or vague thought: We had no *notion* that prices would suddenly rise. *Notion* should be avoided in international correspondence.

### connotation, denotation

*Connotation* is the suggested meaning of words beyond the dictionary definition. For example, *shrewdness* suggests intelligence to some people.

*Denotation* is the primary dictionary meaning of words. For example, *shrewd* is defined in the dictionary as "clever, discerning awareness."

### consistently, constantly

*Consistently* means "with uniformity or regularity; steady continuity": They have *consistently* voted for Independent candidates.

*Constantly* means "with steadfast resolution; faithfulness" (He has been a *constant* supporter) or "without interruption": The computer ran *constantly*.

### continual, continuous

*Continual* means "repeated over and over at close intervals" and sometimes implies a rapid succession: The fax transmission beep was *continual*.

*Continuous* means "connected; unbroken; going on without interruption": The *continuous* use of our generator is expensive.

*continue, resume*

*Continue* means "to keep on without interruption": She will *continue* working this afternoon.

*Resume* means "to start again after interruptions": The company will *resume* operations as soon as the strike has ended.

*convince, persuade*

*Convince* means "to lead someone to understand, agree, or believe": His strong presentation should *convince* the others.

*Persuade* means "to win someone over": He will try to *persuade* them to drop the suit.

*covert, overt*

*Covert* means "hidden": The government has conducted *covert* operations.

*Overt* means "open to view": The agent's work was not always *overt*.

*credible, creditable*

*Credible* means "believable; reasonable": Her argument is *credible*.

*Creditable* means "deserving credit; worthy of praise": His performance is *creditable*.

*currently, presently*

*Currently* means "the time now passing; belonging to the present time": We are *currently* suspending production.

*Presently* means "shortly or before long": The delegates will be here *presently*.

*customary, usual*

*Customary* means "according to usual practices": The *customary* policy is not always the best policy.

*Usual* means "something common, normal, or ordinary": The office will open at the *usual* time.

### decisive, incisive

*Decisive* means "conclusive; final": The vote was a *decisive* victory for the opponents.

*Incisive* means "direct; cutting; clear-cut": His instructions are *incisive.*

### deduction, induction

*Deduction* refers to reasoning by moving from the general to the particular: Employees have always had trouble understanding the policy manual; therefore, the newcomers will probably have trouble understanding it too.

*Induction* refers to reasoning by moving from the particular to the general: Having seen how helpful our policy manual has been, I am convinced that policy manuals serve a very useful purpose.

### defer, delay, postpone

*Defer* means "to put off something until later": I will *defer* my decision until next week.

*Delay* means "to set aside; to detain; to stop": Let's *delay* further work on that project.

*Postpone* means "to put off something until later, with full intention of undertaking it at a specific time": She will *postpone* her trip until November 1.

### degree, extent

*Degree* refers to a step or stage: The project moved closer to completion by *degrees.*

*Extent* refers to the range or scope of something: The *extent* of the damage is unknown.

Both *degree* and *extent* are overused in business writing ("to the *extent* that," "to the *degree* that," "to some *extent/degree*"), and they should be avoided in international correspondence.

*deny, refute*

*Deny* means "to disclaim; to refuse": Her attorney advised her to *deny* all charges.

*Refute* means "to prove wrong": They were able to *refute* the charges.

*depositary, depository*

*Depositary* means "a person or group entrusted with something": The trustee was appointed as *depositary*.

*Depository* means "a place used for safekeeping something": The bank is the *depository* for quarterly payments.

*different from, different than*

*Different from* is preferred by careful business writers: His goal is *different from* mine.

*Different than* may be used when followed by a clause with a verb: His goal now is *different than* the one he had pursued last year.

*differentiate, distinguish*

*Differentiate* means "to show in detail a difference in": You can *differentiate* among the paper samples by weight and grain.

*Distinguish* also means "to show the difference in" but is used to point out general differences that separate one category from another: You can easily *distinguish* the complexity of standard English from the simplicity of Pidgin English.

*disability, inability*

*Disability* suggests a mental or physical impairment: His *disability* was not severe.

*Inability* suggests a lack of power or capacity: Her *inability* to cope with pressure soon became evident.

*disinterested, uninterested*

*Disinterested* means "objective, free from selfish motive; unbiased": He had to remain *disinterested* while researching the book.

*Uninterested* means "indifferent, not interested": She seemed *uninterested* in the project.

### disorganized, unorganized

*Disorganized* means "lack of an orderly system; lack of coherence": A secretary cannot afford to be *disorganized.*

*Unorganized* means "not characterized by an orderly whole": The people shared similar views but, without a leader, remained *unorganized.*

### displace, misplace

*Displace* means "to move something from its usual place": When he accidentally dropped the carton, it *displaced* the transcription unit.

*Misplace* means "to put in a wrong place": She *misplaced* the Hopkins folder.

### disqualified, unqualified

*Disqualified* means "made ineligible; deprived of": She was *disqualified* from membership.

*Unqualified* means "not having the required qualifications; not fit": He was *unqualified* for the position.

### dissatisfied, unsatisfied

*Dissatisfied* means "unhappy; upset; displeased": Her boss was *dissatisfied* with the new policy.

*Unsatisfied* means "not content, not pleased; wanting something more or better to be done": Her boss was *unsatisfied* with the quality of her work.

### doubt if, doubt that, doubt whether

*Doubt if* should be avoided in business writing.

*Doubt that* is the preferred expression in negative or interrogative sentences when little doubt exists: They *doubt that* the new building will be completed this month.

*Doubt whether* is usually limited to situations involving strong uncertainty: I *doubt whether* the president will resign without a fight.

### *each other, one another*

*Each other* is used when referring to two persons or objects: The executive and his assistant consult *each other* regularly.

*One another* is used when referring to three or more persons or objects: The three committee members were discussing the problem with *one another* last night.

### *effective, effectual, efficient*

*Effective* means "producing or capable of producing a desired result": The strategy was *effective.*

*Effectual* also means "producing or capable of producing a desired result" but generally is used in reference to the action: Her efforts were *effectual* in gaining the necessary support.

*Efficient* means "acting directly to produce an effect" and suggests a minimum of waste or unnecessary effort: Our competitors run an *efficient* organization.

### *elicit, illicit, licit*

*Elicit* means "to bring out": The questions were designed to *elicit* the truth.

*Illicit* means "unlawful": The company was charged with *illicit* operations.

*Licit* means "permissible": She would never engage in anything but strictly *licit* behavior.

### *emigrate, immigrate*

*Emigrate* means "to move from one country to another": O'Neill *emigrated* from Ireland in 1994.

*Immigrate* means "to enter a country to establish permanent residence": O'Neill *immigrated* to the United States in 1994.

*eminent, imminent*

*Eminent* means "distinguished; conspicuous": the *eminent* scientist.

*Imminent* means "impending": an *imminent* disaster.

*endless, innumerable*

*Endless* means "boundless; interminable": The wilderness areas seemed *endless.*

*Innumerable* means "countless; too many to count": There are *innumerable* postal regulations.

*envisage, envision*

*Envisage* means "to confront; to plan; to view in a particular way": I *envisage* an overseas office with a director and staff of six.

*Envision* means "to foresee; to picture": I *envision* a rewarding business relationship with Mr. Vieira and his company.

*especial, special*

*Especial* means "of great importance; highly distinctive": His credentials are of *especial* significance.

*Special* means "having some particular quality or some distinctive identity": This model has a *special* recall feature.

*essential, necessary*

*Essential* means "basic; indispensable; necessary," and suggests a sense of urgency: It is *essential* that we increase sales to survive.

*Necessary* also means "indispensable" but usually sounds less urgent than *essential:* The switch is *necessary* if you want to use both printers.

*essentially, substantially*

*Essentially* is used most often to mean "basically": His duties will be *essentially* the same as always. *Essential* implies something indispensable: A security system is *essential* when data are confidential.

*Substantially* also means "basically" and is used interchangeably with *essentially*. *Substantial* suggests a significant size or quantity and may or may not be indispensable: He invested a *substantial* amount of money in the company.

### example, instance, sample

*Example* means "one of a number of things": The diskette is an *example* of data-storage media. It also means "pattern; model": His attitude sets an *example* for all of us.

*Instance* refers to a situation that is used to illustrate something: In that *instance,* he was wrong.

*Sample* means "a part; a specimen": The fabric *sample* shows the vivid colors being offered this year.

### explicit, implicit

*Explicit* means "clear; fully developed": The supervisor gave them *explicit* instructions.

*Implicit* means "understood but not revealed or expressed": His devotion to the company was *implicit* in his actions. It also means "without doubt or reservation": She has *implicit* faith in the new board.

### extended, extensive

*Extended,* a verb, refers to spatial quality and means "spread out; prolonged": The cables were *extended* from one machine to the other. It is overused by many business writers to mean "offer" or "send."

*Extensive,* an adjective, is similar but more specifically means "having a wide range or extent; broad; far-reaching": Her influence is *extensive* in the business world.

### farther, further

*Farther,* in strict usage, refers to physical distance or spatial measurement: He drove 20 miles *farther* before stopping for the night.

*Further,* in strict usage, refers to quantity or degree: We should discuss the matter *further.* It also means "to promote": He hopes to *further* his career.

Business writers now tend to use both terms interchangeably, often using *further* for all situations.

### fashion, manner, mode

*Fashion* usually means "a particular style at a particular time": Artificial fur is the latest *fashion.*

*Manner* describes "behavior; social conduct": Her *manners* were exemplary.

*Mode* means "a particular form of something": Voice mail is a new *mode* of messaging.

### feasible, possible

*Feasible* means "capable of being done": The procedure is *feasible.*

*Possible* means "within realistic limits; likely to occur": It is *possible* that interest rates will fall.

### fewer, less

*Fewer* is used to describe numbers: *Fewer* applications were received this month.

*Less* is used to describe amounts, quantities, or abstractions: The danger of a recession is *less* today than it was a year ago.

### frequent, recurring

*Frequent* means "habitual; persistent; occurring at short intervals": She made *frequent* complaints.

*Recurring* means "occurring again and again; occurring repeatedly": His *recurring* dissatisfaction suggests a deeper problem.

### gloomy, pessimistic

*Gloomy* implies darkness or depression: She was *gloomy* after hearing that the company had declared bankruptcy.

*Pessimistic* means "an inclination to expect the worst; an inclination to emphasize the negative or adverse aspect": He was *pessimistic* about the prospects for success.

### good, well

*Good,* as an adjective, means "praiseworthy; useful; beneficial; free from problems": It was a *good* performance.

*Well,* as an adjective, means "in good health": She is *well.* As an adverb, it means "in a proper manner; with skill": He conducted the project very *well.*

### guarantee, guaranty

*Guarantee,* as a noun, means "an assurance that some condition will be met": The copier had a three-month *guarantee.* As a verb, it means "to ensure that some debt or obligation will be fulfilled": The company *guaranteed* its work. As a verb, *guarantee* is preferred over *guaranty.*

*Guaranty,* as a noun, is used most often in today's business world to mean "the fact of giving security": contract of *guaranty.*

### handle, manage

*Handle* means "to control or manage; to deal with," and is preferred over *manage* when physical action is involved: He *handled* the controls while his partner rested.

*Manage* also means "to control or handle; to deal with," and is preferred over *handle* when nonphysical action is involved: The secretary *managed* the office in her employer's absence.

### happen, occur, transpire

*Happen* means "to occur by chance": If I *happen* to leave early, I'll stop at the bookstore.

*Occur* means "to take place, often unexpectedly," and usually refers to a specific event: The price increase *occurred* sooner than we expected.

*Transpire* means "to pass off; to excrete as a vapor": The leaves *transpired.* Figuratively, it means "to become apparent": The state of the company became clear as events *transpired.* Any remark used figuratively should be avoided in international correspondence.

### if, whether

*If* is used to introduce one condition and often suggests doubt: *If* we leave now, we can be home by midnight.

*Whether* is used to introduce more than one condition: He couldn't decide *whether* [or not] to accept the offer.

### imagine, suppose

*Imagine,* used strictly, means "to form a mental image of something": I *imagine* that offices in the next century will be completely computerized.

*Suppose* means "to assume or suspect something": I *suppose* you have already heard about the layoffs.

### imply, infer

*Imply* means "to suggest by inference or association": His statement *implies* that there was another reason for the company's failure.

*Infer* means "to reach a conclusion from facts or circumstances": She incorrectly *inferred* from my comments that funding had been approved.

### impracticable, impractical

*Impracticable* means "not capable of being used or accomplished": His recommendations to disband are *impracticable.*

*Impractical* means "not capable of dealing sensibly or practically with something": Her approach is *impractical.*

### ineffective, ineffectual

*Ineffective* means "not producing the intended effect; not effective," and often suggests incompetence in some particular area: She is an *ineffective* speaker.

*Ineffectual* also means "not producing the intended effect; not effective," and often suggests a general lack of competence: No matter what he does, he is *ineffectual.*

### ingenious, ingenuous

*Ingenious* means "resourceful; inventive; clever": That is an *ingenious* strategy.

*Ingenuous* means "innocent; childlike; candid": The new recruits are so *ingenuous.*

### irony, sarcasm, satire

*Irony* means "the use of words or statements to express something other than their literal meaning": "Nice day," she said, as the wind and rain beat against the window.

*Sarcasm* means "a sharp, critical, derisive, often bitter and cruel form of wit": I see that you have a new hairdo. Those birds circling overhead apparently noticed it too.

*Satire* means "a combination of wit and irony, usually directed toward vice or folly": The book is a *satire* about American values.

Avoid all of the foregoing expressions in international correspondence.

### irreversible, irrevocable

*Irreversible* means "not capable of being changed or reversed" and usually refers to some pattern or course of action: The judge's ruling is *irreversible.*

*Irrevocable* means "not capable of being revoked or repealed" and usually refers to a specific action or statement: Her decision to resign was *irrevocable.*

### judicial, judicious

*Judicial* means "of or relating to justice or the judiciary": He has always been interested in *judicial* proceedings.

*Judicious* means "having or exercising sound or wise judgment": He has always made *judicious* use of his money.

*know, realize*

*Know* means "to perceive; to understand": I *know* how you feel.

*Realize* means "to accomplish; to grasp fully," and implies a more thorough understanding than *know:* Do you *realize* what a serious impact this may have?

*lack, need, want*

*Lack,* as a noun, means "a deficiency" or "absence": He has a *lack* of interest in a medical career.

*Need,* as a noun, refers to a lack of something desirable or useful and often is used in an emotional context: She *needs* to be appreciated.

*Want,* as a noun, also refers to a lack of something needed or desired: His *wants* are few.

As verbs, *lack* suggests a deficiency; *need,* a necessity; and *want,* a desire.

*lawful, legal*

*Lawful* means "to be in harmony with some form of law, principle, or doctrine; rightful, ethical": Although smoking cigarettes in one's own home may be *lawful,* many people doubt the wisdom of doing so.

*Legal* means "founded on the law; established by law": The company paid the proper amount of tax according to *legal* requirements.

*libel, slander*

*Libel* means "printed or written defamation causing injury to someone's reputation": His derogatory comments in the magazine constitute *libel.*

*Slander* means "oral defamation causing injury to someone's reputation": His malicious comments at the convention about Mr. Bennett constitute *slander.*

*luxuriant, luxurious*

*Luxuriant* means "abundant growth": The foliage is *luxuriant.*

*Luxurious* means "characterized by self-indulgence or luxury": The president's office is *luxurious.*

*maintain, repair, service*

*Maintain* means "to preserve; to keep in existing condition": The county has to *maintain* this road.

*Repair* means "to restore; to fix": We need to *repair* the old typewriter.

*Service* also means "to keep in existing condition" and implies inspection as well as repair and maintenance: I ordered a monthly *service* contract for our computers.

*majority, minority, plurality*

*Majority* means "a number greater than one-half of the total."

*Minority* means "a number less than one-half of the total."

*Plurality* means "the number of votes in excess of those cast for the closest contender when there are two or more candidates": Mr. Watson received fifty-five thousand votes, Ms. Johnston received forty thousand votes, and Mrs. Jenson received thirty thousand votes; thus Mr. Watson had a *plurality* of fifteen thousand votes.

*meticulous, scrupulous*

*Meticulous* refers to extreme care in attending to details: The secretary does *meticulous* work.

*Scrupulous* refers to high principles and conscientious regard: The company is *scrupulous* in its dealings with customers.

*mysterious, mystical, mythical*

*Mysterious* means "something inexplicable; something puzzling": His behavior seemed *mysterious* even to members of his family.

*Mystical* means "something having a spiritual or unapparent significance": The statues are a *mystical* symbol of a lost culture.

*Mythical* means "something imaginary; something involving a myth": The *mythical* tale was his inspiration for the animated children's series.

### official, officious

*Official* means "relating to an office or position of authority or trust": He is a United Nations *official.*

*Officious* means "meddlesome": Her unwanted interference was *officious.*

### omission, oversight

*Omission* means "something left out; something undone or neglected": The *omission* in the contract was intentional.

*Oversight* means "an inadvertent omission or error": His name was left off the guest list because of an *oversight.*

### oral, verbal

*Oral* means "spoken; by mouth": Mr. Sims and Ms. Jackson had an *oral* agreement but nothing in writing.

*Verbal* means "consisting of words, written or spoken": The *verbal* instructions are unclear.

To be more precise, use *written* instead of *verbal.*

### part, portion, share

*Part* means "a subdivision of the whole": Here is *part* of the assignment.

*Portion* means "a part or share of something usually intended for a specific purpose": His *portion* of the work is easier than hers.

*Share* means "the part or portion of something belonging to or given by someone": I am having my *share* of the profits deposited directly.

### persons, people

*Persons* is often preferred in references to a few individuals or when specific individuals are being discussed: Two *persons* shared the prize.

*People* is often preferred in references to large groups or indefinite numbers: Hundreds of *people* attended the concert.

### point of view, standpoint, viewpoint

*Point of view, standpoint*, and *viewpoint* are used or overused interchangeably by business writers. They refer to an attitude or opinion: From my *point of view*, the plan will not solve anything.

Avoid all of the foregoing terms in international correspondence.

### practical, practicable

*Practical* means "sensible; useful; efficient; realistic; workable; manageable": She has a *practical* solution to the problem.

*Practicable* means "feasible; possible," but not necessarily sensible or useful: There is no *practicable* way to implement the program.

### prescribed, proscribed

*Prescribed* means "laid down as a guide; ordered": The manager *prescribed* a series of exercise breaks.

*Proscribed* means "condemned; outlawed": The company *proscribed* loud music in the workstations.

### presumably, supposedly

*Presumably* means "capable of being taken for granted; reasonably assumed to be true": *Presumably,* her experience will give her an edge over the other candidates.

*Supposedly* means "believed, sometimes mistakenly, to be true; imagined to be true": He *supposedly* wants the job, although he hasn't yet applied for it.

Both of the foregoing terms should be avoided in international correspondence.

### principal, principle

*Principal*, as a noun, means "chief participant or head" (the *principal* in the negotiations) or "a sum of money": *principal* and interest. As an adjective, it means "most important or consequential": the *principal* objective.

*Principle,* a noun, refers to "a rule, doctrine, or assumption": the *principle* of human dignity.

### proved, proven

*Proved* is the past tense and past participle of *prove:* They [have] *proved* their point. *Proved* is preferred over *proven* as a past participle.

*Proven* is an adjective (a *proven* belief) and also a past participle: The employees have *proven* their loyalty.

### purposefully, purposely

*Purposefully,* the stronger of the two terms, means "with a definite aim or purpose; deliberately; with determination": He *purposefully* planned the trip to avoid the holidays.

*Purposely* also means "intentionally; deliberately," but with less determination: He *purposely* avoided the subject.

### qualitative, quantitative

*Qualitative* refers to quality or essential character: Their *qualitative* analysis was intended to identify the components of the substance.

*Quantitative* refers to quantity or a measurement: Their *quantitative* analysis was designed to determine the proportions of the components of the substance.

### raise, rear

*Raise,* as a verb, means "to arouse; to elevate": *raise* the flag. As a noun, it commonly means "an increase in pay": She received a *raise* this year.

*Rear,* as a verb, means "to raise upright" (the horse *rears*) or "to bring up a child" (*rear* one child).

Colloquially, one refers to people who *raise* children as well as animals.

*reaction, reply, response*

*Reaction* means "a response to stimuli": The patient's *reaction* was severe. It should not be used to mean a response that is an "attitude, viewpoint, or feeling."

*Reply* means "a response in words or gestures": She sent a *reply* today.

*Response,* used interchangeably with *reply,* is an answer; a reply: His *response* was negative.

*redundant, superfluous*

*Redundant* means "more than necessary; repetitive," and usually refers to wordiness in oral and written communication: The last comment is *redundant.*

*Superfluous* means "exceeding what is needed," but the emphasis in on anything useless or unnecessary rather than repetitive: The editor's task was to delete all *superfluous* words from the text.

*regardless, disregardless, irregardless*

*Regardless* means "despite everything": *Regardless* of public opinion, the company decided to relocate.

*Disregardless* and *irregardless* are used improperly for *regardless.* In both cases, the prefixes *dis-* and *ir-* are unnecessary.

*reported, reputed*

*Reported* means "made known": The secretary *reported* the theft.

*Reputed* means "considered; believed; supposed": He is a *reputed* leader in the field.

*shall, will*

*Shall,* traditionally, is used in the first person to express future time: I *shall* be there tomorrow.

*Will,* traditionally, is used in the second or third person to express future time: He *will* be there tomorrow.

Some authorities believe *shall* sounds too formal in the first person and prefer to use *will* in all instances: I *will,* you *will,* he *will,* she *will,* they *will.*

### stationary, stationery

*Stationary,* an adjective, means "fixed, immobile": The statue is *stationary.*

*Stationery,* a noun, means "writing paper, envelopes, and related supplies": We buy our *stationery* from XYZ Press.

### strain, stress

*Strain,* as a verb, means "to misuse; to filter; to stretch beyond belief; to overexert": That prospect *strains* the imagination. As a noun, it means "excessive exertion or tension": He is often bothered by back *strain.*

*Stress,* as a verb, means "to accent; to emphasize": The speaker *stressed* the need to be involved. As a noun, it means "pressure; tension": Secretaries often experience increased *stress* during times of peak work loads.

### subconscious, unconscious

*Subconscious* means "mental activities of which one is not conscious or aware": He must have had some *subconscious* motive for his actions.

*Unconscious* means "loss of consciousness or awareness": The victim was *unconscious* when the police arrived.

### that, which

*That* refers to persons, animals, or things and may be used in restrictive clauses, where the clause is essential to explain the preceding information: The committee *that* we formed last month has already disbanded. The clause "that we formed last month" explains *which* committee and hence should not be set off with commas.

*Which* refers to animals and things and may be used in nonrestrictive clauses introduced by *which* where the clause is *not* essential to the rest of the sentence: The Finance Committee, *which* we formed last month, has already disbanded. The clause "which we formed last month" in this case is *not* essential to explain *which* committee and hence should be set off with commas.

### *varied, various*

*Varied* means "diverse; with numerous forms; altered": He has a *varied* educational background.

*Various* means "dissimilar; separate; different": She traveled in *various* African countries.

### *viable, workable*

*Viable,* an overused and misused term, means "capable of existence; likely to produce continued success": By the end of its first year, the new company was a *viable* entity.

*Workable* means "practicable; feasible; capable of working or succeeding if properly managed": The proposed schedule seems *workable.*

### *want, wish*

*Want* suggests a need or longing: He *wants* the assignment.

*Wish* is used more often to suggest hope as well as desire: I *wish* we were able to attend the book fair.

### *who, whom*

*Who* is in the subjective case, for example, the subject of a verb or predicate pronoun: The question of *who* will be selected is on everyone's mind. *Who* is the subject of *will be.*

*Whom* is in the objective case, for example, the object of a verb or preposition: He is the writer *whom* we met on the plane. *Whom* is the object of *met.*

# 16

# FOREIGN LANGUAGE

## TWO HUNDRED FOREIGN WORDS AND PHRASES THAT YOU SHOULD KNOW

Even though we live in a global economy, English-language writers are advised not to overuse foreign words and expressions in domestic correspondence. Yet certain terms frequently appear in business communication, and secretaries and other office professionals should be familiar with them. Here are two hundred common foreign words and expressions that you should know.

*à bon marché (Fr.):* at a bargain price.

*à la carte (Fr.):* according to a menu with items priced separately.

*a la mode (Fr.):* in fashion.

*a priori (Lat.):* reasoned from self-evident propositions.

*apropos (Fr.):* concerning; pertinent to.

*a propos de rien (Fr.):* apropos of nothing; irrelevant.

*arigato (Jpn.):* Thank you.

*atelier (Fr.):* workshop; studio.

*attaché (Fr.):* diplomatic official.

*au contraire (Fr.):* on or to the contrary.

*au revoir (Fr.):* good-bye.

*aussitôt dit, aussitôt fait (Fr.):* no sooner said than done.

*autobahn (Ger.):* German motorway.

*autre temps (Fr.):* other times.

*avec plaisir (Fr.):* with pleasure.

*belles lettres (Fr.):* serious literature.

*bête noire (Fr.):* something or someone feared or disliked.

*bolshoi (Rus.):* large; great.

*bona fide (Lat.):* in good faith; genuine.

*bonhomie (Fr.):* good nature.

*bon jour (Fr.):* good day; hello.

*bon soir (Fr.):* good evening; good night.

*bravura (It.):* display of daring or brilliance.

*cache (Fr.):* something hidden.

*camaraderie (Fr.):* goodwill.

*carpe diem (Lat.):* Enjoy the present.

*carte blanche (Fr.):* unconditional power; complete freedom.

*causa sine qua non (Lat.):* an indispensable condition; fundamental cause.

*caveat emptor (Lat.):* Let the buyer beware.

*c'est à dire (Fr.):* that is to say.

*c'est la vie (Fr.):* Such is life.

*chacun à son goût (Fr.):* everyone to his own taste.

*chef de cuisine (Fr.):* head cook.

*chef d'oeuvre (Fr.):* masterpiece.

*cloisonne (Fr.):* enameled decoration.

*cogito ergo sum (Lat.):* I think, therefore, I am.

*communique (Fr.):* official report; communication.

*connoisseur (Fr.):* expert.

*cortege (Fr.):* funeral or other procession.

*coterie (Fr.):* exclusive group.

*coup d'etat (Fr.):* sudden overthrow.

*critique (Fr.):* critical review.

*danke schön (Ger.):* many thanks.

*debacle (Fr.):* sudden collapse.

*debonair (Fr.):* suave; urbane.

*degustibus non est disputandum (Lat.):* There is no arguing about tastes.

*Dei gratia (Lat.):* by the grace of God.

*denouement (Fr.):* climax; outcome.

*Deo gratias (Lat.):* Thanks be to God.

*Deo volente (Lat.):* God willing.

*de riguer (Fr.):* customary; fashionable; strictly necessary.

*de trop (Fr.):* too much; too many; superfluous.

*ding hao (Ch.):* very good; fine; excellent.

*dossier (Fr.):* documents pertaining to a particular subject.

*do svidaniya (Rus.):* till we meet again; goodbye.

*double-entendre (Fr.):* two meanings.

*ecce homo (Lat.):* Behold the man.

*effendi (Turk.):* man of property; authority; education (eastern Mediterranean).

*elan (Fr.):* vigorous spirit or enthusiasm; flair.

*en famille (Fr.):* in one's family; informally.

*ennui (Fr.):* boredom.

*en plein jour (Fr.):* in full daylight; openly.

*en rapport (Fr.):* in sympathy or agreement.

*entourage (Fr.):* attendants.

*entre nous (Fr.):* between us; confidentially.

*e pluribus unum (Lat.):* one out of many.

*ersatz (Ger.):* imitation; substitute.

*ex cathedra (Lat.):* with the authority derived from one's office.

*ex more (Lat.):* according to custom.

*ex officio (Lat.):* by virtue of or because of an office.

*fait accompli (Fr.):* an accomplished fact or deed.

*finis (Lat.):* the end; the conclusion

*gauche (Fr.):* tactless.

*gomei kaisha (Jpn.):* partnership; association.

*gratis (Lat.):* free of charge.

*habitue (Fr.):* regular.

*hauteur (Fr.):* haughty manner.

*hoc anno (Lat.):* in this year.

*humanum est errare (Lat.):* To err is human.

*imbroglio (It.):* a state of great confusion; a difficult situation; a complicated misunderstanding.

*impasse (Fr.):* deadlock.

*in extremis (Lat.):* at the point of death.

*in loco parentis (Lat.):* in the place of a parent.

*in medias res (Lat.):* in or into the middle of a sequence of events.

*in perpetuum (Lat.):* forever.

*in propria persona (Lat.):* in one's own person.

*in rerum natura (Lat.):* in the nature of things.

*in situ (Lat.):* in its place.

*in statu quo (Lat.):* in the state in which it was before.

*inter alia (Lat.):* among other things.

*in toto (Lat.):* altogether; entirely.

*ipso jure (Lat.):* by the law itself.

*jure divino (Lat.):* by divine law.

*jus canonicum (Lat.):* canon law.

*justitia omnibus (Lat.):* justice for all.

*j'y suis, j'y reste (Fr.):* Here I am, here I stay.

*kapellmeister (Ger.):* director of choir or orchestra.

*laissez faire (Fr.):* governmental policy of noninterference.

*laus Deo (Lat.):* Praise be to God.

*le roi est mort, vive le roi (Fr.):* The king is dead! Long live the king!

*le style, c'est l'homme (Fr.):* The style is the man.

*le tout ensemble (Fr.):* the whole (taken) together.

*liaison (Fr.):* affair; connection.

*locus in quo (Lat.):* the place in which.

*loquitur (Lat.):* He or she speaks.

*macabre (Fr.):* ghastly; dwelling on the gruesome.

*ma foi (Fr.):* really!

*mea culpa (Lat.):* acknowledgment of personal fault or error.

*melee (Fr.):* free-for-all.

*mens sana in corpore (Lat.):* a sound mind in a healthy body.

*mi casa es su casa (Sp.):* My house is your house.

*mikado (Jpn.):* (title of) emperor of Japan.

*millennium (Lat.):* a period of one thousand years.

*mise en scène (Fr.):* a stage setting; environment.

*modus operandi (Lat.):* method of operating.

*mon ami (Fr.):* my friend.

*morituri te salutamus (Lat.):* We who are about to die salute you.

*mutatis mutandis (Lat.):* the necessary changes having been made.

*nee (Fr.):* born.

*nemine contradicente (Lat.):* no one contradicting.

*nemine dissentiente (Lat.):* no one dissenting.

*n'est-ce pas? (Fr.):* Isn't that so?

*nolens volens (Lat.):* whether willing or not.

*nom de guerre (Fr.):* a pseudonym.

*nom de plume (Fr.):* pen name; pseudonym.

*nouveau riche (Fr.):* newly rich.

*nuance (Fr.):* subtle distinction.

*obiit (Lat.):* He or she died.

*objet d'art (Fr.):* a work of art.

*okimono (Jpn.):* decorative objects.

*opere citato (Lat.):* in the work cited.

*panache (Fr.):* stylish; high spirits; verve.

*par excellence (Fr.):* best of a kind.

*pari passu (Lat.):* with equal pace.

*parvenu(e) (Fr.):* upstart.

*pasha (Turk.):* man of high rank or office (e.g., in Turkey or North Africa).

*pax vobiscum (Lat.):* Peace be with you.

*penchant (Fr.):* a strong or habitual inclination.

*per se (Lat.):* in itself; essentially; as such.

*persona grata (Lat.):* fully acceptable.

*persona non grata (Lat.):* personally unacceptable.

*piece de resistance (Fr.):* an outstanding accomplishment.

*pied-à-terre (Fr.):* part-time or temporary lodging.

*pince-nez (Fr.):* eyeglasses clipped to one's nose.

*pis aller (Fr.):* the last resort.

*pleno jure (Lat.):* with full authority.

*plus ça change, plus c'est la même chose (Fr.):* The more it changes, the more it's the same thing.

*potpourri (Fr.):* mixture; medley.

*précis (Fr.):* summary.

*primus inter pares (Lat.):* first among equals.

*pro forma (Lat.):* done in a perfunctory way; as a matter of form.

*pro tempore (Lat.):* for the time being; temporarily.

*protege (Fr.):* someone trained by a person of experience or prominence.

*quod vide (Lat.):* which see.

*quo jure? (Lat.):* by what right?

*raconteur (Fr.):* storyteller.

*raison d'être (Fr.):* reason for existing or being.

*recherchee (Fr.):* choice.

*reich (Ger.):* a state or an empire.

*rendezvous (Fr.):* place for a meeting; the meeting itself.

*requiescat in pace (Lat.):* May he or she rest in peace.

*ricochet (Fr.):* rebound.

*risque (Fr.):* suggestive.

*rococo (Lat.):* elaborate; ornate.

*salon (Fr.):* elegant home or room; fashionable gathering of notables in the home of a prominent person.

*sans doute (Fr.):* without doubt.

*sans gêne (Fr.):* without embarrassment.

*sans pareil (Fr.):* without equal.

*sans peine (Fr.):* without difficulty.

*sans souci (Fr.):* carefree.

*savoir-faire (Fr.):* know-how; knowledge.

*sayonara (Jpn.):* goodbye.

*secundum (Lat.):* according to.

*semper idem (Lat.):* always the same.

*semper paratus (Lat.):* always ready.

*sine die (Lat.):* without a day specified (for a future meeting).

*sine qua non (Lat.):* something essential; precondition.

*spasiba (Rus.):* Thank you.

*sub verbo (Lat.):* under the word.

*summum bonum (Lat.):* the greatest good.

*suo jure (Lat.):* in one's own right.

*suo loco (Lat.):* in one's rightful place.

*suum cuique (Lat.):* to each his own.

*table d'hote (Fr.):* meal served to all guests at a certain time for a certain price.

*tant mieux (Fr.):* so much the better.

*tant pis (Fr.):* so much the worse.

*Tao (Ch.):* pathway; the right way; rational basis of human conduct.

*tempora mutantur (Lat.):* Times change.

*tempus fugit (Lat.):* Time flies.

*tete-a-tete (Fr.):* private conversation.

*tong (Ch.):* meeting place; secret organization.

*trompe-l'oeil (Fr.):* art so real as to deceive the eye.

*ut infra (Lat.):* as below.

*ut supra (Lat.):* as above.

*vale (Lat.):* Farewell.

*verbatim et literatim (Lat.):* word for word and letter for letter.

*voilà (Fr.):* Look! See!

*weltschmerz (Ger.):* mental depression or apathy caused by comparing the actual state of the world with an ideal state.

*wen (Ch.):* literature; letters; culture.

*zdrávstvui (Rus.):* a salutation for all occasions, equivalent to "good morning," "good day," etc.

## TWO DOZEN OVERUSED FOREIGN TERMS

Some foreign words and expressions have been used so often that they have become anglicized. The problem is that English-language writers tend to use them for effect—to impress readers and listeners. When such terms are used over and over, they become pretentious and annoying. The following terms should be used sparingly, if at all.

| | | |
|---|---|---|
| a priori | critique | nouveau riche |
| apropos | entre nous | objet d'art |
| au contraire | finis | par excellence |
| bona fide | gratis | per se |
| carte blanche | inter alia | piece de resistance |
| chef d'oeuvre | in toto | raison d'être |
| communique | melee | savoir-faire |
| coup d'etat | modus operandi | sine qua non |

## ANGLICIZED FOREIGN WORDS THAT NEED NO ACCENTS

Foreign terms that have become completely anglicized need no diacritical marks. It is not incorrect, however, to add accents, and some dictionaries and style guides may still recommend them. Follow the preferred practice in your office.

| | | |
|---|---|---|
| abaca | blase | cliche |
| aide memoire | boutonniere | cloisonne |
| a la carte | brassiere | comedienne |
| a la king | cabana | comme ci comme ca |
| a la mode | cafe | communique |
| angstrom | cafeteria | confrere |
| apertif | caique | consomme |
| applique | canape | cortege |
| apropos | cause celebre | coulee |
| auto(s)-da-fe | chateau | coup de grace |

| | | |
|---|---|---|
| coup d'etat | fiance (*masc., fem.*) | porte cochere |
| coupe | frappe | porte lumiere |
| creme | garcon | portiere |
| crepe | glace | pousse cafe |
| crepe de chine | grille | premiere |
| critique | gruyere | protege (*masc., fem.*) |
| critiquing | habitue | puree |
| debacle | ingenue | rale |
| debris | jardiniere | recherche |
| debut | litterateur | regime |
| debutante | materiel | risque (*masc., fem.*) |
| decollete | matinee | role |
| dejeuner | melange | rotisserie |
| denouement | melee | roue |
| depot | menage | saute |
| dos-a-dos | mesalliance | seance |
| eclair | metier | senor |
| eclat | moire | smorgasbord |
| ecru | naive | soiree |
| elan | naivete | souffle |
| elite | nee | suede |
| entree | opera bouffe | table d'hote |
| etude | opera comique | tete-a-tete |
| facade | papier mache | tragedienne |
| faience | piece de resistance | vicuna |
| fete | pleiade | vis-a-vis |

# PART THREE

# REFERENCE
# SECTION

# 17
# WEIGHTS, MEASURES, AND VALUES

## UNITS IN THE METRIC SYSTEM

The metric system, also known as the SI system (Système International), is increasing in use throughout the world. Secretaries should therefore understand the terminology associated with it and know how to make routine calculations and conversions from the traditional U.S. system of weights and measures. In general, the international system has seven *base units* for independent quantities and two *supplementary units* for geometrical measurement. The *derived units* are expressed in terms of either base or supplementary units.

### BASE UNITS

| *Quantity* | *Unit Name* | *Symbol* |
|------------|-------------|----------|
| length | meter | m |
| mass | kilogram | kg |
| time | second | s |
| temperature | Kelvin | K |

| | | |
|---|---|---|
| electric current | ampere | A |
| luminous intensity | candela | cd |
| amount of substance | mole | mol |

### SUPPLEMENTARY UNITS

| Quantity | Unit Name | Symbol |
|---|---|---|
| plane angle | radian | rad |
| solid angle | steradian | sr |

### DERIVED UNITS: QUANTITY, UNIT NAME, SYMBOL

| Quantity | Unit Name | Symbol |
|---|---|---|
| area | square meter | $m^2$ |
| volume | cubic meter | $m^3$ |
| velocity, speed | meter per second | m/s |
| acceleration | meter per second squared | $m/s^2$ |
| density | kilogram per cubic meter | $kg/m^3$ |
| luminescence | candela per square meter | $cd/m^2$ |

### DERIVED UNITS: QUANTITY, UNIT NAME, SYMBOL, DERIVATION

| Quantity | Unit Name | Symbol | Derivation |
|---|---|---|---|
| frequency | hertz | Hz | $s^{-1}$ |
| force | Newton | N | $m \bullet kg/s^2$ |
| pressure | Newton per square meter | $N/m^2$ | |
| work, energy, quantity of heat | joule | J | $N \bullet m$ |
| power | watt | W | J/s |
| electric charge, quantity of electricity | coulomb | C | $A \bullet s$ |
| voltage, potential difference | volt | V | W/A |

## SPELLING AND SYMBOLS FOR UNITS

This list provides the spelling of common metric names of units and the associated symbols. Notice that common U.S. abbreviations, such as *oz.* (ounce), are punctuated in this list as they would be in general business usage, whereas the metric symbols, such as *mm* (millimeter), are not. (*Note*: In some contexts and in some organizations, traditional U.S. abbreviations may not be punctuated. The National Bureau of Standards, for example, uses no punctuation after either metric units or conventional U.S. units; thus, *in, ft, lb,* and so on. Other organizations observe the rule that a period should be used when the abbreviation might be mistaken for an actual word. Hence, *in.,* with a period, denotes an abbreviation, and *in,* without punctuation, denotes an actual word.)

| *Unit* | *Symbol* |
|---|---|
| acre | acre |
| are | a |
| barrel | bbl |
| board foot | fbm |
| bushel | bu. |
| carat | c |
| Celsius, degree | °C |
| centare | ca |
| centigram | cg |
| centiliter | cl |
| centimeter | cm |
| chain | ch |
| cubic centimeter | $cm^3$ |
| cubic decimeter | $dm^3$ |
| cubic dekameter | $dam^3$ |
| cubic foot | $ft.^3$ |
| cubic hectometer | $hm^3$ |
| cubic inch | $in.^3$ |
| cubic kilometer | $km^3$ |
| cubic meter | $m^3$ |

| Unit | Symbol |
|---|---|
| cubic mile | mi.$^3$ |
| cubic millimeter | mm$^3$ |
| cubic yard | yd.$^3$ |
| decigram | dg |
| deciliter | dl |
| decimeter | dm |
| dekagram | dag |
| dekaliter | dal |
| dekameter | dam |
| dram, avoirdupois | dr., avdp. |
| fathom | fath. |
| foot | ft. |
| furlong | furlong |
| gallon | gal. |
| grain | grain |
| gram | g |
| hectare | ha |
| hectogram | hg |
| hectoliter | hl |
| hectometer | hm |
| hogshead | hhd |
| hundredweight | cwt |
| inch | in. |
| International Nautical Mile | INM |
| Kelvin | K |
| kilogram | kg |
| kiloliter | kl |
| kilometer | km |
| link | link |
| liquid | liq. |
| liter | liter |
| meter | m |
| microgram | μg |

| Unit | Symbol |
| --- | --- |
| microinch | μin. |
| microliter | μl |
| micrometer | μm |
| mile | mi. |
| milligram | mg |
| milliliter | ml |
| millimeter | mm |
| minim | minim |
| ounce | oz. |
| ounce, avoirdupois | oz., avdp. |
| ounce, fluid, (or liquid) | fl. oz. (liq. oz.) |
| ounce, troy | oz., tr. |
| peck | peck |
| pennyweight | dwt |
| pint, liquid | liq. pt. |
| pound | lb. |
| pound, avoirdupois | lb., avdp. |
| pound, troy | lb., tr. |
| quart, liquid | liq. qt. |
| rod | rod |
| second | s |
| square centimeter | $cm^2$ |
| square decimeter | $dm^2$ |
| square dekameter | $dam^2$ |
| square foot | $ft.^2$ |
| square hectometer | $hm^2$ |
| square inch | $in.^2$ |
| square kilometer | $km^2$ |
| square meter | $m^2$ |
| square mile | $mi.^2$ |
| square millimeter | $mm^2$ |
| square yard | $yd.^2$ |

| *Unit* | *Symbol* |
|--------|----------|
| ton, long | long ton |
| ton, metric | t |
| ton, short | short ton |
| yard | yd. |

## PREFIXES OF METRIC UNITS

The following table provides sixteen prefixes that can be combined with the base units to form multiples and submultiples of the metric system. Hence the prefix *kilo* when added to the unit *meter* becomes *kilometer.* As indicated in this table: 1 kilometer = 1,000 meters.

| *Prefix* | *Multiplication Factor* | *Symbol* |
|----------|------------------------|----------|
| exa | 1,000,000,000,000,000,000 ($10^{18}$) (one quintillion) | E |
| peta | 1,000,000,000,000,000 ($10^{15}$) (one quadrillion) | P |
| tera | 1,000,000,000,000 ($10^{12}$) (one trillion) | T |
| giga | 1,000,000,000 ($10^{9}$) (one billion) | G |
| mega | 1,000,000 ($10^{6}$) (one million) | M |
| kilo | 1,000 ($10^{3}$) (one thousand) | k |
| hecto | 100 ($10^{2}$) (one hundred) | h |
| deka | 10 (ten) | da |
| deci | 0.1 ($10^{-1}$) (one-tenth) | d |
| centi | 0.01 ($10^{-2}$) (one-hundredth) | c |
| milli | 0.001 ($10^{-3}$) (one-thousandth) | m |
| micro | 0.000,001 ($10^{-6}$) (one-millionth) | μ |

| Prefix | Multiplication Factor | Symbol |
|--------|----------------------|--------|
| nano | 0.000,000,001 ($10^{-9}$) (one-billionth) | n |
| pico | 0.000,000,000,001 ($10^{-12}$) (one-trillionth) | p |
| femto | 0.000,000,000,000,001 ($10^{-15}$) (one-quadrillionth) | f |
| atto | 0.000,000,000,000,000,001 ($10^{-18}$) (one-quintillionth) | a |

## METRIC PREFIXES AND MULTIPLICATION FACTORS

This list indicates how the addition of a prefix to a base unit increases the unit's value. For example, 1 hectometer = 100 meters.

*Weight*

1 *kilo*gram = 1,000 grams

1 *hecto*gram = 100 grams

1 *deka*gram = 10 grams

1 gram = 1 gram

1 *deci*gram = 0.1 gram

1 *centi*gram = 0.01 gram

1 *milli*gram = 0.001 gram

*Length*

1 *kilo*meter = 1,000 meters

1 *hecto*meter = 100 meters

1 *deka*meter = 10 meters

1 meter = 1 meter

1 *deci*meter = 0.1 meter

1 *centi*meter = 0.01 meter

1 *milli*meter = 0.001 meter

*Volume*

1 *hecto*liter = 100 liters

1 *deka*liter = 10 liters

1 liter = 1 liter

1 *centi*liter = 0.01 liter

1 *milli*liter = 0.001 liter

## TRADITIONAL WEIGHTS, MEASURES, AND VALUES AND THE METRIC EQUIVALENTS

This table provides the traditional U.S. equivalent and the metric equivalent for each unit. The units are arranged in categories of length, area, weight, and volume or capacity.

### LENGTH

| *Unit* | *U.S. Equivalent* | *Metric Equivalent* |
| --- | --- | --- |
| inch | 0.083 foot | 2.540 centimeters |
| foot | 1/3 yard, 12 inches | 0.305 meter |
| yard | 3 feet, 36 inches | 0.914 meter |
| rod | 5 1/2 yards, 16 1/2 feet | 5.029 meters |
| mile (statute, land) | 1,760 yards, 5,280 feet, 320 rods | 1.609 kilometers |
| mile (nautical, international) | 1.152 statute miles | 1.852 kilometers |

### AREA

| *Unit* | *U.S. Equivalent* | *Metric Equivalent* |
| --- | --- | --- |
| square inch | 0.007 square foot | 6.452 square centimeters |
| square foot | 144 square inches | 929.030 square centimeters |

| square yard | 1,296 square inches, 9 square feet | 0.836 square meters |
| square rod | 272 1/4 square feet, 30 1/4 square yards | 25.293 square meters |
| acre | 43,560 square feet, 4,840 square yards | 4,047 square meters |
| square mile | 640 acres | 2.590 square kilometers |

## WEIGHT: AVOIRDUPOIS

| *Unit* | *U.S. Equivalent* | *Metric Equivalent* |
|---|---|---|
| grain | 0.036 dram, 0.002285 ounce | 64.799 milligrams |
| dram | 27.344 grains, 0.0625 ounce | 1.772 grams |
| ounce | 16 drams, 437.5 grains | 28.350 grams |
| pound | 16 ounces, 7,000 grains | 453.592 grams |
| ton (short) | 2,000 pounds | 0.907 metric ton (1,000 kilograms) |
| ton (long) | 1.12 short tons, 2,240 pounds | 1.016 metric tons |

## WEIGHT: APOTHECARY

| *Unit* | *U.S. Equivalent* | *Metric Equivalent* |
|---|---|---|
| scruple | 20 grains | 1.296 grams |
| dram | 60 grains | 3.888 grams |
| ounce | 480 grains, 1.097 avoirdupois ounces | 31.103 grams |
| pound | 5,760 grains, 0.823 avoirdupois pound | 373.242 grams |

## VOLUME OR CAPACITY: AREA

| Unit | U.S. Equivalent | Metric Equivalent |
| --- | --- | --- |
| cubic inch | 0.00058 cubic foot | 16.387 cubic centimeters |
| cubic foot | 1,728 cubic inches | 0.028 cubic meter |
| cubic yard | 27 cubic feet | 0.765 cubic meter |

## VOLUME OR CAPACITY: LIQUID MEASURE

| Unit | U.S. Equivalent | Metric Equivalent |
| --- | --- | --- |
| fluid ounce | 8 fluid drams, 1.804 cubic inches | 29.573 milliliters |
| gill | 4 fluid ounces, 7.219 cubic inches | 118.291 milliliters |
| pint | 16 fluid ounces, 28.875 cubic inches | 0.473 liter |
| quart | 2 pints, 57.75 cubic inches | 0.946 liter |
| gallon | 4 quarts, 231 cubic inches | 3.785 liters |
| barrel | varies from 31 to 42 gallons, established by law or usage | varies from 117.35 liters to 158.99 liters |

## VOLUME OR CAPACITY: DRY MEASURE

| Unit | U.S. Equivalent | Metric Equivalent |
| --- | --- | --- |
| pint | 1/2 quart, 33.6 cubic inches | 0.551 liter |
| quart | 2 pints, 67.2 cubic inches | 1.101 liters |
| peck | 8 quarts, 537.605 cubic inches | 8.810 liters |
| bushel | 4 pecks, 2,140.420 cubic inches | 35.239 liters |

### VOLUME OR CAPACITY: BRITISH IMPERIAL LIQUID AND DRY MEASURE

| Unit | U.S. Equivalent | Metric Equivalent |
|---|---|---|
| fluid ounce | 0.961 U.S. fluid ounce, 1.734 cubic inches | 28.413 milliliters |
| pint | 1.032 U.S. dry pints, 1.201 U.S. liquid pints, 34.678 cubic inches | 568.245 milliliters |
| quart | 1.032 U.S. dry quarts, 1.201 U.S. liquid quarts, 69.354 cubic inches | 1.136 liters |
| gallon | 1.201 U.S. gallons, 277.420 cubic inches | 4.546 liters |
| peck | 554.84 cubic inches | 0.009 cubic meter |
| bushel | 1.032 U.S. bushels, 2,219.36 cubic inches | 0.035 cubic meter |

## METRIC MEASUREMENT CONVERSIONS

Sometimes it is necessary to convert conventional U.S. measures into the metric equivalents. The first group of tables in this section gives the metric value or amount of a unit followed by the U.S. equivalent. The last group of tables tells you the multiplication factor to use to convert from metric to conventional.

*Metric Units and U.S. Equivalents*

### LENGTH

| Unit | Meters | U.S. Equivalent |
|---|---|---|
| myriameter | 10,000 | 6.214 miles |

| kilometer | 1,000 | 0.621 miles |
| hectometer | 100 | 109.361 yards |
| dekameter | 10 | 32.808 feet |
| meter | 1 | 39.370 inches |
| decimeter | 0.1 | 3.937 inches |
| centimeter | 0.01 | 0.394 inch |
| millimeter | 0.001 | 0.039 inch |

## AREA

| Unit | Square Meters | U.S. Equivalent |
| --- | --- | --- |
| square kilometer | 1,000,000 | 0.386 square mile |
| hectare | 10,000 | 2.471 acres |
| are | 100 | 119.599 square yards |
| dekiare | 10 | 11.960 square yards |
| centare | 1 | 10.764 square feet |
| square centimeter | 0.0001 | 0.155 square inch |

## VOLUME

| Unit | Cubic Meters | U.S. Equivalent |
| --- | --- | --- |
| dekastere | 10 | 13.079 cubic yards |
| stere | 1 | 1.308 cubic yards |
| decistere | 0.10 | 3.532 cubic feet |
| cubic centimeter | 0.000001 | 0.061 cubic inch |

## CAPACITY

| Unit | Liters | Cubic Measure |
| --- | --- | --- |
| kiloliter | 1,000 | 1.308 cubic yards |
| hectoliter | 100 | 3.532 cubic feet |
| dekaliter | 10 | 0.353 cubic foot |
| liter | 1 | 61.024 cubic inches |
| deciliter | 0.10 | 6.102 cubic inches |

| | | |
|---|---|---|
| centiliter | 0.01 | 0.610 cubic inch |
| milliliter | 0.001 | 0.061 cubic inch |

## MASS AND WEIGHT

| Unit | Grams | U.S. Equivalent |
|---|---|---|
| metric ton | 1,000,000 | 1.102 tons |
| quintal | 100,000 | 220.462 pounds |
| kilogram | 1,000 | 2.205 pounds |
| hectogram | 100 | 3.527 ounces |
| dekagram | 10 | 0.353 ounce |
| gram | 1 | 0.035 ounce |
| decigram | 0.10 | 1.543 grains |
| centigram | 0.01 | 0.154 grain |
| milligram | 0.001 | 0.015 grain |

## *Multiplication Factors for Conversion*

### LENGTH

| When You Know | Multiply by | To Find |
|---|---|---|
| millimeters | 0.04 | inches |
| centimeters | 0.39 | inches |
| meters | 3.28 | feet |
| meters | 1.09 | yards |
| kilometers | 0.62 | miles |
| inches | 25.40 | millimeters |
| inches | 2.54 | centimeters |
| feet | 30.48 | centimeters |
| yards | 0.91 | meters |
| miles | 1.61 | kilometers |

### AREA

| When You Know | Multiply by | To Find |
|---|---|---|
| square centimeters | 0.16 | square inches |

| square meters | 1.20 | square yards |
| square kilometers | 0.39 | square miles |
| hectares (10,000 m$^2$) | 2.47 | acres |
| square inches | 6.45 | square centimeters |
| square feet | 0.09 | square meters |
| square yards | 0.84 | square meters |
| square miles | 2.60 | square kilometers |
| acres | 0.40 | hectares |

## MASS AND WEIGHT

| When You Know | Multiply by | To Find |
| --- | --- | --- |
| grams | 0.035 | ounce |
| kilograms | 2.21 | pounds |
| metric tons (1000 kg) | 1.10 | short tons |
| ounces | 28.35 | grams |
| pounds | 0.45 | kilograms |
| short tons (2000 lbs.) | 0.91 | tons (metric) |

## VOLUME

| When You Know | Multiply by | To Find |
| --- | --- | --- |
| milliliters | 0.20 | teaspoons |
| milliliters | 0.06 | tablespoons |
| milliliters | 0.03 | fluid ounces |
| liters | 4.23 | cups |
| liters | 2.12 | pints |
| liters | 1.06 | quarts |
| liters | 0.26 | gallons |
| cubic meters | 35.32 | cubic feet |
| cubic meters | 1.35 | cubic yards |
| teaspoons | 4.93 | milliliters |
| tablespoons | 14.79 | milliliters |
| fluid ounces | 29.57 | milliliters |

| cups | 0.24 | liters |
| pints | 0.47 | liters |
| quarts | 0.95 | liters |
| gallons | 3.79 | liters |
| cubic feet | 0.03 | cubic meters |
| cubic yards | 0.76 | cubic meters |

## SPEED

| When You Know | Multiply by | To Find |
|---|---|---|
| miles per hour | 1.61 | kilometers per hour |
| kilometers per hour | 0.62 | miles per hour |

## TEMPERATURE (EXACT)

1. To convert from °C to °F: (multiply by 9/5 and add 32) °F = (9/5 x °C) + 32

2. To convert from °F to °C: (deduct 32, and multiply by 5/9) °C = 5/9 (°F - 32)

| Celsius | Fahrenheit |
|---|---|
| 0°C | Freezing point of water (32°F) |
| 10°C | A warm winter day (50°F) |
| 20°C | A mild spring day (68°F) |
| 30°C | A hot summer day (86°F) |
| 37°C | Normal body temperature (98.6°F) |
| 40°C | Heat wave conditions (104°F) |
| 100°C | Boiling point of water (212°F) |

# 18
# OFFICE RECYCLING GUIDE

## HINTS FOR ESTABLISHING A RECYCLING PROGRAM

As most secretaries know, offices are notorious wasters. The main culprit is paper, but all sorts of other products, from copier toner to printer ribbons, are also added to the annual accumulation of trash. In addition to discarding draft copies, handwritten notes, and so on, secretaries and executives regularly throw out old copies of journals, newspapers, and other printed matter. By 1990, for example, newspapers alone had already accounted for 13 million tons of the municipal solid waste stream in the United States before recycling. Many companies now recognize that society is quickly using up its resources while creating a planet that is a threat to our health. This awareness has led to an increasing interest in developing office recycling programs. Although each office must devise a program appropriate for its individual situation, the following recycling guidelines may help you get started.

- Begin with a waste audit. Before you can set up a program, you need to know which products—and how much per day—end up in the trash in your office.

- Talk to community leaders involved in local waste-disposal management and others who have a serious interest, such as waste-disposal educators and environmentalists in local schools and elsewhere.

- Talk to people in other offices in other companies that recycle to learn about their successes and failures and how they got started.

- Visit your library to make a list of recent magazines and books on this subject and to compile an address list of associations that deal with waste-disposal topics and may have literature about recycling.

- Analyze your current waste-disposal costs (collection, transportation, and so on) compared to costs if you were to recycle products, factoring in any income you would receive from selling certain recyclables.

- Make a list of all recyclable products in your office (see the next section for examples).

- Ask independent collection contractors (check your Yellow Pages for addresses) for cost estimates on collection, transportation to recycling sites, and other needs.

- Find out if independent contractors will give you a confidentiality agreement to provide security for proprietary information, and consider what additional needs you may have for the shredding of documents.

- Secure the support of senior management by providing full facts, including costs and savings, and a sensible, workable recycling plan for your office. (*Note:* Most offices start slowly and work up to a full-fledged program.)

- Study your office layout, and decide where to place collection bins so that everyone will be encouraged to use them.

- Set up and label the collection bins according to the classification required by your community and by the collection contractor—paper, glass, plastics, hazardous fluids and other materials, and so on.

- Decide whether participation should be voluntary or mandatory, and discuss with recycle educators how you can encourage employee participation (e.g., distribute informative literature, display posters in prominent places).

- Set targets or objectives for certain periods, such as every six months, and keep everyone informed of progress.

- Appoint a quality-control supervisor to evaluate the program periodically, provide a list of weaknesses, and recommend improvements.

- Establish a task force to recommend ways that everyone can reduce the amount of material used and to find ways to reuse what you already have (see the last section in this chapter).

## RECYCLING PRODUCT LIST

People are often surprised to learn how many office products can be recycled. Many products made of paper, plastic, glass, and aluminum, for example, can be recycled, depending on the recycling program being used. Some may not allow certain products, such as adhesive labels, blueprints, laser printouts, and colored paper. Potentially hazardous materials, however, such as oil, rubber tires, and batteries, are now routinely recycled by industry in many locations. Here are general categories of recyclable office products. (*Note:* Whether or not specific products can be sent to a recycling site depends on available programs and community policies and regulations.)

- Office paper (all types of stationery and envelopes, copier paper, adding machine rolls, computer paper, etc.)

- File folders, file dividers, binders, and report covers

- Paper towels

- Paper bags

- Newspapers and newsletters

- Magazines and journals
- Flyers and bulletins
- Advertising mail
- Aluminum cans and foil
- Steel cans
- Glass containers
- Plastic containers
- Packaging material (boxes, tubes, envelopes, peanuts, chips, etc.)
- Trash bags
- Food-service containers (plastic or paper plates, plastic utensils, and plastic or paper cups, lids, and straws)
- Tissue paper (napkins, paper towels, etc.)
- Toner cartridges (laser printer and copier)
- Printer and typewriter ribbons
- Old office machines (for plastic and other parts)
- Fluorescent lamps

## What You Can Do

Recycle guides usually recommend a three-point approach: (1) *reduce* the amount of material you use (eliminate unnecessary, excessive, and generally wasteful practices); (2) *reuse* the things you already have whenever possible (rather than buy replacements after one-time use); and (3) *recycle* what you can no longer use. Here are examples of specific steps you can take to put the reduce-reuse-recycle concept into effect.

- Choose reusable products over one-time-use products.
- Use recycled paper and other products whenever they are suitable for your machines and your needs.
- Buy products that are packaged simply (tell your suppliers that you will only accept products packaged in recyclable material).

- Avoid excessive packaging when you are the mailer.
- Reuse the packaging material that you receive when you do your own mailings.
- Donate packaging material that you cannot use to another mailer.
- Use your shredded paper as packaging material.
- Take along a reusable shopping bag when you pick up supplies.
- Save the containers in which you receive supplies, and reuse them for mailings, supplies storage, and so on.
- Donate containers you cannot reuse to a school or other facility.
- Use small-size sheets, rather than the standard 8 1/2 by 11 inches, for memos, fax cover sheets, and other messages that do not require full-size paper.
- Eliminate cover sheets entirely with your mailings if a small self-sticking note will suffice.
- Use E-mail, telex, voice mail, and other nonpaper forms of communication.
- Use white rather than colored paper and flat rather than glossy paper, since they are usually easier to recycle.
- Contact local authorities to ask if you should bundle glossy or colored paper apart from white, uncoated paper.
- Use unlaminated products, which are biodegradable.
- Use the back sides of discarded paper for notes and draft work.
- Circulate a notice and post a sign by the copier to print on both sides of the paper whenever practical.
- Make use of the blank page that is often wasted when you pull a document off a printer that has a tractor feeder.
- Use a routing slip with a single copy of a memo rather than send everyone a separate copy.

- Use a bulletin board to post notices rather than send individual memos to everyone.

- Route magazines or have one copy in a company reference room rather than carry a lot of individual subscriptions.

- Donate used books and magazines to schools, nursing homes, and other facilities that can make further use of them.

- Ask direct-mail advertisers to remove your name from their lists if you have no interest in the mailings.

- Use recyclable toner cartridges and, after use, recycle them again.

- Have your printer and typewriter ribbons relinked for further use.

- Use pens and pencils that accept replaceable ink and lead cartridges.

- Use cleaning materials and similar products in concentrated form.

- Avoid petroleum-based products that give off carbon monoxide when burned.

- Avoid plastic and polystyrene-foam containers that are not biodegradable.

- Use unbleached, recycled napkins, towels, coffee filters, and so on.

- Collect and recycle plastic cups, straws, and lids from your office drink machine.

- Urge coworkers to use ceramic coffee mugs for beverages rather than disposable plastic and paper cups.

- Donate used furniture and accessories to charitable organizations rather than send them to a landfill.

- Ask employees with home gardens to consider using organic office waste (lunch and other food scraps) for their garden composting.

- If your company has a landscaped area, suggest starting a company compost pile. (*Note*: You could even start small compost piles on office balconies that have plants and shrubs.)

# INDEX

## A

Abbreviations, mailing abbreviations, 143-51
Abstract, reports, 155
Academic degrees, forms of address, 105, 126-28
Accounting
  bookkeeping, 179
  database, 185-86
  financial statements, 180
  journals and ledgers for, 178-79
  spreadsheet, 180, 184-85
Action words, listing of, 316-18
Active voice, 246
Addenda, proposals, 159
Adjective pronoun, function of, 246
Adjectives, function of, 245
Adverbs, function of, 245
Agenda, meeting topics, 199-200
Airfone, 35
Air Force officials, forms of address, 121
Antecedents, function of, 247
Apostrophe, guidelines for use, 296-97
Appendix, reports, 158
Appositives, function of, 247
Area codes, 46-50
Army officials, forms of address, 119-20
Articles, function of, 247
Association of Records Managers and Administrators, 189
Attention line, letters, 76, 78, 81
  writing tips, 94-95
Audioconferencing, 36, 197
Audiographic conference, 197
Auxiliary verb, function of, 247

## B

Background information, reports, 158
Balance sheet, 180, 181
Bibliography
  reports, 158
  style for, 163-64
Body language, projecting favorable image, 16
Body, letters, 77, 79, 81
  writing tips, 97
Body, memos, 83, 87

writing tips, 102
Body, tables, 160
Bond paper, 172
Bookkeeping
  credit transactions, 179
  debit transactions, 179
  journals for, 178-79
Brackets, guidelines for use, 297
Budget section, proposals, 159
Business cards, for international business, 217
Business stationary memo
  model, 85
  parts of, 86-87

## C

Canadian provinces, mailing abbreviations, 144
Case (grammatical), function of, 247
Cash flow statement, 180, 183
Catholic dignitaries, forms of address, 122-24
Cell reference, of spreadsheet, 184
Cells, of spreadsheet, 184
Cellular telephone service, 36
Certification
  Certified Professional Secretary® (CPS®) rating, 20-21
  Office Proficiency Assessment and Certification® (OPAC), 20
*Chicago Manual of Style,* 162
Cliches, listing of, 347-57
Coast Guard officials, forms of address, 121
Collective nouns, function of, 247
College officials, forms of address, 126-28
Colon, guidelines for use, 297-98
Column heads, tables, 160
Columns, of spreadsheet, 184
Comma, guidelines for use, 298-99
Common nouns, function of, 247
Communication activities, of secretaries, 5
Comparative degree, function of, 247
Comparison (adverbs and adjectives), function of, 247
Complement, function of, 247
Complimentary close, letters, 77, 79, 82
  writing tips, 97-98
Compound predicate, function of, 247
Compound sentence, function of, 247

Compound subject, function of, 247
Compound terms
    closed compounds, 291
    common terms, listing of, 292-95
    function of, 248
    hyphenated compounds, 291-92
    open compounds, 290
Computer-document conference, 197
Computers
    computer security guidelines, 174-75
    desktop publishing, 168-70
    diskettes, protection tips, 173
    electronic filing of information, 187-89
    guidelines for injury prevention, 176-77
    scanning, 169-70
    storage media, 187
    word processing, 152-55
Conference calls, 35
Conjunctions
    function of, 245, 248
    listing of, 254-55
Coordinate conjunction
    function of, 248
    listing of, 254-55
Copy-distribution notation, letters, 78, 80, 82
    writing tips, 100-101
Copy-distribution notation, memos, 86
    writing tips, 103
Correlative conjunction
    function of, 248
    listing of, 254-55
Courier mail, types of services, 142
Court officials, forms of address, 115-16
Cover, reports, 155
Cover stock, 172
Credit-card calls, 35
Credit lines, format for, 162
Credits, in bookkeeping, 179
Criticism, tips for constructive criticism, 25-26
Currency, foreign currency, listing of, 222-29

**D**

Dangling modifier, 248
Dash, guidelines for use, 299-300
Data analysis, reports, 158
Database, 185-86
    components of, 185-86
    information processing functions, 186
    maintenance tasks of secretaries, 7
Data-collection tasks, of secretaries, 5

Data file, of database, 185
Date, letters, 76, 78, 80
    writing tips, 91
Debits, in bookkeeping, 179
Decision-making, of secretaries, 6
Delegation, guidelines for, 26-27
Demonstrative pronoun, function of, 248
Dependent clause, function of, 248
Desktop publishing
    business uses for, 168
    improving documents, guidelines for, 168-69
    scanning, 169-70
Diacritical marks, 305-6
    types of, 306
Diplomatic representatives, forms of
    address, 116-17
Direct-distance dialing, 34
Direct object, function of, 248
Discriminatory language, listing of words,
    342-47
Diskettes
    protection of, 173
    protection tips, 173
Documentation tasks, of secretaries, 7
Document conferencing, 36
Document design tasks, of secretaries, 7
Document preparation tasks, of secretaries, 6
*Domestic Mail Manual,* 141

**E**

Editing documents
    checklist for, 165-67
    and word processing, 153
Electronic filing, guidelines for, 188-89
Ellipsis points, guidelines for use, 300
E-mail
    etiquette, guidelines for, 137-38
    nature of, 36
Embassies
    foreign, in U.S., 236-42
    U.S. embassies abroad, 229-36
Enclosure notation, letters, 77, 80, 82
    writing tips, 100
Enclosure notation, memos, 86, 87
    writing tips, 102
Envelope
    OCR format, 88, 89-90
    proper addressing of, 136-37
    sizes of, 103-4
    traditional format, 88, 89

Equal Employment Opportunity
Commission (EEOC), sexual harassment
criteria, 29
Equipment purchasing tasks, of secretaries, 5
Ergonomics, for computer use, 175-77
*Esq.,* 105
Evaluation section, proposals, 159
Exclamation point, guidelines for use, 300-301
Expletive, function of, 248
Express Mail, 142, 143

**F**

Fax mail, 36
Field, of database, 186
Field name, of database, 186
Filing
electronic filing, 187-89
manual filing systems, 189-91
Financial management tasks, of secretaries, 5
Financial statements, 180
balance sheet, 180, 181
income statement, 180, 182
statement of cash flows, 180, 183
Flat forms, 187
Floppy disks, protection of, 173
Flyleaf, reports, 155
Footnotes
reports, 158
style for, 162-63
tables, 160
Foreign countries
access codes, 50-51
country/city codes, 53-71
currency units for, 223-29
foreign embassies in U.S., 236-42
mailing abbreviations, 148-51
noun/adjectives denoting nationality, 261-67
time differences, 52
U.S. embassies abroad, 230-36
Foreign currency
exchanging abroad, 219
listing of, 222-29
reference guide to, 223
Foreign language
anglicized words/terms, 399-400
common expressions, listing of, 391-98
overused terms, listing of, 399
Foreign officials, forms of address, 117-19

Forms of address
for Air Force officials, 121
for Army officials, 119-20
for Catholic dignitaries, 122-24
for Coast Guard officials, 121
for college/university officials, 126-28
for court officials, 115-16
for diplomatic representatives, 116-17
for foreign officials, 117-19
for Jewish dignitaries, 124
for Marine Corps officials, 121
for married/unmarried couples, 107
for men and women, 104-7
for Navy officials, 120-21
for organizations, 107
for Protestant dignitaries, 124-26
for titled persons, 104-5
for United Nations officials, 128-29
for U.S. government officials, 108-15
Full-block letter format
model, 74
parts of, 78-80
Future perfect tense, 260
Future tense, 260

**G**

General ledger, 178
Gerund, function of, 248
Gift giving, international clients, 32-33
Glossary, reports, 158
Goal-setting, guidelines for, 10-11
Government officials, forms of address, 108-15
Grammar
conjunctions, types of, 254-55
grammatical terms, listing of, 246-52
irregular verbs, 255-60
nouns/adjectives denoting nationality, 260-67
parts of speech, 245-46
prepositions, listing of, 252-54
verb tenses, 260
Guide words, memos, 83, 86-87
writing tips, 101-2

**H**

Homophones, problem words, listing of, 334-41
Hyphens
and adding prefixes, 279

Hyphens, *continued*
    guidelines for use, 301
    hyphenated compound terms, 291-92

# I

Identification initials, letters, 77, 80, 82
    writing tips, 99-100
Identification initials, memos, 87
    writing tips, 102
Imperative mood, function of, 249
Income statements, 180, 182
    balance sheet, 180, 181
    cash flow statement, 180, 183
    income statement, 180, 182
Indefinite pronoun, function of, 249
Index, for reports, 158
Indicative mood, function of, 249
Indirect object, function of, 249
Infinitive, function of, 249
Information-distribution tasks, of
    secretaries, 6
Information gathering tasks, of secretaries, 8
Inside address, letters, 76, 78, 81
    writing tips, 92-94
Interjections, function of, 246
International business
    etiquette guidelines, 30-32
    gift giving, 32-33
    international mail, 142-43
    international telephone calls, 35, 50-71
    international travel, 217-29
    *See also* Foreign countries
International mail, U. S. Postal Service, 142-
    43
*International Mail Manual,* 142
International telephone calls
    access codes, 50-51
    country/city codes, 53-71
    direct dial, 35
    time differences, chart of, 52
International travel
    foreign currency, 222-29
    time differences, calculation of, 220-21
    trip preparation tips, 217-20
Interoffice stationary memo
    model, 84
    parts of, 83, 86
Interpersonal relations
    constructive criticism, 25-26
    delegation, 26-27

    effective listening, 22-23
    international business, 30-33
    office politics, 27-28
    sexual harassment, 29-30
    training of others, 23-25
Interrogative pronoun, function of, 249
Intransitive verb, function of, 249
Introduction
    proposals, 159
    reports, 158
Irregular verbs
    function of, 249
    present/past participles, listing of, 255-
    59

# J

Jargon, listing of words/terms, 357-61
Jewish dignitaries, forms of address, 124
Journals, for accounting, 178-79

# L

Labels, of spreadsheet, 184
Label stock, 172
Leased lines, 35
Letter formats
    full-block format, 74, 78-80
    modified-block format, 75, 80-82
    simplified format, 73, 76-78
Letter of transmittal, reports, 155
Letter writing
    attention line, 94-95
    body, 97
    complimentary close, 97-98
    copy-distribution notation, 100-101
    date, 91
    enclosure notation, 100
    identification, 99-100
    inside address, 92-94
    mailing notation, 100
    personal notation, 91-92
    postscript, 101
    reference, 91
    salutation, 95-96
    signature, 98-99
    stationary, sizes of, 103
    subject, 96
Listening, guidelines for effective
    listening, 22-23
List of illustrations/tables, reports, 155

## M

Magnetic media, for information storage, 187
Mail
envelopes, proper addressing of, 136-37
incoming mail, 130-33
mail room security, 140-41
official manuals for, 141-42
outgoing mail, 133-36
private-courier mail, 142
saving money on, 138-40
U.S. Postal Service domestic mail, 142
U.S. Postal Service international mail,
142-43
Mailing abbreviations
for Canadian provinces, 144
for countries, 148-51
for states and territories, 143-44
for streets and place names, 145-48
Mailing notation, letters, 78, 80, 82
writing tips, 100
Mailing notation, memos, 86, 87
writing tips, 102
Mailing tasks, of secretaries, 6
Marine Corps officials, forms of address, 121
Marine radiotelephone, 35
Married couples, forms of address, 107
Meetings
agenda topics, 199-200
gaining more from, 195-97
meeting preparation checklist, 192-94
parliamentary motions, meanings of, 205-8
preparation of minutes, 201-5
presentation, guidelines for
preparation, 194-95
taking minutes, 200-201
teleconferencing, 197-99
Memo formats
business stationary memo format, 85, 86-
87
interoffice stationary format, 83-84
Memo writing
body, 102
copy-distribution notation, 103
enclosure notation, 102
guide words, 101-2
identification, 102
mailing notation, 102
postscript (P.S.), 103
stationary for memos, 103
Men, forms of address for, 105-7

Metric system
base units, 403-4
derived units, 404
equivalents for traditional
weights/measures, 410-13
metric measurement conversions, 413-17
prefixes of units, 408-9
prefix and multiplication factors, 409-10
spelling/symbols for units, 405-8
supplementary units, 404
Microimage media, for information storage,
187
Military officials, forms of address
Air Force officials, 121
Coast Guard officials, 121
Marine Corps officials, 121
Navy organizations, 120-21
Minutes of meetings
example of, 202-3
preparation guidelines, 201, 204-5
time saving tips, 200-201
Misplaced modifier, 249
*Miss,* 106
Modified-block letter format
model, 75
parts of, 80-82
Modifiers
dangling, 248
function of, 249
misplaced, 249
Mood (grammatical), function of, 249
*Mr.,* 104-5, 107
*MRI Bankers' Guide to Foreign Currency,* 223
*Mrs.,* 106-7
*Ms.,* 106

## N

Names, and titles, 104-7
Nationality, noun/adjectives denoting
nationality, 261-67
*National Zip Code Directory,* 143
Navy officials, forms of address, 120-21
Negative words, listing of, 332-34
Networking
guidelines for, 17-18
and international business, 220
vehicles for, 17
Network tasks, of secretaries, 6
Nominative case, function of, 249
Nonrestrictive clause, function of, 250

Notes
  reports, 158
  source citations, 162-63
Nouns, function of, 246

**O**

Objective case, function of, 250
Objectives, proposals, 159
OCR format, envelope, 88, 89-90
Office politics, dealing with, 27-28
Office Proficiency Assessment and
Certification (OPAC), 20
Office tasks, of secretaries, 5-6
Optical memory media, for information
  storage, 187
Organizational abilities, improvement of, 11-12
Organizations, forms of address, 107
Overnight mail, types of services, 142

**P**

Paper
  as information storage media, 187
  letter/memo stationary, 103
  types of business paper, 172
Parchment paper, 172
Parentheses, guidelines for use, 301-2
Parliamentary motions, meanings of, 205-8
Participle, function of, 250
Parts of speech, 245-46
  adjective, 245
  adverb, 245
  conjunction, 245
  interjection, 246
  noun, 246
  preposition, 246
  pronoun, 246
  verb, 246
Passive voice, function of, 250
Past perfect tense, 260
Past tense, 260
Perforated-forms paper, 172
Period, guidelines for use, 302
Personal notation, letters, 76, 78, 81
  writing tips, 91-92
Personal pronoun, function of, 250
Person (grammatical), function of, 250
Personnel section, proposals, 159
Person-to-person calls, 34
*Ph.D.,* 105

Phrasal preposition
  function of, 250
  listing of, 253-54
Place names, mailing abbreviations, 145-48
Plurals, apostrophe, use of, 297
Positive words, listing of, 313-15
Possessive case
  apostrophe, use of, 296-97
  function of, 250
Postal Union mail, 142
Postscript (P.S.), letters, 78, 80, 82
  writing tips, 101
Postscript (P.S.), memos, 87
  writing tips, 103
Predicate, function of, 250
Predicate adjective, function of, 250
Prefixes
  adding to words, 278-79
  common prefixes, listing of, 279-82
  in metric system, 408-9
*Prentice Hall Style Manual, The,* 162
Prepositional phrase, function of, 250
Prepositions
  function of, 246, 250
  listing of, 252-54
  phrasal prepositions, 253-54
Presentations, guidelines for, 194-95
Present perfect tense, 260
Present tense, 260
Problem section, proposals, 159
Procedure section, proposals, 159
Procrastination
  guidelines for overcoming, 15-16
  reasons for, 14-15
Productivity, guidelines for increasing, 8-9
Professional Secretaries International (PSI®), iv
Programming tasks, of secretaries, 7
Pronouns, function of, 246, 251
Proofreading
  common errors found in, 310-11
  of database, 186
  placement of marks, 307-8
  proofreading marks, 308-9
  and word processing, 153
Proper noun, function of, 251
Proposals
  addenda, 159
  budget section, 159
  editing guidelines, 165-67
  evaluation section, 159
  introduction, 159

Proposals, *continued*
    objectives, 159
    personnel section, 159
    problem section, 159
    procedure section, 159
    references, 162-64
Protestant dignitaries, forms of address, 124-26
Punctuation
    apostrophe, 296-97
    brackets, 297
    colon, 297-98
    comma, 298-99
    dash, 299-300
    diacritical marks, 305-6
    ellipsis points, 300
    exclamation point, 300-301
    hyphen, 301
    parentheses, 301-2
    period, 302
    question mark, 302-3
    quotation marks, 303-4
    semicolon, 304-5
    virgule, 305

**Q**

Question mark, guidelines for use, 302-3
Quotation marks, guidelines for use, 303-4

**R**

Railfone, 35
Reading, speed reading, 18-19
Recommendations, reports, 158
Record, of database, 185
Recycling program
    products for recycling, 420-21
    reducing amount of material for, 421-23
    starting program, 418-20
Redundant expressions, 325-31
Reference, letters, 76, 78, 80
    writing tips, 91
References
    bibliography style, 163-64
    notes, 162-63
    reference lists, style for, 164
Reflexive noun, function of, 251
Relative adjective, function of, 251
Relative pronoun, function of, 251
Religious dignitaries, titles

Catholic dignitaries, 122-24
    Jewish dignitaries, 124
    Protestant dignitaries, 124-26
Reports
    abstract, 155
    appendix, 158
    background information, 158
    bibliography, 158
    cover, 155
    data analysis, 158
    editing checklist, 165-67
    editing guidelines, 165-67
    flyleaf, 155
    glossary, 158
    index, 158
    introduction, 158
    letter of transmittal, 155
    list of illustrations/tables, 155
    notes, 158
    recommendations, 158
    references, 162-64
    table of contents, 155, 157
    title page, 155, 156
Restrictive clause, function of, 251
*Robert's Rules of Order*, 205-8
Rows, of spreadsheet, 184

**S**

Safety paper, 172
Salutation, letters, 76, 79, 81
    writing tips, 95-96
Scanning, 169-70
    good results, guidelines for, 170
*Sc.D.*, 105
Scheduling tasks, of secretaries, 4
Secretaries
    goal-setting guidelines, 10-11
    job tasks of, 4-8
    strategies for job success, 9-10
    titles of, 3
Security
    computer security, 174-75
    mail room, 140-41
Semicolon, guidelines for use, 304-5
Sexist language, troublesome words, listing of, 342-47
Sexual harassment
    dealing with, 29-30
    Equal Opportunity Employment Commission criteria, 29

Signature, letters, 77, 79, 82
  writing tips, 98-99
Signature, memos, 83, 86, 87
  writing tips, 102
Simplified letter format
  model, 73
  parts of, 76-78
Slash, guidelines for use, 305
Solidus, guidelines for use, 305
Sorting, of database, 186
Source notes, tables, 160
Speed reading, guidelines for, 18-19
Spell-check program, 153
Spelling
  commonly misspelled words, 268-78
  of compound terms, 289-92
  for metric units, 405-8
  and prefixes, 278-82
  and suffixes, 282-86
Spreadsheet, 180, 184-85
  data manipulation commands, 185
  parts of, 184
States, mailing abbreviations, 143-44
Stationary, sizes of, 103
Storage, media for document storage, 173, 187
Streets, mailing abbreviations, 145-48
Stress management, tips for, 19-20
Stub, tables, 160
Subject, letters, 77, 79, 81
  writing tips, 96
Subject of sentence, 251
Subjunctive mood, function of, 251
Subordinate conjunction
  function of, 251
  listing of, 254-55
Subsidiary ledger, 179
Suffixes
  common suffixes, listing of, 286-89
  spelling rules for, 282-86
Superlative degree, function of, 251
Supervisory tasks, of secretaries, 4

**T**

Table of contents, reports, 155, 157
Tables
  model of, 161
  positioning parts of, 160
Telecommunications services, 36
  cellular telephone service, 36
  E-mail, 36

  fax mail, 36
  telecomputing, 36
  teleconferencing, 36
  voice mail, 36
Teleconferencing, 197-99
  audioconferencing, 197
  audiographic conference, 197
  computer-document conference, 197
  steps in, 198-99
  videoconference, 197
Telemarketing fraud, 43-44
  guidelines for avoiding, 44
Telephone
  answering phone, guidelines for, 37-40
  area codes, 46-50
  country/city codes, 53-71
  international access codes, 50-51
  leased lines, 35
  most frequently used numbers, 45-46
  telecommunications services, 36
  telemarketing fraud, 43-44
  telephone business services, 34-35
  and time management, 42-43
  voice-mail, use of, 40-42
Tense of verb, 251
  listing of tenses, 260
Territories, mailing abbreviations, 143-44
Time differences
  calculation of, 220-22
  international, 52
  United States, 47
Time management
  guidelines for, 12-14
  procrastination, overcoming, 14-16
  and telephone, 42-43
Title, tables, 160
Title page, reports, 155, 156
Titles
  correct use of, 104-7
  *See also* Forms of address
Training, tips for training others, 23-25
Transcription
  guidelines for efficiency in, 171-72
  tasks of secretaries, 7
Transition words, listing of, 319-20
Transitive verb, function of, 252
Translators, and foreign travel, 219
Transparencies, 172
Travel
  domestic, trip preparation guidelines,
    210-12

Travel, *continued*
    foreign currency, 223-29
    foreign embassies in U.S., 236-42
    international, trip preparation guidelines, 217-20
    safety tips, 212-17
    time differences, calculation of, 220-21
    travel agent, selection of, 209-10
    U.S. embassies abroad, 229-36
Typesetting, drafting manuscripts for, 153-55

## U

United Nations officials, forms of address, 128-29
United States
    area codes, 47-50
    foreign embassies in, 236-42
    time zones, 47

## V

Values, of spreadsheet, 184
Verbal, function of, 252
Verbs
    function of, 246
    tenses, 251, 260
Videoconferencing, 36, 197
Virgule, guidelines for use, 305
Visual aids
    and presentations, 195
    tables, 160, 161

Voice (grammatical), function of, 252
Voice-mail, 36
    leaving messages, 41-42
    messages to callers, 40-41

## W

WATS, inbound and outbound, 35
Women, forms of address for, 105-7
Word processing
    document creation steps, 152-53
    drafting manuscripts for typesetter, 153-55
Word use
    action words, 316-18
    cliches, 347-57
    commonly misused words, listing of, 361-90
    discriminatory language, 342-47
    expressions to avoid, 321-25
    foreign language words/terms, 361-400
    homophones, 334-41
    jargon, 357-61
    negative words, 332-34
    positive words, 313-15
    redundant expressions, 325-31
    transition words, 319-20
Works cited, style for, 163-64

## Z

Zip codes, directory for, 143